Edited by Sasha Waltz and Jochen Sandig
Herausgegeben von Sasha Waltz und Jochen Sandig

Sasha Waltz & Guests

Hatje Cantz Verlag

Creating Space for Imagination – Imagining Space for Creation

Preface

It all begins with »Travelogue«, our first dance piece in 1993 in Berlin. It was with this production that we founded Sasha Waltz & Guests. »Travel« and »Dialogue« merge into »Travelogue«, a travelogue just like this book, which invites you to be our guest on an associative journey through the company's history.

After more than 30 years of intensive artistic work, we dare to take a comprehensive look back. We reflect on ideas and recurring concepts that shape our work as so-called »codes« and rearrange the works accordingly. To broaden the horizon, we have invited writers and philosophers to stimulate further reflection with their texts. This collection is complemented by sources of inspiration from art, literature, music, and sketches from the creation process of our pieces and choreographies. We want to open up a mental exchange between texts, photos and sources of inspiration. Shifting time – from the first thoughts, ideas and sketches to the finished piece and its contextualisation in time – and making paper dance!

We are dreamers in this crazy world. Or perhaps tightrope walkers? Without a net. Our net is art. Those who watch us are excited, maybe holding their breath, and follow us as we cross the circus tent in the air. Risk is our profession. It makes us feel alive. Hey, where is the tightrope stretched now? We feel old age slowly approaching us, a figure at a different pace. It seems still far away but we can already make out the figure in the distance. We feel childhood and youth in our hearts, the storm and stress. But slowly, awareness of our mortality mixes with our dreams and the living past spins its web. It captures us like a ravenous, cunning spider in its delicate yet dangerous web. This book is also a way of feeding the spider with memories.

Our thanks go to the countless dancers, artists, musicians, organisers, technicians and everyone who has been involved in our work over the years and accompanied us along the way – in administration, production, organisation and communication. We also thank our loyal, curious and enthusiastic audiences for the rich years we have been able to spend together in dance, theatres, museums and opera houses worldwide, and in public spaces. Special thanks also go to the many guests from the fields of music, visual arts, architecture, fashion, film and literature. Their imagination, talent, virtuosity, humanity and beauty accompany, move and inspire us again and again.

We are grateful to live in and with art. It saves us!

Sasha Waltz and Jochen Sandig

Vorwort

Alles beginnt mit »Travelogue«, unserem ersten Tanzstück im Jahr 1993 in Berlin. Aus dieser Produktion heraus haben wir Sasha Waltz & Guests gegründet. »Travel« und »Dialogue« verschmelzen zu »Travelogue«, einem Reisebericht, genau wie dieses Buch, das Sie einlädt, unser Gast auf einem assoziativen Weg durch die Geschichte der Compagnie zu sein.

Nach über 30 Jahren intensiver künstlerischer Arbeit wagen wir einen umfassenden Rückblick. Wir reflektieren Ideen und immer wieder auftauchende Begriffe, die unsere Arbeit prägen, als sogenannte »Codes« und ordnen die Werke gemäß diesen »Codes« neu an. Um den Horizont zu erweitern, haben wir Schriftsteller:innen und Philosoph:innen dazu eingeladen, mit ihren Texten zu einer weiterführenden Reflexion anzuregen. Ergänzt wird diese Sammlung durch Inspirationsquellen aus Kunst, Literatur, Musik sowie Skizzen aus dem Entstehungsprozess der Stücke. Wir möchten einen geistigen Austausch zwischen Texten, Fotos und Inspirationsquellen eröffnen. Die Zeit verschieben – von den ersten Gedanken, Ideen und Skizzen bis hin zum fertigen Stück und seiner Einordnung in den zeitlichen Kontext – und das Papier zum Tanzen bringen!

Wir sind Traumtänzer in dieser ver-rückten Welt. Oder doch eher Seiltänzer? Ohne Netz. Unser Netz ist die Kunst. Wer uns zuschaut, ist gespannt, hält vielleicht den Atem an und verfolgt, wie wir das Zirkuszelt in der Luft überqueren. Das Risiko ist unser Beruf. Es macht uns lebendig. Hey, wo ist jetzt das Seil gespannt? Wir spüren das Alter langsam auf uns zukommen, eine Gestalt in anderem Tempo. Sie scheint noch weit entfernt, aber wir können die Gestalt schon in der Ferne ausmachen. Wir spüren die Kindheit und Jugend im Herzen, den Sturm und Drang. Doch langsam mischt sich die Bewusstheit über unsere Endlichkeit in unsere Träume und die lebendige Vergangenheit spinnt ihr Netz. Sie nimmt uns wie eine gefräßige, listige Spinne gefangen in ihrem zarten, doch gefährlichen Netz. Dieses Buch ist auch ein Weg, die Spinne mit Erinnerungen zu füttern.

Unser Dank gilt den unzähligen Tänzer:innen, Künstler:innen, Musiker:innen, Veranstalter:innen, Techniker:innen und allen, die über die Jahre hinweg an unserer Arbeit mitgewirkt und unseren Weg begleitet haben – in Verwaltung, Produktion, Organisation und Kommunikation. Ebenso danken wir unserem treuen, neugierigen und begeisterten Publikum für die reichen Jahre, die wir gemeinsam im Tanz, im Theater, in Museen und Opernhäusern weltweit und auf öffentlichen Plätzen verbringen konnten. Ein besonderer Dank geht auch an die vielen Gäste aus Musik, Bildender Kunst, Architektur, Mode, Film und Literatur. Ihre Imagination, ihr Talent, ihre Virtuosität, Menschlichkeit und Schönheit begleiten, bewegen und inspirieren uns immer wieder aufs Neue.

Wir sind dankbar, in und mit der Kunst zu leben. Sie rettet uns!

Sasha Waltz und Jochen Sandig

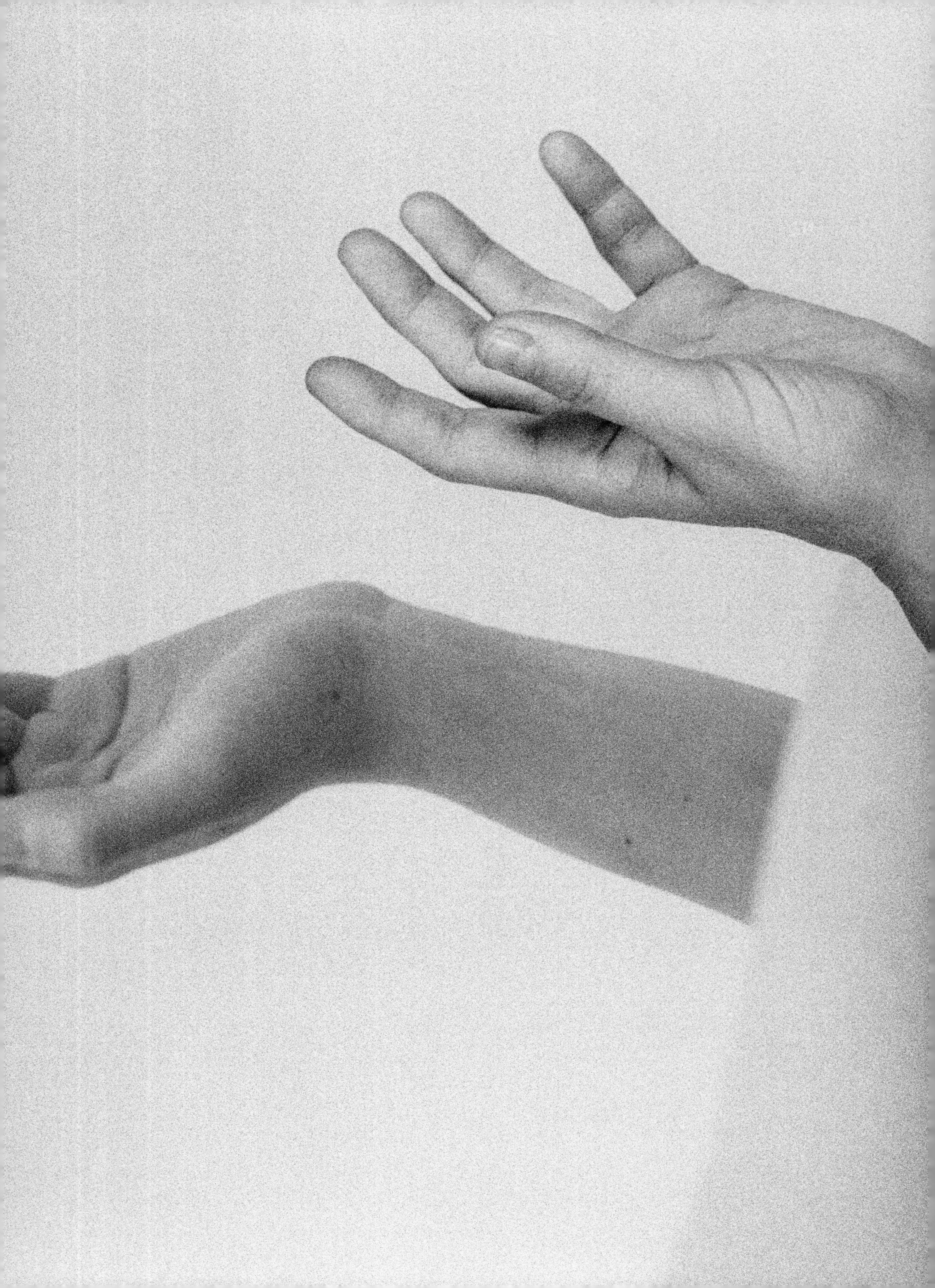

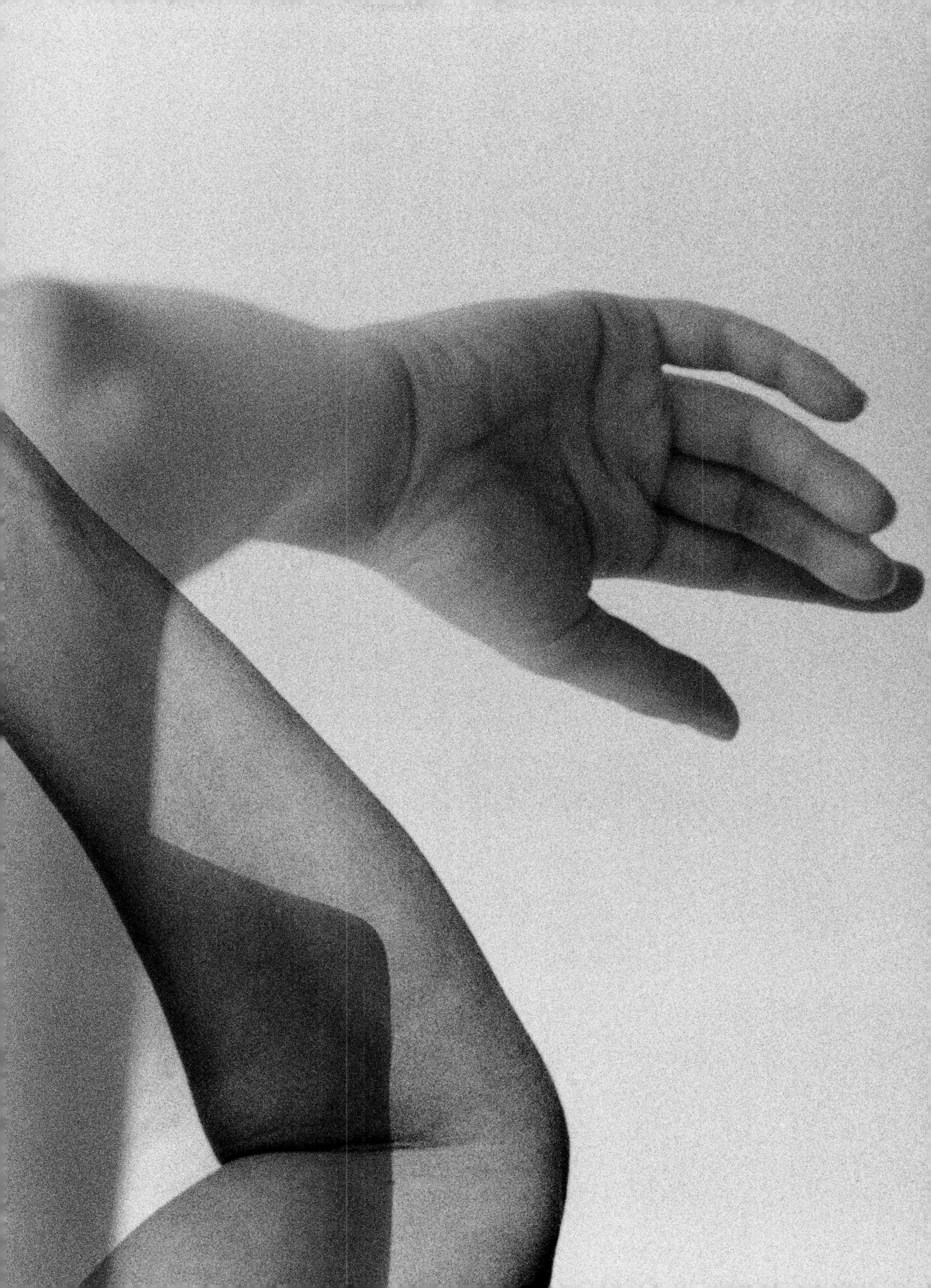

Declining the Body; The Body as Physics

Den Körper deklinieren; der Körper als Physik

Senthuran Varatharajah

Nominative
Paradox and Gravity

A body is a joint: a movable connection of several bones, such as a connected movement held together by bones; a collection of muscles, and the soft surface skin; of size, and weight. The body is bent: bent and declined, according to the cases, according to the four cases, according to the fall as the direction of grammar. The body falls – because it has already fallen, and will fall again and again: into this world, and into the languages it speaks; into the laws of physics, as into the oldest dream of metaphysics; into the measurable vanishing points of space; deep, and deeper into the movement to which it surrenders, into which it enters, and which a body creates in surrender, in the more uncertain falling and letting itself into an imagined and expected form that has yet to be formed, that only it can form, into a form that calls upon its own future. A secret of dancing: lies in this paradox. Only by saying Amen, by resolutely holding on in silent alignment with a promise that the body makes to itself through its joints, by surrendering to gravity, by obeying gravity, by agreeing with gravity: can gravity be overcome. Gravity is the prerequisite for his dignity, as is grace. In dance, in this connected movement, a body is both: the subject, and also the object of transcendence – the transcending and the transcended; a form in formation; a form in the form; a form that forms itself; a gesture that can only explain the enigma of another gesture. Through its weight, a body forgets its weight – the force of gravity, and the gravity of the force that keeps it on the ground; that leads it back to the earth and its comfort. Every body: is lonely, lonely and on the move, falling and falling alone. Every body, pliable and vulnerable as it is, can fall out of this world again. Dance demands this: that the body loses its axis and gives up its centre; that the body can be outside of itself; that the vertical of gravity, even if only for the duration of a broken second, for a second in the break, can be set aside, placed in the horizontal and diagonal, in a direction other than the fall of grammar. For this: the body must obey it; agree to it, belong to it; follow gravity to the end. Only a body can abolish the boundary that it is and that is defined by hair, skin, flesh and bones. A body is a nominative. It names itself, apart from names; in dance it means itself, only there does it want itself. It says who and what it is.

Nominativ
Paradoxie und Schwerkraft

Ein Körper ist ein Gelenk: eine bewegliche Verbindung von mehreren Knochen, so, wie eine verbundene Bewegung, die von Knochen zusammengehalten wird; eine Sammlung von Muskeln, und der weichen Fläche Haut; von Größe, und Gewicht. Der Körper wird gebeugt: gebogen und dekliniert, nach den Kasus, nach den vier Fällen, nach dem Sturz als Richtung der Grammatik. Der Körper fällt – weil er bereits gefallen war, und immer wieder fallen wird: in diese Welt, und in die Sprachen, die sie spricht; in die Gesetze der Physik, wie in den ältesten Traum der Metaphysik; in die vermessbaren Fluchtpunkte des Raumes; tief, und tiefer in die Bewegung, der er sich hingibt, in die er sich hineinbegibt, und die ein Körper in der Hingabe, im ungewisseren Sichfallen- und Einlassen in eine imaginierte und erwartete Form, die noch geformt werden muss, die nur er formen kann, in eine Form, die ihre eigene Zukunft anruft, erzeugt. Ein Geheimnis des Tanzens: liegt in dieser Paradoxie. Allein durch das Amen, durch das entschlossene Festmachen in der stillen Ausrichtung auf ein Versprechen, das der Körper sich, durch seine Gelenke, selbst verspricht, in der Kapitulation vor der Schwerkraft, im Gehorsam gegenüber der Schwerkraft, im Einverständnis mit der Schwerkraft: kann die Schwerkraft überwunden werden. Die Schwerkraft ist die Voraussetzung seiner Würde, wie der Gnade auch. Im Tanz, in dieser verbundenen Bewegung, ist ein Körper beides: das Subjekt, und auch das Objekt der Transzendenz – der Transzendierende und das Transzendierte; eine Gestalt in Gestaltung; eine Gestalt in der Gestalt; eine Gestalt, die sich selbst gestaltet; eine Geste, die nur das Rätsel einer anderen Geste erklären kann. Durch sein Gewicht vergisst ein Körper sein Gewicht – die Kraft der Schwere, und die Schwere der Kraft, die ihn auf dem Boden hält; die ihn wieder zur Erde und zu ihrem Trost zurückführt. Jeder Körper: ist einsam, einsam und unterwegs, im Fall und Einzelfall begriffen. Jeder Körper, biegsam, und verwundbar, wie er ist, kann wieder aus dieser Welt herausfallen. Der Tanz verlangt danach: danach, dass der Körper seine Achse verliert, und dass er sein Zentrum aufgibt; dass der Körper aus sich selbst heraus außer sich sein kann; dass die Vertikale der Schwerkraft, sei es nur für die Dauer einer gebrochenen Sekunde, für eine Sekunde im Bruch, außer Kraft gesetzt, in die Horizontale und Diagonale, in eine andere Richtung als den Sturz der Grammatik gelegt werden kann. Dafür: muss der Körper ihr gehorchen; zustimmen, ihr zugehören; der Schwerkraft bis zum Ende folgen. Nur ein Körper kann die Grenze, die er ist, und die durch Haare, Haut, Fleisch und Knochen definiert wird, aufheben. Ein Körper ist ein Nominativ. Er benennt sich selbst, abseits der Namen; im Tanz meint er sich, nur dort will er sich. Er sagt, wer und was er ist.

Genitive
Testimony and Strong Interaction

Genitiv
Zeugnis und starke Wechselwirkung

II

A body is a poem: a bound, a metrically regulated speech, like a speaking covenant held together by the regularity of metre; a language which, through language, and only language itself, longs for the beginning of silence in the words, like the lost constellations of a night; which expresses the silence with a word; which brings the uncertain reverse side of the words to speech. The body is broken: divided, and arranged, not only by the fourfold traps of grammar, but also by four basic forces, also by the fundamental interaction of physics. The body depends – because only a body that will bear two hearts can give birth to another body: because a body, like a wound, or like a word, is bound to someone else, and to something else; without mass, untouchable and synchronous, dependent on the incidence of diminishing light. The strong interaction holds the atomic nucleus together: it binds what must repel without it – the positively charged protons with the negatively charged neutrons, so that there can be matter; like a word with its first silence; like a body with the shadow to which the body belongs; like the breaks of a verse that make up a poem. A secret of dancing: lies in this testimony. A verse is the breaking, the breaking, and the broken; the break, and the fragility itself: precisely set metrically according to dramaturgical measure, in order to stabilise a movement such as a verse through its destabilisation in the choreography; so that there can be contact; so that neither the body nor the poem must continue to fall. In dance, in this alliance with the shadow and its dark silence, a body is both: a particle, and the force that binds the particle to other particles – the shadow of silence and the silence of the shadow; a doubling, in two areas; in the area of weight, and in the area of its weightlessness. Dance demands this: in order to be able to dance, a body needs its shadow; it must be in contact with it, like a word that only receives its meaning from its silence, which seeks this word in a poem as a repressed memory. Silence: is prior to the word. The shadow: is more original than the body. The poem: is not a sequence of rhythmised words; in a poem each word reveals itself from its beginning and from its end. A dance is not a sequence of movements: in dance, the idea of movement appears as the idea of mobility itself. A body is a genitive: it begets and testifies to itself; in dance it belongs to itself alone; it steps into its shadow. It says whose it is.

Ein Körper ist ein Gedicht: eine gebundene, eine metrisch geregelte Rede, so, wie ein redender Bund, der von der Regelmäßigkeit der Metrik zusammengehalten wird; eine Sprache, die durch die Sprache, und nur die Sprache selbst, sich nach dem Anfang des Schweigens in den Wörtern sehnt, wie nach den verlorenen Konstellationen einer Nacht; die das Schweigen mit einem Wort ausspricht; die die unsichere Rückseite der Wörter zur Sprache bringt. Der Körper wird gebrochen: geteilt, und arrangiert, nicht allein durch die vierfachen Fallen der Grammatik, sondern auch durch vier Grundkräfte, auch durch die fundamentale Wechselwirkung der Physik. Der Körper hängt ab – weil nur ein Körper, der zwei Herzen ertragen wird, einen anderen Körper zur Welt bringen kann: weil ein Körper, wie eine Wunde, oder wie ein Wort, an jemand anderen, und an etwas anderes gebunden ist; ohne Masse, unberührbar und synchron, abhängig vom Einfall des abnehmenden Lichts. Die starke Wechselwirkung hält den Atomkern zusammen: Sie bindet, was sich ohne sie abstoßen muss – die positiv geladenen Protonen mit den negativ geladenen Neutronen, damit es Materie geben kann; wie ein Wort mit seinem ersten Schweigen; wie ein Körper mit dem Schatten, zu dem der Körper gehört; wie die Brüche eines Verses, die ein Gedicht ergeben. Ein Geheimnis des Tanzens: liegt in diesem Zeugnis. Ein Vers ist das Brechen, das Brechende, und das Gebrochene; der Bruch, und die Zerbrechlichkeit selbst: nach dramaturgischem Maß präzise metrisch gesetzt, um eine Bewegung wie eine Strophe durch ihre Destabilisierung in der Choreographie stabilisieren zu können; damit es Berührung geben kann; damit weder der Körper noch das Gedicht weiter stürzen müssen. Im Tanz, in diesem Bündnis mit dem Schatten und seinem dunklen Schweigen, ist ein Körper beides: ein Teilchen, und die Kraft, die das Teilchen an andere Teilchen bindet – der Schatten des Schweigens und das Schweigen des Schattens; eine Verdoppelung, in zwei Bereiche; im Bezirk des Gewichts, und in der Gegend seiner Schwerelosigkeit. Der Tanz verlangt danach: Um tanzen zu können, braucht ein Körper seinen Schatten; er muss mit ihm in Kontakt stehen, wie ein Wort, das nur von seinem Schweigen, das dieses Wort in einem Gedicht als verdrängte Erinnerung sucht, seine Bedeutung erhält. Das Schweigen: ist dem Wort voraus. Der Schatten: ist ursprünglicher als der Körper. Das Gedicht: ist keine Sequenz von rhythmisierten Wörtern; in einem Gedicht zeigt sich jedes Wort von seinem Anfang und von seinem Ende her. Ein Tanz ist keine Folge von Bewegungen: Im Tanz erscheint die Idee der Bewegung als Idee der Beweglichkeit selbst. Ein Körper ist ein Genitiv: Er zeugt, und bezeugt sich; er gehört im Tanz sich selbst allein; er tritt in seinen Schatten. Er sagt, wessen er ist.

Dative
Gift and Electromagnetic Interaction

Dativ
Gabe und elektromagnetische Wechselwirkung

III

A body is a song: the musical use of a voice that produces sound and melody, like the music that needs no voice to produce sound and melody; an aisle cut in air and space until they move; a form of invocation, of call; a song that calls out and into itself; in which the innermost things have been placed in the body of another. The body is carried: accompanied, and guided, by the comprehensible circumference of its lungs, and the expectations in the seconds that imitate the solitary duration of a heartbeat; by the time that a body organises with the muscles and the curves of the spine. The body changes – because it attracts itself, and because it has to repel itself again, like the calculated and controlled breath in singing, which is taken and given, which comes in order to be able to go; because only a body can make itself an instrument, which only the body, only it, and no one beside it, outside of it, plays. The electromagnetic interaction is a microscopic force, which manifests itself in the most improbably small, in the clearest details, and which is significantly weaker than the strong interaction: like charges repel each other, unlike charges attract each other; like a voice that must leave a mouth, and that begins in the diaphragm, in this muscle-tendon plate, at this boundary between the chest and abdomen, as a vibration, a tremor that misses an ear; like a body that sings against the darkness in time; like a body that dances in it. A secret of dancing: lies in this gift. A body is on its way, on its own way to someone else, to whom it can give itself and surrender; to whom it surrenders; to whom it may give itself up. In dance, in this use of the body until it sings, a body is both: its attraction, and repulsion; the one that desires itself, and the one that repels itself; as an event. The dance demands it: the body must be intoned, modulated, paraphrased and varied; it knows the pauses for breath, the whole and the eighth notes; a body must be able to hold the tension, and the distance in it, rootless, and ready to lose its balance; it must tell itself through its flesh, as through a libretto; it must open itself, like the throat, deep from a mouth, through the octave. A body is a dative: it is the given, and the giving; in dance it gives itself because it can give itself: to itself, and to someone else. It says to whom it was given.

Ein Körper ist ein Gesang: der musikalische Gebrauch einer Stimme, die Klang und Melodie erzeugt, so, wie die Musik, die zur Erzeugung von Klang und Melodie keine Stimme braucht; eine Schneise, in Luft und in den Raum geschnitten, bis sie sich bewegen; eine Form der Anrufung, der Aufrufung; ein Lied, das sich hinaus-, und in sich hineinruft; in dem die innersten Dinge in den Körper eines anderen gelegt worden sind. Der Körper wird getragen: begleitet, und gelenkt, vom nachvollziehbaren Umfang seiner Lunge, und den Erwartungen in den Sekunden, die die einsame Dauer eines Herzschlags imitieren; von der Zeit, die ein Körper mit den Muskeln, und mit den Biegungen der Wirbelsäule gliedert. Der Körper verändert sich – weil er sich selbst anzieht, und weil er sich wieder von sich selbst abstoßen muss, wie der kalkulierte und kontrollierte Atem im Singen, der geholt, und gegeben wird, der kommt, um gehen zu können; weil nur ein Körper sich zum Instrument machen kann, das nur der Körper, nur er, und niemand außer ihm, außerhalb von ihm, spielt. Die elektromagnetische Wechselwirkung ist eine mikroskopische Kraft, die sich im unwahrscheinlich Kleinsten, in den deutlichsten Details zeigt, und die signifikant schwächer als die starke Wechselwirkung ist: Gleichnamige Ladungen stoßen sich ab, ungleichnamige ziehen sich an; wie eine Stimme, die einen Mund verlassen muss, und die im Zwerchfell, in dieser Muskel-Sehnenplatte, an dieser Grenze zwischen Brust- und Bauchraum, als Erschütterung, als Zittern beginnt, das ein Ohr vermisst; wie ein Körper, der gegen die Dunkelheit in der Zeit singt; wie ein Körper, der in ihr tanzt. Ein Geheimnis des Tanzens: liegt in dieser Gabe. Ein Körper ist auf dem Weg, auf seinem eigenen Weg zu jemand anderem, dem er sich geben, und hingeben kann; vor dem er sich ergibt; vor dem er sich aufgeben darf. Im Tanz, in diesem Gebrauch des Körpers, bis er singt, ist ein Körper beides: seine Attraktion, und Repulsion; der, der sich selbst begehrt, und der, der sich selbst zurückstößt; als ein Ereignis. Der Tanz verlangt danach: Der Körper muss intoniert, moduliert, paraphrasiert, und variiert werden; er kennt die Atempausen, die Ganzen und die Achtel; ein Körper muss die Spannung, und den Abstand in ihr, halten können, wurzellos, und bereit, sein Gleichgewicht zu verlieren; er muss sich durch sein Fleisch erzählen, wie durch ein Libretto; er muss sich öffnen, wie der Rachen, tief aus einem Mund, durch die Oktave. Ein Körper ist ein Dativ: Er ist das Gegebene, und das Geben; im Tanz gibt er sich, weil er sich geben kann: sich selbst, und jemand anderem. Er sagt, wem er gegeben wurde.

Accusative
Willingness and Weak Interaction

Akkusativ
Bereitschaft und schwache Wechselwirkung

IV

A body is a prayer: a request, and a deep thanks, addressed to another, like the direction that asks for thanks, and gratefully says please; an utterance and address; a speaking out, addressing and being addressed; the trust, a confiding, and being confided in; being allowed to be meant, in a community. The body is blessed: marked, and authenticated, by the rules and order of grammar, by the declensions through which it falls, and by the fundamental forces of nature to which every single phenomenon in the physical world can be traced back; which are its foundation – by gravity, through which every mass strives towards the interior of the earth, by the strong interaction that holds an atom together in its nucleus, by the electromagnetic interaction, the conflict of charges in the heart of atoms, and by the weak interaction as well. The body accuses – a philosophy that defines truth as the opposite of the body, and of dancing; as that which should remain and remain the same: as the eternal, because a body that dances is fleeting and transient; because a body is only grasped in coming, in arriving, in movement. The weak interaction is the power of transformation, and that of decay: it binds no particles and has the shortest range below the radius of the atomic nucleus – like a body that consents to its death; like a body that transforms as it falls; like a voice that falls into it: vertically, horizontally, and diagonally, from every direction, so that it can call it by its name and call it to itself, into these arms. A secret of the dance: lies in this readiness. In the decision that has to be made again every second: to become another; to be allowed to become another; to have been another. A prayer means every centimetre of skin: because it gets under the skin, and means the vulnerability of the arteries and veins; because a prayer believes that a body no longer has to be what it was made to be, and what it had made itself to be. A prayer is threefold: it can be sung, spoken aloud and formulated in silence; alone, and with others. In dance, in this orientation in the sign of asking and giving thanks, a body is both: the object, as well as the subject of transformation – the transformed, and the transforming, which stands in its service, in worship, in the service of a community. Dance demands this: that another movement is possible together; that other movements can still be dreamt of. The body is an accusative: a lament. In dance, it wants a future, which it names, testifies to and gives itself. It asks – for whom.

Ein Körper ist ein Gebet: eine Bitte, und ein tiefer Dank, die an einen anderen gerichtet sind, so, wie die Richtung, die um einen Dank bittet, und dankend Bitte sagt; eine Aussprache und Ansprache; ein Aussprechen, Ansprechen und Angesprochensein; das Vertrauen, ein Sichanvertrauen, und das Anvertraut-werden; gemeint sein dürfen, in einer Gemeinschaft. Der Körper wird gesegnet: gezeichnet, und beglaubigt, durch die Regeln und Ordnung der Grammatik, durch die Deklinationen, durch die er stürzt, und von den Fundamentalkräften der Natur, auf die jede einzelne Erscheinung in der physischen Welt zurückgeführt werden kann; die ihre Grundlegung sind – von der Schwerkraft, durch die jede Masse ins Innere der Erde strebt, von der starken Wechselwirkung, die ein Atom in seinem Kern zusammenhält, von der elektromagnetischen Wechselwirkung, dem Konflikt der Ladungen im Herzen der Atome, und von der schwachen Wechselwirkung auch. Der Körper klagt an – eine Philosophie, die Wahrheit als das Gegenteil des Körpers, und des Tanzens, definiert; als das, was bleiben und gleich bleiben soll: als das Ewige, weil ein Körper, der tanzt, flüchtig und vergänglich ist; weil ein Körper im Kommen, im Ankommen, in der Bewegung nur begriffen wird. Die schwache Wechselwirkung ist die Kraft der Umwandlung, und die des Zerfalls: Sie bindet keine Teilchen und besitzt die kürzeste Reichweite unterhalb des Atomkernradius – wie ein Körper, der seinem Tod zustimmt; wie ein Körper, der im Fallen sich verwandelt; wie eine Stimme, die in ihn hineinfällt: vertikal, horizontal, und diagonal, aus jeder Richtung, damit sie ihn bei seinem Namen nennt, und zu sich, in diese Arme rufen kann. Ein Geheimnis des Tanzes: liegt in dieser Bereitschaft. In der Entscheidung, die in jeder Sekunde noch einmal getroffen werden muss: ein anderer zu werden; ein anderer werden zu dürfen; ein anderer gewesen zu sein. Ein Gebet meint jeden Zentimeter Haut: weil es unter die Haut geht, und die Verletzbarkeit der Arterien und Venen meint; weil ein Gebet glaubt, dass ein Körper nicht länger der sein muss, zu dem er gemacht wurde, und zu dem er sich selbst gemacht hatte. Ein Gebet ist dreifaltig: Es kann gesungen, laut gesprochen und im Schweigen formuliert werden; allein, und mit anderen. Im Tanz, in dieser Ausrichtung im Zeichen des Bittens und Dankens, ist ein Körper beides: das Objekt, so, wie das Subjekt der Transformation – der Transformierte, und das Transformierende, der in seinem Dienst, im Gottesdienst, im Dienst einer Gemeinschaft steht. Der Tanz verlangt danach: danach, dass eine andere Bewegung gemeinsam möglich ist; dass von anderen Bewegungen immer noch geträumt werden kann. Der Körper ist ein Akkusativ: eine Klage. Im Tanz will er eine Zukunft, die er benennt, bezeugt, und sich gibt. Er fragt – nach wen.

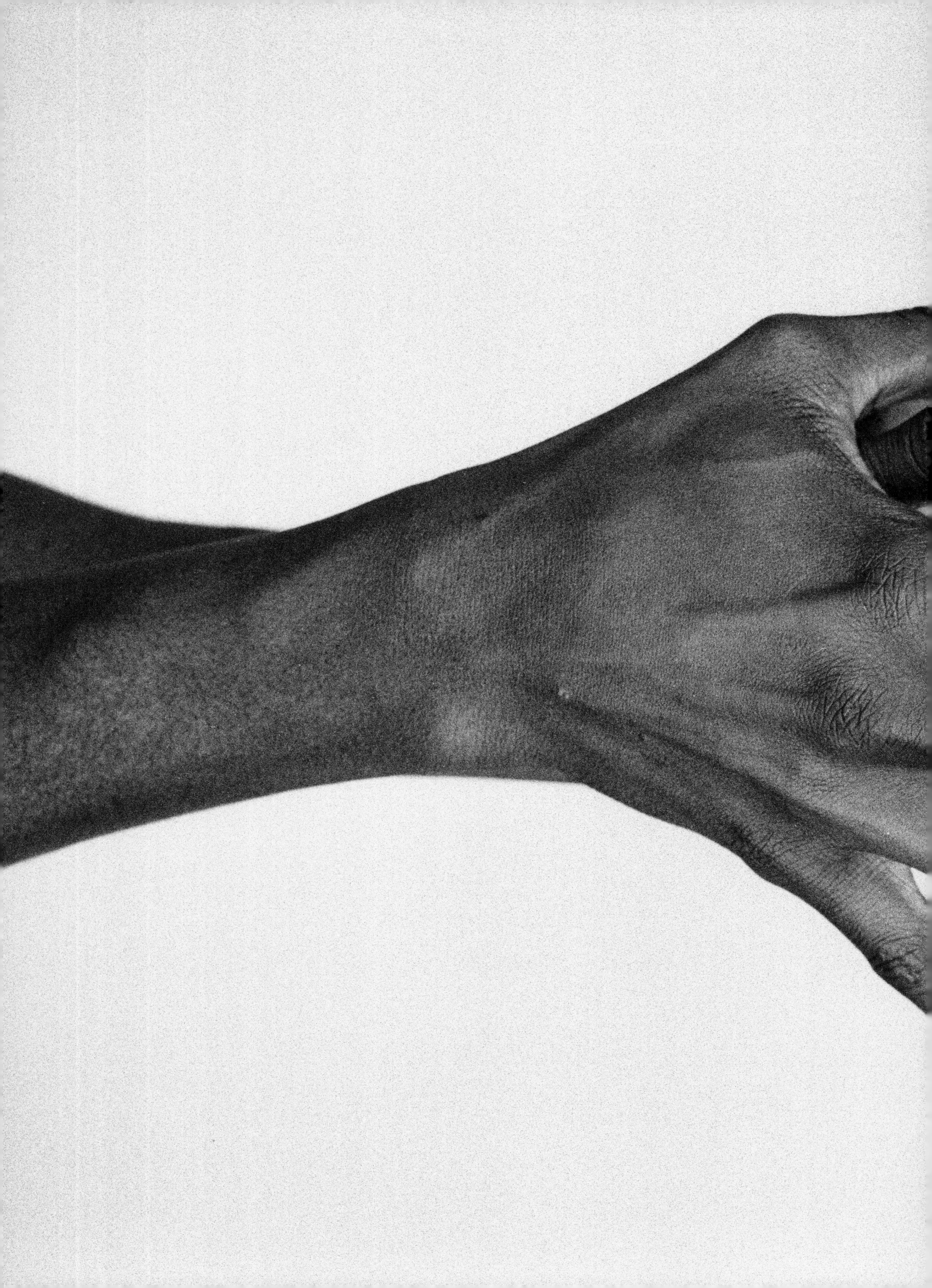

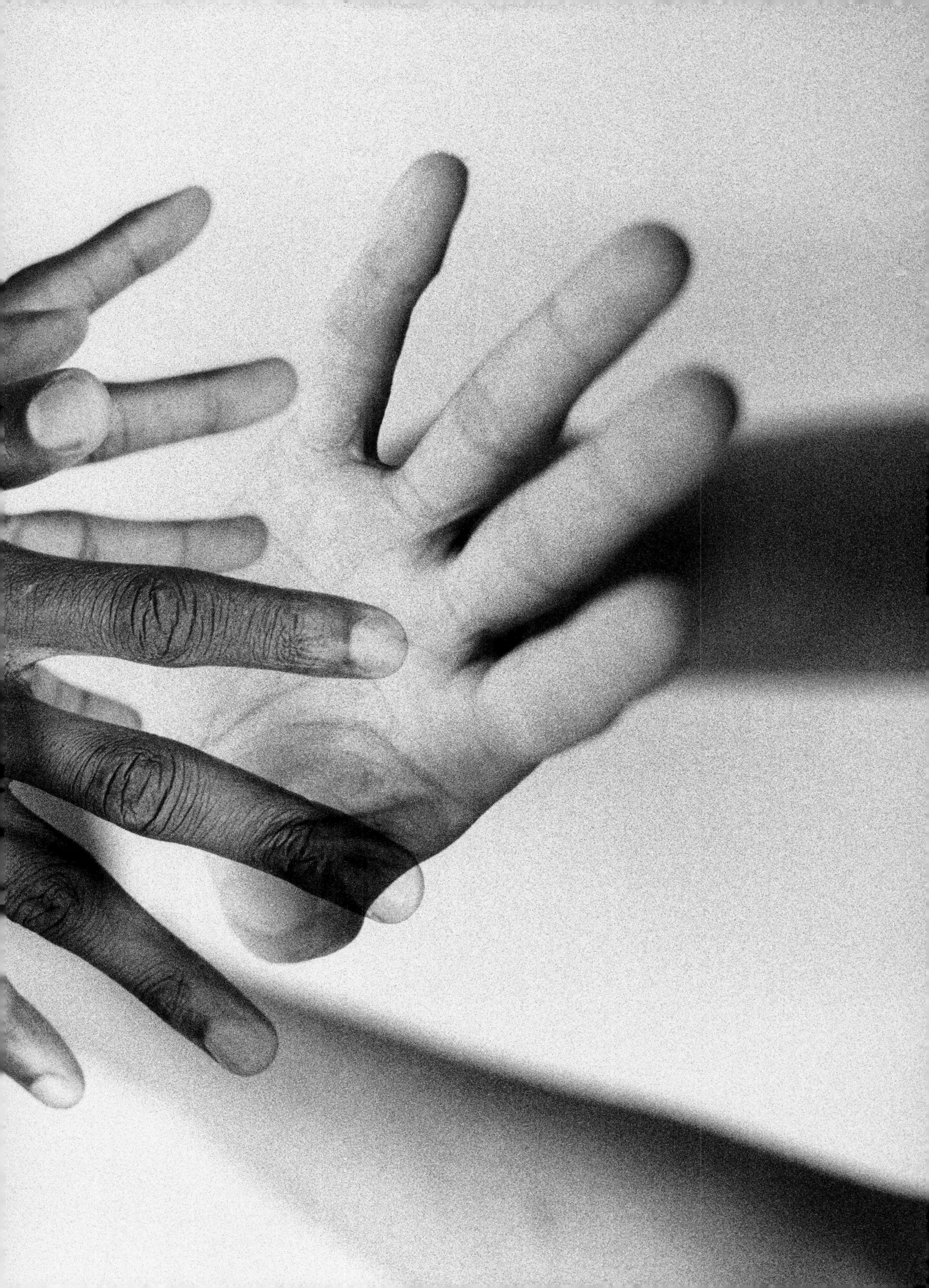

The »scores« of Sasha Waltz's works consist of many different terms, each of which denotes a specific choreographic figure – the so-called »codes«. These codes are created in different ways: some are clearly defined and planned from the beginning, others develop spontaneously during rehearsals, long before their place in the later piece is determined.
A movement sequence becomes a code the moment something special is recognised in it that is to be worked with further. The names created in this way are the preliminary stage of a notation that makes the reproducibility of dance possible in the first place. These are often concrete terms from everyday life, sometimes German, sometimes English, working titles that arise spontaneously and unsystematically and are not intended to become public. Some names appear again and again in different works. They stand for similar, but not always for the same choreographic figures.
Listing them here and using them as a structure for this chapter is the starting point of an experiment. On the following pages, 65 selected codes are not used to present finished works, but to create connections across Sasha Waltz's oeuvre, detached from their original context in words and images. Photos from the productions and rehearsals, as well as sketches and research material by Sasha Waltz and associatively assigned works from art history serve as the source of this encyclopaedic cabinet of curiosities. The picture tableaux are supplemented by texts from the productions, but also by specially requested contributions that create their own reference to the codes.
In addition to the production references, you will also find the respective year of origin, which will help you to find the corresponding productions in the second part of the book, in the »Chronology«.

Die »Partituren« von Sasha Waltz' Arbeiten bestehen aus vielen verschiedenen Begriffen, die jeweils eine bestimmte choreographische Figur bezeichnen – den sogenannten »Codes«. Diese Codes entstehen auf unterschiedliche Weise: Manche sind von Anfang an klar definiert und geplant, andere entwickeln sich spontan während der Proben, lange bevor ihr Platz im späteren Stück festgelegt ist.
Eine Bewegungssequenz wird in dem Moment zum Code, wenn in ihr etwas Besonderes erkannt wird, mit dem weitergearbeitet werden soll. Die so entstehenden Namen sind die Vorstufe einer Notation, die die Wiederholbarkeit von Tanz erst ermöglicht. Oft handelt es sich dabei um konkrete Begriffe aus dem Alltag, mal deutsch, mal englisch, Arbeitstitel, die spontan und unsystematisch entstehen und nicht dafür gedacht sind, öffentlich zu werden. Manche Namen tauchen in unterschiedlichen Werken immer wieder auf. Sie stehen für ähnliche, aber nicht immer für dieselben choreographischen Figuren.
Sie hier aufzulisten und als Gliederung für dieses Kapitel zu verwenden, ist Ausgangspunkt eines Experiments. Auf den folgenden Seiten werden anhand von 65 ausgewählten Codes keine fertigen Werke präsentiert, sondern Verbindungen hergestellt, quer durch das Œuvre von Sasha Waltz, losgelöst von ihrem ursprünglichen Kontext in Wort und Bild. Als Quelle dieser enzyklopädischen Wunderkammer dienen Fotos aus den Produktionen und den Proben, aber auch Skizzen und Recherchematerial von Sasha Waltz sowie assoziativ zugeordnete Werke der Kunstgeschichte. Die Bildertableaus werden ergänzt durch Texte aus den Produktionen, aber auch eigens angefragte Beiträge, die einen ganz eigenen Bezug zu den Codes herstellen.
Neben den Produktionsverweisen finden Sie auch das jeweilige Entstehungsjahr, das Ihnen hilft, die entsprechenden Produktionen im zweiten Teil des Buches, der »Chronologie«, zu finden.

Codes

Anfang Beginning

When you start a piece, it's like jumping off a cliff. You always think you can't do it. At least, that's how it is for me. The process that follows is similar. You're constantly overcoming yourself because you're searching. After all, it's about something that doesn't yet exist. Experience doesn't change that.
SASHA WALTZ

Wenn man ein Stück anfängt, ist das, als ob man von einem Riesenfelsen hinunterspringt. Man denkt immer, man kann es eigentlich gar nicht. Mir geht es so. Der Prozess ist auch so. Man überwindet sich permanent, weil man auf der Suche ist, weil es um etwas geht, das noch nicht existiert. Daran ändert sich auch mit Erfahrung nichts.
SASHA WALTZ

A

A »Roméo et Juliette« ↘2007 B »Johannes-Passion« ↘2024 C »Tomb of the Diver«, c. 480 AD, detail D »Dido & Aeneas« ↘2005 E »S« ↘2000

C

D

B

E

A

Look. Here. Zwischen meinem Körper und meiner Leidenschaft. A man. Animale. Prends-moi. Prends-moi. Parce-que j'attends. J'attends depuis trop longtemps. Open the floor and call the darkness, the beast will not stop. (cry) Remember who? Me. Who? You. Everything is falling down. And there is no one to put it back standing. Stelios chante. Chante pour moi.
CLÉMENTINE DELUY
IN »RAUSCHEN«

Schau. Hier. Zwischen meinem Körper und meiner Leidenschaft. Ein Mann. Tier. Nimm mich. Nimm mich. Denn ich warte. Ich warte schon viel zu lange. Öffne den Boden und ruf die Dunkelheit, das Biest wird nicht aufhören (Schrei) Erinnerst du dich, wer? Ich. Wer? Du. Alles bricht zusammen. Und niemand ist hier, um es wieder aufzustellen. Stelios sing. Sing für mich.
CLÉMENTINE DELUY
IN »RAUSCHEN«

B

A **»Beethoven 7«** ↘2023 B **»Dido & Aeneas«** ↘2005 C **Sasha Waltz, drawing, 2015**

C

A

B

C

A **»In C«** ↘2021 B **Hieronymus Bosch, »The Garden of Earthly Delights«, 1490–1500, detail** C+F **»Kreatur«** ↘2017

D

E

F

D **Sasha Waltz, study for »Sacre«** ↘2013 E **»Sacre«** ↘2013

A

B

A **»In C« at Berliner Dom** ↘2021 B **»Dialoge 09 – Neues Museum«** ↘2009 C+D **»noBody«** ↘2002 E **»ΕΞΟΔΟΣ | Exodos«** ↘2018

C

D

In an arc, two poles are joined by a series of connecting links that exist only in tension with one another. They are held in place by the precisely directed transfer of force between each point on the spectrum. In this way, an opposition is established and at the same time canceled.
The link between our bodies and the world can also be conceived of as an arc: an »intentional arc« (Merleau-Ponty), in which our changing relationship to the world is formed.
As a power that connects and gives direction, this arc creates a dynamic toward the things around us, making it possible to perceive and act. Such connectedness as power and tension is always a link between body and world, a link that is in constant oscillation, moving to the never-ending rhythm of to-ward and away-from.
UNDINE EBERLEIN

Im Bogen sind Pole miteinander verbunden: durch eine Reihe von Zwischengliedern, die nur in elastischer Spannung existieren kann. Sie wird erhalten mittels der exakt gerichteten Kraftübertragung jedes einzelnen Moments im Spektrum zwischen den Polen. So wird ein Gegensatz fixiert und zugleich überwunden.
Auch das Verhältnis unserer Körper zur Welt kann als ein Bogen verstanden werden: In diesem »intentionalen Bogen« (Merleau-Ponty) entwickelt sich unsere bewegte Beziehung zur Welt.
Als Verbindungs- und Richtungskraft stiftet dieser Bogen eine Dynamik auf die Dinge der Umgebung hin, eine Möglichkeit der Wahrnehmung und Handlung. Diese Bezogenheit als Kraft und Spannung ist immer schon ein Band zwischen Körper und Welt, in einem permanent oszillierenden Wechsel, im unendlichen Rhythmus des Hin-zu und Weg-von.
UNDINE EBERLEIN

E

Auflösung Dissolution

When a conflict is solved, the pent-up energy evaporates. When an excruciatingly long wait comes to an end, fear and anxiety melt away. When a human body stops breathing, it stiffens and then decays. But what if something calls a halt to these processes? The Japanese Noh play »Matsukaze« tells the story of two women in love whose lives aren't over when they die because an unfulfilled longing keeps them trapped in a kind of limbo. At night they return to earth as ghosts and unite in an ecstatic dance with the man they love; at dawn they become wind in the pines and wild autumn rain. Dance can represent the liberation of unconscious yearnings like no other aesthetic medium. The effortless metamorphosis of human individuals into an organic mass, a wave, a gust of wind, dynamic energy – is central to the opera »Matsukaze« which tells the story of people who merge with something larger and become part of nature itself. This work is a timely reminder that we are all part of nature, connected to it by every breath we take – that we, too, are all wind and water.

HANNAH DÜBGEN ON »MATSUKAZE«

Wenn sich Konflikte lösen, verflüchtigt sich die angestaute Energie. Wenn quälendes Warten ein Ende hat, lösen sich Angst und Unruhe auf. Wenn ein menschlicher Körper nicht mehr atmet, erstarrt er und zerfällt. Doch was, wenn etwas diese Prozesse aufhält? Das japanische Nō-Theaterstück »Matsukaze« erzählt von zwei Liebenden, deren Leben mit dem Tod nicht zu Ende sind, da eine unerlöste Sehnsucht sie in einem Zwischenreich gefangen hält. Als Geister kehren die Beiden nachts zurück auf die Erde und vereinigen sich in einem ekstatischen Tanz mit dem Geliebten, bevor sie sich im Morgengrauen auflösen, Wind in den Kiefern und stürmischer Herbstregen werden. Der Tanz kann die Befreiung unbewusster Sehnsüchte darstellen wie kein anderes ästhetisches Medium. Die mühelose Metamorphose menschlicher Individuen in eine organische Masse, eine Welle, einen Windstoß, bewegte Energie, wird in »Matsukaze« zum Herzstück einer Oper, die vom Aufgehen der Menschen in etwas Größerem erzählt: der Natur. Dass wir alle zur Natur gehören, uns jeder Atemzug mit ihr verbindet, wir alle auch Wind und Wasser sind, erzählt uns das Werk heute mit neuer Dringlichkeit.

HANNAH DÜBGEN ÜBER »MATSUKAZE«

A

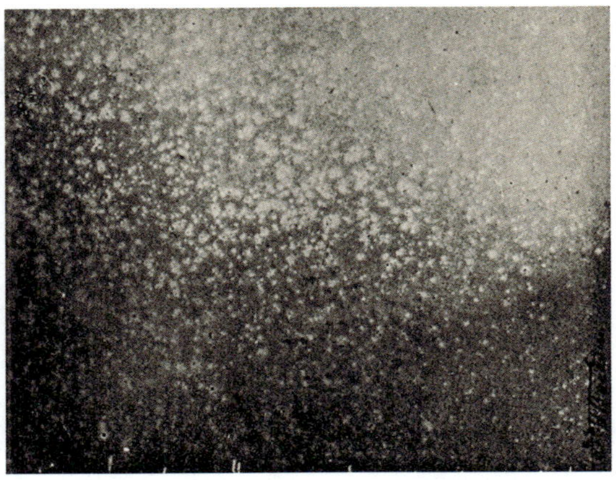

B

C

A+B+D **Hippolyte Baraduc, »L'âme humaine«, 1896, figures** C **»Matsukaze«** ↘2011 E **Sasha Waltz, study for »Medea«** ↘2007 F **»SYM-PHONIE MMXX«** ↘2022

D

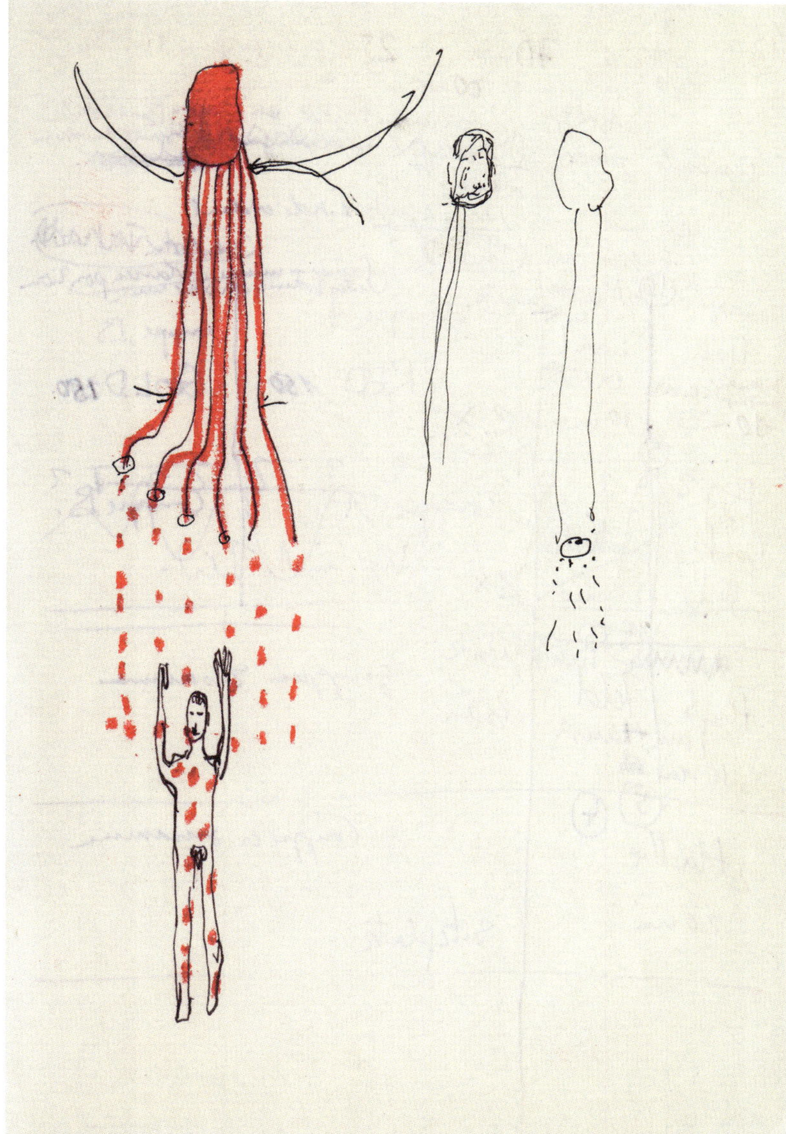

E

F

following page **»noBody« at ZKM** ↘2002 ↘2013

Balance

A

The word balance derives from the Proto-Romance word bilancia, made up of two parts, bi- meaning two and -lancia meaning scale pan. When something is balanced the scales are in equilibrium. They are not necessarily identical, but they are identically weighted. The relationship between the two scale pans need not be bilaterally symmetrical; they are not necessarily mirror images of one another. A bilaterally symmetrical figure is in equilibrium with its own mirror image; it exists only in relation to itself and allows for no other possibilities. In such a figure, appearance and weight are synonymous.
But there are other forms of symmetry in which the two parts of a figure stand in a more complex relationship to one another – in which appearance and weight differ and the two sides can relate to and connect with one another in a variety of different ways, without copying one another, without excluding other forms of interaction.
In the etymological development of the word, the bi- becomes ba-; the Late Latin word ballare, meaning to dance, imposes itself on the Proto-Romance bilancia. Dancing becomes part of balance. If you want to keep your balance you have to dance without stopping – keep moving, reaching out in all directions, always in search of equilibrium.
HANNAH JONAS

Die Balance besteht aus zwei Wortteilen. Im frühromanischen bilancia zeigt sich uns noch das bi- für zwei und das -lancia für die (Waag-)schale. Ist etwas in Balance, stehen die beiden Schalen in ausgeglichenem Gewicht. Sie sind hierbei nicht unbedingt beidseitig gleich – aber gleich gewichtet.
Die Beziehung der beiden Schalen zueinander ist nicht zwingend symmetrisch im Sinne der Spiegelsymmetrie, in der es, will die Balance gehalten werden, nur eine Spiegelachse gibt. Die spiegelsymmetrische Figur balanciert mit ihrem eigenen Spiegelbild, bezieht sich nur auf sich selbst, lässt keine anderen Richtungen zu. Erscheinung und Gewichtung der Figur sind hier gleichbedeutend.
Die Symmetrie aber kennt noch andere Möglichkeiten, in denen die beiden Teile einer Figur in komplexeren Verhältnissen zueinander stehen, in denen Erscheinung und Gewichtung voneinander abweichen, in denen die beiden Seiten unterschiedliche Bezüge eingehen und eröffnen dürfen. Um dabei dennoch, letztendlich, sich auf ihr Gegenüber zu beziehen – ohne es zu kopieren und damit anderes ausschließen zu müssen.
Etymologisch wird aus dem bi- ein ba-, es schiebt sich ins frühromanische bilancia das spätlateinische ballare für tanzen. Das Tanzen wird Teil der Balance. Will man Balance halten, muss man tanzen, nicht stehen bleiben, sondern sich bewegen, in alle Richtungen Beziehung aufbauen, immer wieder nach dem Gleichgewicht suchend. HANNAH JONAS

B

C

A »Dialoge 06 – Radiale Systeme« ↘2006 B »Dialoge – 17-25/4« ↘2001 C »Figure Humaine« ↘2017 D »Impromptus« ↘2004 E Sasha Waltz, sketchbook, undated

D

E

Bird Vogel

A

I am Music, who in sweet accents,
Can make peaceful every troubled heart,
And so with noble anger, and so with love,
Can I inflame the coldest minds.

Singing with my golden Lyre, I like
To charm, now and then, mortal ears,
And in such a fashion that I make their souls aspire more
For the resounding harmony of the lyre of Heaven.

Hence desire spurs me to tell you of Orfeo:
Of Orfeo who tamed wild beasts with his song
And made Hades answer his prayers,
To the immortal glory of Pindus and Helicon.

While I vary my songs, now happy, now sad,
No small bird shall move among these bushes,
Nor on these banks a sounding wave be heard,
And every breeze shall stay its wanderings.

LIBRETTO »L'ORFEO«
CLAUDIO MONTEVERDI

B

Ich bin die Musik, die mit lieblichen Tönen
dem verwirrten Herzen Ruhe schenkt.
Bald zu edlem Zorn, bald zur Liebe vermag ich
selbst eiserstarrte Sinne zu entfachen.

Singend zum Klang der goldenen Zither
entzücke ich zuweilen das Ohr des Sterblichen
und erwecke in der Seele die Freude an den
klangvollen Harmonien der Himmelsleier.

Nun will ich euch von Orpheus berichten,
der mit seinem Gesang die Tiere zähmte
der durch sein Bitten sogar die Hölle bezwang,
und unsterblichen Ruhm auf dem Pindos und dem Helikon errang.

Wenn ich nun meine Lieder singe, mal heiter, mal traurig,
soll der Vogel im Baum unbewegt lauschen,
soll keine Welle an die Ufer schlagen
und jedes Lüftchen still verweilen.

LIBRETTO »L'ORFEO«
CLAUDIO MONTEVERDI

C

A »Passion« ↘2010 B Anonymous, »La chasse à la chouette«, 18th century C »SYM-PHONIE MMXX« ↘2022 D »In C«, video tutorial ↘2021

D

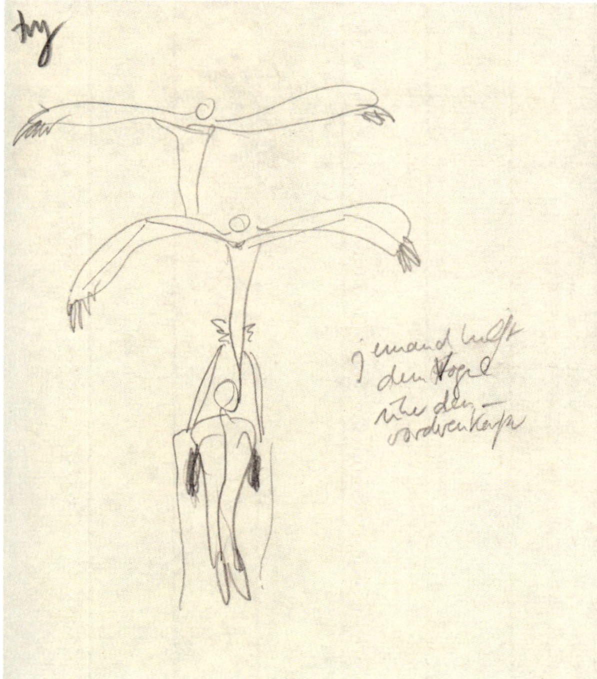

E

F

G

H

I

E **Sasha Waltz, study for »Matsukaze«** ↘2011 F **»Gezeiten«** ↘2005 G **»Continu«** ↘2010 H **»In C«** ↘2021 I **John James Audubon, »American Flamingo«, 1827**

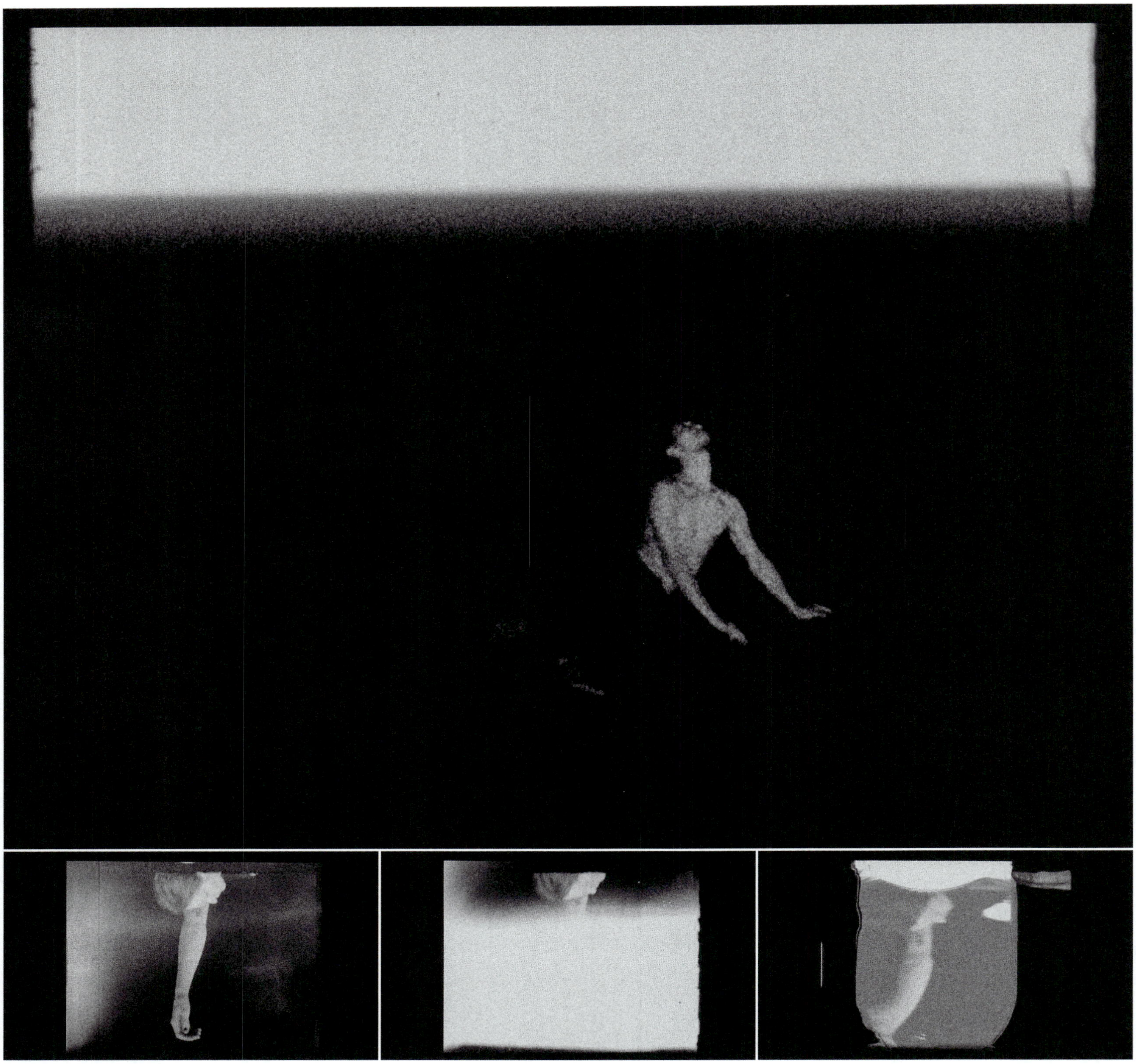

A

B

C

A **»SYM-PHONIE MMXX«, film stills** ↘2022 B **»Roméo et Juliette«** ↘2007 C **»ΕΞΟΔΟΣ | Exodos«** ↘2018 D **»Kreatur«** ↘2017 E **»noBody«** ↘2002

D

E

Body Körper

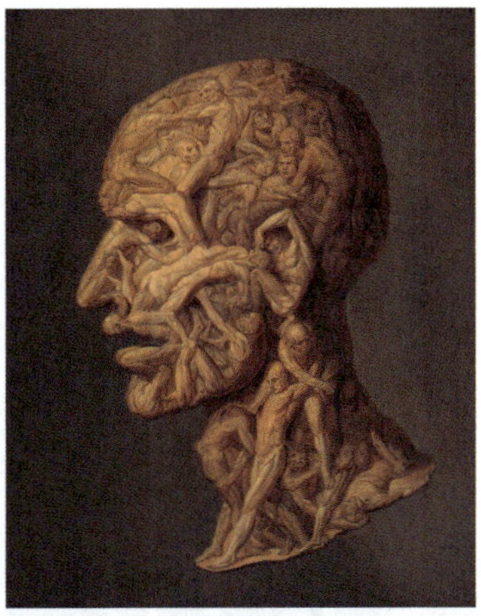

A

B

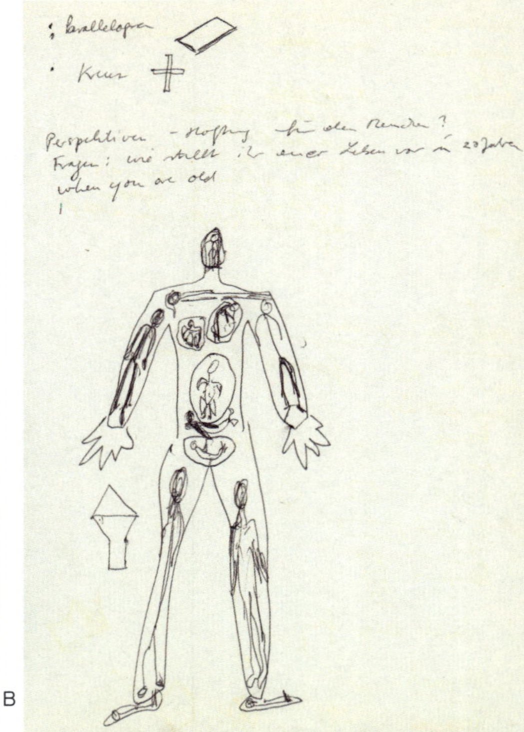

C

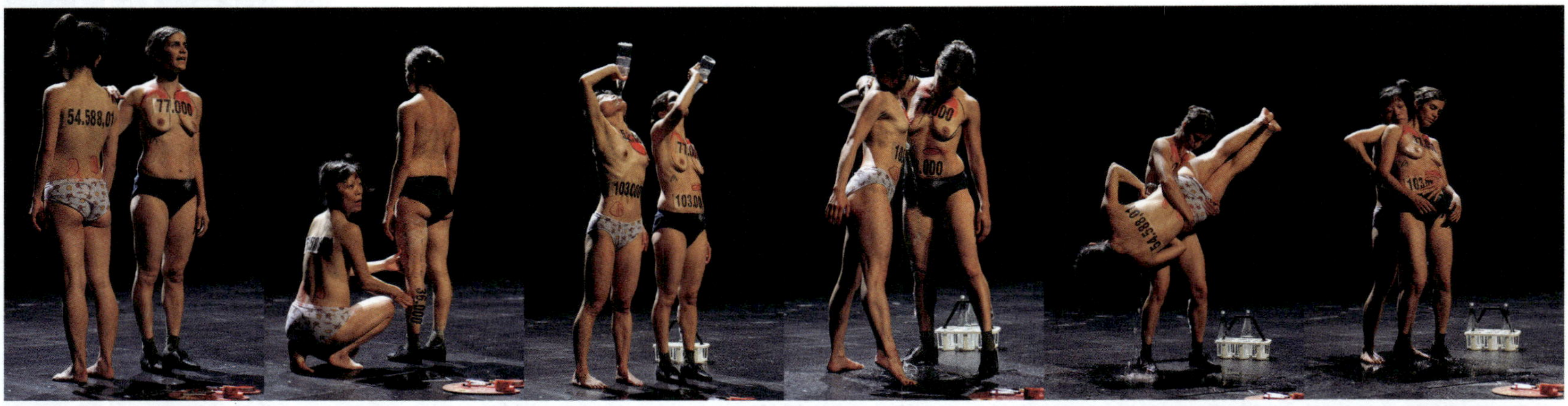

D

E

A **Filippo Balbi, »Testa anatomica«, c. 1850** B **Johannes and Lucas van Doetechum, »Caritas«, 1556** C **Sasha Waltz, study for »Körper«** ↘2000

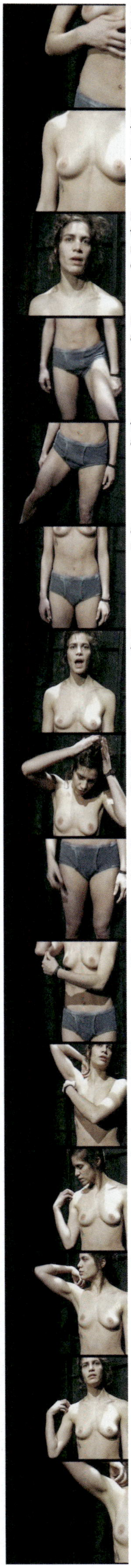

SIGAL'S STORY IN »KÖRPER«

First thing in the morning I open my two eyes.

Most of the time I found myself lying on my back.

I stretch one arm,

the second arm

and I shake my legs.

If I stand up too quickly

I feel how my blood pressure goes down

and my legs start to collapse.

Then I need to sit again

and to breath from my mouth,

3 count in,

3 count out.

3 count in,

3 count out.

F

CLAUDIA'S STORY IN »KÖRPER«

This is my body: Back side,

profile

and front side.

I didn't really choose it. I was just born more or less like this.

Now, I am 1.84 m, my weight is 21 kg and a half

and inside my whole body I have 12 litres of water.

I have a head,

a small mouth

and two

big brown eyes.

G

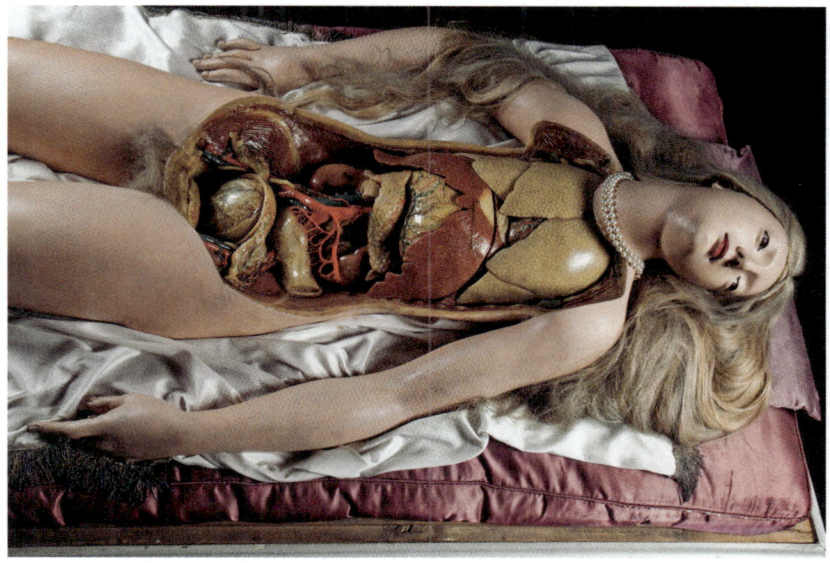

H

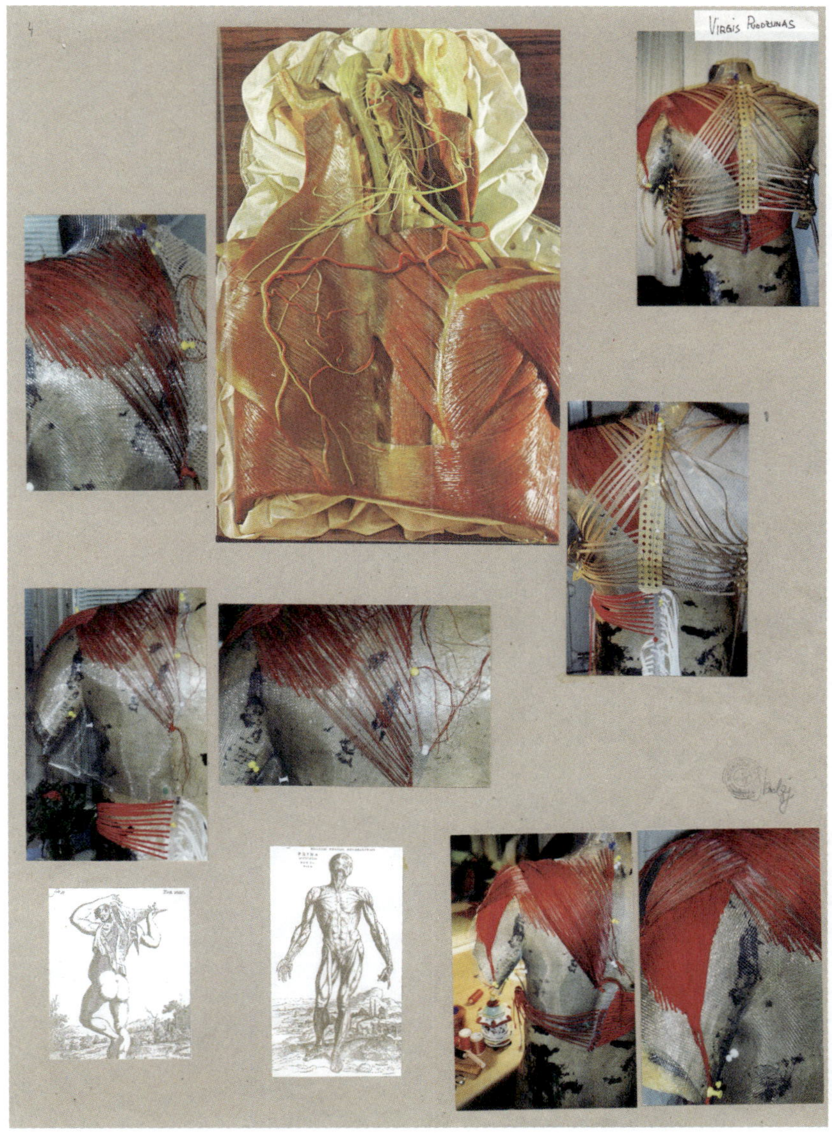

I

J

D+F+G »Körper«, film stills and transcription ↘2000 E+J »Women« ↘2017 H Body model with removable organs, 1781–86 I Bernd Skodzig, costume study for »Körper«

Bodymountain Körperberg

A

B

C

A **»Dialoge '99/II – Jüdisches Museum«** ↘1999 B **»Körper« at ZKM** ↘2000 ↘2013 C **Francisco de Goya, »Harvest of the Dead«, 1810–23**

Almost motionless, but not quite: a gentle flowing movement

painted in the air by five or six bodies: by elbows, calves, the slightly curled fingers of a relaxed hand; you screw up your eyes and motion merges with imagination.

Blurred boundaries where skin meets skin.

They slow down for a moment
creating an image
that we want to hold on to.

We want to capture it
pause it, so that we can say: There it is.
Look, we want to say, a movement
but it's only almost, not quite.

Without grasping, the hand supports an arm and the shoulder blade bears the warm weight of another body. The weight of stories very close. Vulnerable they become to being grasped.

LÁSZLÓ SANDIG

Fast bewegungslos, aber nicht ganz: Ein leichtes Fließen

in die Luft gestrichen mit fünf oder sechs Körpern, durch Ellbogen, Unterschenkel, leicht gebeugte Finger einer entspannten Hand, sodass die Augen zusammengekniffen werden müssen und die Bewegung mit der Einbildung sich vermischt.

Verschwimmende Grenzen, wenn Haut und Haut zusammentrifft.

Kurz verlangsamen sie sich,
dass ein Bild zu stehen scheint,
das wir festhalten wollen.

Wir wollen es erfassen:
dass es stehen bleibt und wir sagen können, das ist Das.
Da, wollen wir sagen: eine Bewegung,
aber hier ist das nur fast.

Ohne zu greifen trägt die Hand den Arm, das Schulterblatt das warme Gewicht eines weiteren Körpers. Das Gewicht von Geschichten ganz nah. Verletzlich werden sie, begriffen zu werden.

LÁSZLÓ SANDIG

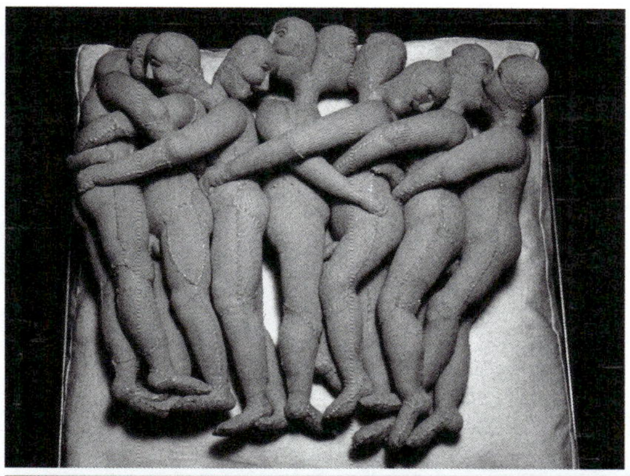

D

E

F

D Louise Bourgeois, »Seven in Bed«, 2001 E Rehearsal at ZKM ↘2013 F »Körper« ↘2000

B

A **»Körper«** ↘2000 B **»Medea«** ↘2007

A

C

D

C **Abraham Bosse, ink drawing of »Leviathan«, 1651, detail** D **»SYM-PHONIE MMXX«, rehearsal** ↘2022

Box

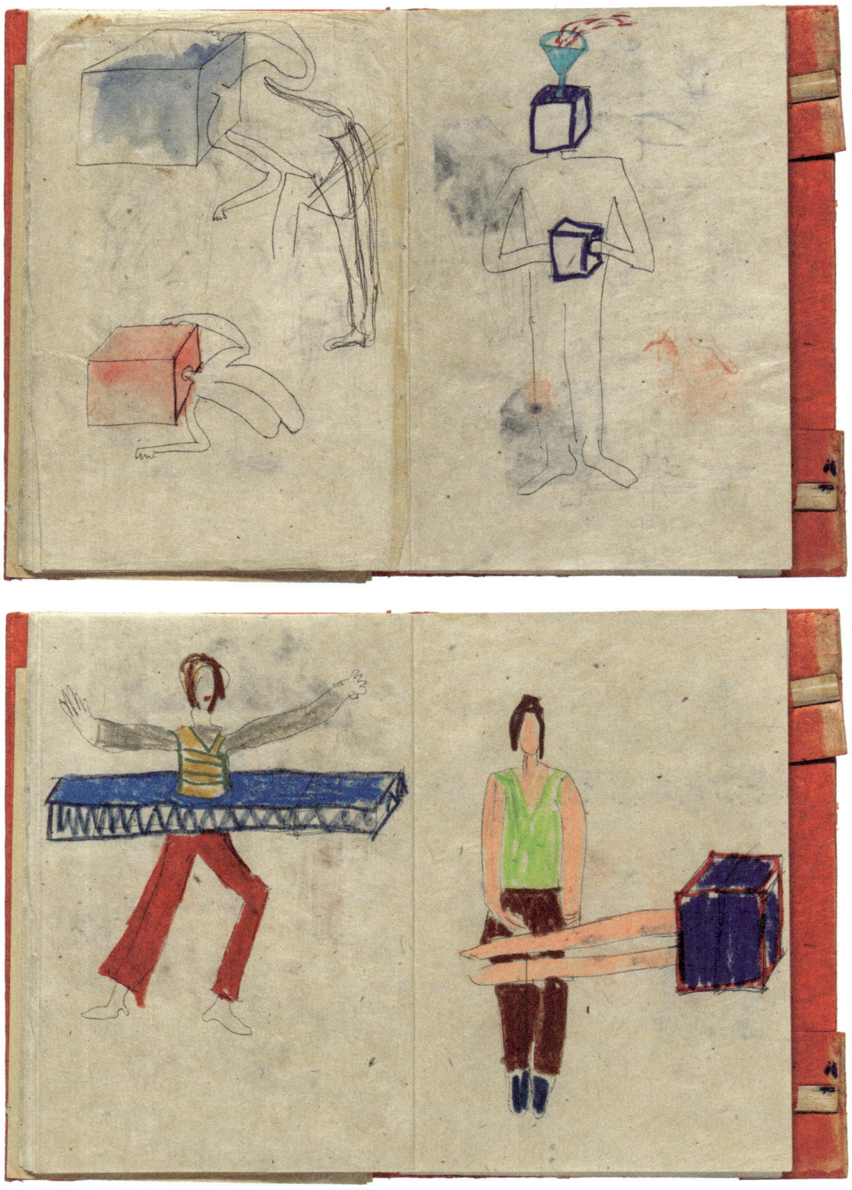

A

B

C

D

U-U-Uto-to-to-to-piaaaaaa-pia-pia Utopia! He! He! Heavvvvven Heaven, Heafam, Hfam, FamilY LylylyLY They HEY EY're THEY'RE COMING!!! WHO'S.COM-INGINGING !?! Shehehehe is coming. NO STOpPIng stoppinggo shop ping ping ping [no visaaaa]
gogo IiZzZza# human :Huwman:Wuman:Woman:Moman.Noman. N0 MAN YOW YOU!Who?YouWHOYOu !!!!! I I>you>she>we>theeeeewvvewe ususus www.WAWAVEWaveR@V€! safe place Sameplace Simbel Simpel Simple Symple Symbol

A **Sasha Waltz, sketchbook »Allee der Kosmonauten«** ↘1996 B+E **»ΕΞΟΔΟΣ | Exodos«** ↘2018 C **»Körper«** ↘2000 D+H **»insideout«** ↘2003 F **»Zweiland«, research**

III'm blackSlackHlackShe'sbackShe's black You"re blÄck I'M_B. she'syellowOWoWOWSshe's w h i t e —Ha-Ha—HA^H^AND^S^u p, raise up, stay UP--->go out <---get in --->go out <---get in --->go out......... »ΕΞΟΔΟΣ | EXODOS«

E

F

G

I

H

J

G »Zweiland« ↘1997 I »Dialoge – Künstlerhaus Bethanien« ↘1993 J »Allee der Kosmonauten« ↘1996

following page »ΕΞΟΔΟΣ | Exodos« ↘2018

Chair Stuhl

A

B

C

D

A Stuhl is not the same as a stool. A Stuhl has a back; in German the backless chair or stool is a Hocker. Seats are an expression of hierarchical relations: at the top the throne; at the bottom the footstool. Power relations are reflected in the height and breadth of the backrest, in the materials used, and in details such as castors and armrests, or even springs. The ergonomic chairs required by law in the modern workplace reflect the democratisation of our society: everyone has a right to comfort and support. The hierarchy is dissolved, but it lives on as a reference even in its dissolution.

Yet in the course of history there have also been moments of rebellion against the dominant power structures, when the body has been regarded not as something to be shored up and constrained and pressed into shape, but as something to be set in motion. In the cantilever chair, even the seated body is to be free, to move freely, you might almost say, to fly. The cantilever chair has no back legs; its front legs bend round in an L to bear the weight of the sitter who, thanks to the elasticity of the tubular steel, is permitted to move freely.

The original model for this chair was made not of steel but of gas pipes – a readymade of semi-finished products. We often forget or overlook the fact that our present-day form of freedom – for which the cantilever chair is only a placeholder – had its origins in the industrial domination of nature which we now know results in climate change and the destruction of global ecological equilibrium. Thus new power structures are built into the act of liberation. Not for nothing is the word possession related to the Latin word sedere, to sit.

FRIEDRICH VON BORRIES

Ein chair ist kein einfacher Stuhl. Ein chair hat eine Rückenlehne, anders als der stool, der eher nur ein Hocker ist. Sitzgelegenheiten drücken hierarchische Verhältnisse aus. Vom Thron bis zum Schemel sind die Machtverhältnisse geordnet. Sie spiegeln sich in der Höhe und Breite der Rückenlehne, in der Materialität der Oberflächen und in Ausstattungsdetails wie Rollen und Armlehnen oder gar wippenden Federungen. In der gesetzlich geregelten Ausstattung des Arbeitsplatzes mit ergonomischen Stühlen spiegelt sich die Demokratisierung: Jede:r hat Anrecht auf Komfort und Stütze, die Hierarchie wird aufgelöst, aber in ihrer Auflösung bleibt sie als Verweis noch erhalten.

Die Geschichte kennt aber auch kurze Aufzuckungen gegen die Machtdispositive des Sitzens, wenn der Körper nicht weiter gehalten, gestützt und formiert werden soll, sondern im Gegenteil in Bewegung gebracht, in Schwingung versetzt werden soll. Im Freischwinger soll der Körper frei sein, fast könnte man meinen: Er soll fliegen.

Der Freischwinger hat keine Hinterbeine, er kragt aus, um das Gewicht des Körpers zu tragen, und versetzt selbigen dank der Elastizität des Stahlrohrs dabei in befreiende Schwingungen.

Die Urform dieses Stuhls war noch nicht aus Stahl gebogen, sondern aus den Rohren, mit denen Gasleitungen verlegt werden, zusammengesteckt, ein Readymade aus Halbfertigzeugen. – Oft übersehen, missachten, verdrängen wir, dass unsere heutige Form von Freiheit – für die der schwingende Stuhl hier nur ein Platzhalter ist – ihren Ursprung in einer Form der industriellen Naturbeherrschung hat, die, wie wir inzwischen wissen, zum Klimawandel und zur Zerstörung des globalen ökologischen Gleichgewichts führt. Und so ist in den Akt der Befreiung eben auch ein neues Machtverhältnis eingeschrieben. Das Sitzen, das eben immer auch ein Besitzen ist, kann davon nicht lassen.

FRIEDRICH VON BORRIES

A+E **»Gezeiten«** ↘2005 B **»Zweiland«** ↘1997 C **»Travelogue II – Tears break fast«** ↘1994 D **»insideout«** ↘2003

E

F

G

H

I

F **»Women«** ↘2017 G **»Dialoge 2020 – Relevante Systeme II«** ↘2020 H **»Travelogue I – Twenty to eight«** ↘1993 I **»Dialoge 2013 – Kolkata«** ↘2013

Channel Kanal

A

What is it that a self channels when it channels itself? Is there a self to be channelled at all? Or is the self itself a channel – an unstable flow of merging and intersecting impulses, constraints, desires and inputs that are never entirely our own to calibrate or control, to govern or direct? It is when the channels that we like to refer to as our »selves« gently or violently coalesce, flowing over and through each other (no matter how momentarily or awkwardly) that we find ourselves in community. There are many words to describe the power of collective channelling: Union. Coalition. Collaboration. Amalgamation. Alliance. Chorus. Ensemble. Company. Revolution. Movement. Movement begins beyond the imagined walls of the self.
CANDICE BREITZ

Was ist es, das ein Selbst kanalisiert, wenn es sich selbst kanalisiert? Gibt es überhaupt ein Selbst, das kanalisiert wird? Oder ist das Selbst selbst ein Kanal – ein unbeständiger Fluss verschmelzender und sich überschneidender Impulse, Zwänge, Sehnsüchte und Vorgaben, bei denen es nie ganz alleine uns obliegt, sie zu kalibrieren oder zu kontrollieren, sie zu steuern oder zu leiten? Wenn die Kanäle, die wir gerne als unser »Selbst« bezeichnen, sanft oder brutal zusammenlaufen, über- und durcheinanderfließen (egal wie vorübergehend oder umständlich), dann finden wir uns selbst in Gemeinschaft wieder. Es gibt viele Wörter, um die Mächte kollektiver Kanalisierung zu beschreiben: Union. Koalition. Kollaboration. Zusammenschluss. Allianz. Chor. Ensemble. Kompanie. Revolution. Bewegung. Bewegung beginnt jenseits der imaginierten Mauern des Selbst.
CANDICE BREITZ

B

C

A »Dialoge 07 – Pergamonmuseum« ↘2007 B Sasha Waltz, research, 2022 C »Na Zemlje« ↘1998

D

E

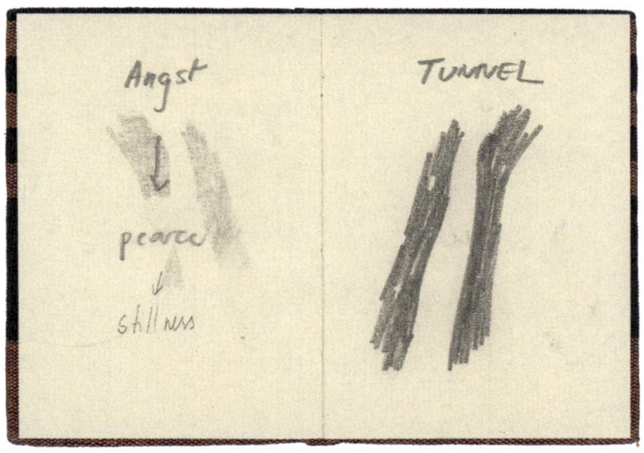

F

G

D »ΕΞΟΔΟΣ | Exodos« ↘2018 E Hieronymus Bosch, »Ascent of the Blessed«, c. 1505–15, detail F Sasha Waltz, sketchbook, undated G »Tannhäuser« ↘2014

Circle Kreis

A

B

The circle is a magical shape. It marks a place where magic happens, a place of cult and ritual. »Khorovod« is an old Slavic term for a circle dance. The dance sets the circle in motion in order to close the zone of the sacred and circumscribe the site of ritual. When Igor Stravinsky was asked to compose a ballet based on this dance he had romantic images of pagan Russia in mind. Inspired by such images, he wanted to use dance and music to bring back to life an ancient mystery. But Stravinsky's »Rite of Spring« is not a regression into pagan rites and customs; it is a ritual in the form of art. In his artwork, the archaic is fused with the modern in the mythical form of the circle dance.
JAN ASSMANN

Der Kreis ist eine magische Gestalt. Er markiert einen Ort, an dem sich ein Zauber vollzieht, ein Ritual, eine kultische Handlung. »Horovod« ist eine altslawische Bezeichnung für den Kreistanz. Er setzt den Kreis in Bewegung, um die Zone des Heiligen abzuschließen und den Ort des Rituals zu umschließen.
Als Igor Strawinsky gebeten wurde, eine Ballettmusik zu diesem Tanz zu schreiben, hatte er dafür romantische Bilder aus dem heidnischen Russland im Kopf. Angelehnt an diese Bilder sollten Tanz und Musik auf der Bühne noch einmal ein altes Mysterium zum Er-Leben bringen. Strawinskys »Le Sacre du Printemps« ist aber kein Abstieg in die Tiefe heidnischer Riten und Bräuche, sondern ein Ritual im Medium der Kunst. Dieser Kunst gelingt es, das Moderne mit dem Archaischen zur Deckung zu bringen – in der mythischen Form des Kreistanzes.
JAN ASSMANN

C

A Sasha Waltz, study for »Sacre« ↘2013 B »Sacre« ↘2013 C Hieronymus Bosch, »The Garden of Earthly Delights«, 1490–1500, detail

D

E

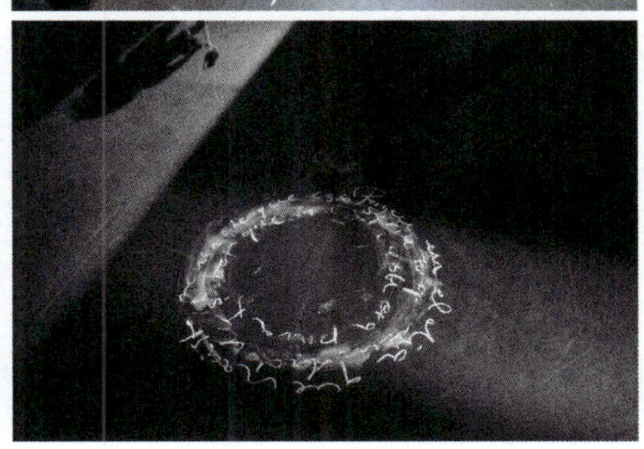

F

G

H

D **»Women«** ↘2017 E **»insideout«** ↘2003 F **»ΕΞΟΔΟΣ | Exodos«** ↘2018 G **»Dialoge '99/I – Sophiensæle«** ↘1999 H **»rauschen«** ↘2019

A

B

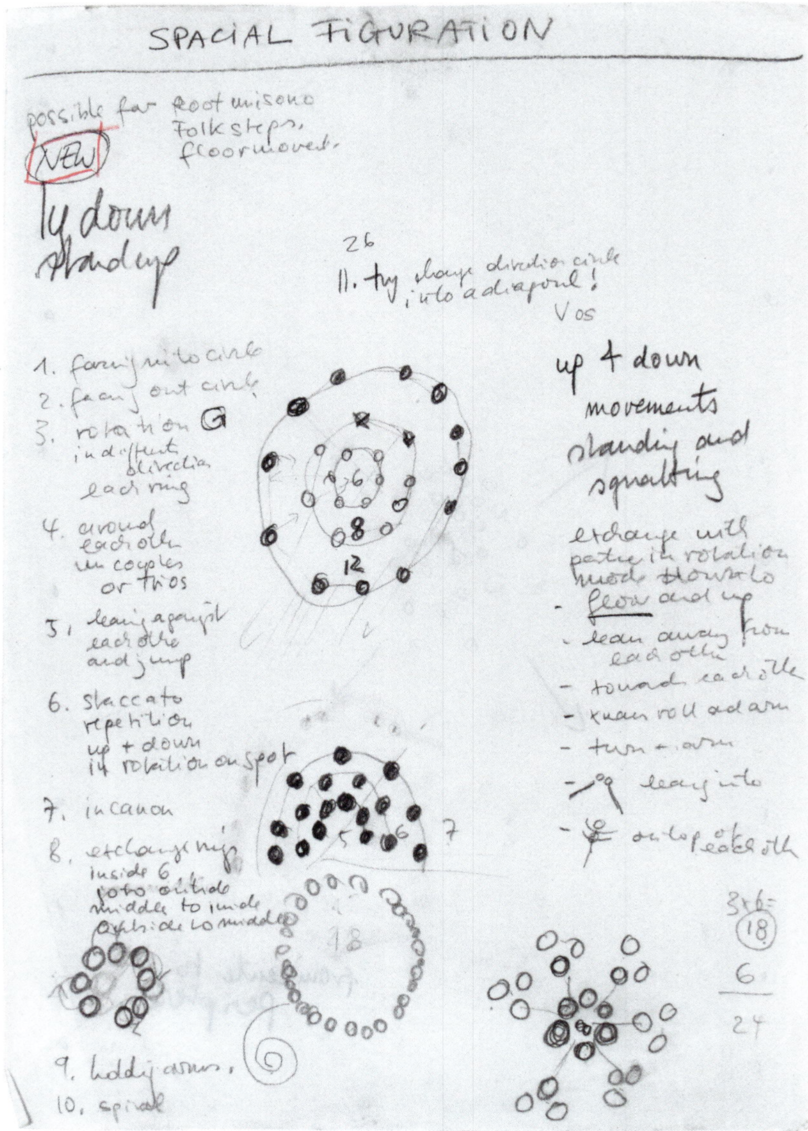

C

D

A **»Dialoge 07 – Pergamonmuseum«** ↘2007 B **»ΕΞΟΔΟΣ | Exodos«** ↘2018 C **Sasha Waltz, study for »Sacre«** ↘2013 D+G **»Medea«** ↘2007

E

F

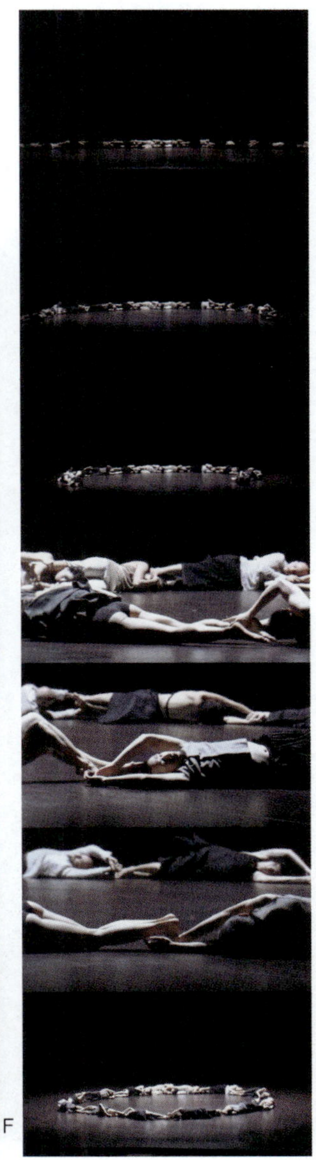

G

E »Dialoge 2013 – Kolkata« ↘2013 F »Johannes-Passion« ↘2024

following page »Körper« ↘2000

Cloud Wolke

A

cloudprayer

once gnarly once thorny
once smooth
where it flies and it crawls
they wait
body buddy birdy
c c c c
loud loud loud loud
clouds

when I stretch out my arms
when I run faster
I manage to jump out of my body
do clouds have the same problems
or are they trying to hold onto their bodies
like I do when I cut it or embrace it
I lend my body to the wind and try out
what the clouds tell me about it

I ask
if the body were a sentence
would the big toe be the beginning or the end
they answer
if the body were a sentence
it would never stop going on and on
its metamorphoses are too slow for the sky
too fast for the earth

what connects us is warmth and water
take these clouds into your eyes
and be their continuation

ahh mmm e n

VOLHA HAPEYEVA

wolkengebet

mal eckig mal dornig
mal glattlinig
wo er fliegt und er kriecht
wartet sie
körp er körp sie körp ich
wo wo wo wo
wo wo wo wo
lke

wenn ich die arme ausbreite
wenn ich jetzt schneller laufe
gelingt es aus dem körper herauszuspringen
haben die wolken dieselben probleme
oder versuchen sie ihre körper festzuhalten
wie ich wenn ich ihn ritze oder umarme
ich leihe meinen körper dem wind und taste
was mir die wolken über ihn erzählen

ich frage
wenn der körper ein satz wäre
wäre die große zehe der anfang oder das ende
sie antworten
wäre der körper ein satz
würde er nie aufhören zu dauern
seine metamorphosen sind zu langsam für den himmel
zu schnell für die erde

was uns verbindet sind wärme und wasser
nimm diese wolke in deine augen
und sei ihre fortsetzung

atem

VOLHA HAPEYEVA

B

A »Kreatur« ↘2017 B »noBody« in Avignon ↘2002 C »noBody« at ZKM ↘2002 ↘2013

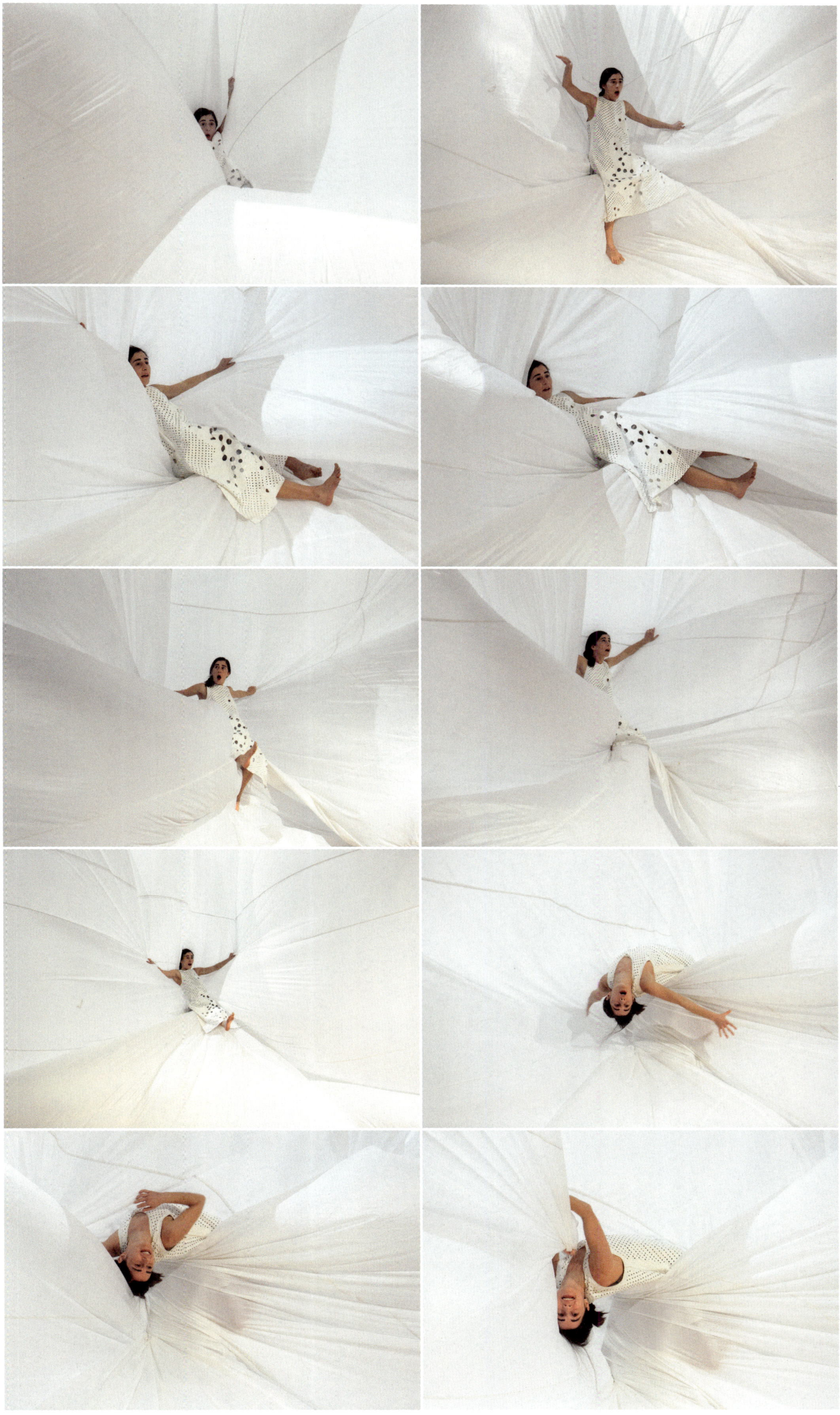

C

following page **»noBody« at ZKM** ↘2002 ↘2013

Clump Knäuel

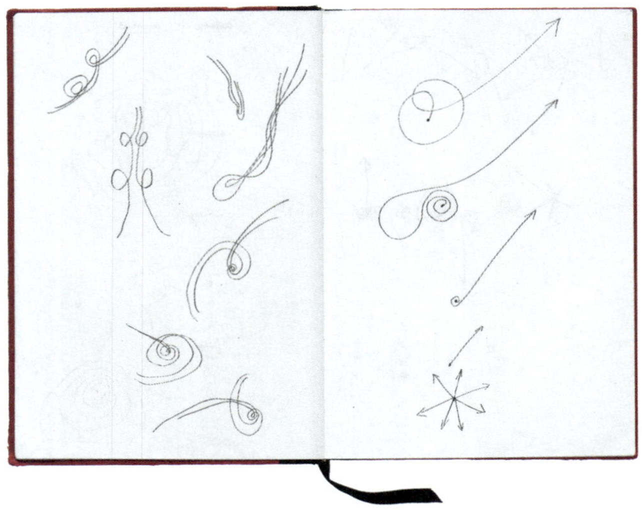

C

A

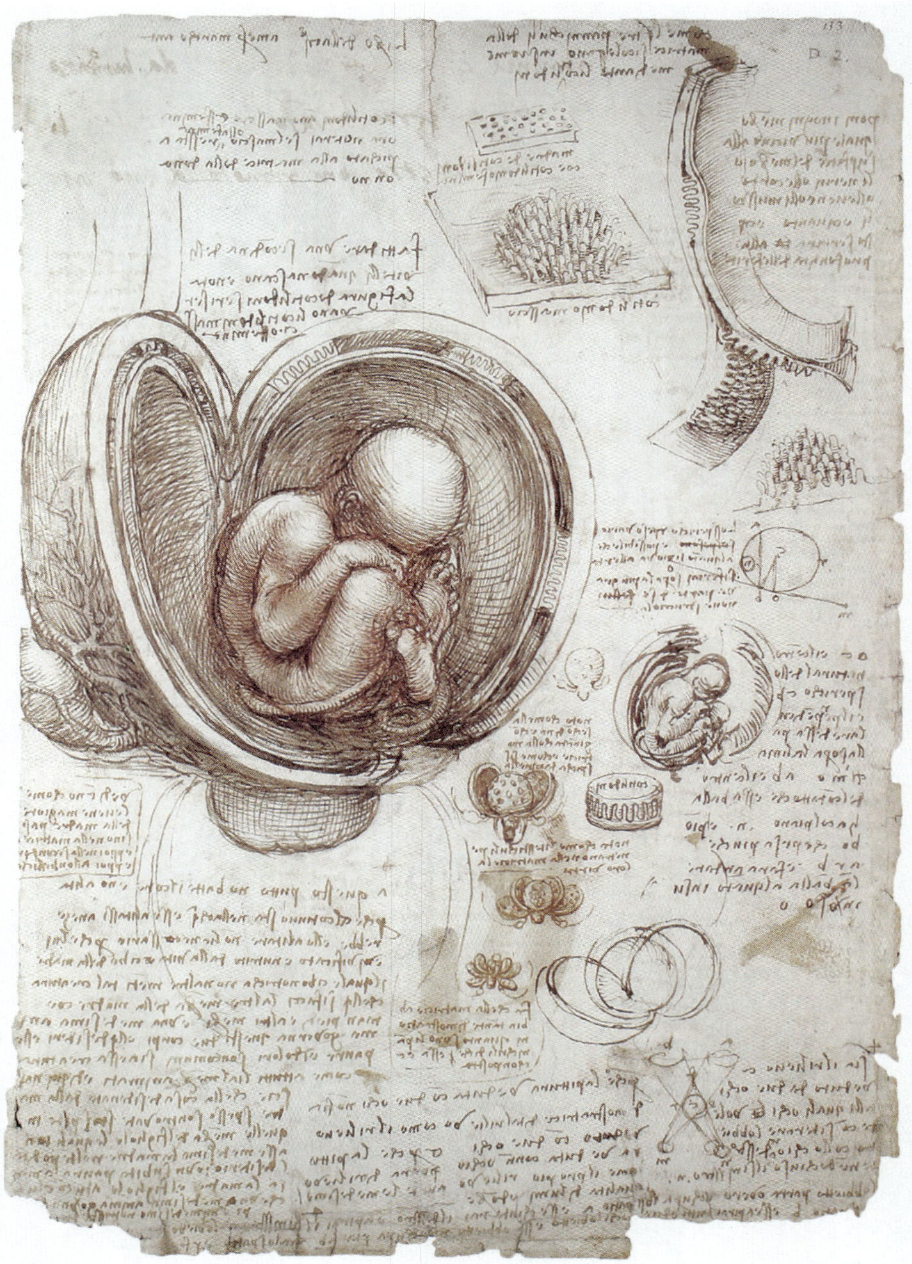

D

B

E

F

A **»Dialoge 09 – MAXXI«** ↘2009 B+F **»ΕΞΟΔΟΣ | Exodos«** ↘2018 C **Sasha Waltz, sketchbook, 2008** D **Leonardo da Vinci, study of the fetus in the womb, c. 1511**

G

H

I

J

E **Newspaper clipping from Sasha Waltz's sketchbook, undated** G–J **»noBody«** ↘2002 H **»Kreatur«, rehearsal (edited), 2017** I **Rachel Kneebone, »Balance«, 2017**

Connection Verbindung

A

B

A **Sasha Waltz, drawing, undated** B **»Na Zemlje«** ↘1998 C **»Gezeiten«** ↘2005 D **»Beethoven 7 in Delphi«** ↘2021 E **Sasha Waltz, notes »Continu«** ↘2010

D

Anything that connects ceases to belong only to itself: borders and contours blur and even vanish when connections are made. Inside intertwines with outside, self with other.
In dance as in life, connecting and letting go alternate with one another, often defying our plans in the process. Form and motion, acceptance and abandon flow into one another and merge, generating new, creative, and surprising things. Physical-corporeal affect and resonance create a tangible in-between; in this »intercorporeality« (Merleau-Ponty) we are always already together and coupled with the »flesh of the world«. But such connection and resonance need not be harmonious; they can also imply violence and injury.
Radical concepts of a comprehensive connectivity tell us that it is not only we who connect ourselves to one another and to things, but also the things as »agents« that determine connections between entities.
UNDINE EBERLEIN

Was sich verbindet, gehört sich nicht mehr nur allein: Konturen und Grenzen werden unscharf, können zeitweise verschwinden. Innen und Außen, Eigenes und Fremdes verflechten sich in solcher Ver-Bindung.
Im Tanz wie im Leben wechseln Ver-Bindung und Ab-Lösung einander ab, entziehen sich oft unserer Planung im Transit des Geschehens. Bewegung und Gestaltung, Hinnahme und Hingabe wechseln, gehen ineinander über.
So kann Neues, Überraschendes und Kreatives entstehen.
Körperlich-leibliche Affizierung und Resonanz schaffen ein erfahrbares Dazwischen: In dieser »Zwischenleiblichkeit« (Merleau-Ponty) sind wir immer schon mit einander und dem »Stoff der Welt« verwoben. Aber solche Verbindung und Resonanz muss keineswegs harmonisch sein, kann auch Gewalt und Verletzung bedeuten.
Radikale Ansätze einer umfassenden Konnektivität sagen: Nicht nur wir verbinden uns durch unser Handeln aktiv mit einander und den Dingen, sondern diese bestimmen als »Aktanten« das Verbindungs-Geschehen mit.
UNDINE EBERLEIN

C

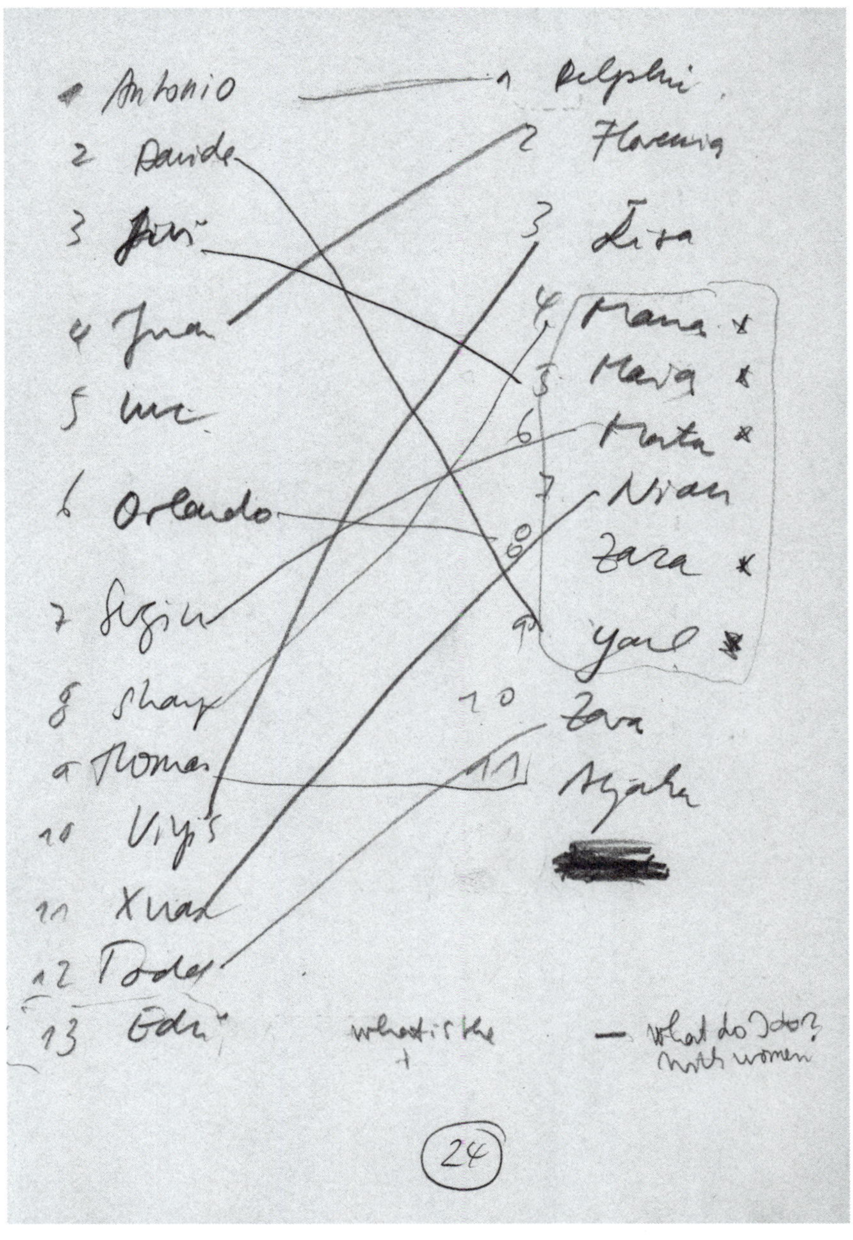

E

Egg Ei

A

B

C

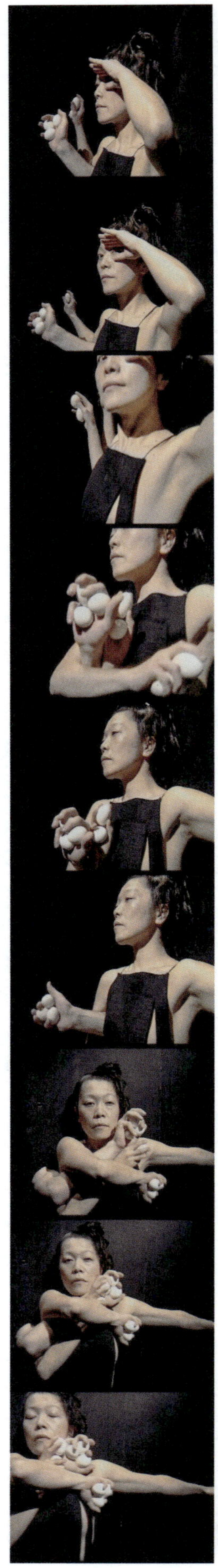

D

A+C **»Medea«** ↘2007 B **Sasha Waltz, 1967** D **»Körper«** ↘2000

E

F

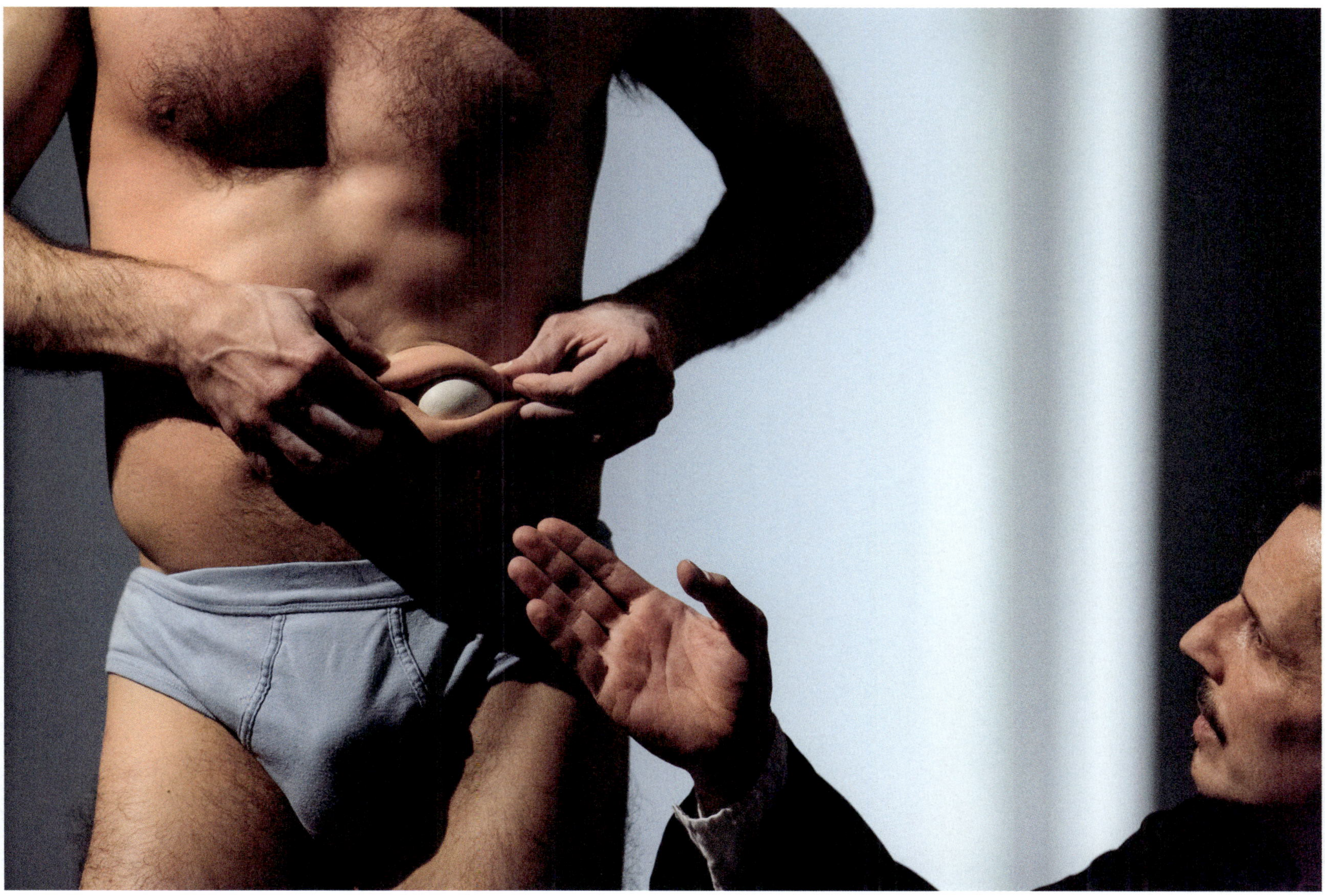
G

E »S« ↘2000 F **Hieronymus Bosch, »The Garden of Earthly Delights«, 1490–1500, detail** G **»Körper« at ZKM** ↘2000 ↘2013

Ende End

The curtain falls. This is usually a sign that the performance has come to an end. The curtain that was raised at the start falls; the game is over. Whatever happens after the end is not meant to be seen; the stage is kept hidden. Its untheatrical reality. Its mechanisms. Its lights shining on the stagehand who has to clear up. The curtain is a boundary beyond which all is secret.
Here the curtain falls at the start. A blood-red curtain over the orchestra pit – a long, oversize piece of cloth imitating what we are used to seeing while the orchestra is playing. This boundary marker is released from its anchoring and falls noisily, following gravity, vertically from top to bottom in a hard cut, not just to the floor but lower, below stage where it comes to rest, hidden from view. We know that this curtain isn't going to go up again. As if a beginning is no longer possible. Although the performance is only just starting. And we see the big, empty space. And we hear a single buzzing tone, coming from far away, filling the room like the echo of something that's already starting to fade. There is nothing else. Beginning or end – there's no way of knowing. Do we want everything to remain undecided, so that there's no need for farther drama? Is the stagnant story of monotonous quiet in near-dark emptiness in fact the benevolent sublime trying to tell us beware?
CHRISTIAN RUZICSKA ON »MEDEA«

Der Vorhang fällt. Damit ist für gewöhnlich das Ende einer Vorstellung gemeint. Der zu Beginn hochgezogene Vorhang fällt, das Spiel ist aus. Was nach dem Ende folgt, darf nicht zu sehen sein, der Raum der Bühne wird verborgen gehalten. Seine nicht theatrale Wirklichkeit. Seine Mechanik. Sein Licht, das auf den Bühnenarbeiter fällt, der aufzuräumen hat. Der Vorhang als Grenze markiert das Geheimnis der Erscheinung.
Hier fällt der Vorhang im Beginn. Blutrot, über den Orchestergraben verlängert, ein überdimensional langes Tuch, nachahmend, was wir gewohnt sind zu sehen, während die Ouvertüre üblicher Weise zu hören ist, wird diese Grenzmarkierung nun aus ihrer Verankerung gelöst und fällt laut, der Schwerkraft folgend, senkrecht von oben nach unten und im harten Schnitt nicht nur zu Boden, sondern tiefer, auf die Unterbühne, wo er verborgen ruht für unsere Augen. Wir wissen, dieser Vorhang wird sich nicht mehr heben können. Als ob kein Anfang mehr möglich wäre. Mitten im Beginn. Und wir sehen den leeren, weiten Raum. Und wir hören einen einzigen sirrenden Ton, von weit her kommend, den Raum ausfüllend, wie ein Echo, von etwas, das beginnt, zu verhallen. Nichts ist außer diesem Anfang oder Ende, es ist nicht zu entscheiden. Möchte man wünschen, das Ununterscheidbare möge in der Schwebe verharren, damit sich nicht abspielen müsse ein weiteres Drama? Ist die stillstehende Erzählung der eintönigen Ruhe in fast dunkler Leere schon die wohltuende Erhabenheit, die uns einflüstern möchte: Hüte dich!?
CHRISTIAN RUZICSKA ÜBER »MEDEA«

A

A

It's no longer a maze, this place where, one after the other, we stood at the entrance, obeying the bitter fate we had chosen. We decorated it with everything we wanted to find. Everything we imagined to be safe and promising.
It's no longer a maze, this place we wandered through for years, unable to escape. Now we are trapped in an earthly limbo, palpating our hearts to reassure ourselves that they're still beating. We are searching for what hope is trying to tell us. That the humanity that we are robbed of daily – through destructive classifications and the invention of new names for us – has dwindled almost to nothing, barely enough to face the world with.
We laughed till we cried whenever one of us was gripped by fear. We fled with our voices that had become too cramped for comfort in our country. We went through the fires of war with our voices until we came to the boats, and the boats carried us to nothingness when we drowned and into the maze when we were saved. We sold what was left of our dreams and memories. We console ourselves, turning our backs on everything and telling ourselves that with a little peace and quiet, a little time, we can get away from it all – we just have to forget; we just have to wake up in the morning safe and sound, without the noise and the oppression of war. How, after all that, can we be a source of fear?
We're the ones, we say, who make the curtains around us fall in order to brighten up the stage and overcome our sorrow. With a smile and an outstretched hand, reaching out to our frightened audience.
This is our chance to tell the story of water before it's filled into bottles, giving shape and color to the distorted image.
I write to put an end to the time of isolation that is demoralising us and to salvage the wreckage of ruined humanity.
I try to whisper stories into the ears of the world. Stories about what we have sown in our country and are still sowing today. We do not want the soil of fear to go on spoiling the harvest.
YASMINE NAYEF MEREI

Es ist kein Irrgarten mehr, an dessen Anfang wir standen, einer nach dem anderen, dem Schicksal gehorchend, das wir in seiner Bitterkeit wählten. Geschmückt haben wir es, mit all dem, was wir uns anzutreffen wünschten. All jenem, das wir uns als sicher und vielversprechend erträumten.
Es ist kein Irrgarten mehr, in dem wir über Jahre umhergezogen und stecken geblieben sind. Nun stehen wir im irdischen Limbus, tasten jede Faser unseres Herzens ab, um uns zu vergewissern, dass es schlägt. Wir suchen nach dem, was die Hoffnung uns mitzuteilen sucht. Dass von der Menschlichkeit, die uns täglich geraubt wird – durch das Untergehen in Klassifikationen und die Erfindung neuer Namen für uns – nur noch wenig übrig geblieben ist, um der Welt um uns herum zu begegnen.
Wir lachen, bis wir weinen, jedes Mal wenn die Angst einen von uns gepackt hat. Wir flohen mit unseren Stimmen, denen der Raum eng geworden war in unserem Land. Die Feuer des Krieges durchquerten wir mit ihnen, bis hin zu den Booten, die uns ins Nichts trugen, wenn wir ertranken, und in den Irrgarten, wenn wir gerettet wurden. Wir verkauften, was uns blieb an Erinnerungen und Träumen. Wir trösten uns selbst, während wir alldem den Rücken kehren und denken, wir entkommen dem Spiel mit ein wenig Ruhe, Zeit, dem Vergessen oder schließlich den sicheren Morgenstunden, ohne den Lärm des Krieges und seine Unterdrückung.
Wie also können wir nach alldem eine Quelle der Angst sein?
Wir sind es, die die Vorhänge zum Fallen bringen, die uns umgeben – so sagen wir das –, um die Bühne zu verschönern und unsere Trauer zu bezwingen. Mit einem Lächeln und einer Hand, ausgestreckt, hin zu unserem verängstigten Gegenüber.
Dies ist unsere Gelegenheit, die Geschichte des Wassers zu erzählen, bevor es in die Flasche gefüllt wird und so dem verzerrten Bild seine Dimensionen und Farben gibt, die es sichtbar machen.
Der Grund, warum ich schreibe, ist der Versuch, der Zeit der Isolation, die uns zermürbt, ein Ende zu setzen und die Trümmer der untergegangenen Menschheit zu bergen.
Ein Versuch, Geschichten in die Ohren der Welt zu flüstern. Geschichten über das, was wir in unserem Land gesät haben und immer noch neu säen. Nur wollen wir nicht, dass der Boden der Angst die Ernte weiter verdirbt.
YASMINE NAYEF MEREI

B

C

A Théodore Géricault, »The Raft of the Medusa«, 1818–19 B »ΕΞΟΔΟΣ | Exodos« ↘2018 C »Dido & Aeneas« ↘2005 D »Kreatur« ↘2017

D

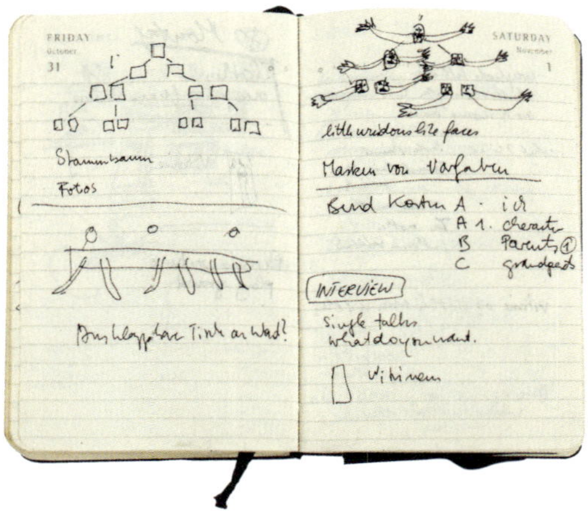

A

B

C

D

E

A **Sasha Waltz, sketchbook »insideout«** ↘2003 B–D **»insideout«** ↘2003 E **»insideout« at ZKM** ↘2003 ↘2013

F

G

Did you say with Creon's daughter Yes
Why not with Creon's daughter who has power
Over her father Creon who alone
Can grant to us the right to live in Corinth
Or drive us out to other foreign shores
Right now perhaps he is embracing Jason
In supplication her unwrinkled knees
For me and for his sons whom he loves
Are you crying or laughing Nurse
[…]
And my brother oh my brother Jason
Whom I threw into your pursuers path
Dismembered he by these my sister hands
To help you to escape from our father
You'd robbed His father and mine Do you love
Your sons You want to have them back your sons
You still owe me a brother Jason

HEINER MÜLLER
»MEDEAMATERIAL«

Hast du gesagt bei Kreons Tochter Ja
Warum bei Kreons Tochter nicht die Macht hat
Wohl über Kreon ihren Vater Der
Uns geben kann das Wohnrecht in Korinth
Oder austreiben in ein andres Ausland
Gerade jetzt vielleicht umfaßt er Jason
Mit Bitten ihre faltenlosen Knie
Für mich und seine Söhne die er liebt
Weinst oder lachst du Amme
[…]
Und meinen Bruder Meinen Bruder Jason
Den ich deinen Verfolgern in den Weg warf
Zerstückt von diesen meinen Schwesternhänden
Für deine Flucht vor dem beraubten Vater
Meinem und seinem Liebst du deine Söhne
Willst du sie wiederhaben deine Söhne
Du bist mir einen Bruder schuldig Jason

HEINER MÜLLER
»MEDEAMATERIAL«

H

I

F »Allee der Kosmonauten«, photo shoot ↘1996 G »Dido & Aeneas« ↘2005 H Federico Barocci, »Aeneas Carrying His Father Out of Troy«, before 1598 I »Sacre« ↘2013

A

I have to confess: even after six weeks when I arrive home I go through a very specific procedure. First turn of the key, second turn of the key. Closing the second door. Switch the light on the right side. Entering the first room. Left, right, behind me. Further step … light on the right. The first bedroom. Looking under the first bed. Left, right, 360°. Switch the light. This time on the left side. The second bedroom. Looking under the second bed. Carefully. It's where I sleep … five steps. It's actually six steps. I checked yesterday, yesterday, yesterday, yesterday …
CLÉMENTINE DELUY IN »RAUSCHEN«

Ich muss gestehen: Selbst nach sechs Wochen durchlaufe ich eine ganz bestimmte Prozedur, wenn ich nach Hause komme. Erste Drehung des Schlüssels, zweite Drehung des Schlüssels. Schließen der zweiten Türe. Das Licht auf der rechten Seite einschalten. Den ersten Raum betreten. Links, rechts, hinter mir. Noch ein Schritt … Licht auf der rechten Seite. Das erste Schlafzimmer. Ein Blick unter das erste Bett. Links, rechts, 360°. Licht einschalten. Diesmal auf der linken Seite. Das zweite Schlafzimmer. Ein Blick unter das zweite Bett. Vorsichtig. Dort schlafe ich … fünf Schritte. Eigentlich sind es sechs Schritte. Ich überprüfte es gestern, gestern, gestern, gestern …
CLÉMENTINE DELUY IN »RAUSCHEN«

Fliegen Flying

A

B

C

D

A **Sasha Waltz, sketchbook, undated** B **»Passion«** ↘2010 C **»Medea«** ↘2007 D **»Dialoge – 17-25/4«, video installation** ↘2001

E

F

E **»Dialoge 09 – MAXXI«** ↘2009 F **»Matsukaze«** ↘2011

Flower Blume

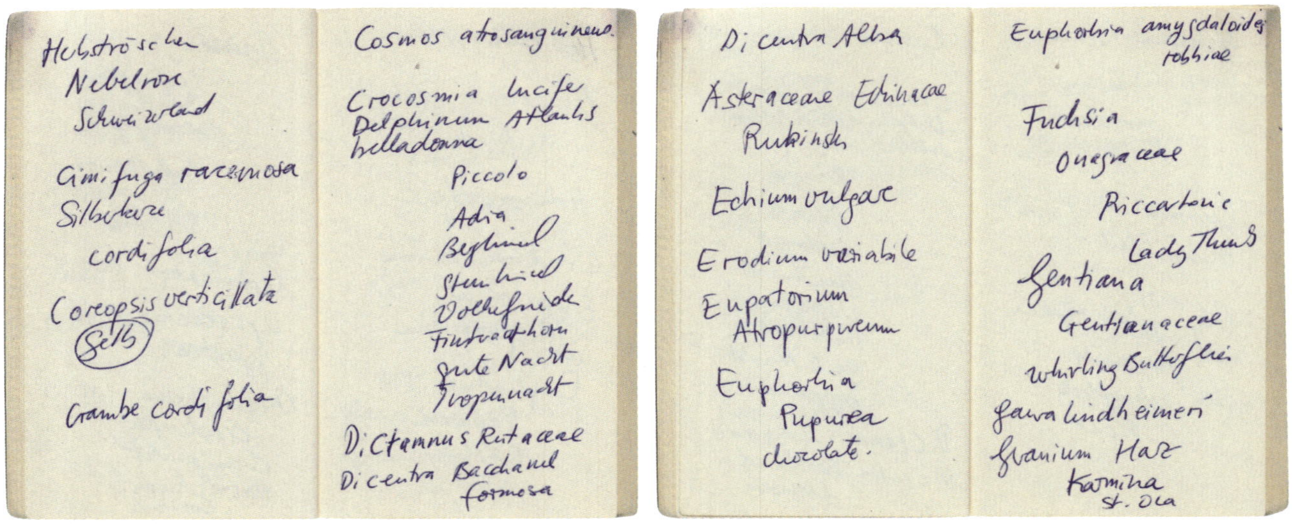

A

B

C

D

A **Sasha Waltz, notebook, 2020** B **»Orfeo«** ↘2014 C **Joos van Cleve, »Madonna and Child«, 1530–35, detail** D **»Kreatur«** ↘2017

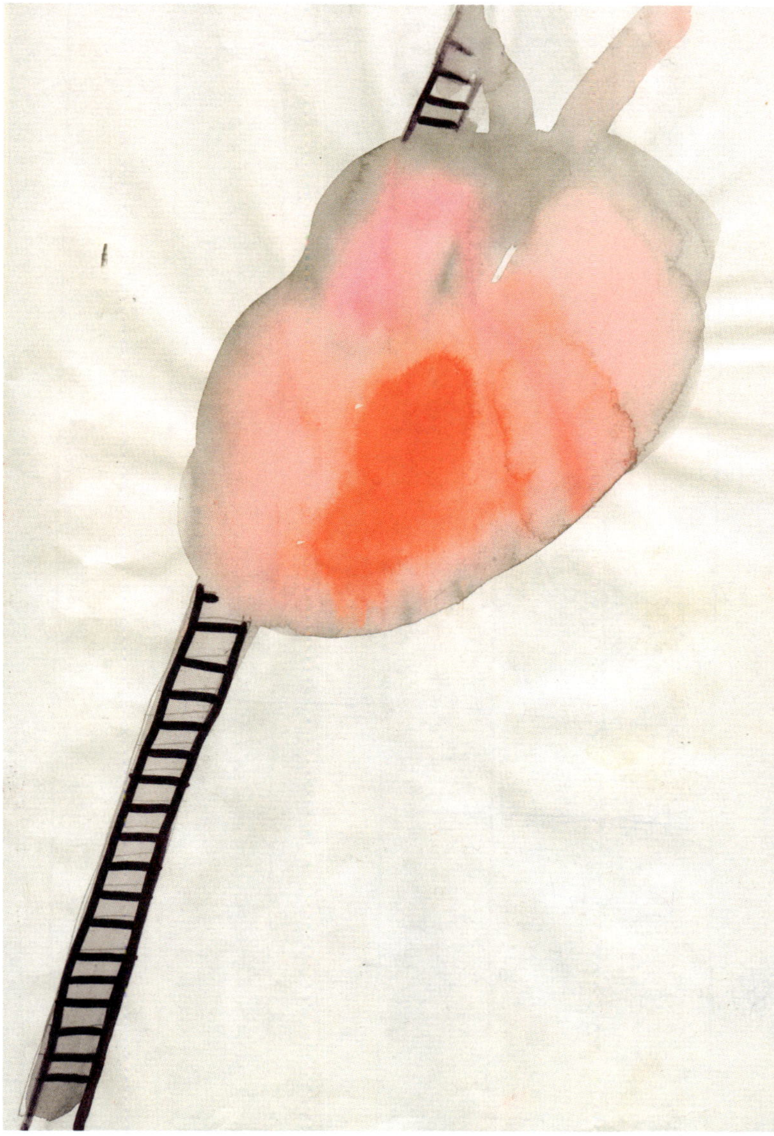

E

G

F

H

E **Sasha Waltz, watercolour, undated** F **Cosimo Tura, »Month of August«, c. 1470, detail** G+H **»Dialoge 09 – MAXXI«** ↘2009

Haare Hair

A

That moment
my legs
wanted to curl
around his.
I left my head at the bar.
So I really need
to wash my hair
before tomorrow.

»TRAVELOGUE I – TWENTY TO EIGHT«

B

C

A **»Travelogue I – Twenty to eight«** ↘1993 B **»Dido & Aeneas«, rehearsal** ↘2005 C **»Kreatur«** ↘2017 D **»Dialoge 09 – MAXXI«** ↘2009

D

A

B

C

D

A **»Gezeiten«** ↘2005 B **»Dialoge 2020 – Relevante Systeme«** ↘2020 C **Francisco de Goya, »The Duchess of Alba Arranging Her Hair«, 1795** D **»Zweiland«** ↘1997

E

Hanging Hängen

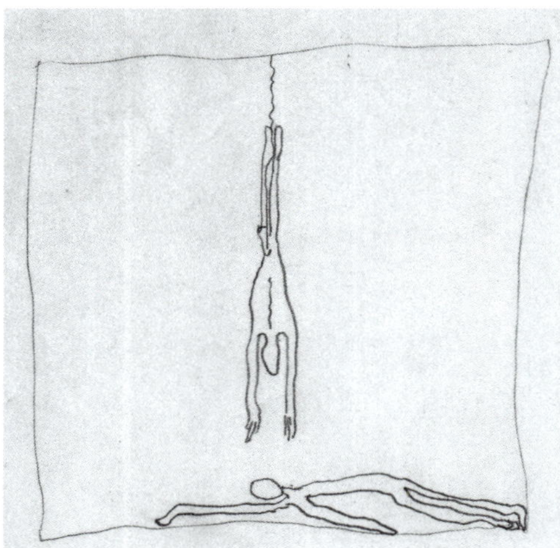

A

B

C

D

A **Sasha Waltz, drawing, undated** B **Andrea del Sarto, two studies of a man suspended by his left leg, 1530** C **»Dialoge 09 – MAXXI«** ↘2009

E

D »**Dialoge – Künstlerhaus Bethanien**« ↘1993 E »**Dialoge 09 – Neues Museum**« ↘2009

following page »**ΕΞΟΔΟΣ | Exodos**« ↘2018

A

A **»Kreatur«** ↘2017 B **»SYM-PHONIE MMXX«, rehearsal** ↘2022 C **»SYM-PHONIE MMXX«** ↘2022

B

C

Impulse, to impel, to set in motion. From within or without, often suddenly, surprisingly.
When impulses are transmitted it can create a complex ensemble of movement, energy, and emotion, often at the same time and in synchrony. Such resonance need not mean homogenisation; difference and otherness can be preserved.
The transfer of or response to impulses can never be completely controlled; their modulation through the material and living body is always unpredictable. Self-awareness and self-denial co-exist, activity and passivity, own and other.
How exactly it begins, how it will go on, eludes all plans and stipulations: »… at the still point, there the dance is, / But neither arrest nor movement. And do not call it fixity, / Where past and future are gathered. Neither movement from nor towards, / Neither ascent nor decline. Except for the point, the still point, / There would be no dance, and there is only the dance.« (T. S. Eliot, »Burnt Norton«)

UNDINE EBERLEIN

Anstoß, antreiben, in Bewegung setzen. Von außen oder innen, oft plötzlich und überraschend.
Wenn Impulse sich übertragen, kann ein komplexes Ensemble von Bewegungen, Energien und Emotionen entstehen, oft synchron und in gleichgerichteter Dynamik. Solche Resonanz muss nicht Homogenisierung bedeuten, kann Differenz und Fremdheit bewahren.
Die Weitergabe oder Beantwortung der Impulse ist nie ganz kontrollierbar, ihre Modulation durch den eigenen Körper-Leib immer auch Widerfahrnis. Selbstbezug und Selbstentzug, Aktivität und Passivität, Eigenes und Fremdes sind ko-existent.
Wie genau es anfängt oder weitergeht, entzieht sich Plan und Verfügung: »… at the stillpoint, there the dance is, / But neither arrest nor movement. And do not call it fixity, / Where past and future are gathered. Neither movement from nor towards, / Neither ascent nor decline. Except for the point, the still point, / There would be no dance, and there is only the dance.« (T. S. Eliot, »Burnt Norton«)

UNDINE EBERLEIN

following page **»Kreatur«** ↘2017

Kiss Kuss

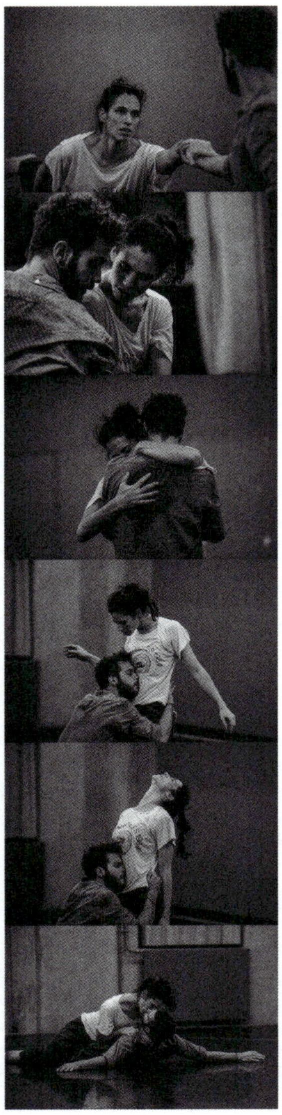
A

B

C

When I was a child, approaching puberty, and started to touch my lips to the softest part of my arm, I thought that kisses were another form of speaking – one that spoke not to our ears, but to our mouths. I thought that to kiss another person was to speak into their mouth without uttering a word, and that if someone kissed me and then abandoned me – when my mouth remembered the loneliness of its existence and began to grieve – all the words that the other person had spoken into my mouth would begin to move inside me, down my throat and into my gullet; they would begin to shift my organs around to stop the ache, a few millimetres down, a few centimetres to the right. These words would rearrange my body as they saw fit. And I would have no choice but to play the submissive host, faithful to the end.
SENTHURAN VARATHARAJAH

Als ich ein Kind war, kurz vor der Pubertät, als ich anfing, auf der weichsten Stelle meines Oberarms meine Lippen abzulegen, dachte ich, der Kuss sei eine andere Form des Sprechens, die den Mund meint, nicht unsere Ohren. Als ich ein Kind war, dachte ich, küssen heißt, in den Mund eines anderen Menschen zu sprechen: ohne ein Wort dabei zu sagen. Und sobald der Mensch, der uns noch küsste, uns verlassen haben wird, wenn unser Mund sich an die Einsamkeit seiner Existenz erinnert und zu trauern beginnt, dachte ich, müssten die Wörter, die nur ein anderer Mensch in unseren Mund sprechen kann, anfangen, sich zu bewegen, in uns, durch den Rachen, und die Speiseröhre hindurch; sie würden beginnen, unsere Organe zu verschieben, ein paar Zentimeter nach rechts, nur ein paar Millimeter nach unten, wo es nicht mehr wehtun soll. Nach ihrem Willen: würden diese Wörter meinen Körper ordnen. Und mir würde nichts anderes übrig bleiben, als ihr gehorsamer Gastgeber zu sein; treu, bis zu meinem Ende. SENTHURAN VARATHARAJAH

D

A **»Roméo et Juliette«, rehearsal** ↘2007 B+C **»Kreatur«** ↘2017 D **»Sacre«** ↘2013 E **»Roméo et Juliette«, photo shoot** ↘2007

E

Kneeling Knien

A

We pray on our knees. We read on our knees. We speak on our knees. In a word: we kneel. Our legs bend, obeying grace, not gravity. Our skin, which is thin at the knee, with no flesh separating it from the bone, touches the floor, which is hard enough to break it. Our kneecaps know the floor; they know how cold it is, how smooth. We rest them on the floor. We are silent on our knees. We cry on our knees. We write on our knees. Our knees connect the two longest bones in our body. They know the angles that come and go; we bend them like words, according to person, number, tense, and mood. And case, from the Latin for »fall.« Our knees pull us down; they allow us to crouch and to stand upright. We want to read on them, to listen to them, and so we dance – on our knees.
SENTHURAN VARATHARAJAH

Wir beten auf unseren Knien. Wir lesen auf unseren Knien. Wir sprechen auf unseren Knien. In einem Namen: knien wir. Die Beine biegen sich: Sie folgen der Gnade, nicht der Schwerkraft. Die Haut , die hier dünn ist, und die kein Fleisch von den Knochen trennt, berührt den Boden, der sie brechen könnte. Unsere Kniescheiben: kennen ihn, sie kennen seine Kälte, sie wissen, wie glatt er ist; wir legen sie auf ihm ab. Wir schweigen auf unseren Knien. Wir weinen auf unseren Knien. Wir schreiben auf unseren Knien. Unsere Knie: verbinden die beiden längsten Knochen unseres Körpers. Sie kennen den Abschied der Winkel, die sie vermessen können, wie ein Wort werden sie gebeugt, auch sie: nach Person, Numerus, Tempus, Modus; nach ihrem Fall. Die Knie führen uns nach unten; sie erlauben uns, uns nach unten zu bewegen, und aufrecht zu stehen. Damit wir auf ihnen lesen werden, damit wir auf ihnen hören können, wir tanzen: auf unseren Knien.
SENTHURAN VARATHARAJAH

B

C

A »Dialoge '99/II – Jüdisches Museum« ↘1999 B Willy Brandt Monument in Warsaw, 2000, detail C Hieronymus Bosch, »The Garden of Earthly Delights«, 1490–1500, detail

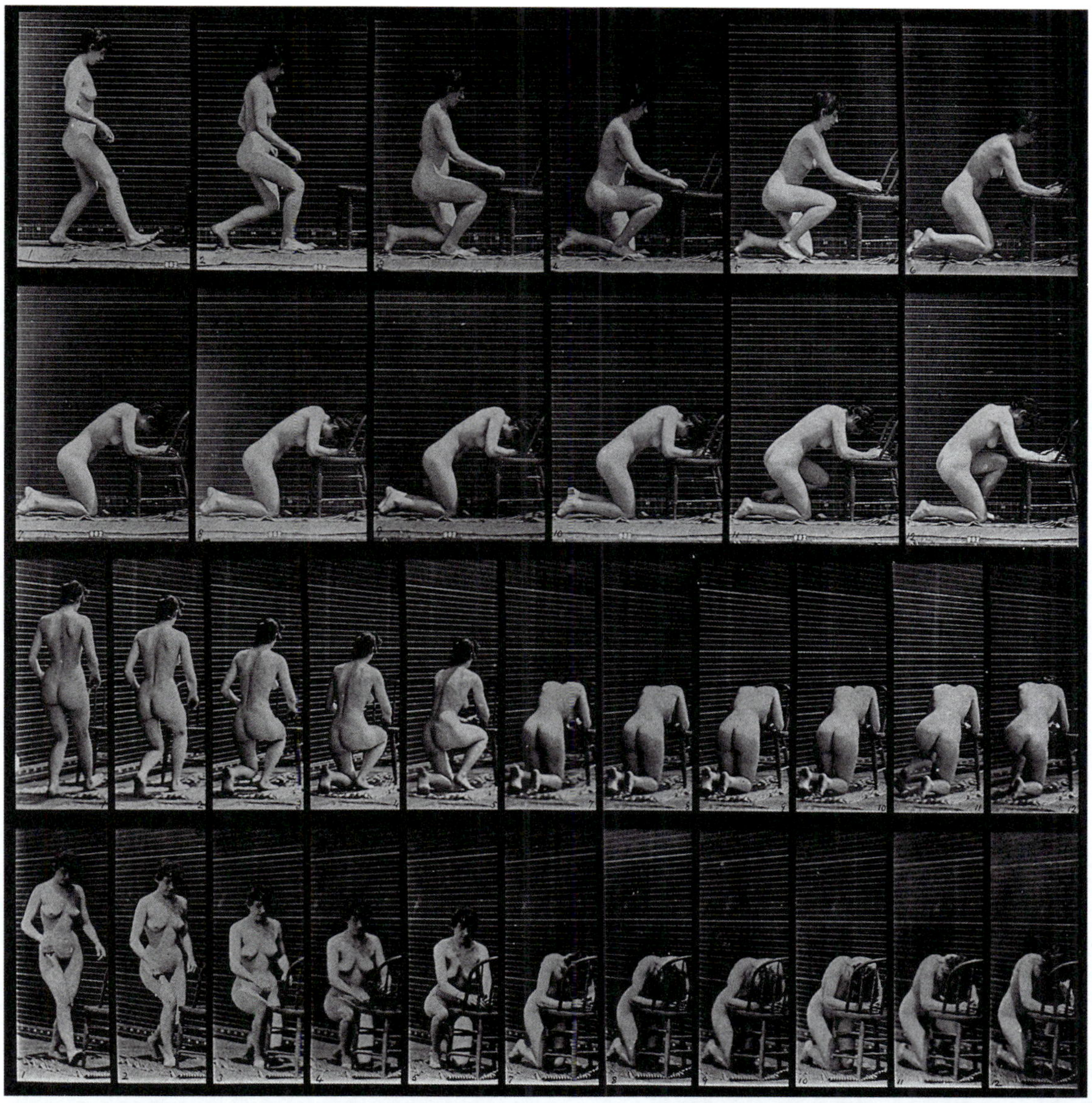

D

E

F

D **Collotype after Eadweard Muybridge, 1887** E **»Dialoge 09 – MAXXI«** ↘2009 F **»Sacre«** ↘2013

Liebende Lovers

B

A

She didn't know her.
She heard about her
from someone else.
He didn't come back.
She saw her.
She knew her
from somewhere.
She waited.

Which side to stand still.
Simple movements.
She stopped him.
She passed out.
She cried.
He stayed with her.
Which side to stand still.
Simple movements.

He called.
He said
he couldn't come.
She fell.
She ran.
She was standing still.
She
was waiting.
She was laughing.
He had to stay with her.
He said
he had to stay with her.
He said she was.
She called her.

He didn't come back.
She saw her.
She knew her
from somewhere else.
She waited.
She waited.
She went home.
She went.

Because
it's so easy
to see the ceiling
when you're lying
on the ground and then
you can put it up
on the shelf
without preparing
the bed alone with you
on the ground
of the kitchen.
The fridge is full of food.
The shelf collapsed
and it made a big noise.

Under the door
was nothing but light
that crept in.
The night
arriving between doors.

That day
I came into the kitchen
and all keys
were dropped
on the floor.
Then the telephone rang.
But she forgot about it.

The ice
became too liquid.
The wall became near.

»TRAVELOGUE I – TWENTY TO EIGHT«

C

A+C **»Travelogue I – Twenty to eight«** ↘1993 B **»Zweiland«** ↘1997 D **Sasha Waltz, drawings »Roméo et Juliette«, premiere gifts, 2018** E **»Roméo et Juliette«** ↘2007

D

E

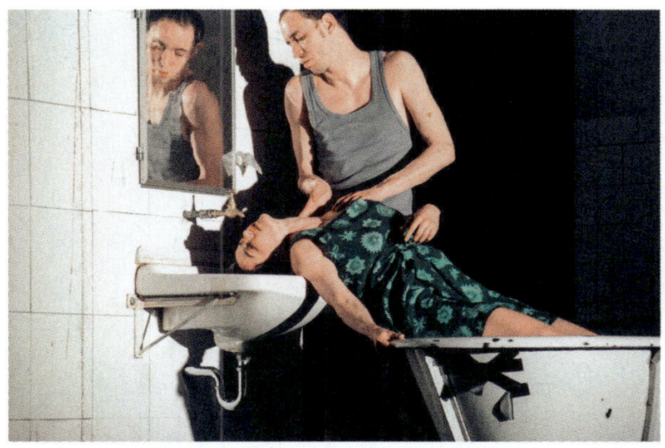

F

G

H

F **»Travelogue II – Tears break fast«** ↘1994 G **»Dido & Aeneas«** ↘2005 H **»Kreatur«** ↘2017

following page **»Roméo et Juliette«** ↘2007

 A **»Körper« at ZKM** ↘2000 ↘2013 B **»Dialoge 2018 – Wirbel«** ↘2018

A

B

The dancers move as one body from left to right, the hands of one hooked into the feet of the next, who in turn is clasping the feet of the one after, and so on. The chain winds its way forwards and slowly forms a circle with nothing inside it – an empty centre which, as soon as the circle is closed, reveals a force that bursts the chain. The fastenings are broken, the individual links roll apart with centrifugal force and become isolated from one another. The energy of the circle is destroyed; the links of the broken chain become visible as individual entities, demanding attention.
CHRISTIAN RUZICSKA

Die Hände des einen über den Kopf mit den Füßen des nächsten verhakt, dessen Arme die Füße des nächsten umfassen und wieder so, von ganz links nach ganz rechts, bewegen sich die Tänzer als Einheit. Die Kette windet sich nach vorn und wird sich langsam zu einem Kreis schließen, dessen Mitte leer ist. – Ein leeres Zentrum, das, sobald sich der Kreis schließt, eine Kraft offenbart, die die Kette sprengt. Die Verhakungen werden gelöst, die einzelnen Glieder rollen zentrifugal auseinander, werden isoliert voneinander. Die energetische Form des Kreises zerbirst, das einzelne Glied einer zerbrochenen Kette wird sichtbar und verlangt nach Aufmerksamkeit.
CHRISTIAN RUZICSKA

A

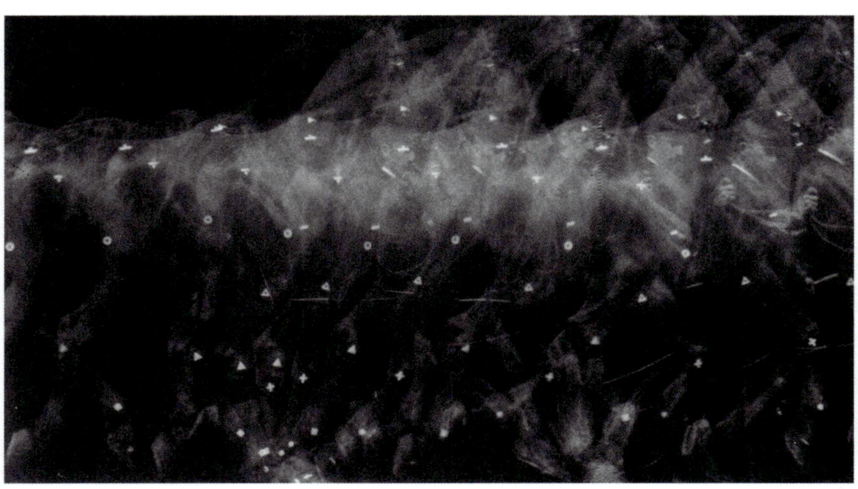

B

C

A **»Figure Humaine«** ↘2017 B **Étienne-Jules Marey, chronophotograph of a trotting horse, 1886** C **»Continu«** ↘2010

D

E

F

D **»Dialoge 09 – MAXXI«** ↘2009   E **Rehearsal at ZKM** ↘2013   F **»ΕΞΟΔΟΣ | Exodos«** ↘2018

Liquid Flüssigkeit

A

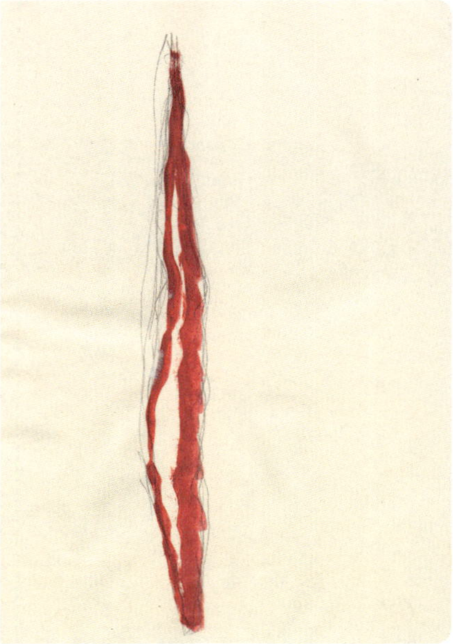

B

I am dancing through a group of half-naked people, their shoulders steadily turning, their heads circling, their feet poised in constantly changing constellations. We don't know what it's all for or why we move this way or that way, but it happens and we act, if you can call it acting, this acceptance of energy that comes from no one knows where. I am here, where you were just a moment ago, and the tension that your body exerts on mine when we come close is discharged when I raise my hand and it glides, open, fingers alert, up your back and then on into the air, like a thought coming to rest here and there in someone's consciousness. Nothing is still; everything drifts and glides and collides, coming together like clouds of gas in the Andromeda Galaxy as it moves slowly towards our Milky Way, preparing for a grand dance. Over there someone jumps, making my torso spin to the floor, and you shift your weight, bringing it to rest on someone else's back. LÁSZLÓ SANDIG

Ich durchtanze eine Gruppe halb nackter Menschen mit stetig rotierenden Schultern und kreisenden Köpfen und schwebenden Füßen in ständig sich verändernden Konstellationen. Wir wissen nicht, wofür das Ganze, wofür diese einzelne Bewegung hier oder dort, und trotzdem passiert es, und wir handeln, wenn man das so nennen kann, dieses Zulassen der Energie, die irgendwo herkommt. Wo du warst, bin jetzt ich, und die Spannung, die dein Körper auf den meinen ausübt, wenn wir uns nähern, entlädt sich im Heben meiner Hand, die offen, mit wachen Fingern deinen Rücken entlanggleitet und dann weiter durch die Luft treibt wie ein Gedanke, der sich mal hier, mal dort in einem Bewusstsein niederlässt. Nichts bleibt stehen, sondern treibt, gleitet, kollidiert, vermengt wie Gaswolken in der Andromedagalaxie, die sich langsam auf unsere Milchstraße zubewegt und zu einem großen Tanze vorbereitet. Der Sprung dort drüben lässt meinen Oberkörper sich rotierend dem Boden nähern, verlagert dein Gewicht, das jetzt an einem anderen Rücken Halt findet. LÁSZLÓ SANDIG

C

D

A »Dialoge 2020 – Relevante Systeme« ↘2020 B Sasha Waltz, study for »Medea« ↘2007 C Hans Namuth, photograph of Jackson Pollock, 1950 D »Impromptus« ↘2004

E

A

B

A **Katsushika Hokusai, »Hokusai Manga«, vol. 7, 1819, details** B **»Matsukaze«** ↘2011 C **»rauschen«** ↘2019 D **»S«** ↘2000

C

D

Melancholia Melancholie

A

B

C

The starting point for my work on »Impromptus« was Schubert's biography. His not-feeling-at-home-anywhere, not-being-rooted-in-himself, his lack of stability, his loneliness – all Romantic themes.
The theme of rootlessness is central to the music. Everything tilts and tips; there's no equilibrium. This instability helped shape the set. The stage slopes; the surface offers no stability – the bodies struggle permanently to keep their balance. The dancers fall from one movement into the next; they have to keep re-establishing their equilibrium, which creates a sense of extreme fragility.
SASHA WALTZ ON »IMPROMPTUS«

Der Ansatzpunkt bei der Arbeit an »Impromptus« war für mich die Biographie Schuberts. Dieses Sich-nirgends-zu-Hause-Fühlen, Nicht-in-sich-verwurzelt-Sein, Keinen-richtigen-Halt-Haben, die Einsamkeit, das sind gleichzeitig Themen der Romantik.
Das Thema der Nichtverwurzelung ist Thema der Musik, es ist immer am Kippen, nie im Gleichgewicht. Die Instabilität hat das Bühnenbild beeinflusst, es ist gekippt, die Körper haben keinen richtigen Halt auf dieser Fläche, sie müssen sich ihre Balance ununterbrochen erkämpfen. Man fällt von einer Bewegung in die nächste und muss das Gleichgewicht immer neu formen, dadurch entsteht eine extreme Fragilität.
SASHA WALTZ ÜBER »IMPROMPTUS«

A+B **»SYM-PHONIE MMXX«** ↘2022 C **»Impromptus«** ↘2004 D **»Zweiland Tour«** ↘1997 ↘2010 E **»SYM-PHONIE MMXX«, film still** ↘2022

D

E

following page **»Zweiland Tour«** ↘1997 ↘2010

Moon Mond

A

B

We see the moon when it's dark. Its pale white light is a semblance, a reflection, indirect and fractured, but also mysterious. Enigmatic. In moonlight, bodies become silhouettes, reality appears doubtful, fragile. Nothing seems certain, much seems possible. Things look permeable rather than solid. The dancers flit, spin, stroll, slide, glide, shuffle, scurry, run, even fly over the stage. Gravity still exists, but it seems to have lost some of its effect – like on the moon. Formations are formed and transformed. Something new takes shape, making way for the invisible, for whatever it is in us that jostles and runs and spins. Spaces open up in which we discover ourselves. Stories begin in the mysterious white light of the floodlights.
HANNAH DÜBGEN

Wir sehen den Mond leuchten, wenn es bei uns dunkel ist. Sein fahles, weißes Licht ist Schein, Widerschein, ist indirekt und gebrochen, aber auch geheimnisvoll. Hintergründig. Im Mondlicht werden Körper zu Schemen, das Wirkliche wirkt fragwürdig, fragil. Nichts scheint sicher, vieles möglich. Nichts wirkt solide, vieles durchlässig. Die Tanzenden huschen, hasten, wirbeln, wandeln, wischen, schleifen, schweben, rennen, ja fliegen über den Boden. Die Schwerkraft scheint nicht aufgehoben, aber weniger wirksam zu sein – wie auf dem Mond. Formationen finden und verwandeln sich, etwas Neues nimmt Gestalt an. Dem Unsichtbaren wird Platz gemacht, dem, was in uns drängt und rennt und wirbelt. Räume öffnen sich, in denen wir uns wiederfinden. Erzählungen beginnen im weißen, geheimnisvollen Licht der Bühnenscheinwerfer.
HANNAH DÜBGEN

C

A »Matsukaze« ↘2011 B+C »Dialoge 2018 – Wirbel« ↘2018

D

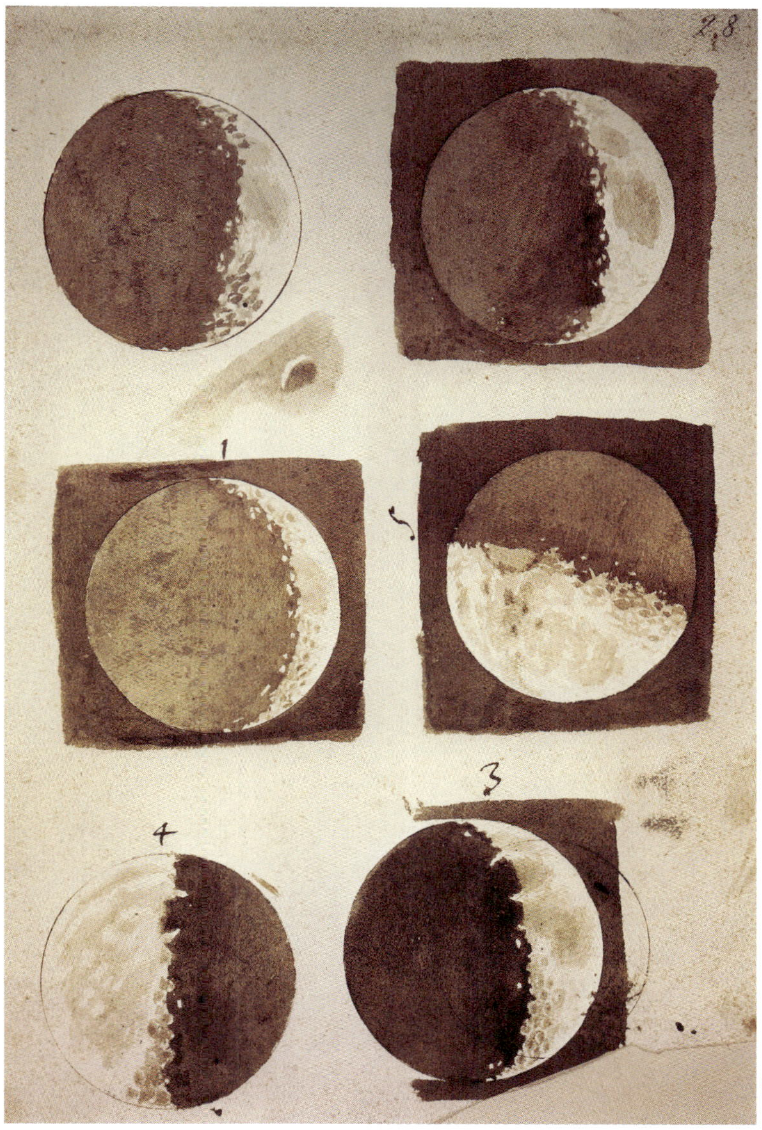

E

F

G

D+G **»Impromptus«** ↘2004 E **Galileo Galilei, »Sidereus Nuncius«, 1610** F **Sasha Waltz, sketchbook »Matsukaze«** ↘2011

Moshpit

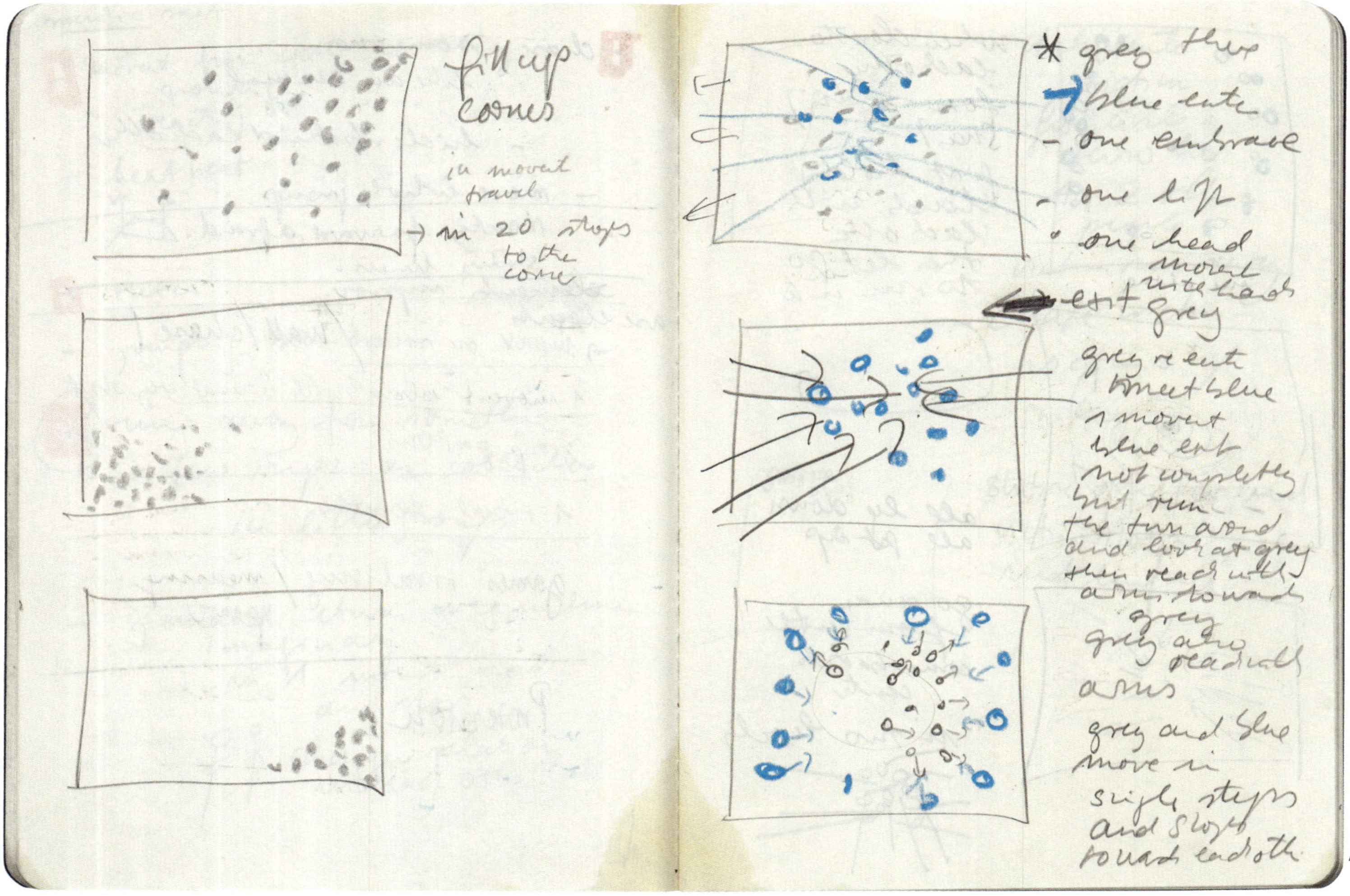

A

B

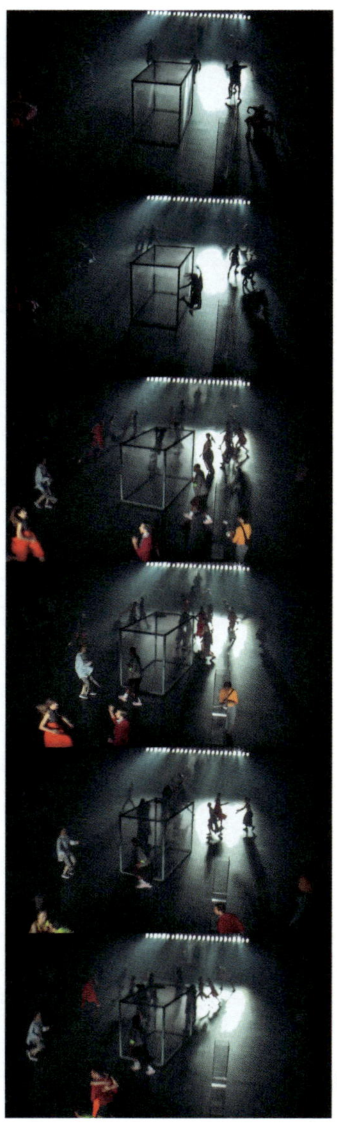

C

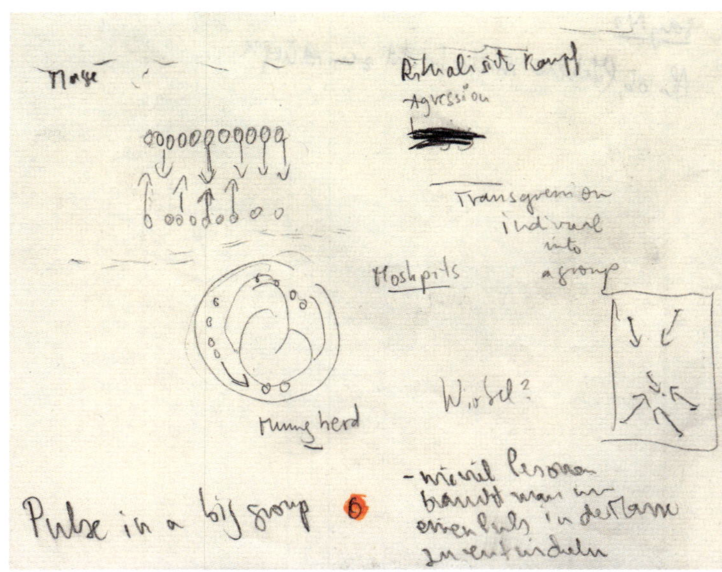

D

In pogo culture, a crisis or collapse of the collective body is simulated or induced, comparable to a state of panic. Moshpits celebrate the rebellion of the collective body against itself and can be read as a form of »swarm« self-harm, a deliberate dysfunctionality or performance of dysfunctionality that also contains elements of subversiveness. [...] The neuralgic point at which the pressure of the crowd becomes unbearable depends on the context. It almost certainly makes a big difference to what extent you have been expecting the phenomenon and psyched yourself up to it. AGNES SCHERER

In der Pogokultur wird eine Krise bzw. der Zerfall des Kollektivkörpers, vergleichbar einem Panikzustand, simuliert bzw. induziert. Moshpits zelebrieren das Aufbegehren des Kollektivkörpers gegen sich selbst, evtl. lesbar als ein selbstverletzendes Verhalten des »Schwarms«, eine vorsätzliche Dysfunktionalität oder Performance von Dysfunktionalität, in der auch eine subversive Motivation mitschwingt. [...] Der neuralgische Punkt, an dem der Druck durch die Masse unerträglich wird, ist kontextabhängig. Entscheidend ist sicher, inwieweit man mit dem Phänomen rechnet und sich innerlich darauf eingestellt hat.
AGNES SCHERER

 A **Sasha Waltz, sketchbook »Sacre«** ↘2013 B **»SYM-PHONIE MMXX«** ↘2022 C+E **»ΕΞΟΔΟΣ | Exodos«** ↘2018 D **Sasha Waltz, study for »ΕΞΟΔΟΣ | Exodos«** ↘2018

E

Nature Natur

A

B

snow sound pure, swimming in time, in rain, dimming
light silver dew swarming from the harp – the darling faun
of russian fairy tales spraying at the wayside in flocks.

mild wild stream lines – breaking trust holding forth.
fixed in flight. shadows swarm and alight.
break out, heave-ho, out of the crowd
in and back, towering high, rearing up,
face-on, biting tone, the air shimmering
with flickering colors, glimmering scent
bridling, reining in anger, burning in the dark
cursing the light, simmering,
catch him and hold him and haul him in.
gleaming and naked as the next.
snake through the smoke of vengeance
sparking joy, blind to the islands.

up and up.

up and over. spellbound, calling out,
people like ants, swarm together, form a raft
and drift,
not long for this world – a deep breath and
in they plunge, sweetly rocked by lethe's waters.

hoary as never before,

flakes of ash around the early brood, colliding
and diving and writhing.
hair-woven willow. feathers spread wide.
throw themselves into the thermal, spin in the wind,
the peaks from above. sycamore keys.

slaughter earlier, stones on stones,
Motes of dust. stinging eyes. racing pain.
tomorrow another will take the hand,
open and waiting.

JULIA FRANCK
ON »SYM-PHONIE MMXX«

schneelaut rein zeitbaden regen sekundenladen.
tau silbern aus der harfe schwarm: russischer märchen,
liebchen faun, sprühen am straßensaum, in herden.

milder wilder strom linien – treu bruch sal badern.
starren flug. schwarm schatten aller.
aus brechen eines, wuchten für sich, raus aus der menge,
hinein und zurück, empor ragen, auf bäumen,
in stellung frontale, beißender ton,
reißende lage in luft farben flimmern, gleißender duft,
auf zäumen, wut zerren, finsternis blaken,
licht fluchten, simmern,
ihn fangen und halten und ein holen.
blank der nackten und nächsten.
ranken im rauch einer rache aus niederen wonnefunken
erblinden zu inseln übriger.

hoch weichen.

hinüber. im bann der zauber bloß, an rufen aus,
menschen wie ameisen zum floß sich schließen
und treiben,
ganz außer sich bald nirgendwo mehr sein,
ein atmen durch, in lethes wassern sich selig wiegen.

rauhreif, wie sie noch nie waren,

ascheflocken um frühe brut, sich in queren kommen
und tauchen und an winden über.
haare flechten weiden. vor teilen aus. federn spreizen.
sich auflegen in die thermik zum wind schrauben,
die gipfel von oben. ahornsamen.

zeitigen früher schlachten, steine an steine,
partikel staub. augen brennen. schmerz rasen.
morgen nimmt ein anderer die hand,
die offen bleibt.

JULIA FRANCK
ÜBER »SYM-PHONIE MMXX«

A »L'Après-midi d'un faune«, video shoot ↘2024 B+C »Dialoge 2020 – Relevante Systeme« ↘2020

D

C

E

D »Dialoge 2020 – Strandbad Tegelsee« ↘2020 E »SYM-PHONIE MMXX« ↘2022

following page »L'Après-midi d'un faune« ↘2024

A

B

C

A **Matthias Grünewald, »Isenheim Altarpiece«, 1512–16** B **»L'Après-midi d'un faune«** ↘2024 C **»Johannes-Passion«** ↘2024

D

E

D **»Dido & Aeneas«** ↘2005 E **»rauschen«** ↘2019

following page **»Medea Fries«, film stills** ↘2007

Perfect body Perfekter Körper

A

B

C

D

E

As a child, I was dismissed from ballet class because I neither fitted into the classic corset of gestures nor possessed the right body for it. I was classified as »imperfect«. Despite this handicap, let us skip light-footed over the next 20 years and land in Berlin. In the late 1990s, Sasha Waltz was not the only choreographer to liberate the dancing body, but she was in the right place at the right time – a place where everything was moving and changing. Beauty didn't come from the static, the given, the normative; it came from movement. Beauty inserted itself into movements that led us back to the body in all its diversity. The perfect body was not a standard; it was expression, gesture. The dance company found its home in an old pump factory (Radialsystem) and their bodies imitate the fluid movements of water – everything flows. The history of the body also found expression in peaceful dance campaigns in museums, where something perfect was created between audience, dancers and the dynamic reliefs and sculptures. A woman in a green peacock dress on the stairs of the Neues Museum; moving frescoes in an aquarium in »Dido & Aeneas«; human figures in »Sacre«; »Medea« and the eternal quest for the expression of the tragic – it was for moments like these that Berlin's loveliest audience always came to Sasha.

KATJA PETROWSKAJA

A+C+D **»Körper«** ↘2000 B **Lucas Cranach the Elder, »Hercules and Antaeus (?)«, after 1505** E **Hans Bellmer, »La poupée«, 1934** F **»Zweiland«** ↘1997

Als Kind wurde ich aus dem Ballett-Unterricht entlassen, da ich weder in die klassischen Gestik-Korsette hineinpasste noch den dafür perfekt geeigneten Körper besaß. Ich wurde als »imperfekt« für Tanz eingestuft. Trotz dieser Voraussetzung überspringen wir jetzt leichtfüßig zwanzig Jahre und landen in Berlin. Sasha Waltz war Ende der Neunziger nicht die Einzige, die den tanzenden Körper befreite, aber sie war rechtzeitig an einem Ort, an dem sich alles bewegte. Die Schönheit entstand nicht aus dem Statischen, Gegebenen, Normativen, sondern aus der Bewegung. Schönheit nistete sich in Bewegungen, die uns zurück zum Körper in seiner Vielfalt führten. Perfect Body war kein Maß, sondern ein Ausdruck, eine Geste. Das Zuhause der Compagnie wurde in einer Pumpfabrik gefunden (Radialsystem), wo die Körper die Wege des Wassers nachahmen, denn alles fließt. Die Geschichte des Körpers entfaltete sich auch in friedlichen Tanz-Feldzügen durch Museen: Es entstand etwas Perfektes zwischen den Zuschauern, Tänzern und den belebten Reliefen und Skulpturen aus Stein. Eine Frau in grünem Pfauenkleid auf der Treppe des neuen Museums, die beweglichen Fresken in einem Aquarium von »Dido & Aeneas«, menschliche Figuren in »Sacre«, »Medea« und die ewige Suche nach dem Ausdruck des Tragischen, dafür kam immer das schönste Publikum Berlins zu Sasha.
KATJA PETROWSKAJA

F

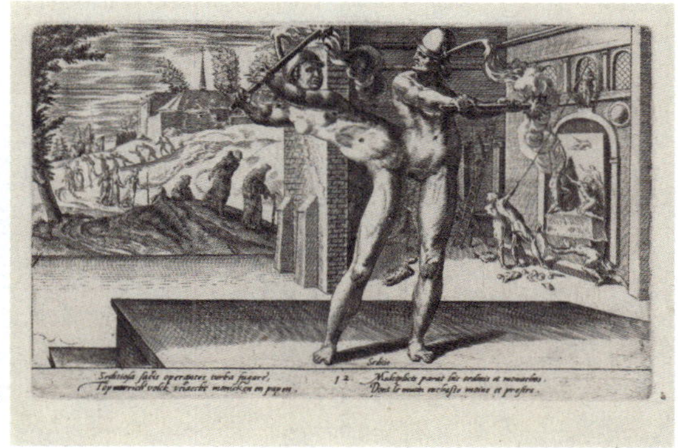
G

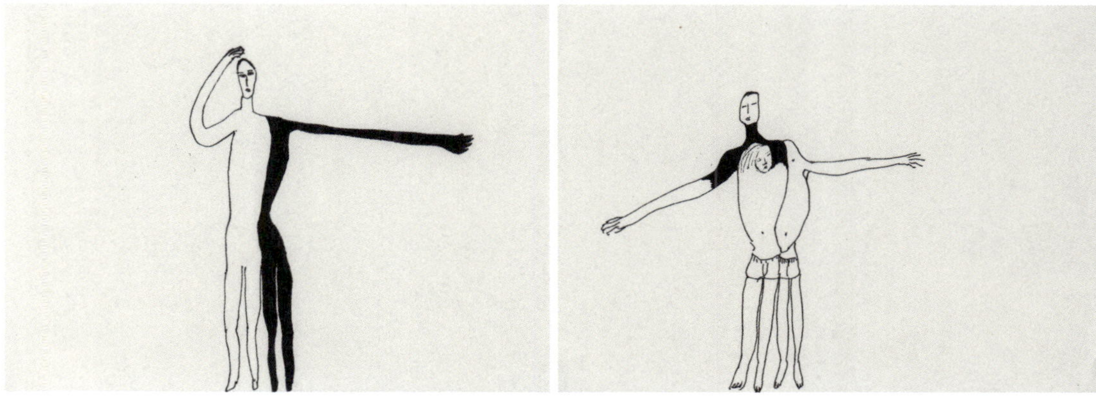
H

I

G **Dirck Volkertszoon Coornhert, »Seditio«, 1604** H **Sasha Waltz, drawings »Zweiland«** ↘1997 I **Hieronymus Bosch, »The Garden of Earthly Delights«, 1490–1500, detail**

Plates Teller

A

B

C

D

A **»Women«** ↘2017 B+H **»Körper«** ↘2000 C+D **Judy Chicago, »The Dinner Party«, 1974–79, plates**

E

F

G

H

E **»Dialoge 09 – MAXXI«** ↘2009 F **»Körper« at ZKM** ↘2000 ↘2013 G **Oval Dining Room, Palazzo Cini, detail**

Pole Pfahl

Pole, pivot, stake, mast, post, prop, axis mundi. A broad spectrum of meanings.
There is atrocity: the mauled and martyred body tied to the stake, impalement or crucifixion. But there is also the signpost to point the way, the prop to give support, the pivot, the axis mundi on which the Earth turns, the tree of life.
The balance beam brings us, dancing and teetering, to nicer images: children, in particular, love to grab hold of a pole and spin around it, abandoning themselves to the joy and pleasure of movement.
And so we move from atrocity to ease and play.
UNDINE EBERLEIN

Pfahl, Drehpunkt, Latte, Mast, Stützpfosten, Weltachse, Pol. Ein breites Spektrum an Bedeutungen.
Da ist Grausamkeit: der an den Pfahl gebundene, zugerichtete, gemarterte Körper, die Pfählung oder Kreuzigung. Aber auch der Weg- und Orientierungspunkt im Gelände, der Stützpfosten als sicherer Halt, der Drehpunkt, die Erd- und Himmelsachse, der Weltenbaum.
Der schwebende oder weitergegebene Balken lässt uns tanzend und balancierend zu freundlicheren Bildern gelangen: Vor allem Kinder ergreifen gerne jede Stange: um sie kreisend sich der Lust und Freude der Bewegung überlassend.
So gelangen wir von Grausamkeit zu Leichtigkeit und Spiel.
UNDINE EBERLEIN

A

A+C+E **»Kreatur«** ↘2017 B **»Allee der Kosmonauten«** ↘1996 D **Sasha Waltz, sketchbook, undated**

B

C

D

E

Rachefrauen Furies

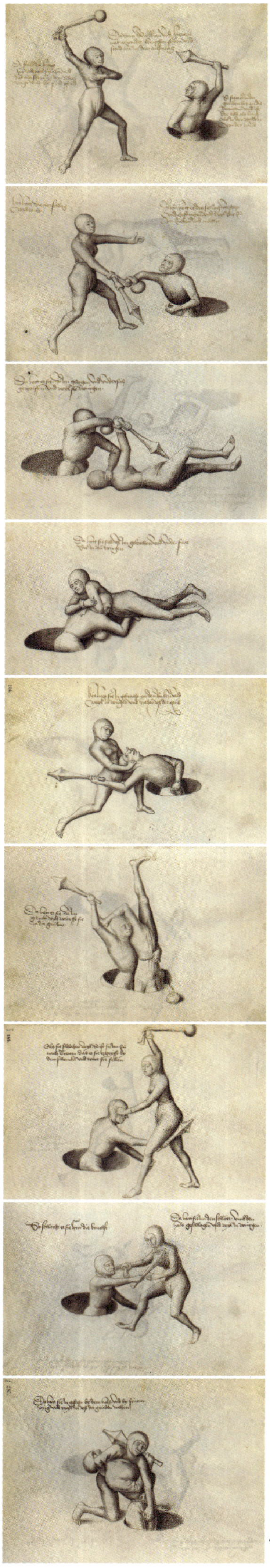

A

B

C

the butterfly you poisoned had a human face
gloomy jet-black wings   are bound to have memory
remember   the feminine madness of its last dive towards you

hatred   thinks itself a flower
in the misconceptions of bright morning
a black powder-puff   puffs the gaudy room full of nightmare
again the butterfly waits on the wall you fear to see

shredded by your hand   it finds you
turned to shadow   shockingly surrounded by the wind's voice
a tiny mouth that bites you   after death

it's bound to belong to someone   invading the green sky backwards
the more you want to forget
the more you see the butterfly is taking its revenge

YANG LIAN »BUTTERFLY OF REVENGE«

A **»Judicial Duel between Man and Woman«, from: Hans Thalhofer, »Fechtbuch«, 1467**   B **»Continu«** ↘2010   C **»SYM-PHONIE MMXX«** ↘2022

D

E

F

D **»ΕΞΟΔΟΣ | Exodos«** ↘2018 E **Giotto di Bondone, »Wrath«, 1303–05** F **»Ira – Zorn – Wrath«** ↘2022

following page **»Women«** ↘2017

Resistance Widerstand

A

B

C

D

E

F

A+B+G+H **»Dialoge 2020 – Relevante Systeme«** ↘2020 C **Demonstration in Valparaiso on 8 March 2023, research** D **»Körper«** ↘2000

G

H

I

J

E **Newspaper clipping of X González at the »March for Our Lives«, research, 2018** F **»SYM-PHONIE MMXX«** ↘2022 I+J **»ΕΞΟΔΟΣ | Exodos«** ↘2018

A

B

A+B+D+E **»Kreatur«** ↘2017 C **Sasha Waltz, study for »Kreatur«** ↘2017

In »Seven Samurai« Akira Kurosawa created a narrative that reached far beyond the boundaries of the film. A group of eccentric samurai help a peaceful rural village in its fight against a gang of ferocious bandits. The conflict between the two groups stands for the drama of human existence, with the samurai acting as mysterious vanishing points. Each has his own personality and develops in his own way. But in order to overcome the fear and the chaos, the individuals join forces to form a single powerful body – a body that disbands again once order has been temporarily reestablished.
ROBERT EIKMEYER

Mit »Seven Samurai« etablierte Akira Kurosawa ein Narrativ, das weit über die Grenzen des Films hinaus wirkte. Eine Gruppe exzentrischer Samurai unterstützt ein friedliches Bauerndorf im Kampf gegen grausame Banditen. Im Konflikt der Gruppen verkörpert sich das Drama der menschlichen Existenz mit den Samurai als mysteriösen Fluchtpunkten. Jeder hat seine eigene Persönlichkeit und Entwicklung. Aber um das Chaos und die Angst zu besiegen, gehen die Elemente Verbindungen ein, bilden einen wehrhaften Körper, der nach der vorübergehenden Herstellung der Ordnung wieder in seine Einzelteile zerfällt.
ROBERT EIKMEYER

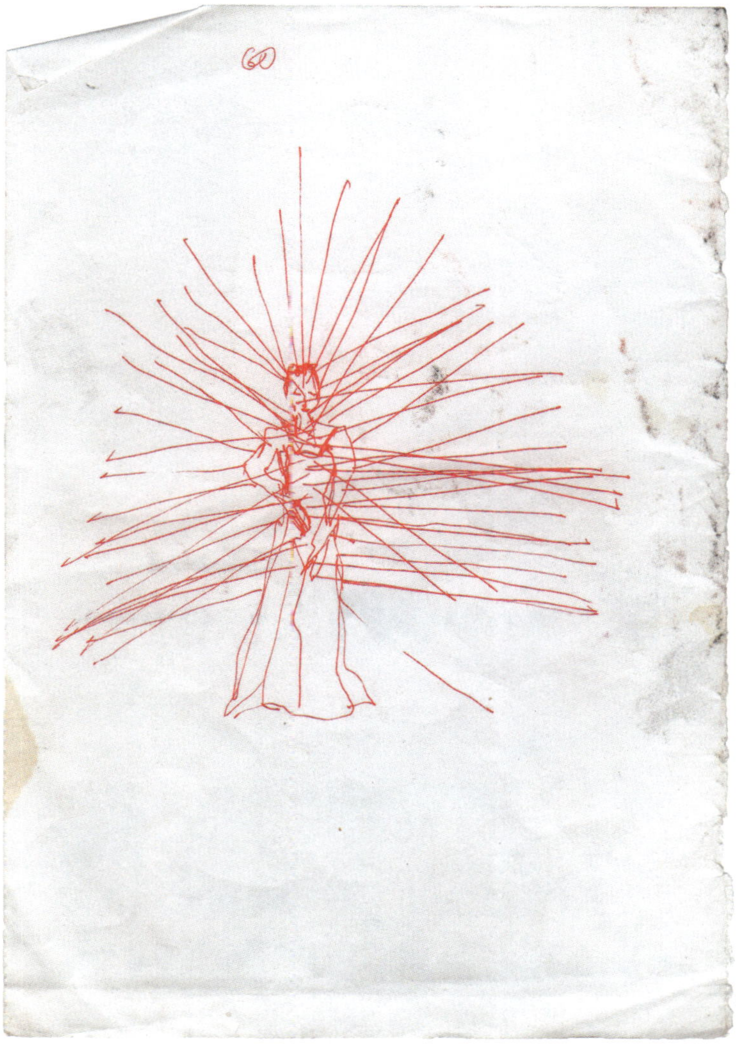

C

D

E

Sculpture Skulptur

A

B

C

D

In 1899 Rodin exhibited the first ever sculpture without a pedestal, a revolutionary approach which he had already proposed for »The Burghers of Calais« in 1893. The arrangement of the burghers on a flat base at ground level allows for face-to-face encounters between sculpture and viewers, an effect that is even more pronounced with the life-size »Eve«. The shock of the »Burghers'« anti-heroism triggered a whole sequence of imitations that influenced not only the development of modern sculpture but also that of expressive dance. Carl Andre, for example, radicalised Rodin's approach with the false-bottom aesthetic of his Minimalist metal-plate sculptures, allowing the viewers themselves to adopt the point of view of the »Burghers«. At the same time, the Judson Dance Theater experimented with mattresses and sculptured elements by Andre, thus preparing the ground for a diverse range of encounters between bodies and objects in the 20th and 21st centuries.
ROBERT EIKMEYER

1899 präsentierte Rodin erstmals eine Skulptur ohne Sockel, ein revolutionärer Ansatz, den er bereits 1893 für »Die Bürger von Calais« empfohlen hatte. Das Arrangement der Figuren auf einer flachen Bodenplatte und besonders die ebenerdige Präsentation der lebensgroßen »Eva« ermöglichten Begegnungen von Skulpturen und Betrachtenden auf Augenhöhe. Die Konfrontation mit der antiheroischen Haltung der »Bürger« startete einen gestischen Reigen, der nicht nur die Entwicklung der modernen Skulptur, sondern auch den Ausdruckstanz beeinflusst hat. Mit der Ästhetik des doppelten Bodens seiner minimalistischen Plastiken aus flachen Metallplatten radikalisierte Carl Andre Rodins Ansatz und erlaubte den Betrachter:innen, nun selbst die Wahrnehmung der »Bürger« einzunehmen. Zeitgleich experimentierte das Judson Dance Theater mit Matratzen oder den skulpturalen Elementen von Andre und bereitete so den Boden für die vielfältigen Begegnungen von Körpern und Objekten im Raum des 20. und 21. Jahrhunderts.
ROBERT EIKMEYER

A **»rauschen«** ↘2019 B **»Dialoge 09 – Neues Museum«** ↘2009 C+F **»Medea Fries«, research** ↘2007 D **»insideout«** ↘2003

E

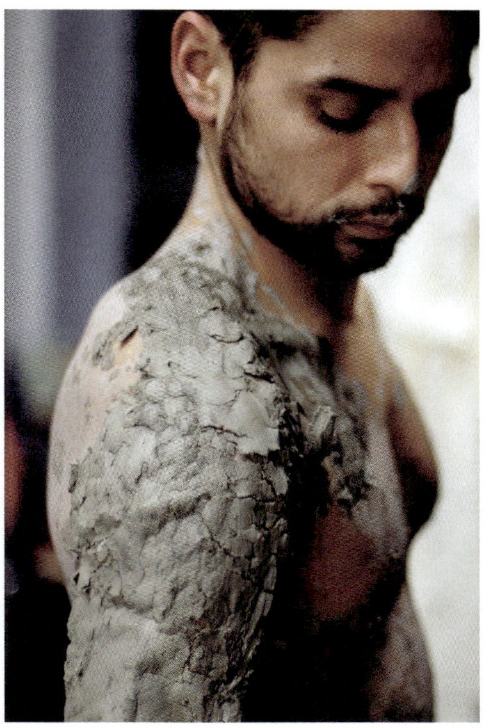

F

G

E **»Dialoge 06 – Radiale Systeme«** ↘2006   G **»Dialoge 07 – Pergamonmuseum«** ↘2007

Seed Saat

Is the sower also the reaper? The dancers are dressed in earth tones and black; their skin provides the third color of the evening which will later flow with red, the pigment of death. At first they form a figure that imitates the good gesture of the sower, the arms rising and falling as they scatter seed – but when, briefly, the movements grow faster and more aggressive, the gesture could equally be that of the grim reaper, the deadly slash of the scythe. Archaic images? Yes, but they are also more than that.
After all, the images were transported and transposed from a story that didn't write itself. The whole troupe, everyone on stage, is seized and united by the gesture of sowing – only to shatter the logic of this gesture a short time afterwards. As in a fugue, the movement develops into its opposite – and cuts deep into flesh. Not just the flesh of memory. Music of gestures: giving and taking, fertility and sacrifice, love and murder oscillate indistinguishably in the first instant of the movement. What am I looking at here? Harmony or dissonance? Am I steeped in the hope of a more hopeful start? In the fear of my bleak experience?
CHRISTIAN RUZICSKA ON »MEDEA«

Der Sämann, ist er der Schnitter? Die in Erdtönen und Schwarz gekleideten Tänzer, deren Haut die dritte Grundfarbe des Abends bildet, in die das Rot der tödlichen Pigmente fließt, finden momentan zu einer Figur, die die Güte des Säens spiegelt, das ewige Auf und Ab der Arme, wenn es kurz darauf heftiger wird, schneller, als Ausholen und Ausführen gelesen, könnte es der tödliche Schnitt der Sichel sein. Archaische Bilder? Ja, aber nicht nur.
Auch diese ja nur transportiert und transponiert von einer sich nicht selbst schreibenden Geschichte. Das gesamte Personal auf der Bühne, die theatrale Menschheit, wird von einer Bewegung des Säens erfasst und vereint. Und sprengt deren Logik nur kurze Zeit später. Fugenartig entwickelt sich aus der einen Bewegung ihr Gegenbild und schneidet ins Fleisch. Nicht nur der Erinnerung. Musik der Gesten: Geben und Nehmen, Fruchtbarkeit und Opferung, Liebe und Mord oszillieren ununterscheidbar im ersten Moment der Bewegung. Worauf richte ich da mein Augenmerk? Wohlklang oder Dissonanz? Bin ich getränkt von einer Hoffnung auf einen hoffnungsvolleren Beginn? Von der Angst meiner hoffnungslosen Erfahrung?
CHRISTIAN RUZICSKA ÜBER »MEDEA«

A

B

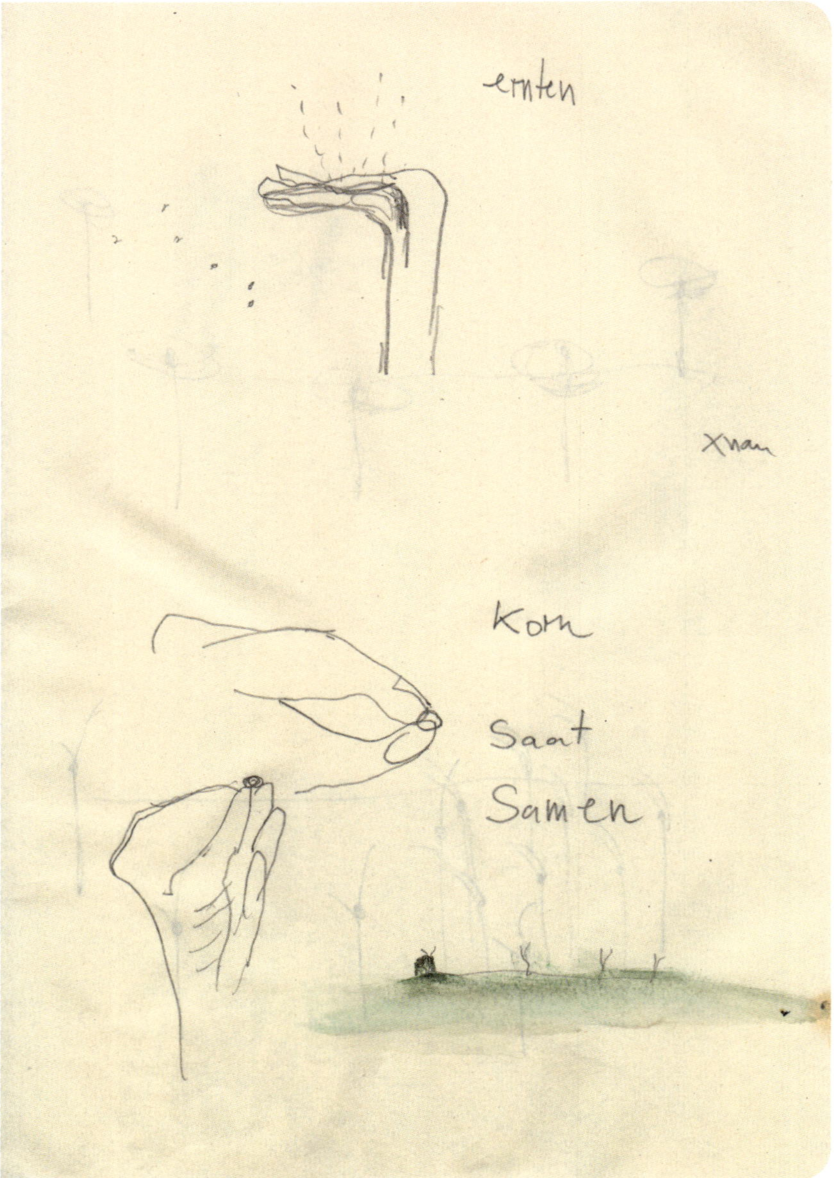

C

A »Dialoge 07 – Pergamonmuseum« ↘2007 B »Medea« ↘2007 C Sasha Waltz, study for »Medea« ↘2007

D

E

D »Sacre« ↘2013 E »Na Zemlje«, »Flower growing machine«, interactive object at ZKM ↘1998 ↘2013

following page »Figure Humaine« ↘2017

Shadow Schatten

B

A

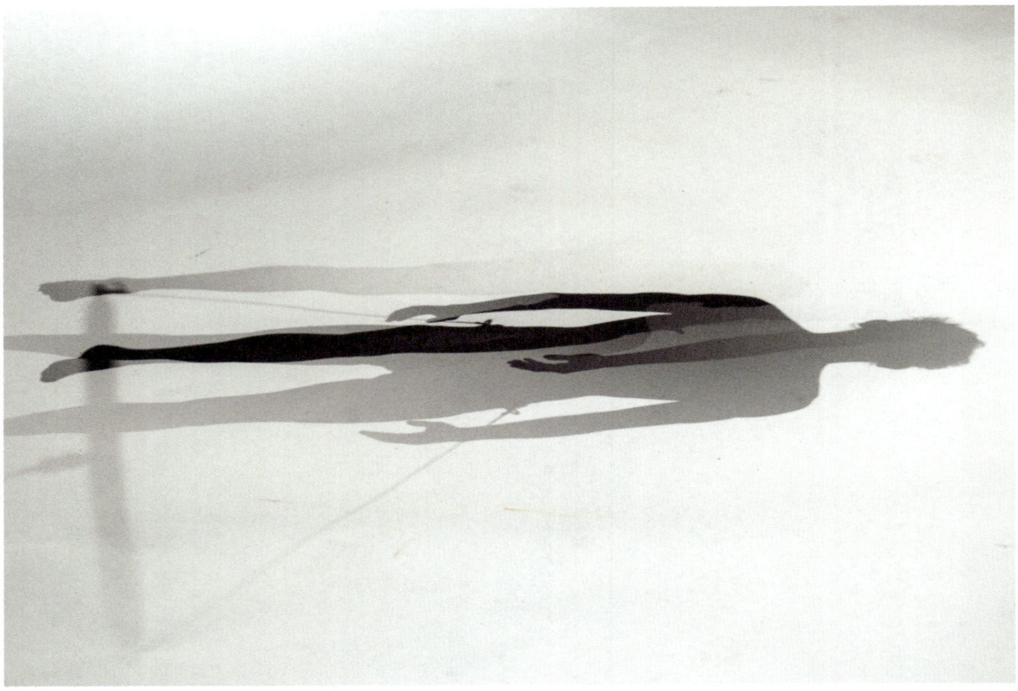

C

D

A **Sasha Waltz, drawing »noBody«** ↘2002 B **Sasha Stone, Nelson-Revue »Lichter von Berlin«, 1927** C **»Continu«** ↘2010 D **»Dialoge – Les Grandes Traversées«** ↘2003

Good night. Sweet nightmares. Don't cry. I'm listening. And you, my shadow, take your last bow for our yearning. Et c'est fini. C'est fini la comédie.
CLÉMENTINE DELUY IN »RAUSCHEN«

Gute Nacht und schönen Albtraum. Don't cry. I'm listening. Und du, mein Schatten, mach die letzte Verbeugung für unsere Sehnsucht. Et c'est fini. C'est fini la comédie.
CLÉMENTINE DELUY IN »RAUSCHEN«

E

F

E **»rauschen«** ↘2019 F **»Passion«** ↘2010

following page **»rauschen«** ↘2019

Shelter Schutz

A

B

A new morning in this dazzling city, quiet and peaceful. The colors shine like in a cartoon movie. There is no mist and the sky is so clear that I can see the houses on the most distant mountaintop.
I still haven't learned how to orient myself according to the cardinal directions. I haven't yet worked out which way this apartment faces. Ten years ago, in our house where the sun fell into the sitting-room window, it was easy. All I had to know was that if I stood to the left of the window I had the south in front of me, the north behind me and the west to my right. Is it normal to lose your bearings when you move into a »new house«? Is it normal that the image we have of our old houses gradually disintegrates?
Whenever I move into a new apartment that gets the morning sun – right now I'm in Apartment Number 26 – I always try to put my bed next to a window that faces east. Ten years after leaving the house where I grew up, I wake up and imagine that I can look out of the window and see the apartment of Uncle Abu Adil and the neighbors drinking tea and stuffing vine leaves in the courtyard.
I guess it's the smells of our mothers' cooking that are missing from our present, temporary homes. Back then we could smell their cooking on our way back from school or work. Maybe our homes here provide us with a space for the many questions we would have liked to ask the people we came into contact with in the course of the day. People who look for stories in us to satisfy their curiosity or their prejudices. Or who offer us help, maybe hoping for the head rush of a clear conscience.
Personally I have trouble explaining to them that I could cry – that I do cry – when I see radicchio leaves at the side of the road. My memory thrusts me back to the roads of the village where I was a child.
It's hard to explain to them that I run up to every plant I come across, buy it and put it in my apartment, just because my mother planted it at home. That I say prayers and spells to try to keep them alive.

YASMINE NAYEF MEREI

Ein neuer, ruhiger und friedlicher Morgen in dieser schillernden Stadt. Die Farben leuchten wie in einem Zeichentrickfilm. Es ist nicht nebelig und der Himmel ist so klar, dass ich die Häuser auf dem weitesten Berggipfel sehen kann.
Ich habe hier immer noch nicht gelernt, mich nach den Himmelsrichtungen zu orientieren. Vor zehn Jahren war das in unserem Haus, wo die Sonne in das Fenster des Wohnzimmers hineinschien, einfach. Es reichte, zu wissen, dass der Süden vor mir, der Norden hinter mir und der Westen rechts von mir lag, wenn ich links vom Fenster stand.
Ist es normal, dass man seine Orientierung in den »neuen Häusern« verliert? Dass das Bild von unseren damaligen Häusern Stück für Stück zerfällt?
Jedes Mal, wenn ich in eine neue Wohnung ziehe, in die morgens die Sonne scheint – ich wohne momentan in Wohnung Nummer 26 – und ich ein östlich liegendes Fenster entdecke, stelle ich mein Bett daneben. Zehn Jahre, nachdem ich unsere Wohnung verlassen habe, wache ich auf und bilde mir ein, die Wohnung von Onkel Abu Adil und den Nachbarn, die Tee trinken und im Hof des Hauses Weinblätter füllen, sehen zu können, wenn ich gleich aus dem Fenster blicke.
Wahrscheinlich sind die Speisegerüche unserer Mütter das, was unseren jetzigen, temporären Häusern fehlt. Damals erreichten uns die Gerüche auf dem Nachhauseweg von der Schule und der Arbeit. Vielleicht bieten uns unsere Häuser hier einen Platz für unsere vielen Fragen, die wir den Menschen gerne draußen im Laufe des Tages gestellt hätten, als wir ihnen begegnet sind. Menschen, die in uns nach Geschichten suchen, um ihre Neugierde zu befriedigen oder um ihre Vorurteile zu bestätigen. Vielleicht wollen sie auch das ekstatische Gefühl eines reinen Gewissens spüren, wenn sie uns Hilfe anbieten.
Mir persönlich fällt es schwer, ihnen zu erklären, dass ich weinen könnte – und ich weine tatsächlich –, wenn ich die Blätter eines Radicchio an einem Wegrand sehe. Meine Erinnerung führt mich zwangsweise in die Straßen meines Dorfes zurück.
Es ist schwer, ihnen zu erklären, dass ich zu jeder Pflanze, die mir begegnet, laufe, sie kaufe und in meine Wohnung stelle, nur weil meine Mutter sie zu Hause gepflanzt hat. Ich versuche sie dann mit Gebeten und Sprüchen am Leben zu halten.

YASMINE NAYEF MEREI

C

D

E

A **»Kreatur«** ↘2017 B **»Gezeiten«** ↘2005 C **»Dialoge 2013 – Kolkata«** ↘2013 D **»SYM-PHONIE MMXX«** ↘2022 E **»insideout«** ↘2003

F

G

H

F **»Dialoge 2020 – Relevante Systeme«** ↘2020 G **»Orfeo«, photo shoot** ↘2014 H **»Beethoven 7«** ↘2023

Skin Haut

So. A will. A load of humanity packed on a back, Atlas: nod, wink: Axis. Shoulders' blades descend, strength rears its head, letting another come and go, carrying oneself, something, another, dropping them, jamming, isolating, becoming an island, being imprisonment, locked, living in the mirror, loving more and more, make them wait until they're sore, boot them out, lame them, lame oneself, make them freeze and embrace them out of the doldrums: delta of a river of a woman.
Out of the drought comes a raging and a wearing, along the banks of a current, landing and rocking. Rid of all thoughts. Being time. Tides high and low. Mud of light on a belly. Lux in flux.
Fiume. Blade of reed. Silv'ry light. A judgement felt. Wind leaps up waves, immerses light, whips people down. Judgement – a molecule from another time, from ancient times. Suspension, distortion in the Now.
Centrifuge of darkness. Hell's Mouth. Ruptured gullet. Guillotine dulls an eye, strangles pain of pulled nails, torn retina. Moon's glow. Eradication.
The horde obliterates the individual. Incorporates him, spits her out. Existere. Expulsion. Blazing of sounds in the beating of limbs: a stingling brumsing and crispeling, shacksling and pladdering, mendling into a fugue. Tasting vortexes made of maple seeds in clouds of smoke, plus swings of time crystals. Wafting of silence when time billows and solidifies to an instant, when symmetry breaks rhythms. Warming a belly on Atlas, where atlas ring turns and twists around axis peg, nods and bends and blue-beats the nooses tighter, man for man. Fumes scourge desire with strength from the chine. So sudden the loss. A forest of veins. Heartbeat thinning from bloodletting. Embracing in free fall. Sailing and springing from that descent. So.
JULIA FRANCK ON »KREATUR«

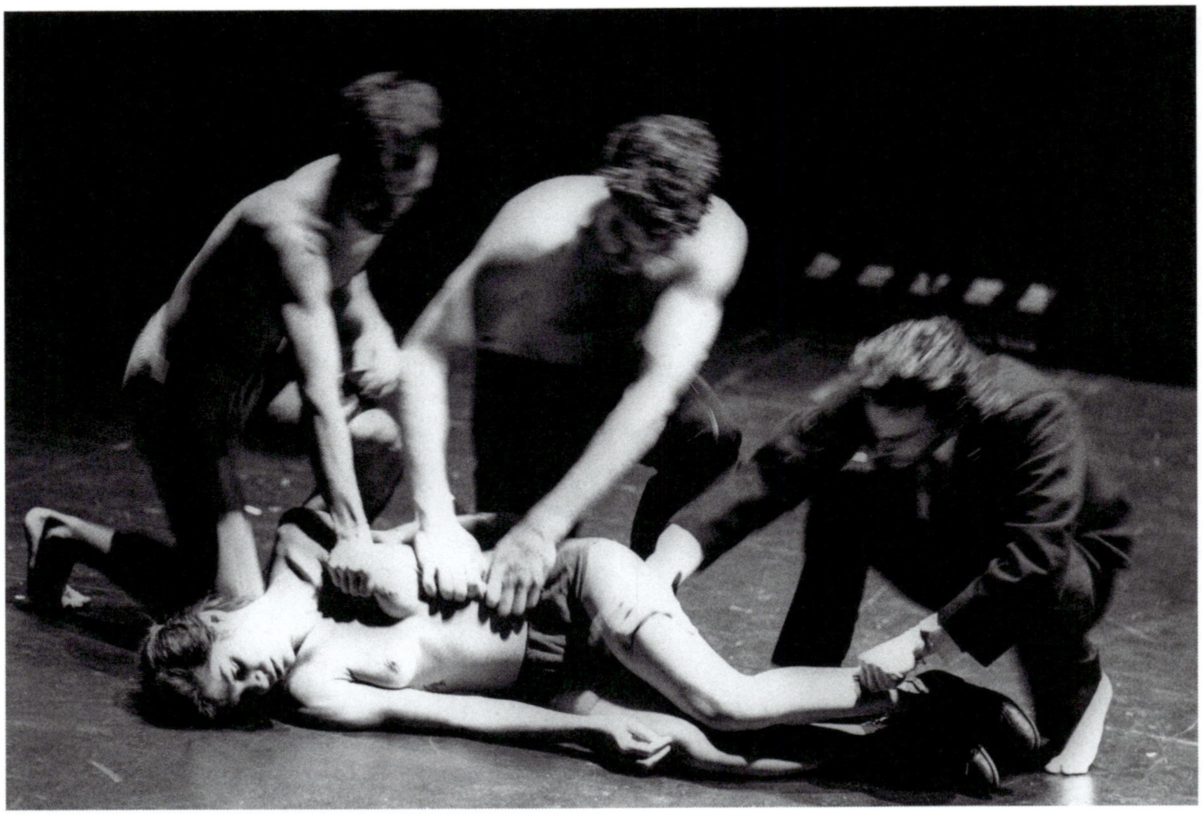
A

Also. Ein Wille. Eine Ladung Mensch auf dem Buckel, Atlas knick knack Axis. Schulters Blätter Fall, bäumt sich Macht, einen anderen kommen und diesen gehen lassen, etwas, sich, einen tragen können, ihn fallen lassen, pferchen, isolieren, Insel werden, Gefangenschaft sein, gesperrt, im Spiegel leben, sich rundlieben, andere wundwarten machen, ausbooten, sich aneinander lähmen, erstarren lassen und aus der Flaute halsen: Delta eines Flusses einer Frau.
Aus der Dürre ein Ragen und Zehren entlang, am Ufer eines Stroms, Landen und Wiegen. Gedanken los sein. Zeit sein. Ebben und Fluten. Lichtschlamm am Bauch. Lux im Flux.
Fiume. Schilfhalm. Silberlichtig. Ein Urteil fällt. Wind springt Wellen auf, taucht Licht ein, peitscht Menschen unter. Urteil – Molekül aus anderer Zeit, aus Urzeit. Aufhebung, Verwerfung im Jetzt.
Zentrifuge der Finsternis. Höllenschlund. Gurgelbruch. Fallbeil stumpft Auge ab, erdrosselt Schmerz gezogener Nägel, gerissener Netzhaut. Mondglut. Ausmerzung.
Die Rotte tilgt das Einzelne. Verleibt ihn sich ein, spuckt sie aus. Existere. Expulsion. Lodern der Geräusche im Schlaglaut von Gliedern: zweubelndes Bromsen und Krispeln, Schackseln und Fladdern zur Fuge sich reugen. Von Ahornsamen erzeugte Luftwirbel in Rauchwolken schmecken, auch Schwingen von Zeitkristallen. Wehen der Stille, wenn Zeit sich bläht und gerinnt zum Augenblick, als Symmetrie noch Takt bricht. Den Bauch am Atlas wärmen, wo Atlasring um Axiszahn sich dreht und wendet, nickt und knickt und Mann um Mann die Schlingen fester bläut. Schäumt Geißel Lust mit Macht vom Grat. Jäh der Verlust. Venenwald. Aus Aderlass sich Herzschlag lichtet. Halsen im freien Fall. Aus dem Fall segeln und springen. Also.
JULIA FRANCK ÜBER »KREATUR«

B

A+C »Körper« ↘2000 B Titian, »Flaying of Marsyas«, 1570–76

C

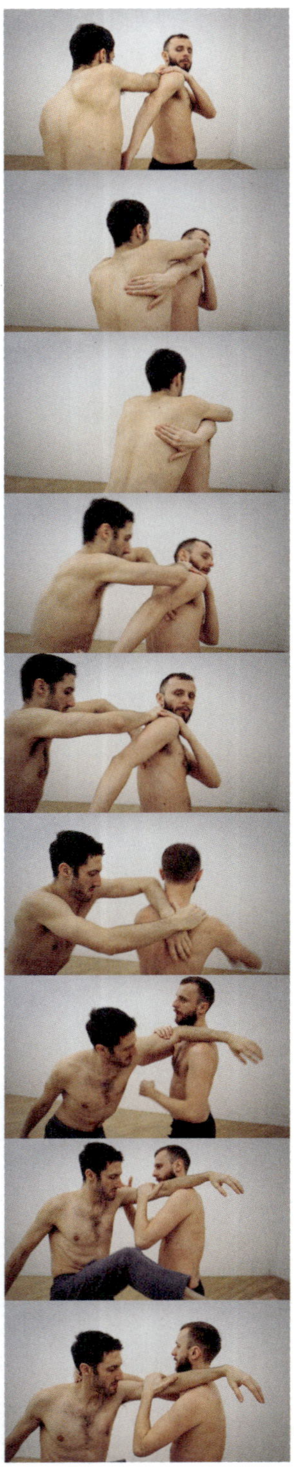

A

B

C

D

A–D **»Figure Humaine«** ↘2017 E **»Kreatur«** ↘2017

E

Snake Schlange

A

Alas
Would I'd remained the animal I was
Before my man made me into his woman
Medea The barbarian Now despised
With these my hands the hands of the barbarian
Well steeped in lye torn by the needle skinned
I want to break mankind apart in two
And live within the empty middle I
No woman and no man What do you scream
Worse than death is to grow old You'd kiss
The hand that gives you death if you knew life
That was Corinth Who are you Who has dressed
You in the bodies of my little children
What animal is hiding in your eyes
Do you play dead You won't deceive the mother
You're actors nothing but liars and traitors
Inhabited by dogs rats snakes you are
It barks it squeaks it hisses I can hear it
O I am wise I am Medea I
Don't you have blood left Now it is all quiet
The screams of Colchis silenced too And nothing left
HEINER MÜLLER »MEDEAMATERIAL«

Ach
Wär ich das Tier geblieben das Ich war
Eh mich ein Mann zu seiner Frau gemacht hat
Medea die Barbarin jetzt verschmäht
Mit diesen meinen Händen der Barbarin
Händen zerlaugt zerstickt zerschunden vielmal
Will ich die Menschheit in zwei Stücke brechen
Und wohnen in der leeren Mitte Ich
Kein Weib kein Mann Was schreit ihr Schlimmer als Tod
Ist alt sein Küssen würdet ihr die Hand
Die euch den Tod schenkt kenntet ihr das Leben
Das war Korinth Wer seid ihr Wer hat euch
Gekleidet in die Leiber meiner Kinder
In euren Augen welches Tier versteckt sich
Stellt ihr euch tot Die Mutter täuscht ihr nicht
Schauspieler seid ihr Lügner und Verräter
Bewohnt von Hunden Ratten Schlangen seid ihr
Das bellt und pfeift und zischt Ich hör es gut
O ich bin klug ich bin Medea Ich
Habt ihr kein Blut mehr Jetzt ist alles still
Die Schreie von Kolchis auch verstummt Und nichts mehr
HEINER MÜLLER »MEDEAMATERIAL«

B

A **»S«, photo shoot** ↘2000 B **»Roméo et Juliette«** ↘2007

C

D

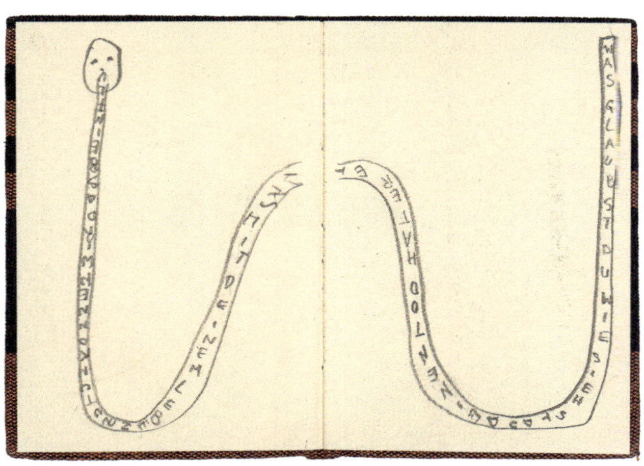

E

F

C **»Figure Humaine«** ↘2017 D **»Beethoven 7 in Delphi«** ↘2021 E **Sasha Waltz, sketchbook, undated** F **»Dialoge 07 – Pergamonmuseum«, rehearsal** ↘2007

Space (white) Raum (weißer)

A

B

White space. Space (white). The unprinted space on a page, the space that gives the other elements room to breathe. White space on its own is boring; no white space is a disaster – enough to make you crazy.
White space is two-dimensional. It's flat.
The White Cube is three-dimensional. Rooms for exhibiting art did not used to be white. Probably no rooms were white in the past. They were different colors and so were the pictures hanging on the walls.
I could mention other forms of whiteness. White noise, a sequence of sounds or noise of a certain frequency that have a soothing effect. Whiteout, an optical phenomenon that occurs in snow- and ice-covered landscapes – a sense of disorientation that comes from not having any landmarks to get your bearings by. People who live in clouds will know how it feels.
The white space of the White Cube is an imposition. It's disorientating. The whiteout blanks out reality. It's not things that have turned against us; we've turned against them. The quest for »freedom from« has led us into a dead end. It has made us less open to »freedom to«, a positive freedom. The freedom to do what is right and good, the freedom to do beautiful things; things that makes sense.
Brian O'Doherty once described the White Cube as a cell. Space (white). The total lack of reference points is a cell, a white cell, a white jail. We have to break out of it, in order to exercise a »freedom to«.
Even those of us who live in the clouds.
FRIEDRICH VON BORRIES

Weißraum. Raum (weißer). Das ist der unbedruckte Raum auf einer Seite – er gibt den anderen Elementen Platz. Nur Weißraum ist langweilig, gar kein Weißraum geht auch nicht, da dreht man durch.
Der Weißraum ist also zweidimensional. Er ist flach.
Dreidimensional ist der White Cube. Früher waren Räume, in denen Kunst gezeigt wird, nicht weiß. Wahrscheinlich waren damals keine Räume weiß. Sie waren farbig und die Bilder, die an den Wänden hingen, auch.
Ich könnte noch die ganzen anderen Weißheiten durchmessen, das Weiße Rauschen, ein Klangphänomen, durch das Geräusche, ja Lärm, in einer bestimmten Frequenz beruhigend wirken; ich könnte in dieser Annäherung an Weiß noch zum Whiteout gelangen, einem optischen Phänomen, das in Schnee- und Eislandschaften auftritt: ein Gefühl von Desorientierung, weil es keine Anhaltspunkte mehr gibt, nichts, woran man sich festhalten kann. Menschen, die in Wolken leben, werden dieses Gefühl kennen.
Der Weißraum, der White Cube ist eine Vermessenheit, er führt zu Desorientierung. Das Whiteout blendet die Wirklichkeit aus. Nicht die Dinge haben sich gegen uns gewendet, sondern wir gegen sie. Die Suche nach »Freiheit von« hat in die Sackgasse geführt. Sie verhindert die Offenheit für eine »Freiheit für«, eine positive Freiheit. Freiheit, das zu tun, was richtig, was gut, was schön, was sinnvoll wäre.
Brian O'Doherty hat den White Cube als eine Zelle beschrieben. Raum (weiß), die Unendlichkeit der Referenzlosigkeit ist eine Zelle, eine weiße Zelle, ein weißes Gefängnis. Wir müssen es verlassen, um eine »Freiheit für« ausüben zu können.
Selbst dann, wenn wir in den Wolken wohnen.
FRIEDRICH VON BORRIES

A George Lucas, »THX 1138«, 1971, film still B »rauschen« ↘2019 C »Continu« ↘2010 D »Continu« at ZKM ↘2010 ↘2013

C

D

A

A »rauschen« ↘2019 B »Dialoge 09 – MAXXI« ↘2009 C »Beethoven 7« ↘2023

We filled our lungs with something that wasn't freedom,
but which felt just like it.
Our lie was an Amber Room,
Full of ancient junk.
We breathed more quickly than them.
We danced more deeply.
We laughed more broadly and we fell.
Out.
Of.
Ourselves.

We shall be carried.

BEHZAD KARIM KHANI

Wir füllten unsere Lungen mit etwas das keine Freiheit war,
sich aber genauso angefühlt hatte.
Unsere Lüge ein Bernsteinzimmer.
Voll mit gestrigem Unrat.
Wir atmeten schneller als sie.
Wir tanzten tiefer.
Wir lachten breiter und wir fielen.
Aus.
Uns.
Heraus.

Uns wird man tragen.

BEHZAD KARIM KHANI

B

C

Spiral Spirale

The spiral is a small miracle from the realm of analogue technology. Spirals came out of the first flashlights; they were pushed into ballpoint pens. Their form is worth thinking about: one open circle leads to another open circle, which leads to another, and so on. The result is a serial repetition, a rigid form with neither beginning nor end, a permanent movement without origin or goal.
The spiral is my image for rhythmised time, time divided into periods. No one moment can be lived more than once. But there is repetition. The feast days in the calendar, for instance – but also dates in history, which become part of the present when we remember them. The distant past returns in the present; once is superimposed on now. What was far away is suddenly close; old becomes new again; the forgotten returns. But the spiral breaks the circle of eternal return and points into the future. New events are reflected in old ones, set themselves apart from them, cut themselves free. ALEIDA ASSMANN

Die Spirale ist ein kleines Wunder aus dem Reich der analogen Technik. Sie sprang aus der ersten Taschenlampe heraus oder wurde in den Kugelschreiber gestopft. Ihre Gestalt gibt zu denken: Sie entsteht aus einem offenen Kreis, der in einen weiteren mündet. Das Ergebnis ist eine serielle Wiederholung, eine strenge Form, ohne Anfang und Ende, das Bild einer dauernden Bewegung ohne Ziel und Ursprung.
Die Spirale ist mein Bild für rhythmisierte Zeit, die Zeit der Perioden. Keinen Augenblick erlebt man zum zweiten Mal. Doch vieles wiederholt sich. Die Feste im Kalender, aber auch entfernte Geschichtsdaten werden noch einmal Gegenwart in der Erinnerung. Das Ferne kehrt in die Gegenwart zurück, das Einst und Jetzt überlagern sich. Das Ferne ist plötzlich nah, das Alte wird noch mal neu, das Vergessene ist wieder da. Doch die Spirale bricht den Kreis der Wiederkehr auf und strebt weiter in die Zukunft. Das neue Ereignis spiegelt sich im Alten, hebt sich von ihm ab und macht sich von ihm los. ALEIDA ASSMANN

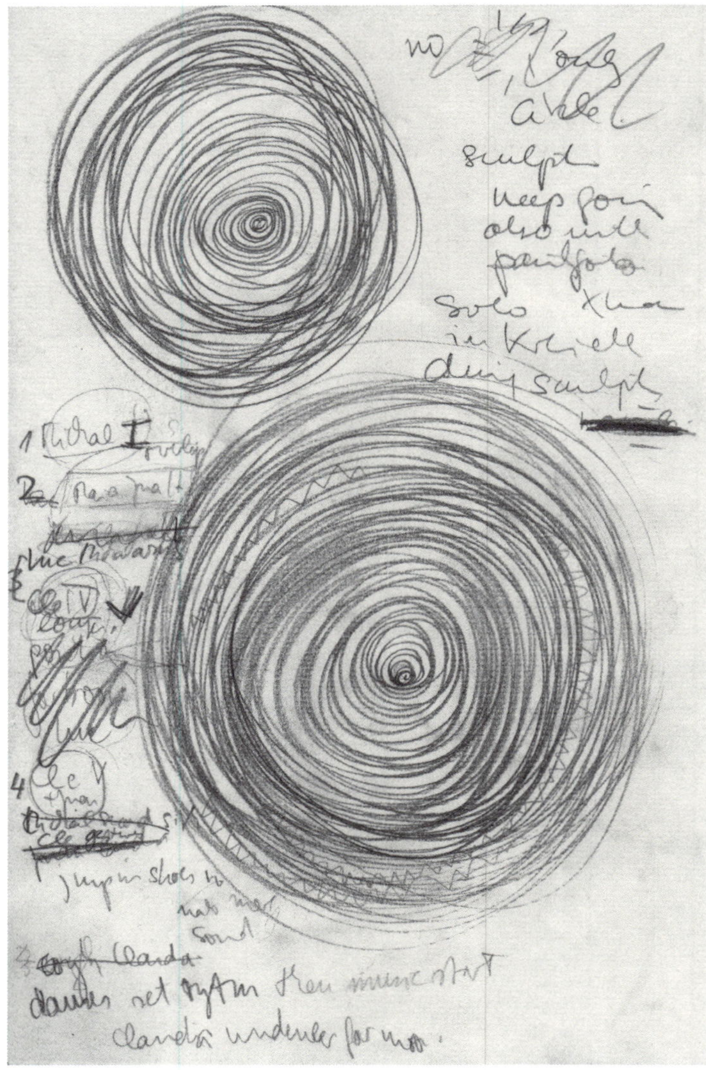

A

B

A **Sasha Waltz, study for »Impromptus«** ↘2004 B **»ΕΞΟΔΟΣ | Exodos«** ↘2018

C

D

E

C »Dialoge 09 – MAXXI« ↘2009 D »Dialoge 07 – Pergamonmuseum« ↘2007 E »Impromptus« ↘2004

Staggering Staffelung

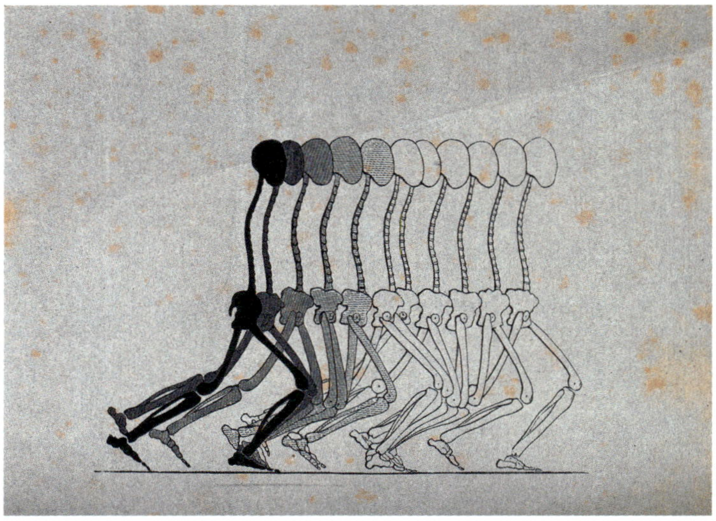

A

B

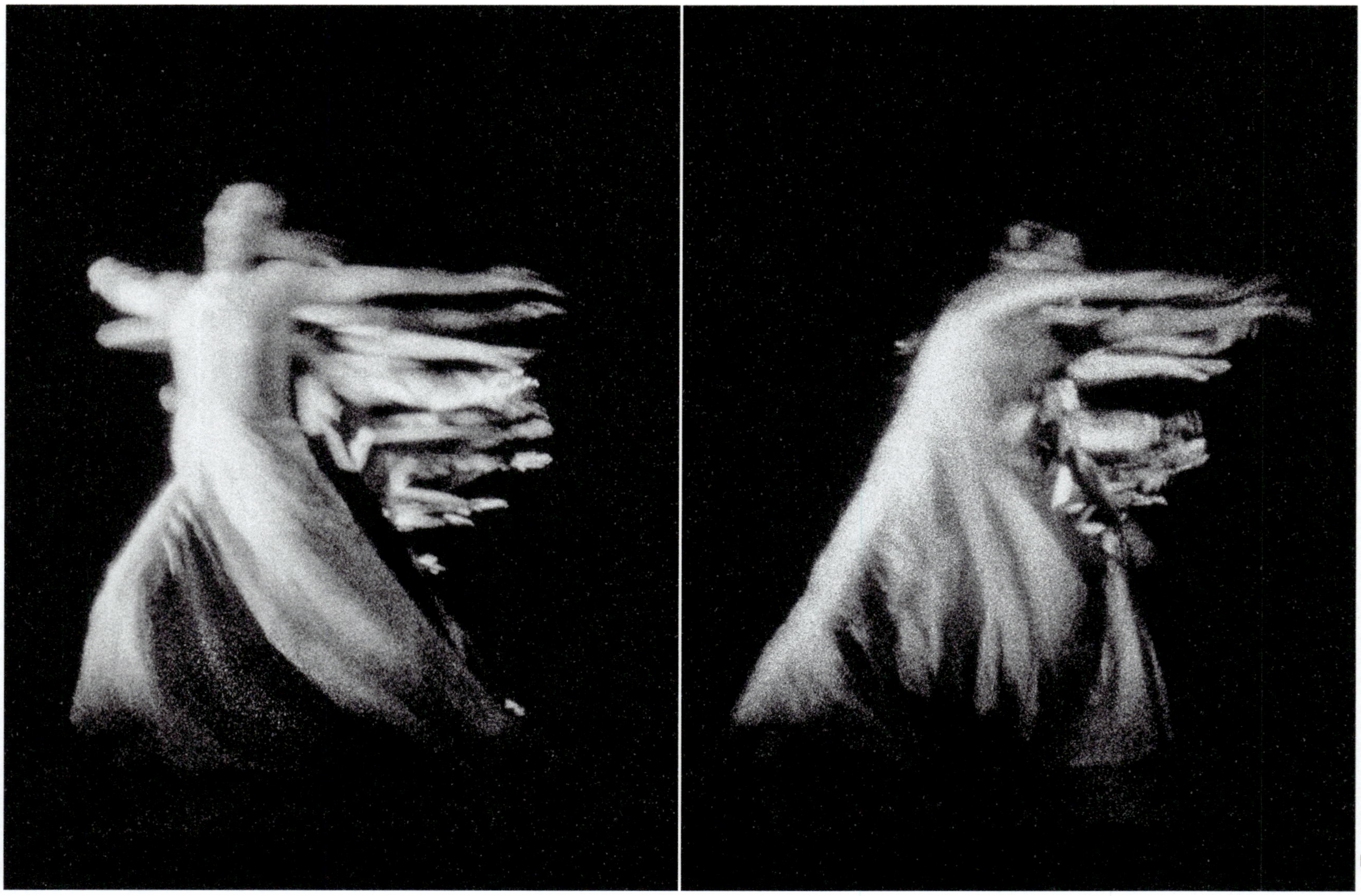

D

A **Wilhelm Eduard Weber, »A skeleton in motion«, lithograph, after 1836** B **»Dialoge 06 – Radiale Systeme«** ↘2006 C **»Gezeiten«** ↘2005 D **»SYM-PHONIE MMXX«** ↘2022

E

F

C

G

E **»Continu«** ↘2010 F **»Roméo et Juliette«** ↘2007 G **»Matsukaze«** ↘2011

Stairs Treppe

A

B

C

Nothing promises more sense, more power than a pedestal. Life is on a level, it's the next degree that counts. Since ancient times convex bodies with crooked glued heads climb up on the ziggurat to where the blue wind blows into the bellows of the bronchi and the brick zenith watches over the death masks of the first words.
The stairway bustle, dream and drive. During the ascent, the world is particularly small and narrow, the air: thin. Not everyone makes it to the firmament, body to body, sweat in sweat on the way, calves and cheeks against the wall. Man is a petrifying being, a bas-relief, a single assemblage of the urge for rank. Of resentment and courage. And more of luck than skill: you can slip even on Jacob's ladder.
HEINRICH KIRSCHBAUM

Nichts verspricht mehr Sinn, mehr Macht als ein Sockel. Alles gestaffelt und eingestuft. Graduiert. Leben sei Level, es zähle das nächste Niveau. Seit alters klimmen konvexe Körper mit krumm geklebten Köpfen empor auf die Zikkurat, dorthin, wo der blaue Wind in die Bälge der Bronchien bläst und der Ziegelzenit wacht über die Totenmasken der ersten Worte.
Treppentraum: Trieb und Betrieb. Die Welt ist beim Anstieg besonders eng, die Luft dünn. Nicht alle schaffen es bis zum Firmament, Leib an Leib unterwegs, Schweiß in Schweiß, mit Waden und Wangen zur Wand. Ein versteinerndes Wesen ist der Mensch, ein Basrelief, eine einzige Assemblage aus dem Drang nach Rang. Aus Ressentiment und Courage. Und eher aus Glück denn Geschick: Ausrutschen kann man ja selbst auf der Jakobsleiter.
HEINRICH KIRSCHBAUM

D

A »Johannes-Passion« ↘2024 B+C »Kreatur« ↘2017 D »In C« at Berliner Dom ↘2021

E

F

G

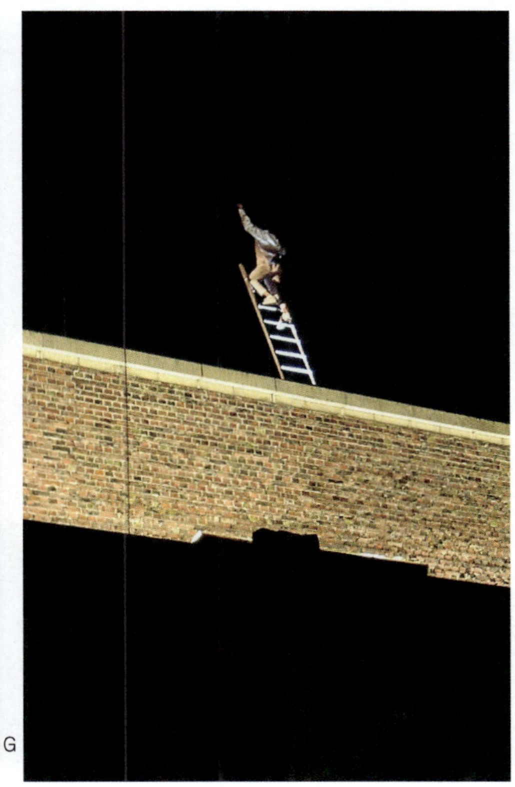
H

E **»Dialoge 09 – Neues Museum«** ↘2009 F **»Dialoge '99/II – Jüdisches Museum«** ↘1999 G **»Dialoge 2013 – Kolkata«** ↘2013 H **»Dialoge – 17-25/4«** ↘2001

A

B

C

A **»Dialoge 2020 – Relevante Systeme«** ↘2020 B **Andrea Mantegna, »St Sebastian«, c. 1470–80** C+D **»Johannes-Passion«** ↘2024

D

E

F

E »Orfeo« ↘2014 F »Dialoge 09 – MAXXI« ↘2009

A

B

C

A **»Travelogue III – All ways six steps«** ↘1995 B **»Gezeiten«** ↘2005 C **»Tannhäuser«** ↘2014 D **Lucas Cranach the Elder, »The Tournament with Lances«, 1509**

D

E

F

Stone Stein

A

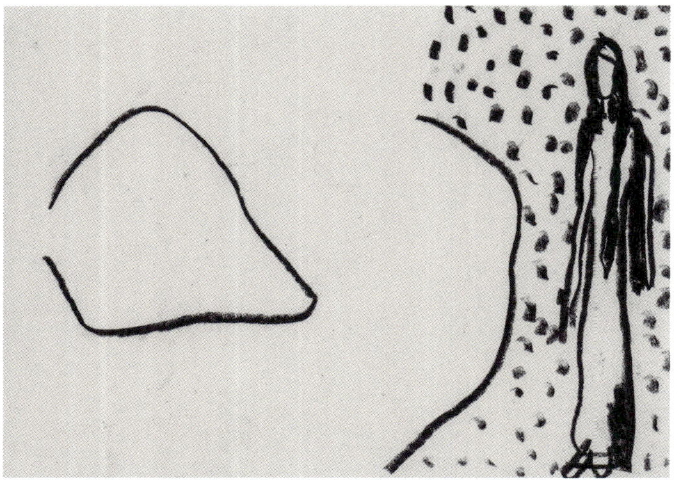
B

C

D

A »Dialoge 06 – Radiale Systeme« ↘2006 B Sasha Waltz, drawing, undated C+F–H »Dialoge 2020 – Relevante Systeme« ↘2020 D »Roméo et Juliette« ↘2007

who comes with you close to each of your deaths
who says the one harvested stone
makes the sea sink to the level of your water
as you look you can only hear birdsong as funeral music
you listen but dream of the ocean's carmine dustjacket
placed on the windowsill
picky nightmares read you more closely still
corpses stuffed with recalled-again chalk
who shares this doleful distance with you

now is furthest away

YANG LIAN »(1)«

E

F

G

H

Transformation

A

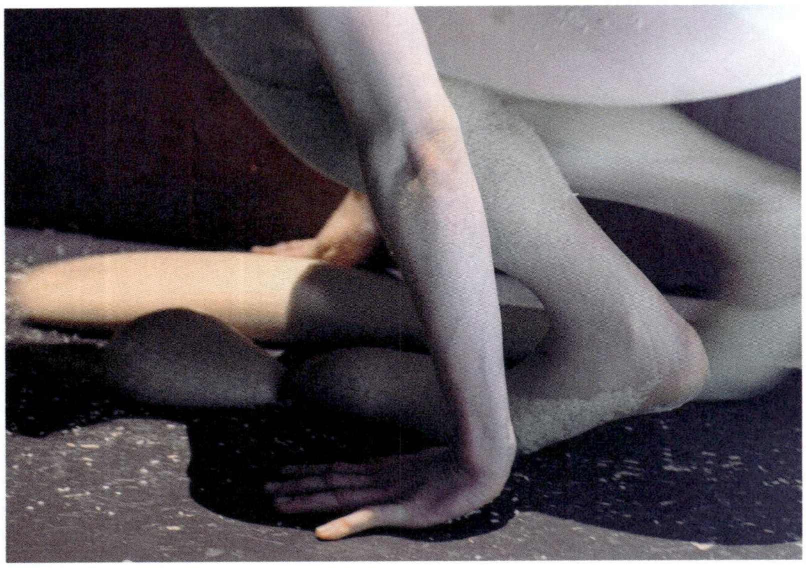

B

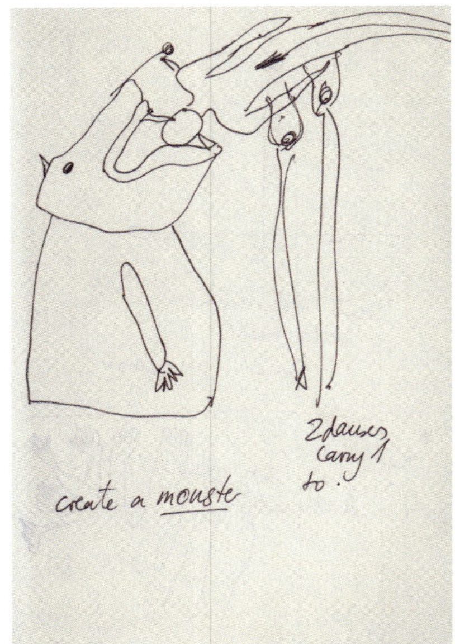

C

D

A **»Dialoge 2020 – Relevante Systeme II«** ↘2020 B **»insideout«** ↘2003 C **Sasha Waltz, study for »Medea«**↘2007 D+E **»S«** ↘2000

E

Form, shape, figure – they have a beginning and an end, a front and a back. Some of them are able to point beyond themselves, to occupy space without touching it. Form unites what it is with what it occupies; it tends toward, it suggests, it seeks to connect. It isn't neutral; it isn't »white« or isolated. Form exists in space and in relation to space. It's a snapshot of space.
If the space changes, the form changes with it. Form changes and is trans-formed in relation to the space around it – but also in relation to itself.
A change in time also brings about a change in form. Form develops in response to transformations in time, changing fundamentally, while also recalling its old self. Every form contains a memory of its previous form, its original form. It is not neutral, not »free«, not without history. Yet the memory of its previous form also contains an awareness of its change, its transformability, its future. Form is a snapshot of time. Transformation is in the nature of form. Change is its continuity.
In changing it unites what it was with what it will be.
HANNAH JONAS

Form, Gestalt, Figur, sie haben einen Anfang, ein Ende, ein Vorne, ein Hinten. Manchen gelingt es, über ihre Form hinaus zu verweisen, Raum einzunehmen, ohne ihn zu berühren. Die Form vereint, was sie ist, und das, was sie einnimmt, ohne es zu sein, sie neigt sich, deutet an, sucht Kontakt. Sie ist nicht neutral, nicht »weiß«, nicht bezugslos.
Die Form existiert in dem Raum, zu dem sie in Beziehung steht. Sie ist eine Momentaufnahme des Raums.
Wandelt sich der Raum, wandelt sich auch die Form. Sie wandelt sich und sie transformiert sich in der Beziehung zu ihrer Umwelt, aber auch im Beziehen auf sich selbst.
Wandelt sich die Zeit, wandelt sich auch die Form. In der Transformation und der Antwort auf die Änderungen der Zeit entwickelt die Form sich weiter, verändert sich fundamental und erinnert sich gleichzeitig ihrer selbst. In jeder Form steckt die Erinnerung an ihre Vor-Form, ihre Ur-Form. Sie ist nicht neutral, nicht »frei«, nicht geschichtslos. In der Erinnerung an ihre Vor-Form allerdings liegt auch die Erkenntnis über ihren Wandel, ihre Wandelbarkeit, ihre Zukunft. Die Form ist eine Momentaufnahme der Zeit.
Die Transformation ist die Natur der Form. Der Wandel ist ihre Kontinuität. Im Wandel vereint sie, was sie war, mit dem, was sie sein wird.
HANNAH JONAS

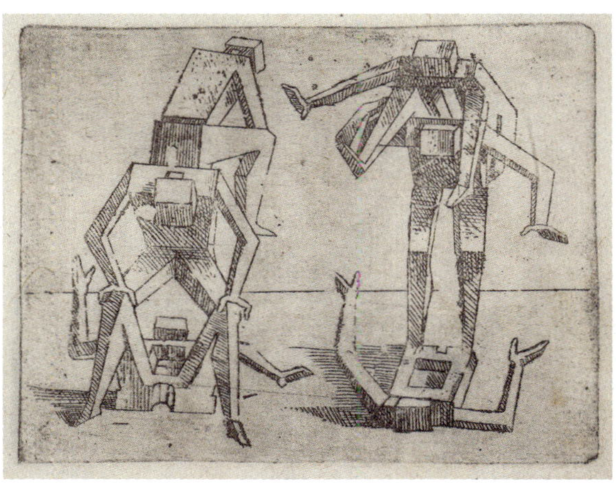

F

G

F Giovanni Battista Bracelli, »Oddities of Various Figures«, 1624, detail   G »Gezeiten« ↘2005

A »**SYM-PHONIE MMXX**«, **poster motif** ↘2022

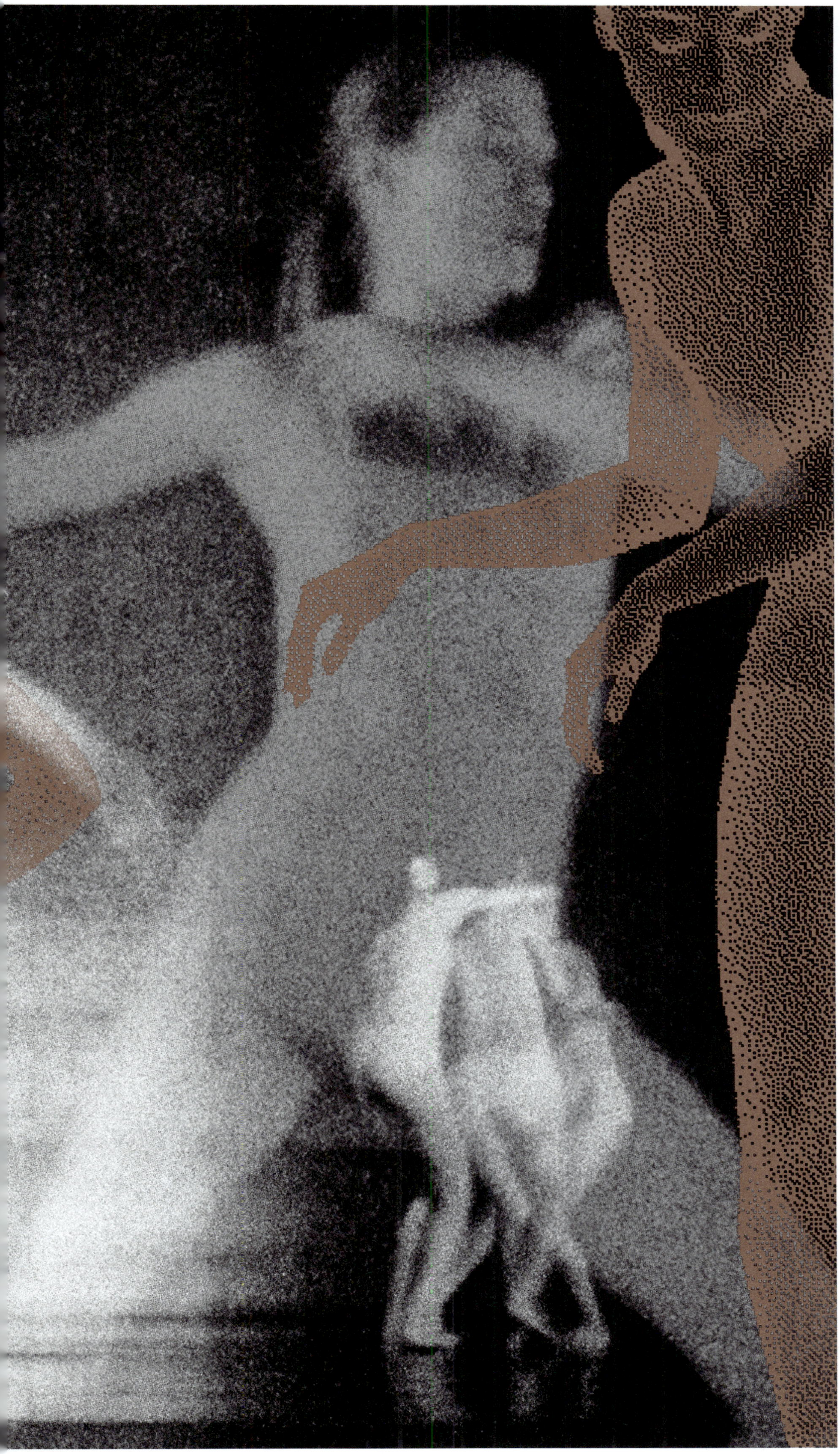

A

Dreams move on a level that we cannot comprehend, and dance – for me – is very congenial. I love this kind of energy when something cannot be grasped rationally, when you cannot precisely say what it is, and when there are no words for it. Some dreams occupy your mind, and you just know that they are about something essential, but you cannot explain it. Creating a new piece is quite similar. It feels like it is already within you, and you seek the right approach. The Surrealists and Dadaists have always been very important to me because they made this kind of boundless freedom an essential foundation of their work. With Luis Buñuel, the layers intertwine so much that you no longer know: What is what? Is it happening in the mind, or is it real? I love this so much because I often perceive life similarly. There is my mind and my perception, and it is so different from what others see. We live in parallel worlds, in different realities. The question is how far one is willing to engage with something like this, with the tangled and confusing. If you succeed and get close to the unconscious, it becomes a center of power you can follow. You must rely on your intuition, trusting it knows where to go, and then you must let yourself drift in that direction. This is essentially how I develop my pieces. The analysis follows the theme – but first, you must swim.
SASHA WALTZ

Träume bewegen sich auf einer Ebene, die wir nicht begreifen können, und Tanz hat für mich etwas sehr Wesensverwandtes. Ich liebe diese Art von Energie, wenn man etwas nicht rational greifen kann, nicht genau sagen kann, was es ist, und keine Worte dafür findet. Es gibt ja diese Träume, man hat sie im Kopf und weiß ganz genau, dass es sich um etwas Essenzielles handelt, aber man kann es nicht erklären. So ähnlich ist auch die Kreation eines neuen Stücks. Man trägt es irgendwie schon in sich, und dann sucht man den richtigen Zugang. Die Surrealisten und Dadaisten sind für mich immer sehr wichtig gewesen, weil sie diese Art von grenzenloser Freiheit zur wesentlichen Grundlage ihrer Arbeit gemacht haben. Bei Luis Buñuel verschieben sich die Ebenen so ineinander, dass man gar nicht mehr weiß: Was ist was? Findet es im Kopf statt, ist es wirklich? Ich liebe das so sehr, weil ich das Leben oft genauso empfinde. Da ist mein Kopf, meine Wahrnehmung, und es ist so anders als das, was die anderen sehen. Wir leben in parallelen Welten, in unterschiedlichen Wirklichkeiten. Die Frage ist, wie weit man bereit ist, sich auf so etwas einzulassen, auf dieses Verworrene und Verwirrende. Wenn es einem gelingt, wenn man nahe am Unbewussten ist, dann wird das zu einem Kraftzentrum, dem man folgen kann. Man muss sich dabei auf die eigene Intuition verlassen, darauf, dass sie weiß, wo es hingeht, und dann muss man sich dahin treiben lassen. So entwickle ich im Wesentlichen meine Stücke. Die Analyse, dem Thema folgen – aber erst einmal muss man schwimmen. SASHA WALTZ

Tree Baum

A

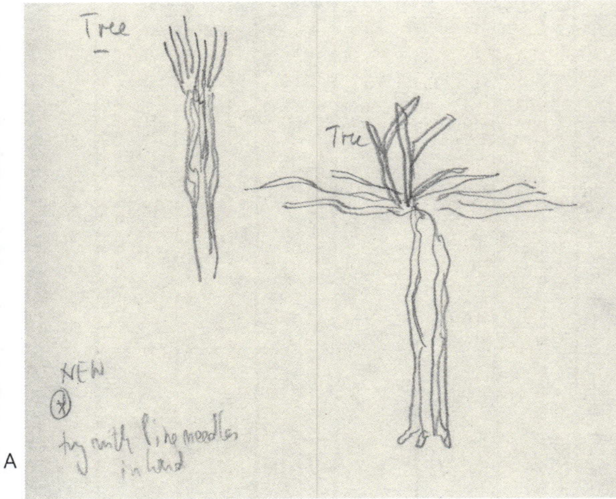

B

C

E

D

A **»Tannhäuser«** ↘2014 B **Sasha Waltz, study for »Matsukaze«** ↘2011 C **Piero del Pollaiuolo, »Apollo and Daphne«, 1470–80** D **»Dido & Aeneas«** ↘2005

F

What I want to do here is to bring the past back to life in this deeply unsettling present – all those incredibly stimulating moments, the experience of seeing and watching dancing bodies, the exhilaration of feeling that I was moving with them, growing light and soaring at the sight of them.
In my memory I see the vigorous, expressive bodies in which pure vitality gave emotional force to so many historically charged moments – and in the present, in the streets of the city where I live, I see trees that are wilting as I write (it's 30 July 2023). Berlin, a place of memory. But also, though less famously, a place of oases – islands of green that make the city so agreeable to live in. The trees are suffering. Clearly suffering. And not only here, and not only the trees. I travel through Europe and see the Po, the Elbe, the Rhone, the Rhine trickling along like little streams; these rivers, once so great and fearless, are suffering. Clearly suffering.
The bodies, our bodies, those that dance and those that watch, they cannot not see this: the signs are everywhere and abundantly clear. They say: something is dying. We remember the times, the good times when we saw the bodies dancing, and we have to be able to hope that those times will come again. When we see trees coming into green we cannot help but feel happy, but what we see now is withering life. We see violence where we should see vitality.
In »Körper« (Bodies), I always saw the injury inflicted on the body by the atrocities of history, to which the dancing bodies offered resistance with vigor and gravity – important, politically important resistance.
Now I see such injury everywhere: in the rivers, woods and oceans, in the faces of fleeing people, in images of war. I see them in us. Dance produces images that are still capable of making us feel happy, but nature – the nature we see today when we bother to look – shows us images of atrophy. It shows us violence. And that violence originates with us. We should gather the power of dance inside ourselves. We should flock together like birds in the sky and remember that we are nature, we are power; it has been granted to us to dance and live in this air, under glorious blue skies or grey seas of clouds, and we cannot continue to look on as it slips into lifelessness. We need to resist.
CHRISTIAN RUZICSKA

Das Vergangene, die vielen unfassbar belebenden Momente des Sehens und Zusehens, des Erlebens tanzender Körper, stets belebt durch das Fühlen, selbst in Schwingung zu geraten und leicht zu werden und zu schweben beim Anblick dieser Körper, nun wiederzubeleben in dieser Gegenwart, die mich zutiefst beunruhigt, ist die Aufforderung.
Ich sehe in meiner Erinnerung die kraftvollen, ausdrucksstarken Körper, in denen pure Vitalität so vielen auch historisch aufgeladenen Momenten emotionale Kraft schenkte, und ich sehe in der Gegenwart in den Straßen der Stadt, in der ich lebe, Bäume, die jetzt, wir schreiben den 30. Juli 2023, verdorrt sind. Berlin, Ort der Erinnerung. Ort auch und selten deswegen besungen, der vielen grünen Oasen, die diese Stadt so lebenswert machen. Sie leiden. Die Bäume. Deutlich. Und nicht nur hier und nicht nur sie. Ich fahre durch Europa und sehe den Po, ich sehe die Elbe, ich sehe die Rhône, den Rhein wie dünne Rinnsale dahinfließen, diese einst großen, arglosen Flüsse, sie leiden. Deutlich.
Die Körper, unsere Körper, die tanzenden wie die schauenden, können dies nicht nicht sehen: Die Zeichen sind überdeutlich, überall zu sehen. In ihnen steht geschrieben: Es geht hier etwas zu Grunde.
Wir können uns erinnern, an die Zeiten, die schönen, da wir die Körper tanzen sahen, und wir müssen wollen dürfen, dass dies auch morgen so sein mag. Wir können beim Anblick grünender Bäume nicht anders als Glück empfinden, wir sehen aber jetzt: verdorrendes Leben. Wir sehen Gewalt, wo wir Vitalität schauen sollten.
In dem Stück »Körper« sah ich stets die Verletzung des Körpers durch die Gewalttaten der Geschichte, dem die tanzenden Körper voller Lebenskraft und tiefem Ernst Widerstand entgegensetzten, einen wichtigen, politisch eminent wichtigen Widerstand.
Jetzt sehe ich diese Verletzung überall, in den Flüssen, den Wäldern, den Meeren, und ich sehe sie in den Gesichtern der Geflüchteten, in den Bildern vom Krieg. Ich sehe sie in uns. Der Tanz hat Bilder erschaffen, die immer auch Glück erzeugen konnten. Die Natur aber, die wir heute sehen, wenn wir hinsehen, zeigt uns ein verwelkendes Bild. Sie zeigt uns Gewalt. Und diese Gewalt geht von uns aus.
Wir sollten die Kraft des Tanzes in uns versammeln und konzentrieren, wir sollten einen Schwarm bilden, gleich dem Vogelschwarm am weiten Himmel, und wissen, dass wir Natur sind und Kraft, und nicht länger bereit sein, die Luft, in der unter herrlichem Blau oder grauem Wolkenmeer wir eingeladen sind zu tanzen, zu leben, ins Leblose gleiten zu lassen, so ganz ohne Widerstand!
CHRISTIAN RUZICSKA

G

H

E Abraham Jamnitzer, statuette of Daphne, 1580–86 F »Matsukaze« ↘2011 G »Dialoge 2020 – Strandbad Tegelsee« ↘2020 H »SYM-PHONIE MMXX« ↘2022

Vitrine

A

B

The history of the museum begins with the cabinet of curiosities as an omnium-gatherum of treasures. The institution of the modern museum as a system of universal representation is a result of the paradigm change in revolutionary France. In the Grande Galerie of the Louvre, de-functionalised works of art were presented to the public as l'art pour l'art, a development that reached its climax in the White Cube. In the 1960s, happenings and the Fluxus movement called on the public to participate, triggering a complex interplay between exhibition space and stage space as illuminated display case. At the same time, Joseph Beuys and others started to use cabinets and vitrines for collections of objects and relicts from their actions – a trend that was later developed on a larger scale in the art of installation, another art form influenced by avant-garde theatre and dance.
ROBERT EIKMEYER

Die Geschichte des Museums beginnt mit der Kunst- und Wunderkammer als Sammelsurium von Kostbarkeiten. Die Institution des modernen Museums als System universeller Repräsentation ist eine Folge des Paradigmenwechsels im revolutionären Frankreich. In der Großen Galerie des Louvre wurden de-funktionalisierte Kunstwerke der Öffentlichkeit präsentiert und traten als l'art pour l'art in Dialog mit den Betrachter:innen, eine Entwicklung, die ihren Höhepunkt im Innenraum des White Cube fand. In den 1960er Jahren forderten Fluxus und Happening das Publikum zur Teilnahme auf und leiteten ein komplexes Wechselspiel zwischen dem Ausstellungs- und Bühnenraum als leuchtenden Schaukasten ein. Gleichzeitig begannen Joseph Beuys und andere, Kästen und Vitrinen für Objektsammlungen und Relikte ihrer Aktionen zu nutzen, was später raumfüllend in die auch vom Avantgarde-Theater und Tanz beeinflusste Kunst der Installation mündete.
ROBERT EIKMEYER

C

D

A »Dialoge '99/I – Sophiensæle« ↘1999 B »ΕΞΟΔΟΣ | Exodos« ↘2018 C Hieronymus Bosch, »The Garden of Earthly Delights«, 1490–1500, detail

E

A

A »Körper« ↘2000 B+E »**ΕΞΟΔΟΣ | Exodos**« ↘2018 C+F »**insideout**« ↘2003 D **Christoph Angermair, »Little Death Clock«, 1624**

B

C

D

E

F

Voice Stimme

A

B

C

A voice transcending into song. Two voices singing the same notes, united in song. Many voices, creating and modulating harmonies as they sing. Solo, duet, ensemble – terms that are used in opera and in dance. Over the course of the last centuries, dance has played an ever smaller part in Western opera. With Sasha Waltz it has made a comeback and is so much more than an interlude or an allusion to court dances. It is a narrative in motion, an expression of elemental forces, it creates a space in which past and present come together and differences vanish – between dream and reality, male and female, individual and collective. E.T.A. Hoffmann supposedly said: »Music begins where language ends.« In Sasha's choreographic operas, it seems that at the point where traditional acting and verbal negotiation of conflict reach their limits, the dance unfolds, begins to enact the work, to express its essence, and to give it space and depth.
HANNAH DÜBGEN

Eine Stimme, die sich singend aufschwingt. Zwei Stimmen, die dasselbe singen und sich im Gesang vereinen. Viele Stimmen, die singend Harmonien kreieren und modulieren. Solo, Duett, Ensemble – Begriffe, die in der Oper und im Tanz verwendet werden. Der Tanz hat sich in den letzten Jahrhunderten immer mehr aus der abendländischen Oper entfernt. Mit Sasha Waltz kehrt er zurück und ist so viel mehr als ein Zwischenspiel, ein Zitat der Tänze bei Hofe. Er ist Erzählung in Bewegung, Ausdruck von Elementarem, schafft einen Raum, in dem Vergangenheit und Gegenwart ineinander fallen und sich Unterschiede auflösen: zwischen Traum und Wirklichkeit, Mann und Frau, Individuum und Kollektiv. Wo die Sprache aufhört, fängt die Musik an, soll E.T.A. Hoffmann gesagt haben. Beim Betrachten von Sashas Operninszenierungen blitzt der Gedanke auf: Wo im Musiktheater das Schauspiel, das verbale Verhandeln von Konflikten aufhört, fängt der Tanz an, das Werk darzustellen, seine Essenz auszudrücken, ihm Flügel und Tiefe zu verleihen. HANNAH DÜBGEN

D

E

A Margaret Watts Hughes, »Untitled Voice Figure«, date unknown B+H+I »Dialoge 2018 – Wirbel« ↘2018 C »insideout« ↘2003

F

G

H

I

D **»Dialoge – Künstlerhaus Bethanien«** ↘1993 E **Sasha Waltz, study for »Medea«** ↘2007 F **»rauschen«** ↘2019 G **»Fantasie«** ↘2006

Wall Wand

A

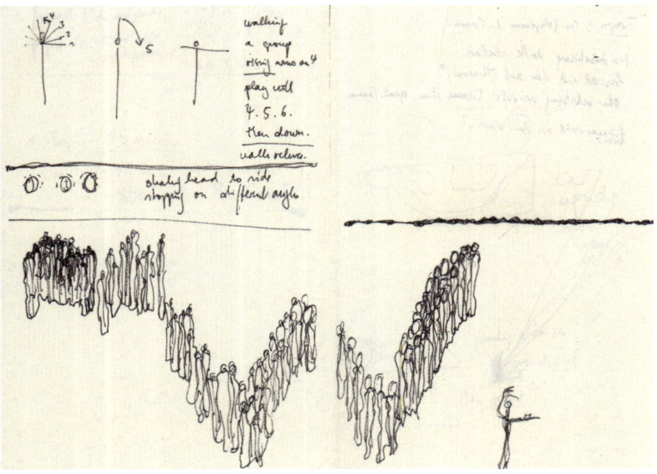

B

C

D

A **»SYM-PHONIE MMXX«** ↘2022 B **Sasha Waltz, study for »SYM-PHONIE MMXX«** ↘2022 C **»Körper«** ↘2000 D+F **»Kreatur«** ↘2017

E

A wall – dark, oppressive, grey. The wall. Fists desperately pounding against it. Is there anybody out there? No reply. Only dust silently falling. The Corona wall, for months on end. Dividing. Separating. Isolating. Chilling. Silencing. Hardening. Ossifying and desiccating. And then, one evening in spring – a first crack. Movement. Four dancers, no more, in the Berlin Cathedral. Powerful walls. Powerful organ music. The walls palpable in every movement, but with every movement they change their nature. They don't come tumbling down. But they have become porous, fluid, creating connections between inside and outside, between people. Only dance can do that, only dance and music. They don't deny the cold horrors of reality; they make them palpable, visible – and in doing so, they take the edge off them. I've never seen so many people cry.
HARTMUT ROSA ON »IN C«

Dunkle, schwere, graue Mauer. The Wall. Verzweifeltes Hämmern dagegen: Is There Anybody Out There?! Nur Schweigen. Staubrieseln als Antwort. Corona-Mauer, über viele Monate. Sie trennte. Vereinsamte. Schnitt ab. Ließ frieren. Verstummen. Verhärten. Erstarren und Ausdörren. Und dann, eines Abends, im Frühling, zum ersten Mal: ein Riss. Eine Bewegung. Vier Tanzende nur, im Berliner Dom. Mächtige Mauern. Mächtige Orgelklänge. In jeder Bewegung die Mauern spürbar, in jeder Bewegung aber verändern sie ihren Charakter: Die Mauern sind nicht eingestürzt. Sie sind durchlässig geworden. Flüssig, Verbindung stiftend zwischen Innen und Außen und zwischen den Menschen. Das kann nur Tanz, das können nur Tanz und Musik. Sie verleugnen nicht das Grauen und die Kälte der Wirklichkeit, sie machen sie fühlbar, führen sie vor Augen und heben sie auf dabei. Nie habe ich so viele Weinende gesehen.
HARTMUT ROSA ÜBER »IN C«

F

G

E **»In C« at Berliner Dom** ↘2021 G **»Roméo et Juliette«** ↘2007

following page **»Körper«** ↘2000

A

B

C

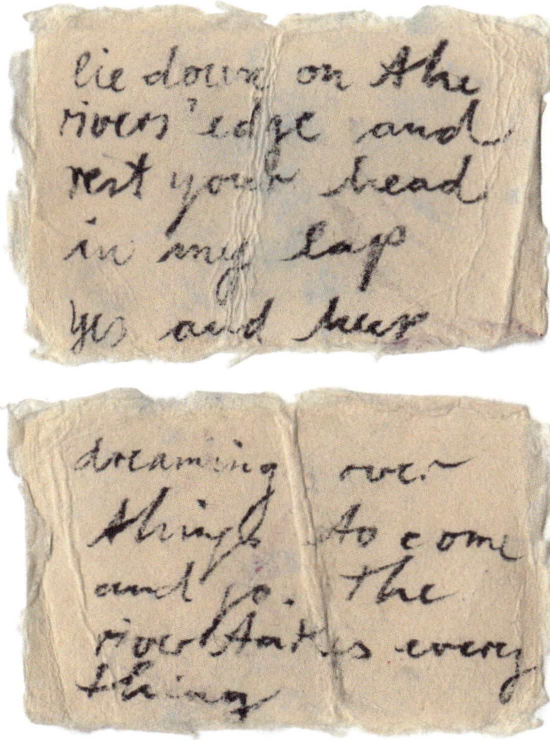

D

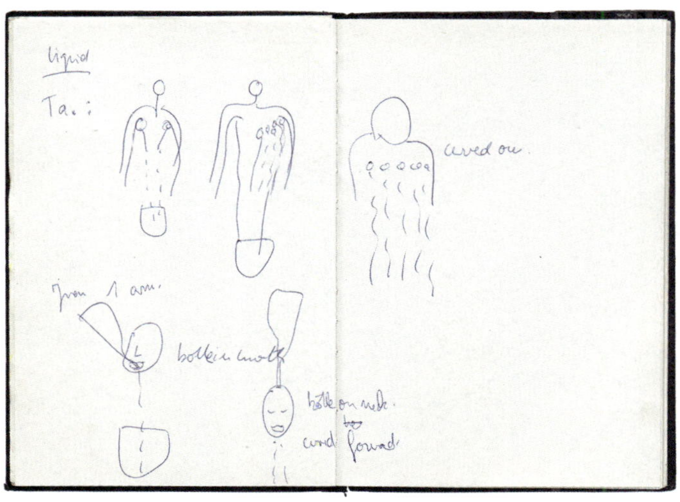

E

F

B **»Orfeo«** ↘2014 C **»Dialoge 2018 – Wirbel«** ↘2018 D **Sasha Waltz, writing, undated** E **Sasha Waltz, sketchbook »Körper«** ↘2000 F **»Impromptus«** ↘2004

A

B

C

A **»Orfeo«** ↘2014 B **»Zweiland«** ↘1997 C **»Gezeiten«** ↘2005 D **»Dido & Aeneas«** ↘2005

D

Wind

B

A

C

D

A+F **»Medea«** ↘2007 B **»Beethoven 7«** ↘2023 C **»Dialoge 2020 – Relevante Systeme«** ↘2020 D **»Dialoge 09 – MAXXI«** ↘2009

E

So debating with herself, her heart inflamed, the goddess
came to Aeolia, to the country of storms, the place
of wild gales. Here in his vast cave, King Aeolus
keeps the writhing winds, and the roaring tempests,
under control, curbs them with chains and imprisonment.
They moan angrily at the doors, with a mountain's vast murmurs:
Aeolus sits, holding his sceptre, in his high stronghold,
softening their passions, tempering their rage: if not,
they'd surely carry off seas and lands and the highest heavens,
with them, in rapid flight, and sweep them through the air.
But the all-powerful Father, fearing this, hid them
in dark caves, and piled a high mountain mass over them
and gave them a king, who, by fixed agreement, would know
how to give the order to tighten or slacken the reins.
VIRGIL »THE AENEID«

Solches wälzte bei sich die Göttin flammenden Herzens,
kam in der Stürme Bereich, ins Land voll fauchender Föhne,
kam nach Aeolien. Hier in weiter Höhle bedrängt mit
hartem Befehl der Winde Gewühl und heulende Stürme
König Aeolus, hält sie mit Fesseln und Kerker im Zaume.
Jene toben empört rings wider Wände und Riegel.
Dumpf dröhnt drinnen der Berg. Doch Aeolus, szeptergewaltig,
thront auf der Burg, stimmt mild ihr Gemüt und zähmt ihre Zornwut.
Täte er's nicht, so rissen sie Meere und Länder und Himmels-
tiefen im Fluge mit fort und fegten sie hin in die Lüfte.
Doch der allmächtige Vater verbarg sie in düsteren Höhlen,
dieses befürchtend, und türmte noch Bergesmassen darauf und
gab einen König den Winden; der sollte nach festem Vertrage
klug, auf Geheiß, bald straff, bald lockerer führen die Zügel.
VERGIL »AENEIS«

F

following page »**Johannes-Passion**« ↘2024

A

B

A **»Johannes-Passion«, recycled planks from »Gezeiten«** ↘2024 B+E **»Gezeiten«** ↘2005

C

F

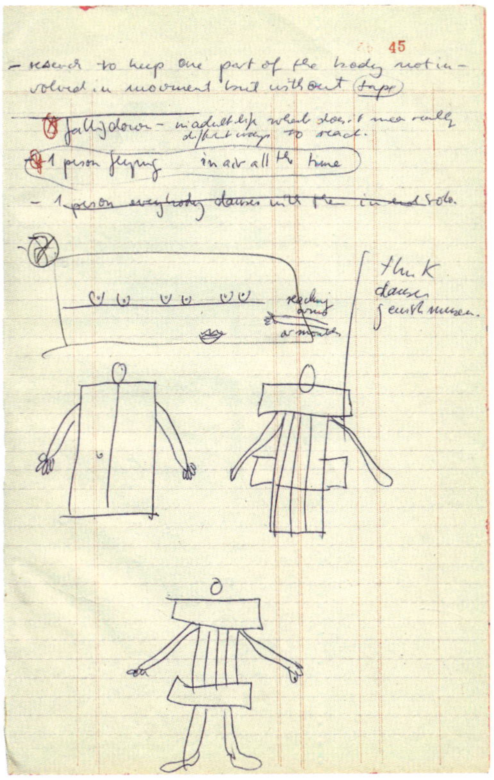

D

E

G

C »Allee der Kosmonauten« ↘1996 D Sasha Waltz, study for »Dialoge '99/I – Sophiensæle« ↘1999 F »noBody« ↘2002 G »Na Zemlje« ↘1998

Yes/No Ja/Nein

As a singular naked body I run through the room. **YES**, I shout and someone else shouts, **NO**. **NO**, another repeats. Then something pulls tight, comes together into one loud voice; we're standing next to each other, facing the same way. **NO** With one voice. It's not clear who hears it. **YES** As one body we cross the room, following in the wake of our voices. **NO** Sucked in by the collective shout. No in-between. No need for a coalition partner. We don't listen to individuals. We divide and sort. Drive clear lines into the mass of chaos. **NO** Polarisation filters protect our eyes from all the confusion out there. In the anatomy of our social body is the eye that sees our world. Can you see the shape of us under the weight of our opinion? The skin, taut over our body, smooth and complete? The collective muscles underneath ready to leap into action. **YES—NO NO—YES** A dancing individual breaks out of the structure. A thought escaping the system. **NO—YES** The dancer flinches, dodging our voices. A something else become visible, a grain of sand in the works, soundless. **YES—NO NO—YES** Mouths growing undisciplined. **YES—YES—NO** Order collapsing into many voices, motley talk. Words in many tongues flying through the air. Points of view splintering into diversity, filters overlapping. **NO—NO—YES—NO** And our bodies are many again. But the rhythm of collective thinking continues to pump: **NO—YES—NO** It's written into our bodies: spines twisting in sync, rotating to the beat: **YES—NO** Heads shake: **NO—YES** Ribcages turn the other way: **NO—YES—YES** Pray for synchronisation, and disorientation will shimmer through. Oscillating in between is the proof of a moving reality. LÁSZLÓ SANDIG

Als einzelner nackter Körper laufe ich durch den Raum. **YES** rufe ich. Ein Gegenüber ruft **NO**. **NO** wiederholt eine andere, dann zurrt sich was zusammen, zu einer großen Stimme kondensiert, denn wir stehen aufrecht nebeneinander und blicken in dieselbe Richtung. **NO** Einstimmig. Nicht sichtbar ist, wen es trifft. **YES** Als gemeinsamer Körper durchschreiten wir den Raum, der Schneise unseres Wortes hinterher. **NO** Sog des gemeinsamen Rufs. Kein Dazwischen. Kein Koalitionspartner nötig. Dem besonderen Gegenüber lauschen wir nicht. Wir sortieren und zerteilen. Schlagen greifbare Kanten in die Masse des Chaos. **NO** Polarisierungsfilter schützen den Blick vor dem konfusen Ganzen da draußen. In der Anatomie unseres sozialen Körpers sitzt der Augapfel, der unsere Welt erfasst. Siehst du unsere Form unter dem Gewicht unserer Meinung und die Haut, wie sie sich um uns spannt, glatt und lückenlos? Darunter Kollektivmuskeln vor dem Sprung in die Handlung. **YES—NO NO—YES** Ein tanzendes Individuum entflieht der Struktur. Ein Gedanke, der dem System entweicht. **NO—YES** Zuckend weicht die Person unseren Stimmen aus. Ein sichtbar gewordenes Anderes, ein Sandkorn im Getriebe, lautlos. **YES—NO NO—YES** Münder verlieren ihre Disziplin. **YES—YES—NO** Ordnung zerfällt in viele Stimmen, buntes Gerede. Wörter vieler Sprachen fliegen durcheinander. Perspektiven zersplittern in Vielfalt, Filter überlappen. **NO—NO—YES—NO** Und unsere Körper werden wieder viele. Doch noch pumpt der Rhythmus eines Denkens **NO—YES—NO** Er schrieb sich in unsere Körper ein: synchron verdrehte, geregelt-rotierende Wirbelsäulen, **YES—NO** Köpfe schütteln **NO—YES** Brustkörbe schrauben entgegengesetzt **NO—YES—YES** Im Gebet der Gleichschaltung schimmert zwanghafte Orientierungslosigkeit. Oszillierend im Dazwischen liegt der Beweis einer beweglichen Wirklichkeit.

LÁSZLÓ SANDIG

A

B

GO

Chronology

Sasha Waltz and Jochen Sandig **found the dance company Sasha Waltz & Guests** in Berlin.

REPERTOIRE

Travelogue I – Twenty to eight
Berlin, Groningen, Freiburg, Münster, Rotterdam, Amsterdam

A

B

1993

Dialoge – Künstlerhaus Bethanien (Showing I–V)
↘pp. 53, 96, 198, **227**

Künstlerhaus Bethanien, Berlin
Concept
Sasha Waltz
I
31 Jan
Dance/Choreography
Frans Poelstra
Sasha Waltz
Music
Tristan Honsinger (Violoncello)
Stage Design
Barbara Steppe
II
27 Feb
Dance/Choreography
Nasser Martin-Gousset
Takako Suzuki
Sasha Waltz
Music
Sibylle Pomorin (Children's Choir)
III
6 Mar
Dance/Choreography
Kitt Johnson
Sasha Waltz
Music
David Moss (Vocals)
IV
13 Mar
Dance/Choreography
Carme Renalias
Sasha Waltz
Music
Dietmar Diesner (Saxophone)
Sven Åke Johansson (Percussion)
V
27 Mar
Dance
Sasha Waltz
David Zambrano
Music
Peter Hollinger (Percussion)

Bungalow

Hackesche Höfe, Berlin
15 May
Direction/Choreography
Sasha Waltz
Dance/Choreography
Takako Suzuki
Sasha Waltz
Music
Peter Hollinger

Travelogue I – Twenty to eight
↘pp. 57, 92, 108, **228**, 238

Grand Theatre Groningen
16 Sep
Direction/Choreography
Sasha Waltz
Dance/Choreography
Thomas Lehmen
Nasser Martin-Gousset
Takako Suzuki
Sasha Waltz
Charlotte Zerbey
Music
Tristan Honsinger Quintett
Jean-Marc Zelwer
Stage Design
Barbara Steppe
Costume Design
Sasha Waltz
Light Design
Tomski Binsert
André Pronk
Coproduction
Grand Theatre Groningen
Supported by
Berliner Senatsverwaltung für Kulturelle Angelegenheiten (Frauenförderung)
Fonds Darstellende Künste
Initiative Neue Musik Berlin e.V.

A **»Bungalow«** B **Künstlerhaus Bethanien**

Dialoge – Künstlerhaus Bethanien (Showing I–V)

In 1992, Sasha Waltz comes to Berlin as part of a residency at Künstlerhaus Bethanien, where she develops the improvisation series »Dialogue« with international guests, stemming from an interdisciplinary approach in her work. This approach forms the foundation for the artist's future processes: »Dialogue« projects are short and intense encounters between musicians, visual artists, dancers and choreographers, each focussed on particular spaces and themes.

1992 kommt Sasha Waltz im Rahmen eines Stipendiums am Künstlerhaus Bethanien nach Berlin, wo sie aus dem Geiste des interdisziplinären Arbeitens heraus die Improvisationsreihe »Dialoge« mit internationalen Gästen entwickelt. Dieser Ansatz bildet das Fundament für zukünftige Arbeitsprozesse der Künstlerin: »Dialoge«-Projekte sind kurze und intensive Begegnungen zwischen Musiker:innen, Bildenden Künstler:innen, Tänzer:innen und Choreograph:innen in jeweils sehr spezifischen Räumen und Themenfeldern.

Travelogue I – Twenty to eight

Subsequent to the »Dialogue« project at Künstlerhaus Bethanien, Sasha Waltz embarks on the first part of the »Travelogue« trilogy, a co-production with the Grand Theatre Groningen. In 1993, Sasha Waltz sketches in »Travelogue I – Twenty to eight« a humorous, aggressive and sensual picture of contemporary morals and customs. Over the following years this piece loses neither its relevance nor its controversial intensity. It is a dance classic and still enthrals its audiences all over the world today.

In einer Koproduktion zwischen dem Grand Theatre Groningen und Sasha Waltz entsteht im Anschluss an das »Dialoge«-Projekt im Künstlerhaus Bethanien der erste Teil der »Travelogue«-Trilogie. Mit Humor, Aggressivität und Sinnlichkeit zeichnet Sasha Waltz in »Travelogue I – Twenty to eight« 1993 ein Sittenbild der Gegenwart, das über die Jahre nichts an Brisanz und Relevanz eingebüßt hat: ein Tanzklassiker. Das Stück begeistert bis heute das Publikum weltweit.

Prize for »Travelogue I – Twenty to eight« at the **International Choreographer's Competition** in Groningen.

»Berliner Zeitung« Critics' Prize for Sasha Waltz.

REPERTOIRE

Travelogue I – Twenty to eight Berlin, Groningen, Zurich, Frankfurt, London, Copenhagen, Prague, Hanover, Hamburg, Nancy, Erlangen
Travelogue II – Tears break fast Berlin, Pforzheim, Kassel, Frankfurt

Paulinchen allein zu Haus

Kunsthaus Tacheles, Berlin
5 May
Choreography
Sasha Waltz
Music
Jochen Sandig

Travelogue II – Tears break fast
↘pp. 56, 109, **231**

Podewil, Berlin
26 Oct
Direction/Choreography
Sasha Waltz
Dance/Choreography
Ákos Hargitai
Nasser Martin-Gousset
Takako Suzuki
Sasha Waltz
Music
Tristan Honsinger Sextett
Stage Design
Barbara Steppe
Sasha Waltz
Costume Design
Sasha Waltz & Guests
Annette Bätz
Light Design
André Pronk
Production
Sasha Waltz & Guests
Supported by
Berliner Senatsverwaltung für Kulturelle Angelegenheiten
Fonds Darstellende Künste
TanzWerkstatt Berlin
Podewil, Berlin
Grand Theatre Groningen
SIEMENS Kulturprogramm

1994

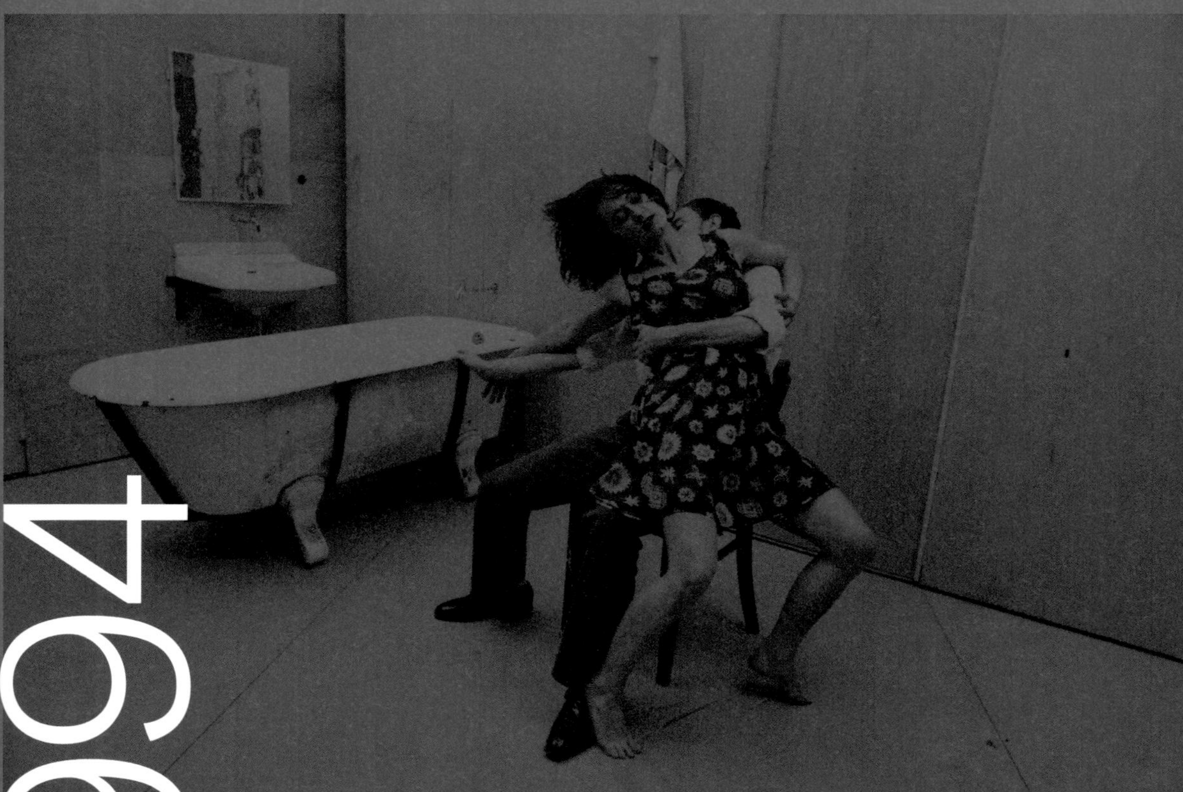

A

A **»Travelogue II – Tears break fast«**

Travelogue II – Tears break fast

Sasha Waltz takes us through everyday spaces in her »Travelogue« trilogy. After the first part, »Twenty to eight«, is set in the kitchen, the action in »Tears break fast« moves to other rooms in a film noir fashion, inspired by the movies »A bout du souffle« by Jean-Luc Godard and »Un chien andalou« by Luis Buñuel. The bathroom is the place of retreat, stripping and secret passions, where cares seem far away. Vanity and superficiality prevail right next door at a bar, as do glamour and unfulfilled dreams. This is where the plot begins, and how it ends remains in the dark. Four individuals – or five? – bathe and drink, dance and daydream. The audience is drawn in, empathising with their desires and loves, their addictions and crimes … and their defeats.

Sasha Waltz führt in ihrer »Travelogue«-Trilogie durch Räume des Alltags. Nach der Küche im ersten Teil »Twenty to eight«, inspiriert von Jean-Luc Godards Film »A bout de souffle« und Luis Buñuels »Un chien andalou«, verlagert sich das Geschehen in »Tears break fast« auf andere Räume im Stil des Film Noirs: Das Badezimmer als Ort des Rückzugs, der Entblößung, der geheimen Passionen und Unbeschwertheit befindet sich Tür an Tür mit einer Bar, dem Ort des schönen Scheins, des Glamours und der unerfüllten Träume. Hier entspinnt sich eine Handlung, deren Ausgang im Dunkeln liegt. Vier Menschen – oder sind es fünf? – baden und trinken, tanzen und träumen. Das Publikum nimmt Teil an ihrem Verlangen und Lieben, ihren Süchten und Verbrechen … und ihrem Scheitern.

First international tour to the USA and Canada with »Travelogue I – Twenty to eight«.

REPERTOIRE

Travelogue I – Twenty to eight Budapest, Oldenburg, Groningen, Munich, Ludwigsburg, Atlanta, New York, Chicago, Houston, Montreal, Los Angeles
Travelogue II – Tears break fast Berlin, Groningen, Munich, London, Ludwigsburg, Erlangen
Travelogue III – All ways six steps Berlin, Munich

Travelogue III – All ways six steps
↘pp. 182, **233**

Hebbel-Theater, Berlin
26 Aug
Direction/Choreography
Sasha Waltz
Dance/Choreography
Bo Madvig
Nasser Martin-Gousset
Cécile Mertens
Takako Suzuki
Sasha Waltz
Music
Tristan Honsinger
Mola Sylla
Stage Design
Thomas Schenk
Sasha Waltz
Costume Design
Sasha Waltz & Guests
Annette Bätz
Light Design
André Pronk
Production
Sasha Waltz & Guests
Coproduction
Sophiensæle, Berlin
Schauburg München
Grand Theatre Groningen
Supported by
Berliner Senatsverwaltung für Kulturelle Angelegenheiten
Fonds Darstellende Künste

A

1995

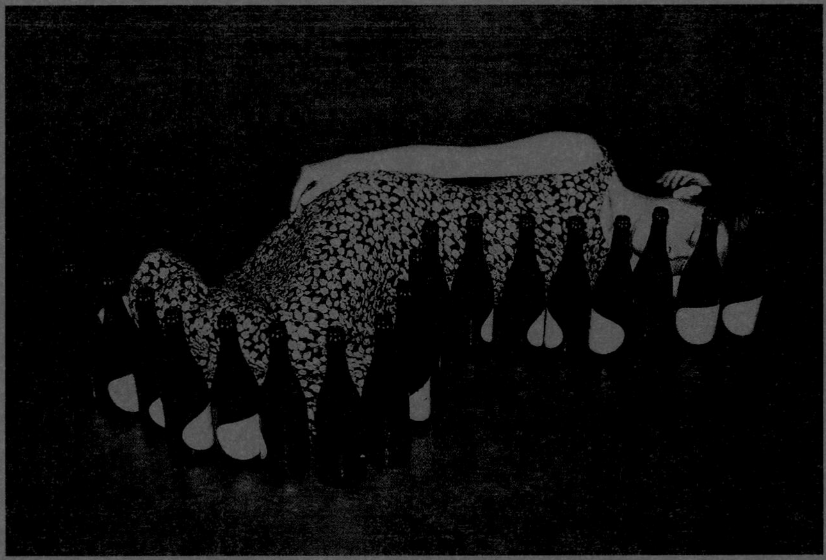
B

A+B **»Travelogue III – All ways six steps«**

Travelogue III – All ways six steps

Compared to the first two parts of the trilogy, domestic space is even more constricted and intimate in the last part, »All ways six steps«. The dancers are now in the bedroom that resembles a life-size doll's house, and in which they face surreal encounters with one another. The claustrophobic scenario, fitted out with a bed, cupboard, table and bedside table, is based on a stylised imitation of a Parisian hotel room where the rehearsals begin.
The courtyard of this confined space represents a parallel and outside world. The stage scenery is thus divided into two levels and symbolises different worlds. The bedroom is on the upper storey and the courtyard on the ground level. The original music for the other two »Travelogue« productions was composed by the American composer Tristan Honsinger. In this one he plays the cello while the Senegalese vocalist Mola Sylla sings. They take on the role of narrators and, in the end, blend into the story themselves.

Im letzten Teil »All ways six steps« ist der Innenraum gegenüber den beiden anderen Produktionen noch kleiner und intimer geworden: Wir befinden uns jetzt im Schlafzimmer, das einer lebensgroßen Puppenstube gleicht, in der es zwischen Tänzer:innen zu surrealen Begegnungen kommt. Dieses beengende Szenario mit seinem Mobiliar aus Bett, Schrank, Tisch, Stuhl und Nachttischschränkchen entsteht als stilisierter Nachbau eines Pariser Hotelzimmers, in dem die Proben ihren Anfang nehmen.
Die Parallel- und Außenwelt zu diesem Ort der Enge ist der Hof des Hauses. Das Bühnenbild ist so in zwei Ebenen unterteilt und symbolisiert unterschiedliche Welten. Das Zimmer befindet sich im ersten Stock und der Hof auf ebener Erde. Der amerikanische Komponist Tristan Honsinger am Cello, der auch die Originalmusik der beiden anderen »Travelogue«-Produktionen komponiert hat, und der senegalesische Sänger Mola Sylla übernehmen die Rolle von Erzählern, die am Ende selbst Teil der Geschichte werden.

The beginning is marked by the search for a permanent rehearsal space. Sasha Waltz worked as a wandering nomad, moving to four different locations over three years before finally securing the Sophiensäle. From Künstlerhaus Bethanien, to Hackesche Höfe, to Podewil, and then a factory floor on Burgstraße – each time, something of the place's identity infused itself into a new production. When the factory was demolished, a historic opportunity arose right next door in a former heritage-protected building by the former Berlin Handicraft Association. A Kairos moment! The company moved into the abandoned building in the rear courtyard at Sophienstraße 18. Dirk Cieslak, Jo Fabian and many others followed to work there, including Peter Brook, Milo Rau, Ulrich Rasche, Constanza Macras and Florentina Holzinger. They found nothing less than artistic freedom and independence beyond the conventional and institutional theatre spaces.

»Sophiensäle« transformed into »Sophiensæle« – a house full of »halls with souls«. The graphic designer used the »æ« symbol as a striking signifier, an invitation to think outside the box or even rethink entirely. Beyond the hectic zeitgeist, a place emerged in the heart of the city, where the ephemeral art forms of theatre and dance found a new, material identity. In theatre as in life, the moment counts – the one where the present and eternity merge. Founding a new theatre holds both hope and risk. Only those who have ever started a theatre know the existential fears and the weight of responsibility. Hope says, »Everything will be fine«, while risk says, »Nothing ventured, nothing gained«. Constant failure looms, the flip side of success that must be hard-won.

It all begins with an empty space. A circle of chairs on a creaking parquet. The bare ballroom without a stage, costumes or lights. Only the audience, who together recite plays by Georg Büchner, each in assigned roles. That alone is enough to create unforgettable moments. With »Danton's Death«, the hall stirs as the crowd rises in revolt, with voices resounding all at once. After »Woyzeck«, there's a bowl of pea soup.

But what is the secret of this place? The Sophiensæle are cloaked in magic. It's the light streaming through the large windows, the radiators quietly humming, the mysterious garden in the second courtyard. It's the smells of old paints, the traces of time. A real space that embodies transience. In a »Dialogue« project in 1999, the hall was restored to its original state. Sasha Waltz emptied it, leaving it as she had found it when she first entered. Here, even before the »Dialogue« project at the Jewish Museum, important groundwork was laid for »Körper«, the piece with which Schaubühne am Lehniner Platz would be reopened under new artistic direction almost a year later. The space has the greatest impact when it is still, empty and dark. That is when Sophie's soul starts to dance.

Am Anfang steht die Suche nach einem dauerhaften Proberaum. Sasha Waltz arbeitet als wandernde Nomadin innerhalb von drei Jahren an vier Orten, bevor sie sich die Sophiensäle erschließt. Vom Künstlerhaus Bethanien zu den Hackeschen Höfen, ins Podewil und in eine Fabriketage in der Burgstraße. Jedes Mal überträgt sich etwas von der Identität des Ortes in eine neue Produktion. Die Fabrik wird abgerissen, da offenbart sich eine historische Chance in unmittelbarer Nachbarschaft, im ehemaligen, denkmalgeschützten Haus des Berliner Handwerkervereins. Das Maxim-Gorki-Theater muss infolge der Schließung des Schiller Theaters in dessen Werkstätten umziehen – ein Kairos-Moment! Die Compagnie zieht in das verlassene Gebäude im Hinterhof der Sophienstraße 18. Dirk Cieslak, Jo Fabian und viele andere folgen, um hier zu arbeiten, darunter auch Peter Brook, Milo Rau, Ulrich Rasche, Constanza Macras und Florentina Holzinger. Sie finden nichts Geringeres als echte Spielräume und künstlerische Freiheit jenseits der konventionellen und institutionellen Theaterräume.

Die »Sophiensäle« verwandeln sich in die »Sophiensæle« – ein Haus voller »Säle mit Seele«. Der Grafiker setzt durch die Verwendung des »æ« ein markantes Zeichen. Eine Einladung, um die Ecke zu denken oder gar umzudenken. Jenseits des hektischen Zeitgeists entsteht im Herzen der Stadt ein Ort, in dem die Kunstformen der Verflüchtigung – Theater und Tanz – eine neue, materielle Identität erhalten. Im Theater wie im Leben zählt der Moment, in dem Augenblick und Ewigkeit sich vereinen. Die Gründung eines neuen Theaters birgt sowohl Hoffnung als auch Risiko. Nur wer selbst ein Theater gegründet hat, kennt die Existenzängste und die Verantwortung. Die Hoffnung sagt: »Alles wird gut«, das Risiko sagt: »Wer wagt, gewinnt«. Ständig droht das Scheitern, die Kehrseite des Erfolgs, der hart erkämpft werden muss.

Mit dem leeren Raum fängt alles an. Ein Kreis aus Stühlen auf knarrendem Parkett. Der nackte Festsaal ohne Bühne, Kostüme und Licht. Nur das Publikum, das selbst gemeinsam Theaterstücke von Georg Büchner in verteilten Rollen spricht. Das allein reicht, um unvergessliche Momente zu schaffen. Bei »Dantons Tod« geht es hoch her, wenn das Volk in Aufruhr gerät, dann erheben sich alle Stimmen gleichzeitig im Saal. Nach »Woyzeck« gibt es einen Teller Erbsensuppe.

Was aber ist das Geheimnis dieses Ortes? Es liegt ein Zauber über den Sophiensælen. Es ist das Licht, das durch die großen Fenster scheint, es ist die Heizung, die vor sich hin tuckert, es ist der geheimnisvolle Garten im zweiten Hof. Es sind die Gerüche nach alten Farben, es sind die Spuren der Zeit. Ein realer Raum, der Vergänglichkeit verkörpert. In einem »Dialoge«-Projekt wird er 1999 in seinen Urzustand versetzt. Sasha Waltz räumt ihn so leer, wie sie ihn vorgefunden hat, als sie einzog. Noch vor dem »Dialoge«-Projekt im Jüdischen Museum werden hier wichtige Grundsteine für »Körper« gelegt, das Stück, mit dem ein knappes Jahr später die Schaubühne am Lehniner Platz unter der neuen Künstlerischen Leitung eröffnet werden soll. Die stärkste Wirkung entfaltet der Raum immer, wenn er still, leer und dunkel ist. Dann tanzt Sophies Seele.

Sasha Waltz and Jochen Sandig **co-found the Sophiensæle in Berlin** – opening on September 26th with the world premiere of »Allee der Kosmonauten«.

REPERTOIRE

Allee der Kosmonauten Berlin, Groningen, Oldenburg, Münster, Belo Horizonte, São Paulo
Travelogue I – Twenty to eight Ferrara, Utrecht, Paris, Moscow, Copenhagen, Bern, Basel
Travelogue II – Tears break fast Hamburg, Frankfurt, Karlsruhe, Copenhagen, Basel
Travelogue III – All ways six steps Frankfurt, Utrecht, London, Copenhagen, Basel

A

Allee der Kosmonauten
↘pp. 52, 53, 83, 141, 215, **237**

Sophiensæle, Berlin
26 Sep
Direction/Choreography
Sasha Waltz
Dance/Choreography
Nadia Cusimano
Juan Kruz Diaz de Garaio Esnaola
Luc Dunberry
Nicola Mascia
Takako Suzuki
Laurie Young
Music
Nicholas Bussmann
Hanno Leichtmann
Lars Rudolph
Juan Kruz Diaz de Garaio Esnaola (Accordion)
Video
Elliot Caplan
Stage Design
Thomas Schenk
Costume Design
Sasha Waltz & Guests
Annette Bätz
Light Design
André Pronk
Production
Sasha Waltz & Guests
Coproduction
Schauburg München
Grand Theatre Groningen
Tollhaus, Karlsruhe
Theater im Pumpenhaus, Münster
Festival Internacional de Dança, Brazil
SIEMENS Kulturprogramm
Supported by
Berliner Senatsverwaltung für Wissenschaft, Forschung und Kultur

1996

B

A+B **»Allee der Kosmonauten«, photo shoot**

Allee der Kosmonauten

The world premiere of »Allee der Kosmonauten« opened the Sophiensæle in 1996. The living room couch of a prefabricated, high-rise apartment building in the Marzahn district of Berlin is the focal point of the action. The piece condenses research and interviews with the dwellers of the building into scenes of anxious sticking it out and waiting during the time after the Wall came down. The feelings, movement and actions of a family of three generations build up in this menacingly confined space. The inhabitants can only bury their feelings in lethargy or succumb to the loop of cause and effect that is linked to the claustrophobic living conditions. The choreographic confrontation with the anxiety in being confined in this way unfolds solutions that challenge the limits of dance and generates an uneasy comic effect in the absence of affection. Original video footage filmed from the prefabricated apartment blocks overlaps the action on the stage and provides more details about the world that the inhabitants live in. »Allee der Kosmonauten« belongs to a series of early pieces by Sasha Waltz in which she captures the worlds of everyday movement, investigating this new space for interpretation in dance. Created on the threshold of a new epoch, the piece tells the story of an era of living together without the possibility of escape.

Die Uraufführung von »Allee der Kosmonauten« eröffnet im Jahr 1996 die Sophiensæle. Mittelpunkt des Geschehens ist die Wohnzimmercouch einer Plattenbauwohnung in Berlin-Marzahn. In dieser Kulisse kondensieren Recherche und Interviews mit den Bewohner:innen zu Szenen angespannten Ausharrens und Wartens in der Zeit nach dem Mauerfall. Gefühle und Bewegungsimpulse einer Dreigenerationenfamilie stauen sich hier in prekärer Nähe, können nur entweder in Lethargie begraben oder dem Rückkopplungseffekt ihrer beengten Wohnsituation ausgesetzt werden. Die choreographische Konfrontation mit diesem nervösen Aufeinandergeworfensein entspinnt Lösungen an den Grenzen des Tanzbaren und entwickelt aus dem Fehlen von Zärtlichkeit eine unbehagliche Komik. Projektionen von Original-Videoaufnahmen aus den Plattenbauwohnungen überlagern das Geschehen auf der Bühne und erweitern den Blick auf die Lebenswelt der Bewohner:innen. »Allee der Kosmonauten« gehört zu einer Reihe früher Projekte von Sasha Waltz, die Bewegungswelten des Alltags dokumentarisch festhalten und als tänzerischen Interpretationsraum neu ergründen. Entstanden an der Schwelle zu einem neuen Zeitalter, erzählt das Stück von der Ära eines Zusammenlebens ohne Hintertür.

László Sandig is born, son of Sasha Waltz and Jochen Sandig.

»Allee der Kosmonauten« is invited to the **34th Theatertreffen,** Berlin.

REPERTOIRE

Allee der Kosmonauten Berlin, Moscow, Wilhelmshaven, Karlsruhe, Munich, Utrecht, Dresden, Barcelona, Seoul, Lisbon, Plzeň, Antwerp, Zurich, Düsseldorf
Travelogue I – Twenty to eight Bordeaux
Travelogue III – All ways six steps Barcelona, Bordeaux
Zweiland Berlin, Groningen

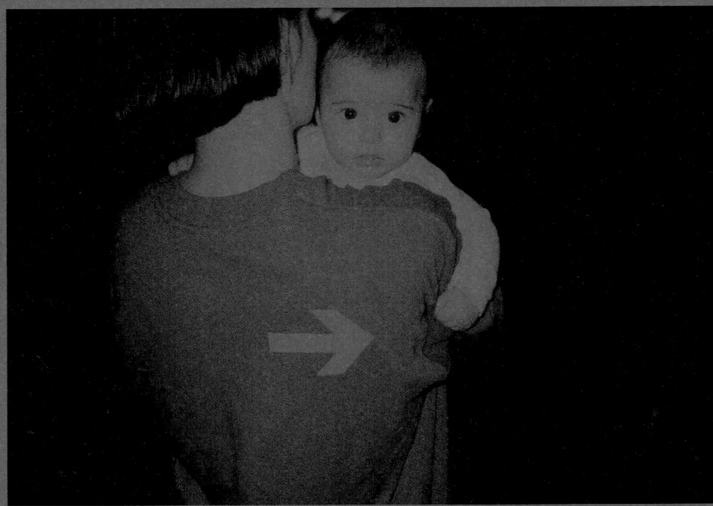
A

Zweiland
↘pp. 53, 56, 94, 108, 121, 122, 137, 206, **239,** 280

Sophiensæle, Berlin
25 Sep
Direction/Choreography
Sasha Waltz
Dance/Choreography
Juan Kruz Diaz de Garaio Esnaola
Luc Dunberry
Klaus Jürgens
Nicola Mascia
Vivianne Rodrigues de Brito
Takako Suzuki
Laurie Young
Music
Juan Kruz Diaz de Garaio Esnaola
Sasha Waltz
Stage Design
Thomas Schenk
Sasha Waltz
Costume Design
Sasha Waltz & Guests
Annette Bätz
Light Design
Martin Hauk
Production
Sasha Waltz & Guests
Sophiensæle, Berlin
Coproduction
Berliner Festspiele
Grand Theatre Groningen
Schauburg München
Staatsschauspiel Dresden
Supported by
Berliner Senatsverwaltung für Wissenschaft, Forschung und Kultur

1997

B

C

A **Sasha Waltz with son László** B+C **Jochen Sandig with son László during »Travelogue I – Twenty to eight« tour to Bordeaux**

Zweiland

Following the interiors of the previous four pieces, »Zweiland« takes us to a public space, the street. The rhythmic movement sequences mirror the dynamism and vibrant life on urban streets. Whereas Sasha Waltz is open to inspiration from existing social living conditions and bringing them to the stage in a mode of alienated realism in »Allee der Kosmonauten«, in »Zweiland« she seeks a poetic approach to the topic of »Images from Germany«. Social conditions are represented in the shape of relationships, so we easily empathise with the experience. Absurd everyday situations alternate with character studies and fairytale-like images.
Rubble and junk lie on the streets of East Berlin in the 1990s. The Wall is down. Years of division have left their scars. There is little to be handed around and much destroyed. Long queues line up at the kiosk, the busy hub of activity on stage. The people waiting there yearn impatiently for a future in which both sides harmonise as one after the time of division, a future that must be searched for, built up and sung for. In the changing city we encounter individuals filled with hopes and dreams. Common ground, buried in the past, literature, folk and art songs from many centuries are the building material for reunified Germany's new self-identity.

Nach den Innenräumen der vorangegangenen vier Stücke führt die Produktion »Zweiland« in einen öffentlichen Raum: die Straße. Die Dynamik und das pulsierende urbane Lebensgefühl der Straße spiegeln sich in den rhythmischen Bewegungssequenzen wider. Im Unterschied zu »Allee der Kosmonauten«, wo sich Sasha Waltz durch konkrete soziale Lebensverhältnisse inspirieren ließ und diese in einem verfremdeten Realismus auf die Bühne brachte, sucht sie in »Zweiland« eine poetische Annäherung an das Thema »Bilder aus Deutschland«. Gesellschaftliche Verhältnisse werden auf der zwischenmenschlichen Ebene dargestellt und dadurch ganz unmittelbar erfahrbar. Absurde Alltagssituationen wechseln sich mit Charakterstudien und märchenhaften Bildern ab.
Schutt und Gerümpel liegen auf den Straßen Ost-Berlins der 90er Jahre. Die Mauer ist gefallen. Das Trennende hat Spuren hinterlassen. Es gibt wenig und viel ist zerstört. Am Kiosk, der bewegten Achse des Geschehens auf der Bühne, bilden sich Schlangen der Wartenden. Ungeduldig sehnen sie sich. Nach einer Zukunft, die nach der Zeit der Trennung wieder zusammenfließt und gesucht, gebaut, gesungen werden muss. In der Stadt im Aufbruch treffen wir auf Gestalten voller Träume und Hoffnungen. Verschüttete Gemeinsamkeiten, Literatur, Volks- und Kunstlieder aus verschiedenen Jahrhunderten, sind das Baumaterial für ein neues Selbstverständnis eines wiedervereinten Deutschlands.

REPERTOIRE

Allee der Kosmonauten Hong Kong, Munich, Ferrara, London, Toruń, Ludwigsburg, Stockholm, Gothenburg, Budapest
Na Zemlje Berlin
Travelogue I – Twenty to eight Berlin
Travelogue II – Tears break fast Berlin
Travelogue III – All ways six steps Berlin, Brussels
Zweiland Berlin, Dresden, Ferrara, Munich, Brussels, Freiburg, Heidelberg, Ludwigsburg, Essen, Cologne, Düsseldorf, Sera Dro, Copenhagen, Gothenburg, Wilhelmshaven

FILM

Allee der Kosmonauten [58']
Director Sasha Waltz
Collaboration Elliot Caplan
Producers Jochen Sandig, Sasha Waltz
Production kosmonaut films for Arte/ZDF

1998

A

Rötung (work in progress)

Sophiensæle, Berlin
29 Jan
Direction/Choreography
Sasha Waltz
Dance/Choreography
Benoît Lachambre
Robert Meilleur

Na Zemlje
↘pp. 58, 72, 153, 215, **241**

Sophiensæle, Berlin
11 Nov
Direction/Choreography
Sasha Waltz
Dance/Choreography
Albert Albert
Nadia Cusimano
Juan Kruz Diaz de Garaio Esnaola
Luc Dunberry
Elena Golovašova
Irina Gontovaja
Vasilij Juščenko
Alexandra Konnikova
Nicola Mascia
Konstantin Mišin
Takako Suzuki
Laurie Young
Musical Concept
Sasha Waltz
Music
Juan Kruz Diaz de Garaio Esnaola
Stage Design
Thomas Schenk
Sasha Waltz
Costume Design
Annette Bätz
Sasha Waltz
Light Design
Thilo Reuther
Dramaturgy
Jochen Sandig
Production
Sasha Waltz & Guests
Cooperation
School for Dramatic Art, Moscow
Sophiensæle, Berlin
Coproduction
Düsseldorfer Schauspielhaus
Goethe-Institutes Moscow and Munich
Theatre Festival Basel 1999
Supported by
Culture committee of the government of the city of Moscow
Berliner Senatsverwaltung für Wissenschaft, Forschung und Kultur
Stanislavskij Charity Foundation
Sponsoring
»Wella«

A **»Na Zemlje«**

Na Zemlje

»Na Zemlje« (On Earth) portrays a rural society with all its potential for conflict. The production is the outcome of an invitation by the Goethe Institute in Moscow as a German-Russian coproduction of the Sasha Waltz Company and the legendary Moscow theatre's »School of Dramatic Art« of Anatoly Vasilyev and »Class of Expressive Plastic Movement« of Gennady Abramov. The encounter between two cultures in the German-Russian ensemble of 12 dancers is pivotal in the creative process of the production. In »Na Zemlje«, Sasha Waltz tackles the topic of humankind's relationship to nature as well as the nature of humankind. The latter leads to segregation, domination and relentless fighting, finally ending in a tragic sacrificial ritual. Arranged by Martin Berg at the Goethe Institute in Moscow, the first three weeks of rehearsals take place at Konstantin S. Stanislavski's former country estate in Ljubimovka outside of Moscow. This is where the director had the rehearsals in 1896 for the first performance of Anton Chekhov's »The Seagull«. It is also where Chekhov wrote »The Cherry Orchard« in 1903. Devastated nature and ruined landscapes dating back to different epochs often expose cracks in the idyll of bygone days in the post-Soviet era – as well as the insecurity and brutality that can be felt everywhere in Russia today. Much of this reminds us of films like Andrei Tarkowski's »Mirror« or »Stalker«. Sasha Waltz found inspiration for the project in the region in which the country estate lies and in the ambience created by Pieter Bruegel in his paintings. A Chekhovian melancholy flows into the dramatic nature of her piece. The dancers sing and make music, as we already experienced in »Zweiland«; Russian folk songs meld together with new compositions. The thunder of a jetfighter tears the community out of its daily routines, and the rock band Europe's hit »Final Countdown« from 1986 delivers a moment of ecstasy that breaks into the desolate dystopia.

»Na Zemlje« (Auf Erde) ist das Porträt einer dörflichen Gemeinschaft mit all ihren Konfliktpotenzialen. Es entsteht auf Einladung des Goethe-Instituts Moskau als deutsch-russische Koproduktion der Compagnie mit dem legendären Moskauer Theater »Schule für Dramatische Kunst« von Anatolij Vasiliev und der »Klasse für Expressive Bewegung« von Gennadij Abramov. Das Zusammentreffen zweier Kulturen im zwölfköpfigen deutsch-russischen Ensemble ist für den Entstehungsprozess von zentraler Bedeutung. In »Na Zemlje« verhandelt Sasha Waltz thematisch das Verhältnis des Menschen zur Natur sowie die Natur des Menschen, die zu Ausgrenzung, Dominanz und unerbittlichem Kampf führt und schließlich in einem tragischen Opferritual mündet. Vermittelt durch Martin Berg vom Goethe-Institut Moskau, finden die ersten drei Probenwochen auf dem ehemaligen Landgut von Konstantin S. Stanislawski in Ljubimovka außerhalb von Moskau statt. Hier probte der Regisseur 1896 für die Uraufführung der »Möwe« von Anton P. Tschechow, und hier schrieb dieser seinen »Kirschgarten« im Jahr 1903. Die Idylle vergangener Zeiten ist in der post-sowjetischen Ära vielfach gebrochen durch eine zerstörte Natur, Ruinenlandschaften unterschiedlicher Epochen sowie die überall spürbare Ungewissheit und Härte der russischen Gegenwart. Vieles hier erinnert an Filme wie »Der Spiegel« oder »Stalker« von Andrei Tarkowski. Die Umgebung des Landguts und die Atmosphäre der Gemälde Pieter Bruegels inspirierten Sasha Waltz zu dieser Arbeit, die in ihrer Theatralität auch eine Tschechow'sche Melancholie erzeugt. Wie bereits in »Zweiland« wird die Musik von den Tänzern selbst gesungen und gespielt. Russische Volkslieder vermischen sich mit neuen Kompositionen. Der Lärm eines Düsenflugzeugs reißt die Gemeinschaft aus ihrem Alltag, und der Hit »Final Countdown« der Band Europe aus dem Jahr 1986 erzeugt einen Moment der Ekstase, der die dystopische Trostlosigkeit durchbricht.

REPERTOIRE

Allee der Kosmonauten Berlin, Mumbai, New Delhi, Kolkata, Colombo, Metz, Geneva, Novosibirsk, Omsk, Lörrach, Tokyo, Osaka **Na Zemlje** Düsseldorf, Charleroi, Moscow, Avignon, Aarhus, Basel, Hamburg **Zweiland** Amsterdam, The Hague, Leeuwarden, Leiden, Remscheid, Lyon, Rouen, Avignon, Berkeley

1999

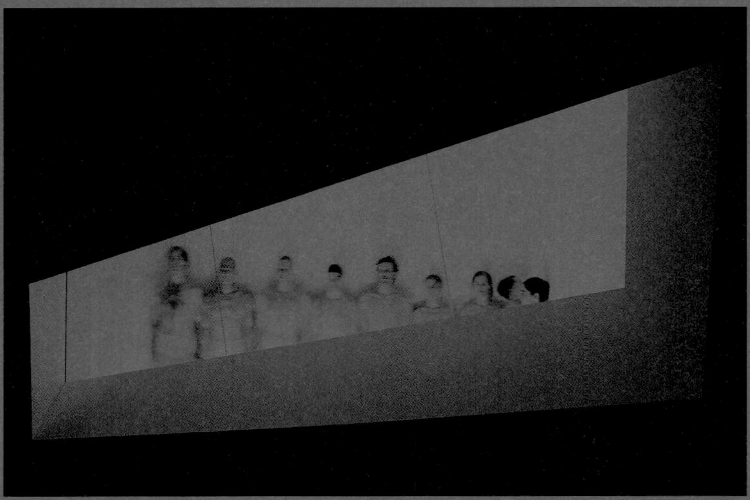

A

B

Dialoge '99/I – Sophiensæle
↘pp. 61, 194, 215, 234, **243**

Sophiensæle, Berlin
21 May
Direction/Concept
Sasha Waltz
Soundinstallation
Joanna Dudley
Dance/Choreography
Julie Bougard
Davide Camplani
Nadia Cusimano
Juan Kruz Diaz de Garaio Esnaola
Luc Dunberry
Siggi Keil
Nicola Mascia
Joakim NaBi Olsson
Claudia de Serpa Soares
Takako Suzuki
Maria Clara Villa-Lobos
Laurie Young
Stage Design
Heike Schuppelius
Costume Design
Bernd Skodzig
Light Design
Jörg Bittner
Production
Sasha Waltz & Guests

Dialoge '99/II – Jüdisches Museum
↘pp. 48, 106, 179, **244**

Jüdisches Museum, Berlin
11 Jun
Direction/Concept
Sasha Waltz
Soundinstallation
Hans Peter Kuhn
Dance/Choreography
Alexandra Bachzetsis
Julie Bougard
Davide Camplani
Nadia Cusimano
Lisa Densem
Juan Kruz Diaz de Garaio Esnaola
Luc Dunberry
Alan Good
Nicola Mascia
Joakim NaBi Olsson
Virgis Puodziunas
Claudia de Serpa Soares
Takako Suzuki
Maria Clara Villa-Lobos
Junko Wada
Laurie Young
Sigal Zouk
Stage Design
Rufus Didwiszius
Costume Design
Bernd Skodzig
Light Design
Thilo Reuther
Production
Sasha Waltz & Guests
Coproduction
»Berlin offene Stadt«/Berliner Festspiele

A **»Dialoge '99/II – Jüdisches Museum«** B **»Dialoge '99/I – Sophiensæle«**

In 1999, Sasha Waltz and her dancers perform in the interior and outside areas of the Sophiensæle in Berlin on the topic of being human. The audience explores the performance by moving around freely as in an exhibition. Novel body formations evolve indoors, inspired by the large-format sculptures of the Norwegian sculptor Gustav Vigeland. Hanging, reclining, sitting, skewered and fragile bodies – in their proximity and radical nudity – are discomfiting in comparison to what the audience normally sees. The large Sophiensæle Festsaal, too, is empty and completely stripped. Here the first »Körper« images such as »Body Mountains« und »Vitrine« emerge, which lead to the opening production for Schaubühne am Lehniner Platz in 2000. The three-wing windowpanes facing the courtyard are transformed into contemporary triptych images featuring naked bodies. In this project, Sasha Waltz works with the costume designer Bernd Skodzig for the first time. His aesthetic will also influence many pieces in the future. It marks the beginning of surveying the body in Sasha Waltz's art.

1999 bespielt Sasha Waltz mit ihren Tänzer:innen den Innen- und Außenbereich der Sophiensæle zum Thema »Menschsein«. Das Publikum erkundet die Performance frei wie in einer Ausstellung. Inspiriert durch die großformatigen Skulpturen des norwegischen Bildhauers Gustav Vigeland, entstehen im Innenraum neuartige Körperformationen. Hängende, liegende, sitzende, aufgespießte und fragile Körper irritieren die Sehgewohnheiten der Zuschauer:innen in ihrer Nähe und radikalen Nacktheit. Auch der große Festsaal der Sophiensæle ist leer und komplett entblößt. Hier entstehen die ersten »Körper«-Bilder wie »Body Mountains« und »Vitrine«, die 2000 in die Eröffnungsproduktion an der Schaubühne am Lehniner Platz münden werden. Die dreiflügeligen Fensterscheiben zum Hof verwandeln sich in zeitgenössische Altarbilder mit entkleideten Leibern. Zum ersten Mal arbeitet Sasha Waltz hier mit dem Kostümbildner Bernd Skodzig zusammen, dessen Ästhetik auch viele Werke in Zukunft prägen wird. Die Vermessung des Körpers nimmt hier ihren Anfang im künstlerischen Schaffen von Sasha Waltz.

Dialoge '99/II – Jüdisches Museum

At the invitation of Tom Freudenheim, deputy director of the newly founded Jewish Museum Berlin, Sasha Waltz conceives a spatially expansive choreography together with 17 international dancers in 1999 in the empty new building designed by Daniel Libeskind. The choreography is staged before the official opening in 2001. The production enters into an intense dialogue with the architecture of the building. Daniel Libeskind not only creates a museum: he generates a memorial in the shape of a spatial sculpture. The so-called »Voids«, in particular, underscore the lacunae and symbolise the annihilation of Jewish life in Berlin and Germany, making it a physical experience.
Sasha Waltz acknowledges responsibility for the atrocities perpetrated by Germany and is in search of a choreographic language that can adequately reflect the horrors of the Shoah. She finds a form which is simultaneously abstract and physical. »Körper« again takes up the historical references and further explores them in a radical und uncompromising way.
The sound artist Hans Peter Kuhn creates an elusive sound installation that acoustically interweaves the individual spaces on all levels with one another into a great unity. From afar we hear Arnold Schoenberg's oratorio »Jacob's Ladder«. This first collaboration with Hans Peter Kuhn is continued in the compositions for the subsequent productions »Körper« and »noBody«.

Auf Einladung von Tom Freudenheim, stellvertretender Direktor des neu gegründeten Jüdischen Museums Berlin, konzipiert Sasha Waltz im Juni 1999, noch vor der offiziellen Eröffnung im Jahre 2001, gemeinsam mit 17 internationalen Tänzer:innen im leeren Neubau von Daniel Libeskind eine raumgreifende Choreographie, die in einen intensiven Dialog mit der Architektur tritt.
Daniel Libeskind schuf nicht nur ein Museum, sondern einen Erinnerungsort in Form einer Raumskulptur. Insbesondere die sogenannten »Voids« markieren Leerstellen, die das Auslöschen des jüdischen Lebens in Berlin und Deutschland sinnbildlich und körperlich erfahrbar machen.
Sasha Waltz stellt sich der Verantwortung der Täterschaft in der deutschen Geschichte und versucht, hierfür eine choreographische Sprache zu finden, die die Grausamkeit der Shoah reflektiert. Sie findet hier zu einer gleichermaßen abstrakten wie auch physischen Form. Diese historischen Bezüge werden in »Körper« radikal und schonungslos weitergeführt.
Der Klangkünstler Hans Peter Kuhn schreibt eine subtile Klanginstallation, die die einzelnen Räume auf allen Ebenen miteinander akustisch zu einem Ganzen verwebt. Von Ferne erklingt Arnold Schönbergs Oratorium »Die Jakobsleiter«. Diese erste Zusammenarbeit findet ihre Fortsetzung in Hans Peter Kuhns Kompositionen für die nachfolgenden Produktionen »Körper« und »noBody«.

SCHAUBÜHNE

Schaubühne am Lehniner Platz

A programmatic re-appropriation of the building marks the beginning of a new era at the Schaubühne in Berlin. Sasha Waltz's »Körper« resembles a cleansing ritual. The stage is stripped bare down to the naked concrete of the architecture, and the theatre machine is reduced to zero. No curtain, no scenery, no illusion: only the presence of the bodies fuels the imagination.
The decision to place »Körper« at the beginning of the programme holds a promise: that the equality of dance and theatre, which has rarely been practised in other theatres, is taken seriously. This is stated in the manifesto of the gang of four, Sasha Waltz, Thomas Ostermeier, Jens Hillje and Jochen Sandig, who form the artistic directorship of the Schaubühne. There they assign dance a role as a sensual instrument of knowledge that helps to overcome the limitations of language and rational science. As an exclamation mark for a return to experience and a sought-after contact with reality, the piece »Körper« marks a break with outdated theatre literature. Dance pieces are not codified. They are created through collaboration. Allowing the choreographer and their dancers to make their first appearance also means understanding this form of production as a model for ensemble work. »Körper« is an homage to the Schaubüne.
The Schaubühne has never seemed so big. From the steep tiers, the view is of a deep semicircle bordered by a three-storey concrete wall, like an ancient arena. The theatre, built in 1927/28 according to plans by Erich Mendelsohn as a cinema and converted for the Schaubühne between 1978 and 1981, is one of the few incunabula of classical modernism in Berlin. But rarely has the dramatic expressiveness of its constructive skeleton been experienced so purely. Circus, bear pit, anatomical theatre, waxworks and cooling tower: everything becomes space on this evening. This versatility of the Schaubühne, which has rarely been used to date, was one of the reasons why Sasha Waltz moved from her romantic residence in the Sophiensæle in Berlin Mitte to Ku'damm.
KATRIN BETTINA MÜLLER

Mit einer programmatischen Aneignung des Hauses beginnt die neue Zeitrechnung an der Berliner Schaubühne. »Körper« von Sasha Waltz gleicht einem Ritual der Reinigung. Bis auf den nackten Beton der Architektur wird die Bühne von allem entkleidet und die Theatermaschine zurückgefahren auf den Nullpunkt. Kein Vorhang, keine Kulissen, keine Illusion: Allein die Präsenz der Körper treibt die Imagination an.
Den »Körper« an den Anfang zu stellen, beinhaltet ein Versprechen: dass es ernst gemeint ist mit der Gleichberechtigung zwischen Tanz und Theater, die bisher an kaum einem anderen Haus praktiziert wird. So steht es im Manifest der Viererbande von Sasha Waltz, Thomas Ostermeier, Jens Hillje und Jochen Sandig, die die Intendanz der Schaubühne bilden. Dort weisen sie dem Tanz eine Rolle als sinnliches Instrument der Erkenntnis zu, das die Grenzen der Sprache und der rationalen Wissenschaften überwinden hilft. Als ein Ausrufezeichen für die Rückkehr zur Erfahrung und den gesuchten Kontakt zur Wirklichkeit markiert das Stück »Körper« den Bruch mit abgelagerter Theaterliteratur. Tanzstücke sind nirgendwo festgeschrieben. Sie entstehen in der Zusammenarbeit. Der Choreographin und ihren Tänzer:innen den ersten Auftritt zu lassen, bedeutet auch, diese Produktionsform modellhaft zu begreifen für die Ensemblearbeit. »Körper« ist die Hommage an das Haus.
Nie wirkte die Schaubühne so groß. Von den steilen Rängen blickt man wie in einer antiken Arena in ein tiefes Halbrund, das von einer dreigeschossigen Betonwand begrenzt wird. Das Theater, das 1927/28 nach Plänen von Erich Mendelsohn als Kino errichtet und 1978 bis 1981 für die Schaubühne umgebaut wurde, ist eine der wenigen Inkunabeln der klassischen Moderne in Berlin. Doch selten erfuhr man so pur die dramatische Expressivität seines konstruktiven Skeletts. Zirkus, Bärenzwinger, anatomisches Theater, Panoptikum und Kühlturm: Alles wird der Raum an diesem Abend. Diese bisher kaum genutzte Vielseitigkeit der Schaubühne war nicht zuletzt ein Grund für Sasha Waltz, von ihrem romantischen Domizil in den Sophiensælen in Berlin Mitte an den Ku'damm zu wechseln.
KATRIN BETTINA MÜLLER

2000

Jens Hillje, Thomas Ostermeier, Jochen Sandig and Sasha Waltz are appointed as the **artistic direction of the Schaubühne am Lehniner Platz, Berlin.**

»Emmy Award« nomination for the film »Körper«.

»Körper« is invited to the **37th Theatertreffen, Berlin.**

»Grimme-Preis« for the film »Allee der Kosmonauten«.

»Grand Prix« at the Belgrade BITEF Festival for »Körper«.

Critics' Prize from the Association of German Critics for Sasha Waltz.

First tour through Asia with »Allee der Kosmonauten«.

REPERTOIRE

Allee der Kosmonauten Berlin, Jakarta, Rouen, Manila, Bangkok, Singapore
Körper Berlin, Amsterdam, Edinburgh, Belgrade, Paris
Na Zemlje Berlin, Rouen, Amsterdam
S Berlin
Zweiland Berlin

PRODUCTIONS SCHAUBÜHNE AM LEHNINER PLATZ

9×9 *Christine De Smedt, Mårten Spångberg, Les ballets C de la B* Berlin
Anything else *Luc Dunberry* Berlin
Iets op Bach *Les ballets C de la B* Berlin
Tanz Soli Berlin
The rest of you *Luc Dunberry* Berlin

FILM

Körper Sasha Waltz, Hans Peter Kuhn [57'] A film by Jörg Jeshel, Brigitte Kramer Production Schaubühne am Lehniner Platz, nachtaktivfilm commissioned by ZDF/Arte/ZDFtheaterkanal Cooperation Goethe-Institut Distribution DVD, Arthaus Musik 2011
S Sasha Waltz [66'] Filmed by Jörg Jeshel, Brigitte Kramer Production Schaubühne am Lehniner Platz, nachtaktivfilm Distribution DVD, Arthaus Musik 2011

A

Körper

↘pp. 46, 47, 48, 49, 50, 52, 64, 76, 77, 95, 112, 117, 136, 138, 139, 146, 162, 163, 195, 196, 200, 202, 205, 217, **249**, 268, 344

Schaubühne am Lehniner Platz, Berlin
22 Jan
Direction/Choreography
Sasha Waltz
Music
Hans Peter Kuhn
Dance/Choreography
Davide Camplani
Nadia Cusimano
Lisa Densem
Juan Kruz Diaz de Garaio Esnaola
Luc Dunberry
Nicola Mascia
Grayson Millwood
Joakim NaBi Olsson
Virgis Puodziunas
Claudia de Serpa Soares
Takako Suzuki
Laurie Young
Sigal Zouk
Stage Design
Thomas Schenk
Heike Schuppelius
Sasha Waltz
Costume Design
Bernd Skodzig
Light Design
Valentin Gallé
Martin Hauk
Dramaturgy
Jochen Sandig
Production
Schaubühne am Lehniner Platz, Berlin
Coproduction
Théâtre de la Ville, Paris

Dialoge – La chapelle des Pénitents blancs

La chapelle des Pénitents blancs, Festival d'Avignon
22 Jul
Direction/Concept
Sasha Waltz
Dance/Choreography
Benoît Lachambre
Nicola Mascia
Sasha Waltz
David Zambrano
Music/Performance
Joanna Dudley
Robyn Schulkowsky

S

↘pp. 29, 77, 119, 166, 168, 188, 189, **250**

Schaubühne am Lehniner Platz, Berlin
7 Nov
Direction/Choreography
Sasha Waltz
Music
Jonathan Bepler
Stage Design
Heike Schuppelius
Sasha Waltz
Costume Design
Sylvia Hagen-Schäfer
Sasha Waltz
Video
Eve Sussman
Heike Schuppelius
Light Design
Martin Hauk
Dramaturgy
Jochen Sandig
Dance/Choreography
Lisa Densem
Nicola Mascia
Grayson Millwood
Joakim NaBi Olsson
Virgis Puodziunas
Claudia de Serpa Soares
Takako Suzuki
Laurie Young
Production
Schaubühne am Lehniner Platz, Berlin

Dialoge – Schaubühne am Lehniner Platz

Schaubühne am Lehniner Platz, Berlin
1 Dec
Direction/Concept
Sasha Waltz
Dance/Choreography
Benoît Lachambre
Sasha Waltz
Music/Performance
Joanna Dudley
Robyn Schulkowsky
Production
Schaubühne am Lehniner Platz, Berlin

B

A **Artistic direction of Schaubühne am Lehniner Platz** B **»Körper« rehearsal**

Körper

In 2000, Sasha Waltz opens the Schaubühne am Lehniner Platz under new artistic direction with »Körper«. Together with Thomas Ostermeier, Jens Hillje and Jochen Sandig, she forms the artistic direction for five years. This work marks the beginning of the legendary »Körper« trilogy and is considered a cornerstone of classical modernism in dance. The explored human anatomy resonates in both the cathedral-like concrete architecture of the open Schaubühne and in the sound compositions by Hans Peter Kuhn.
In her choreography, Sasha Waltz visualises the exterior and interior of the human body with her Schaubühne ensemble comprising 13 dancers, showcasing its beauty and fragility. What is the body? How is it composed? The substance of life can be twisted, thrown, piled up and dissected. By soberly acknowledging the human body's materiality, the piece approaches an understanding of the disjunction that our bodily existence imposes. It questions cultural patterns of movement, brutal forms of pleasure, performance enhancement and the surgical perfection of the body, as well as the treatment of the body as a resource.
Why do we confront our vulnerability with such harshness? Why does the narrative about our body continually skirt around what we truly feel? Naked to the bone, revealed beneath the skin, the piece subjects the body to an even more radical disrobing: the stripping away the labels that cling to it and obscure its essence. Twisting and winding it, diverting its path, the work on this true visibility begins anew each time. The body appears as something never before seen.

Mit »Körper« eröffnet Sasha Waltz im Jahr 2000 die Schaubühne am Lehniner Platz unter neuer Künstlerischer Leitung. Thomas Ostermeier, Jens Hillje und Jochen Sandig bilden gemeinsam mit ihr für fünf Jahre das Leitungsteam. Das Werk ist Auftakt der legendären »Körper«-Trilogie und wird zum Kanon der klassischen Moderne gezählt. Die untersuchte menschliche Anatomie findet ihre Resonanz sowohl in der kathedralenartigen Beton-Architektur der offenen Schaubühne als auch in den Klangkompositionen von Hans Peter Kuhn.
Sasha Waltz visualisiert in der Choreographie mit ihrem Schaubühnenensemble, bestehend aus 13 Tänzer:innen, die Hülle und das Innere des menschlichen Körpers, führt uns seine Schönheit und seine Fragilität vor Augen. Was ist der Körper? Wie setzt er sich zusammen? Die Substanz des Lebens kann herumgezerrt, geworfen, zu Haufen aufgeschichtet, zergliedert werden. Über die nüchterne Anerkennung der Stofflichkeit des menschlichen Körpers nähert sich das Stück einem Verständnis der Entzweiung, die das Körper-Sein uns auferlegt. Es hinterfragt kulturelle Bewegungsmuster, brachiale Formen des Vergnügens, der Leistungssteigerung und chirurgischen Perfektionierung sowie die Behandlung des Körpers als Ressource. Warum begegnen wir unserer Verletzlichkeit mit solcher Härte? Warum gleitet das Erzählen über unseren Körper immer wieder an dem vorbei, was wir eigentlich empfinden? Nackt bis auf die Knochen, offenbart bis unter die Haut, unterzieht das Stück den Körper einer noch radikaleren Entkleidung: dem Abstreifen der Benennungen, die ihm überall anhaften und ihn verdecken. Ihn drehend und windend, auf Abwege lenkend, beginnt die Arbeit an dieser eigentlichen Sichtbarmachung dauernd aufs Neue. Der Körper erscheint als nie Gesehenes.

S

»S« is the middle part of the trilogy of the body and is the connecting link between the confrontation with the physical constitution of the human body in »Körper« and the metaphysical side of human existence in »noBody«. Whereas sexuality and eros are all but absent in the first and the third parts of the trilogy, in »S« they are central themes. The impact of Hieronymus Bosch's art is clearly recognisable in the sensual ease of the Garden of Eden and Expulsion from Paradise. The New York musician Jonathan Bepler, renowned for his compositions for Matthew Barney's »Cremaster Cycle«, is responsible for the original music of the production. The stage set is designed in collaboration with Heike Schuppelius.

»S« bildet den Mittelteil der »Körper«-Trilogie. So wirkt das Stück als Bindeglied zwischen der Auseinandersetzung mit der Physis des Menschen in »Körper« einerseits und der Metaphysik menschlichen Seins in »noBody« andererseits. Wurden Sexualität und Eros in den beiden anderen Werken fast vollständig ausgespart, stehen sie in »S« thematisch im Zentrum. Starken Einfluss haben die Bilder von Hieronymus Bosch, die sinnliche Unbeschwertheit im Garten Eden und die Vertreibung aus dem Paradies. Der New Yorker Musiker Jonathan Bepler, bekannt durch die Komposition für Matthew Barneys »Cremaster-Zyklus«, schreibt die Originalmusik der Inszenierung. Das Bühnenbild entsteht in Zusammenarbeit mit Heike Schuppelius.

2001

Death of Margot Waltz, Sasha Waltz's mother.

REPERTOIRE

Allee der Kosmonauten Irvine, Berkeley
Körper Berlin, Lubljana, Antwerp, Frankfurt, Buenos Aires, Tel Aviv
Na Zemlje Paris
S Berlin
Travelogue I – Twenty to eight Wuppertal
Zweiland Antwerp, Zagreb, Buenos Aires, Rome, Porto Alegre, Bonn, Paris

PRODUCTIONS SCHAUBÜHNE AM LEHNINER PLATZ

Anything else Berlin, Sarajevo, Freiburg
My dearest… My fairest *Joanna Dudley, Juan Kruz Diaz de Garaio Esnaola* Berlin
Seriously *Luc Dunberry* Berlin
Tanz Soli Berlin

A

B

Dialoge – Mumbai

Mumbai
16 Mar
Direction/Concept/Dance
Sasha Waltz
Music/Performance
Rajesh Mehta
Robyn Schulkowsky
Production
Goethe-Institut Mumbai

Dialoge – 17-25/4
↘pp. 40, 88, 179, **253**

Schaubühne am Lehniner Platz, Berlin
29 Jun
Direction/Concept
Sasha Waltz
Music
Hans Peter Kuhn
Dance/Choreography
Mikel Aristegui
Robert Beyer
Jule Böwe
Davide Camplani
Lisa Densem
Juan Kruz Diaz de Garaio Esnaola
Luc Dunberry
Swantje Henke
Norbert Kliesch
Hans-Werner Klohe
Anna Koch
Nicola Mascia
Grayson Millwood
Jorge Morro
Michal Mualem
Joakim NaBi Olsson
Shaun Parker
Virgis Puodziunas
Sasa Queliz
Claudia de Serpa Soares
Laura Siegmund
Norbert Steinwarz
Takako Suzuki
André Szymanski
Nir Tamir
Junko Wada
Laurie Young
Sigal Zouk
Vocals
Zoe Tuvia
Costume Design
Bernd Skodzig
Video
Heike Schuppelius
Dramaturgy
Jochen Sandig
Production
Schaubühne am Lehniner Platz, Berlin

A **Artistic team of »noBody«** B **»Dialoge – 17-25/4«**

The Schaubühne and the surrounding buildings are registered at the state surveyor's office in Berlin as lot 25/4 on block 17. This is taken up in the title of the choreographic piece. In the course of the evening, the dancers occupy the space in and around the Schaubühne am Lehniner Platz and comprehend the site in the terms of an artistic analysis of Erich Mendelsohn's architecture.

Die Schaubühne und die umliegenden Gebäude sind beim Landesvermessungsamt in Berlin als Flurstück 25/4 auf Block 17 eingetragen, worauf sich auch der Titel bezieht. Im Verlauf des Abends nehmen die Tänzer:innen den Raum in und um die Schaubühne am Lehniner Platz für sich ein und erschließen den Ort in einer künstlerischen Analyse der Architektur Erich Mendelsohns.

Sophia Sandig is born, daughter of Sasha Waltz and Jochen Sandig.

REPERTOIRE

Körper Berlin, Paris, Mulhouse, Istanbul, Ludwigsburg, Guanajuato, Mexico City, New York
noBody Berlin, Bruges, Avignon, Hamburg, Salamanca
S Berlin, Paris
Zweiland Marseille

PRODUCTIONS SCHAUBÜHNE AM LEHNINER PLATZ

Anything else Berlin, Marseille
d'avant *Juan Kruz Diaz de Garaio Esnaola, Sidi Larbi Cherkaoui, Luc Dunberry, Damien Jalet* Berlin, Paris
He taught me to yodel *Joanna Dudley* Berlin
My dearest… My fairest Berlin
Seriously Berlin, Leipzig, Marseille

FILM

noBody [85'] A film by Sasha Waltz Producer Brigitte Kramer Production Schaubühne am Lehniner Platz, nachtaktivfilm commissioned by ZDF Cooperation Arte and ZDFtheaterkanal Distribution DVD, Arthaus Musik 2011

2002

noBody
↘pp. 35, 38, 45, 66, 67, 68, 71, 156, 215, 252, **255,** 292

Schaubühne am Lehniner Platz, Berlin
23 Feb
Direction/Choreography
Sasha Waltz
Music
Hans Peter Kuhn
Dance/Choreography
Mikel Aristegui
Rita Aozane Bilibio
Hsuan Cheng
Clémentine Deluy
Lisa Densem
Juan Kruz Diaz de Garaio Esnaola
Luc Dunberry
Andreas Ebbert-Scholl
Su-Mi Jang
Hans-Werner Klohe
Nicola Mascia
Thusnelda Mercy
Grayson Millwood
Michal Mualem
Joakim NaBi Olsson
Sasa Queliz
Davide de Robertis
Claudia de Serpa Soares
Laura Siegmund
Norbert Steinwarz
Takako Suzuki
Mohan Thomas
Junko Wada
Laurie Young
Matan Zamir
Sigal Zouk
Stage Design
Thomas Schenk
Sasha Waltz
Costume Design
Bernd Skodzig
Light Design
Martin Hauk
Dramaturgy
Jochen Sandig
Production
Schaubühne am Lehniner Platz, Berlin
Coproduction
Festival d'Avignon

A

B

A+B **»noBody«**

noBody

»noBody« concludes the three-part cycle on humanity and the body created by Sasha Waltz at the turn of the millennium. Following an exploration of the materiality of the human form and the origins of life, the choreographer, alongside 26 dancers, endeavours in »noBody« to make the non-corporeal and the spiritual visible. The work raises questions about the metaphysical existence of humanity, addressing the absence of the body and the mystery of death. What is humankind beyond its physical form? Is there something immortal within us that transcends our being?
In this melancholic and tragic piece, Sasha Waltz also processes a personal and transformative moment in her life: the unexpected early death of her mother. This creates a radical and cathartic confrontation with the emotions that the awareness of mortality evokes. She presents abstract and concrete images of farewell, loss, grief and pain, juxtaposed with poignant images of comfort and tenderness amidst collective chaos and destruction. The stage design features a space with translucent windows. A giant cloud gradually fills the space, making the void palpable. Hans Peter Kuhn composes music with an increasingly immersive quality.

»noBody« bildet den Abschluss des dreiteiligen Zyklus über den Menschen und seinen Körper, den Sasha Waltz zur Jahrtausendwende schafft. Nach der Untersuchung der Materialität des Menschen und dem Ursprung des Lebens stellt sich die Choreographin in »noBody« gemeinsam mit 26 Tänzer:innen die Aufgabe, das Nicht-Körperliche und das Geistige sichtbar zu machen. Die Arbeit formuliert die Frage nach der metaphysischen Existenz des Menschen, thematisiert die Abwesenheit des Körpers und das Mysterium des Todes. Was ist der Mensch über seinen Körper hinaus? Gibt es etwas Unsterbliches in uns, das unser Sein überdauert? Sasha Waltz verarbeitet in diesem melancholischen und tragischen Werk auch einen persönlichen und einschneidenden Wendepunkt in ihrem eigenen Leben, den unerwarteten frühen Tod ihrer Mutter. Es entsteht eine radikale und kathartische Konfrontation mit den Gefühlen, die die Erkenntnis der Sterblichkeit in uns auslöst. Sie findet dabei sowohl abstrakte als auch konkrete Bilder des Abschieds, des Verlusts, der Trauer, des Schmerzes, auch von kollektivem Chaos und Zerstörung, denen sie berührende Bilder des Trostes und der Zärtlichkeit gegenüberstellt. Das Bühnenbild besteht aus einem leeren Raum mit transluziden Fenstern. Es erscheint eine überdimensionale Wolke, die immer mehr den Raum verdrängt und so das Nichts spürbar macht. Hans Peter Kuhn ersinnt Musik von wachsender Sogwirkung.

10th anniversary of Sasha Waltz & Guests in Bordeaux.

REPERTOIRE

insideout Berlin, Graz
Körper Berlin, Paris, London, Forbach
noBody Berlin, Antwerp, Paris, Chalon-sur-Saône, Saint Petersburg
S Antwerp, Rouen
Zweiland Berlin, Venice, Bordeaux

PRODUCTIONS SCHAUBÜHNE AM LEHNINER PLATZ

Anything else Berlin
Cucina Erotica *Constanza Macras* Berlin, Bordeaux
d'avant Berlin, Leuven, Forbach, Buenos Aires, Bordeaux, Ferrara
Foi *Sidi Larbi Cherkaoui, Schaubühne am Lehniner Platz, Les ballets C de la B & Capilla Flamenca* Berlin
My dearest… My fairest Berlin, London, Buenos Aires, Bordeaux
Paper Doll *Padmini Chettur* Berlin, Bordeaux
Seriously Berlin, Nancy

2003

A

B

insideout
↘pp. 52, 53, 56, 61, 82, 150, 160, 188, 197, 198, **257**, 270

Helmut-List-Halle, Graz
18 Sep
Concept/Direction/Choreography
Sasha Waltz
Music
Rebecca Saunders
Dance/Choreography
Mikel Aristegui
Jiří Bartovanec
Maria Marta Colusi
Clémentine Deluy
Lisa Densem
Juan Kruz Diaz de Garaio Esnaola
Luc Dunberry
Charlotte Engelkes
Nicola Mascia
Michal Mualem
Manuel Alfonso Pérez Torres
Sasa Queliz
Paolo dos Santos
Claudia de Serpa Soares
Xuan Shi
Takako Suzuki
Laurie Young
Matan Zamir
Sigal Zouk
Music
Ensemble Musikfabrik
Stage Design
Thomas Schenk
Sasha Waltz
Costume Design
Sasha Waltz & Guests
Video
Philip Bussmann
Light Design
Martin Hauk
Dramaturgy/Concept
Jochen Sandig
Science
Karl Stocker
Production
Schaubühne am Lehniner Platz, Berlin
Coproduction
European Capital of Culture 2003 – Graz, steirischer herbst
Supported by
Kulturstiftung des Bundes

Dialoge – Les Grandes Traversées
↘p. 156

Salle A. Vitez/Grand Théâtre, Bordeaux
27 Nov
Direction/Concept
Sasha Waltz
Jochen Sandig
Dance/Choreography
Lindy Annis
Mikel Aristegui
Jiří Bartovanec
Laurie Booth
Sidi Larbi Cherkaoui
Padmini Chettur
Maria Marta Colusi
Clémentine Deluy
Lisa Densem
Juan Kruz Diaz de Garaio Esnaola
Luc Dunberry
Charlotte Engelkes
Lisi Estaràs
Benoît Lachambre
Constanza Macras
Nasser Martin-Gousset
Nicola Mascia
Grayson Millwood
Fatima Miranda
Michal Mualem
Erna Ómarsdóttir
Manuel Alfonso Pérez Torres
Frans Poelstra
Virgis Puodziunas
Sasa Queliz
Claudia de Serpa Soares
Xuan Shi
Kirstie Simson
Norbert Steinwarz
Takako Suzuki
Michael Tiepold
Mark Tompkins
Laurie Young
Sigal Zouk
Music/Performance
Jonathan Bepler
Marco Blaauw
Nicholas Bussmann
Joanna Dudley
Reinhold Friedl
Hanayo
Hanno Leichtmann
Friedrich Liechtenstein
Ulrich Löffler
Thomas Oesterdiekhoff
Adrian Pereyra
Carl Rosman
Burkhard Schlothauer
Michael Vorfeld
Visual Arts/Video
Jean-Louis Badet
Philip Bussmann
Thomas Schenk
Heike Schuppelius
Barbara Steppe

A **Sasha Waltz with daughter Sophia and Thomas Schenk working on the stage design of »insideout«** B **»insideout« model**

insideout

On the initiative of the European Capital of Culture Graz, 2003, Sasha Waltz arranges »insideout« as a choreographic exhibition in a walk-through architectural space in the shape of different buildings with a central marketplace. This symbolic global village allows the audience to become part of the choreography, and an individual cosmos opens up for each visitor.
The interdisciplinary production is based on the private biographies of the participants: 19 performers and ten musicians from Asia, Europe, the United States and South America. Thematically the piece addresses individual and social values, lifestyles and status symbols. What do we need to unfold our identities? What relevance do origins, family and history have? The various individual persons and life histories contribute to make a multi-faceted kaleidoscope of a diverse society. Living sculptures, animated objects, intimacy between the audience and performers as well as the overlap of simultaneous actions, images and sounds characterise the production. In the book published for it, the cultural studies scholar and co-initiator Karl Stocker juxtaposes interviews with the members of the dance ensemble with sociological ideas put forward by Jean Baudrillard, Ulrich Beck and Pierre Bourdieu. In her first score for the stage, the composer Rebecca Saunders condenses individual solos, duets and trios for the ten musicians of the Ensemble Musikfabrik – who are distributed throughout the space – as well as mechanical music sources such as musical clocks and record players into a multi-layered composition. The video artist Philip Bussmann associatively widens the scope of the layers in visual perception with his projections, which are generated live in vastly different spaces. The spectacular stage set created by Thomas Schenk and Sasha Waltz is awarded the OPUS Preis for »Bühnenbild des Jahres« (stage set of the year) in 2004.

Auf Initiative der Europäischen Kulturhauptstadt Graz 2003 ersinnt Sasha Waltz »insideout« als eine choreographische Ausstellung in begehbarer Raumarchitektur aus unterschiedlichen Gebäuden mit einem zentralen Marktplatz. Dieses symbolische Global Village lässt das Publikum Teil der Choreographie werden, und für jede:n Besucher:in erschließt sich ein eigener Kosmos.
Die interdisziplinäre Produktion mit 19 Darsteller:innen und zehn Musiker:innen aus Asien, Europa, Nord- und Südamerika behandelt auf Grundlage der persönlichen Biographien der Mitwirkenden die individuellen und gesellschaftlichen Werte, Lebensstile und Statussymbole. Was benötigen wir zur Entwicklung unserer Identitäten? Welche Bedeutung haben Herkunft, Familie und Geschichte? Die Vielfältigkeit der einzelnen Persönlichkeiten und Lebensgeschichten lässt ein facettenreiches Kaleidoskop einer diversen Gesellschaft entstehen. Lebendige Skulpturen, animierte Objekte, eine intime Nähe zwischen Publikum und Darsteller:innen sowie die Überlagerung von simultanen Aktionen, Bildern und Klängen kennzeichnen die Aufführung. In einem produktionsbegleitenden Buch stellt der Kulturwissenschaftler und Mitinitiator Karl Stocker Interviews mit Mitgliedern des Tanzensembles soziologischen Thesen von Jean Baudrillard, Ulrich Beck und Pierre Bourdieu gegenüber. Die Komponistin Rebecca Saunders verdichtet in ihrem ersten musikalischen Werk für die Bühne einzelne Soli, Duette und Trios für zehn im Raum verteilte Musiker:innen des Ensemble Musikfabrik sowie mechanische Musikquellen wie Spieluhren und Plattenspieler zu einer vielschichtigen Gesamtkomposition. Der Videokünstler Philip Bussmann erweitert mit seinen live generierten Projektionen in den unterschiedlichsten Räumen assoziative visuelle Wahrnehmungsebenen. Das spektakuläre Bühnenbild von Thomas Schenk und Sasha Waltz erhält 2004 den OPUS-Preis »Bühnenbild des Jahres«.

»OPUS-Preis« for the best set design of the year to »insideout« (Thomas Schenk and Sasha Waltz).

REPERTOIRE

Impromptus Berlin, Avignon, Paris, Ferrara
insideout Berlin, Amsterdam
Körper Berlin, Moscow, Seoul, Reykjavik, Düsseldorf
noBody Stockholm
Zweiland Berlin, Genoa

PRODUCTIONS SCHAUBÜHNE AM LEHNINER PLATZ

colours may fade… *Joanna Dudley, Juan Kruz Diaz de Garaio Esnaola* Berlin
d'avant Berlin, Düsseldorf, Athens, Lyon
My dearest… My fairest Berlin, Gmunden

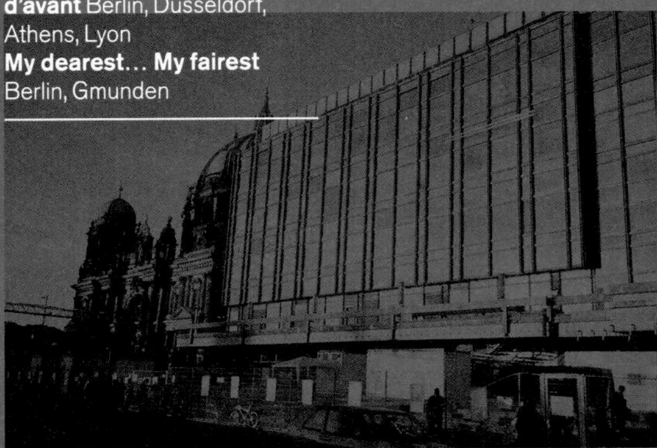
A

B

C

2004

Dialoge – Paris

Le ferme du Buisson, Festival Les Presqu'îles de Danse, Paris
17 Jan
Direction/Concept
Sasha Waltz
Dance/Choreography
Boris Charmatz
Nicola Mascia
Claudia de Serpa Soares
Sasha Waltz
Music/Performance
Joanna Dudley
Anton Lukoszevieze
Adrian Pereyra
Production
Schaubühne am Lehniner Platz, Berlin

Impromptus
↘pp. 41, 116, 120, 125, 174, 175, 205, **259**, 308

Schaubühne am Lehniner Platz, Berlin
17 Apr
Direction/Choreography
Sasha Waltz
Music
Franz Schubert
Dance/Choreography
Maria Marta Colusi
Clémentine Deluy
Juan Kruz Diaz de Garaio Esnaola
Luc Dunberry
Michal Mualem
Claudia de Serpa Soares
Xuan Shi
Music
Andreas Kern (Piano)
Judith Simonis (Vocals)
Stage Design
Thomas Schenk
Sasha Waltz
Costume Design
Christine Birkle
Light Design
Martin Hauk
Dramaturgy
Jochen Sandig
Yoreme Waltz
Production
Schaubühne am Lehniner Platz, Berlin
Coproduction
Teatro Comunale di Ferrara

Dialoge – Passages

Studio Bagouet/Les Ursulines, Festival Montpellier Danse, Montpellier
4 Jul
Direction/Concept
Sasha Waltz
Dance/Choreography
Mikel Aristegui
Davide Camplani
Sidi Larbi Cherkaoui
Maria Marta Colusi
Tomas Danielis
Clémentine Deluy
Lisa Densem
Juan Kruz Diaz de Garaio Esnaola
Luc Dunberry
Charlotte Engelkes
Damien Jalet
Benoît Lachambre
Nicola Mascia
Grayson Millwood
Michal Mualem
Virgis Puodziunas
Claudia de Serpa Soares
Xuan Shi
Takako Suzuki
Laurie Young
David Zambrano
Sigal Zouk
Music/Performance
Joanna Dudley
Anton Lukoszevieze
Adrian Pereyra
Carl Rosman
Eva Stahler
zeitkratzer
Visual Arts
Regina Frank
Sissel Tolaas

Dialoge 04 – St. Elisabeth I–IV
↘p. **260**

St. Elisabeth-Kirche, Berlin
Direction/Concept
Sasha Waltz
Jochen Sandig
Visual Arts
Thora Sólveig Bergsteinsdóttir
Brad Hwang
Erwin van der Werve
Production
Sasha Waltz & Guests
Coproduction
Tanz im August – Internationales Festival Berlin
Kulturbüro SOPHIEN
Funded by
Hauptstadtkulturfonds
I
21 Aug
Dance/Choreography/ Performance
Milli Bitterli
Lisi Estaràs
Thomas Hauert
Benoît Lachambre
Susanne Linke
Nicola Mascia
Friederike Plafki
Frans Poelstra
Christopher Roman
Takako Suzuki
Sasha Waltz
Music
zeitkratzer
II
22 Aug
Dance/Choreography/ Performance
Milli Bitterli
Lisi Estaràs
Thomas Hauert
Benoît Lachambre
Susanne Linke
Nicola Mascia
Friederike Plafki
Frans Poelstra
Christopher Roman
László Sandig
Takako Suzuki
Sasha Waltz
Music
zeitkratzer
III
28 Aug
Dance/Choreography
Simone Forti
Yasmeen Godder
John Jasperse
Nicola Mascia
Andréya Ouamba
Friederike Plafki
Claudia de Serpa Soares
Takako Suzuki
Mat Voorter
Junko Wada
Sasha Waltz
David Zambrano
Matan Zamir
Sigal Zouk
Music
Jonathan Bepler (Electronics)
Nicholas Bussmann (Cello)
Hanno Leichtmann (Electronics)
Axel Dörner (Trumpet)
Reinhold Friedl (Piano)
Maurice de Martin (Percussion)
Michael Vorfeld (Percussion)
Hanayo (Vocals)
IV
29 Aug
Dance/Choreography
Lisa Densem
Joséphine Evran
Simone Forti
John Jasperse
Benoît Lachambre
Nicola Mascia
Lars Rudolph
László Sandig
Claudia de Serpa Soares
Meg Stuart
Mat Voorter
Sasha Waltz
David Zambrano
Music
Jonathan Bepler (Electronics)
Nicholas Bussmann (Cello)
Hanno Leichtmann (Electronics)
Reinhold Friedl (Piano)
Maurice de Martin (Percussion)
Michael Vorfeld (Percussion)
Hahn Rowe (DJ)
Hanayo (Vocals)

Dialoge 04 – Palast der Republik
↘p. **261**

Palast der Republik, Berlin
17 Sep
Direction/Concept
Sasha Waltz
Jochen Sandig
Dance/Choreography
Zaida Ballesteros
Jiří Bartovanec
Dagmar Bock
Joris Camelin
Davide Camplani
Maria Marta Colusi
Clémentine Deluy
Lisa Densem
Juan Kruz Diaz de Garaio Esnaola
Luc Dunberry
Kazue Ikeda
Nikos Kamondo
Iztok Kovac
Nicola Mascia
Michal Mualem
Friederike Plafki
Virgis Puodziunas
Sasa Queliz
Mata Sakka
Claudia de Serpa Soares
Xuan Shi
Takako Suzuki
Vanessa Thrull
Junko Wada
Sasha Waltz
Laurie Young
Matan Zamir
Sigal Zouk
Music
Nicholas Bussmann
Arnold Keser
Hans Peter Kuhn
Hanno Leichtmann
Friedrich Liechtenstein
zeitkratzer
Visual Arts
Brad Hwang
Video
Philip Bussmann
Christopher Roman (Dance)
Production
Sasha Waltz & Guests
Supported by
Hauptstadtkulturfonds

A+B **»Dialoge 04 – Palast der Republik«** C **»Dialoge 04 – St. Elisabeth I–IV«**

Impromptus

This piece probes the emotional states from loss of orientation to exhilaration on two strongly inclined planes that are wedged together like masses of ice, searching for choreographic pendants to existential instability as found in the Romantic music of Franz Schubert. »Impromptus« is the beginning of an extended creative period in which Sasha Waltz mainly choreographs to classical music, including operas and symphonies. Three intimate duets constitute the core of the piece, contrasted by spirited and spatially expansive group scenes. The focus is on the unfilled yearning for felicity and harmony that Schubert sublimated in his music and on the recurring wanderer motif in his work. The wanderer is Schubert's alter ego, damned to loneliness without a home – symbolising the creative individual who feels alienated in this world. The continuous rhythms in the composition are evocative of a never-ending journey that never leads to a homecoming. The melancholy choreography takes up this thread and develops it further in subtle rhythms in the movement sequences. The four songs in the voice of a mezzo soprano also reflect yearning and inner emptiness. Franz Schubert composed the two »Impromptus« D.899 and D.935 in 1827, a year before he died at the end of a period of sickness and nevertheless extremely productive creative phase. They are among his most successful piano compositions. In the darkest moment of the piece, the movement of the bodies shapes an outsized drawing rendered in red and black pigments on the floor of the stage. Water runs over the drawing, which is on a slant, so that the image blurs into a large painting.

Auf zwei Flächen in extremer Schräglage, wie ineinandergekeilte Eisschollen, ergründet dieses Werk emotionale Zustände zwischen Haltlosigkeit und Schweben und findet damit choreographische Entsprechungen zu der existenziellen Instabilität, die sich in Franz Schuberts Musik der Romantik vermittelt. »Impromptus« ist der Beginn einer ausgedehnten Schaffensphase, in der Sasha Waltz hauptsächlich zu klassischer Musik choreographieren wird, darunter Opern und sinfonische Werke.
Drei zärtliche Duette bilden das Herzstück. Sie werden von dynamischen und raumgreifenden Gruppenszenen kontrastiert. Die von der Musik angestoßene Emotion – die bei Schubert sublimierte, unerfüllte Sehnsucht nach Glück und Harmonie – und das in seinem Werk vielfach auftauchende Motiv des Wanderers stehen im Vordergrund. Der zu Heimatlosigkeit und Einsamkeit verdammte Wanderer ist als Sinnbild des schöpferischen Menschen, der sich nicht von dieser Welt fühlt, Schuberts Alter Ego. Fortlaufende Rhythmen bringen kompositorisch eine endlose Wanderschaft ohne Heimkehr zum Ausdruck. Die melancholische Choreographie nimmt diesen Faden auf und spinnt ihn in einer subtilen Rhythmik in den Bewegungssequenzen weiter. Sehnsucht und innere Leere spiegeln sich auch in den vier Liedern wider, die von einer Mezzosopranistin vorgetragen werden. Franz Schubert komponierte die beiden »Impromptus« D.899 / D.935, die zu seinen erfolgreichsten Klavierkompositionen zählen, 1827 – ein Jahr vor seinem Tod, in einer von Krankheit geprägten und dennoch äußerst schaffensreichen Phase. Im dunkelsten Moment des Stücks entsteht aus rotem und schwarzem Pigment eine überdimensionale Zeichnung auf dem Bühnenboden durch die Bewegung der Körper. Eine Zeichnung, über deren Schräge herablaufendes Wasser die Farben zu einem großen Gemälde verschwimmen lässt.

Dialoge 04 – St. Elisabeth I–IV

A new open space for the arts in Berlin is founded in St Elisabeth Church in conjunction with one of Sasha Waltz & Guests' »Dialogue« projects. »Dialoge 04« presents an homage to the legendary Judson Memorial Church in New York, where, after Merce Cunningham, American post-modernism found its artistic home in the figures of Steve Paxton, Trisha Brown, Simone Forti and many others. Over four days, Sasha Waltz meets with various artists for improvisation sessions as a font of artistic exchange on the sand-covered floor of the church. Sasha Waltz brings younger dancers and experimental musicians together with icons of dance from the older generation, such as Simone Forti and Susanne Linke.

Mit einem »Dialoge«-Projekt von Sasha Waltz & Guests wird die St. Elisabeth-Kirche als ein neuer offener Raum für die Künste in Berlin gegründet. »Dialoge 04« stellt eine Hommage an die legendäre New Yorker Judson Memorial Church dar, in der die amerikanische Postmoderne nach Merce Cunningham um Steve Paxton, Trisha Brown, Simone Forti und viele andere ihre künstlerische Heimat fand. An vier Tagen versammelt Sasha Waltz verschiedene Künstler:innen zur Improvisation, als Quelle künstlerischen Austauschs auf dem mit Sand bedeckten Boden der Kirche. Sasha Waltz bringt Tanz-Ikonen der älteren Generation wie Simone Forti und Susanne Linke mit jüngeren Tänzer:innen und experimentellen Musiker:innen zusammen.

Dialoge 04 – Palast der Republik

Sasha Waltz presents a »Dialogue« project on three evenings in the gutted Palast der Republik in September 2004. It is performed on different levels and in all three sections of the impressive culture palace as part of the »Volkspalast« programme, with Ensemble zeitkratzer, Friedrich Liechtenstein and Hans Peter Kuhn, Sasha Waltz's company and other international guests. Turf has been rolled out at the centre of the former assembly room of the building. Many scenes take place on it. It anticipates the future interim function of an open area of turf in the centre of the city – before it too is supplanted by the reconstruction of the reformistic building of the Royal Palace.

Im September 2004 zeigt Sasha Waltz im entkernten Palast der Republik an drei Abenden ein »Dialoge«-Projekt, das auf verschiedenen Ebenen und in allen drei Gebäudeteilen des imposanten Kulturpalastes stattfindet. Es wird als Teil des Programms »Volkspalast« mit dem Ensemble zeitkratzer, Friedrich Liechtenstein und Hans Peter Kuhn, ihrer Compagnie sowie weiteren internationalen Gästen aufgeführt. Ein ausgerollter Rasen in der Mitte des ehemaligen Versammlungssaal des Palastes, auf dem sich viele Szenen abspielen, nimmt die spätere Zwischennutzung als offene Grasfläche im Zentrum der Stadt vorweg, bevor auch diese später von der reformistischen Form des rekonstruierten Schlosses verdrängt wird.

2005

After five years at Schaubühne am Lehniner Platz Sasha Waltz & Guests is becoming an **independent company** again.

First movement group for children by Sasha Waltz – a project in cooperation with »TanzZeit – Tanz in Schulen«.

REPERTOIRE

Dido & Aeneas Berlin, Luxembourg, Montpellier
Gezeiten Berlin
Impromptus Berlin, Paris, Weimar, Lille, Antwerp, Edinburgh, New York
insideout Berlin
Körper Toulouse, Lisbon, Warsaw, Turin, Oslo
noBody Berlin

GUEST PRODUCTIONS

89 Seconds at Alcázar *Eve Sussman, Claudia de Serpa Soares, Jonathan Bepler* Berlin
Anything else Luxembourg
colours may fade… Berlin
d'avant Barcelona, Seville, Lille, Amsterdam, Otsu, Guanajuato, Ottawa
Don't we *Luc Dunberry* Berlin, Groningen
Foi Berlin
lawn *Splintergroup* Berlin
My dearest… My fairest Luxembourg
Paper Doll Berlin
Persona *Christopher Roman, Philip Bussmann* Berlin
under *matanicola vs. Yasmeen Godder* Berlin, Groningen

FILM

Dido & Aeneas Henry Purcell, Sasha Waltz [90'] Director for TV and Video Peter Schönhofer TV Editors Wolfgang Bergmann, Dieter Schneider Production ZDF in collaboration with Arte Coproduction ZDFtheaterkanal, Sasha Waltz & Guests Distribution DVD, Arthaus Musik 2008

A

Dido & Aeneas
↘pp. 29, 30, 80, 83, 92, 109, 133, 192, 207, 208, **263**, 284, 308

Grand Théâtre de la Ville de Luxembourg
29 Jan
Music
Henry Purcell
Libretto
Nahum Tate
Direction/Choreography
Sasha Waltz
Musical Direction/Reconstruction
Attilio Cremonesi
Dance/Choreography
Jiří Bartovanec (Second Witch/A Spirit)
Maria Marta Colusi (Second Woman)
Clémentine Deluy (Dido)
Juan Kruz Diaz de Garaio Esnaola (Sorceress)
Luc Dunberry (Train of Aeneas)
Charlotte Engelkes (Narrator)
Michal Mualem (Dido)
Manuel Alfonso Pérez Torres (Train of Aeneas)
Virgis Puodziunas (Aeneas)
Sasa Queliz (Belinda)
László Sandig (Ascanius)
Xuan Shi (Sorceress)
Takako Suzuki (First Witch/A Sailor)
Soloists
Aurore Ugolin (Dido)
Reuben Willcox (Aeneas)
Deborah York (Belinda)
Céline Ricci (Second Woman)
Fabrice Mantegna (Sorceress)
Eberhard Francesco Lorenz (First Witch/A Sailor)
Michael Bennett (Second Witch/A Spirit)
Stage Design
Thomas Schenk
Pia Maier Schriever
Sasha Waltz
Costume Design
Christine Birkle
Light Design
Thilo Reuther
Dramaturgy
Jochen Sandig
Yoreme Waltz
Choir
Vocalconsort Berlin
Orchestra
Akademie für Alte Musik Berlin
Production
Sasha Waltz & Guests
Akademie für Alte Musik Berlin
Coproduction
Les Théâtres de la Ville de Luxembourg
Staatsoper Unter den Linden, Berlin
Opéra National de Montpellier
Supported by
Hauptstadtkulturfonds

Dialoge – Happy Day

Opéra de Lille
7 May
Direction/Concept
Sasha Waltz
Jochen Sandig
Dance/Choreography
Maria Marta Colusi
Clémentine Deluy
Luc Dunberry
Nicola Mascia
Michal Mualem
Friederike Plafki
Christopher Roman
Claudia de Serpa Soares
Xuan Shi
Laurie Young
Sasha Waltz
Music
Ensemble Musikfabrik
Production
Sasha Waltz & Guests

Dialoge 2005 – Open Church

St. Elisabeth-Kirche, Berlin
17 Aug
Concept
Sasha Waltz
Production
Sasha Waltz & Guests
Kulturbüro SOPHIEN
Tanz im August – Internationales Festival Berlin

Gezeiten
↘pp. 43, 56, 57, 72, 94, 160, 176, 182, 189, 206, 214, 215, **264**

Schaubühne am Lehniner Platz, Berlin
19 Nov
Direction/Choreography
Sasha Waltz
Music
Jonathan Bepler
Dance/Choreography
Davide Camplani
Maria Marta Colusi
Koen De Preter
Juan Kruz Diaz de Garaio Esnaola
Matija Ferlin
Gabriel Galindez Cruz
Maria Öhman
Pinar Ömerbeyoglu
Friederike Plafki
Virgis Puodziunas
Sasa Queliz
Mata Sakka
Claudia de Serpa Soares
Xuan Shi
Davide Sportelli
Laurie Young
Stage Design
Thomas Schenk
Sasha Waltz
Costume Design
Beate Borrmann
Light Design
Martin Hauk
Baroque Cello
James Bush
Production
Sasha Waltz & Guests
Schaubühne am Lehniner Platz, Berlin

A **First movement group for children by Sasha Waltz**

Dido & Aeneas

Sasha Waltz pursues a totally new approach in her notions of dance with her first opera production in 2005. She chooses the Baroque period and Henry Purcell's most famous opera »Dido & Aeneas«. She stages the piece as music theatre with 13 dancers from her ensemble together with 28 musicians, 16 vocalists for the choir and seven soloists.
It is a tragic love story against the background of a war. The queen, Dido, grants Aeneas and his companions asylum in the seaport Carthage after they've fled from Troy in flames. The gods thwart the fulfilment of her love for Aeneas, intervening because they see his fate tied up in founding the city of Rome. Dido despairs when Aeneas unexpectedly departs. Her lament »When I Am Laid in Earth« is one of the saddest and most beautiful arias in music history.
In order to illustrate the inner conflict of the two lovers, Sasha Waltz allocates their roles to several dancers and soloists, who in unison express the various emotions. As one of the pioneers among modern female opera directors, Sasha Waltz generates a piece out of the complex feelings of the protagonists that involves the opera singers in the dancing processes and in this way merges dance and opera into a single art form: the choreographic opera. Attilio Cremonesi and Sasha Waltz supplement Purcell's opera with a prologue comprised of musical fragments from his compositions. With playful ease, the dancers introduce the mythical story in an elongated water basin that spans the proscenium and transposes the scene to the Mediterranean Sea. Phoebus the sun god rises out of the ocean in his sun chariot. Together with the Nereids, he sings of the arrival of Venus. The audience joins the narrators and dives into the waters where the sunken city of Carthage is discovered beneath the ocean's depths.

Sasha Waltz beschreitet mit ihrer ersten Opernregie 2005 einen völlig neuen Weg in ihrem künstlerischen Schaffen. Sie entscheidet sich für die Epoche des Barock und erwählt Henry Purcells berühmteste Oper »Dido & Aeneas« als das Werk, das sie als Musiktheater mit 13 Tänzer:innen ihres Ensembles sowie 28 Musiker:innen, 16 Chorist:innen und sieben Solist:innen inszeniert.
Es erzählt von einer tragischen Liebe vor dem Hintergrund eines Krieges. Die Königin Dido bietet dem trojanischen Helden Aeneas und seinem Gefolge, die dem brennenden Troja entflohen sind, Zuflucht an ihrem Hof in der Hafenstadt Karthago. Die Erfüllung ihrer Liebe wird vereitelt durch die Einwirkung der Götter, die sein Schicksal an die Gründung der Stadt Rom binden. Dido zerbricht an dem unerwarteten Aufbruch von Aeneas. Ihr Lamento »When I am Laid in Earth« zählt zu den traurigsten und schönsten Arien der Musikgeschichte.
Um die innere Zerrissenheit der beiden Liebenden zu verbildlichen, besetzt Sasha Waltz ihre Rollen mit mehreren Tänzer:innen und Solist:innen, die vereint unterschiedliche Emotionen zum Ausdruck bringen. Als eine der ersten unter den modernen Opernregisseur:innen entwickelt Sasha Waltz aus den komplexen Gefühlswelten der Protagonisten ein Werk, das die Sänger:innen in tänzerische Prozesse involviert und somit Tanz und Oper zu einer einzigen Kunstform verschmilzt: der Choreographischen Oper. Attilio Cremonesi und Sasha Waltz erweitern die Oper um einen Prolog aus musikalischen Fragmenten Purcells.
In einem das Bühnenportal ausfüllenden länglichen Wasserbecken leiten die Tänzer:innen spielerisch in den Mythos ein und verlagern den Handlungsrahmen an das Mittelmeer: Der Sonnengott Phoebus entsteigt dem Meer mit seinem Sonnenwagen. Zusammen mit den Nereiden besingt er die Ankunft der Venus, gemeinsam mit den Erzähler:innen tauchen die Betrachtenden in die Fluten und entdecken am Grund die versunkene Stadt Karthago.

Gezeiten

A room marked by signs and upheavals of the past is the last refuge and sanctuary for a group of people. They are threatened by a catastrophe that is destroying the world outside. The dancers find themselves trapped as disaster increasingly closes in on them. In »Gezeiten« (Tides), Sasha Waltz and her ensemble of 16 dancers probe the transformations that life permanently faces. The piece centres around the reciprocal actions of destruction and reconstruction and seeks expression in plumbing their physical and metaphysical layers. Sasha Waltz adopts various perspectives – aesthetically and content-wise – and combines the objectivity and surreal theatricality of her early pieces with the abstraction and dance dynamic of her later works. Crises that disrupt the natural course of things especially interest her: overtones of certain natural catastrophes are recognisable in »Gezeiten«, such as Hurricane Katrina or the dystopian themes of »climate change« and »pandemics«. What remains after collapse and destruction? How do we continually reshape our world anew? What is worth saving?

Ein Raum, in dem Spuren und Verwerfungen der Vergangenheit eingeschrieben sind, ist letzter Zufluchtsort und wird zum Schutzraum einer Gruppe von Menschen. Eine Katastrophe zerstört das Außen, bedroht die Eingeschlossenen, dringt immer tiefer in diese Schicksalsgemeinschaft ein. In »Gezeiten« beschäftigt sich Sasha Waltz gemeinsam mit ihrem Ensemble von 16 Tänzer:innen mit den Transformationen, denen das Leben permanent unterworfen ist. Das Stück kreist um die Wechselwirkung von Zerstörung und Neugestaltung und sucht nach einem Ausdruck, indem es deren physische und metaphysische Ebenen auslotet. Sasha Waltz nimmt verschiedene ästhetische und inhaltliche Blickwinkel ein und verbindet die Gegenständlichkeit und surreale Theatralik ihrer frühen Stücke mit der Abstraktion und tänzerischen Dynamik späterer Arbeiten. Besonderes Interesse richtet sie dabei auf Krisensituationen, die den natürlichen Rhythmus stören: Konkrete Naturkatastrophen wie Hurrikan Katrina, aber auch die dystopischen Themen »Klimawandel« und »Pandemie« schwingen in »Gezeiten« bereits mit. Was bleibt nach Zusammenbruch und Zerstörung? Wie gestalten wir unsere Welt immer wieder neu? Was ist es wert, gerettet zu werden?

On 9 September 2006, the Radialsystem opens with a moving inaugural speech by Prof. Ivan Nagel: »A miracle is happening here before our eyes. It is no mystical miracle, but a sober and necessary one. This house is needed.« Indeed, the founding of this institution is a miracle, defying all economic rationale. While no one doubts its necessity, the path will be long and challenging.
Sasha Waltz & Guests is the driving force behind the establishment of Radialsystem. Developed and led over many years by Jochen Sandig and Folkert Uhde, it was envisioned as a »Space for Arts and Ideas«. Influences from Tacheles, Sophiensæle and Schaubühne am Lehniner Platz helped shape its interior design for maximum flexibility of use. This transformation of space results in a space of transformation, reflecting the openness and creativity of the city in a dual sense – due to its location on the banks of the Spree and its proximity to Holzmarkt, a utopian urban village. The result is a unique »space of possibilities« in Berlin, located in what was once a no-man's land between Kreuzberg, Mitte and Friedrichshain. The building becomes an instrument, constantly reimagined. Here, music dances!
The international success of »Dido & Aeneas« marked the beginning of a new era and became the initial spark for Radialsystem. Folkert Uhde, manager of the Academy for Ancient Music, collaborated with Sasha Waltz to develop her first choreographic opera, while Jochen Sandig found in him the perfect partner to realise their shared dream of a production house. The founders were driven by the idea of creating a space that transcends individual art forms, envisioning it as an open, cross-disciplinary radiation in all directions – a true »radial system«. In 1860, James Hobrecht, alongside Rudolf Virchow, invented the sustainable circular economy of »Radialsystems« in Berlin, 12 pumping stations with sewage fields used for agriculture outside the city. The »dialogical principle« between tradition and innovation finds its ideal stage in the landmarked »Radialsystem V«, hosting artistic creations, future congresses and conferences – a place where arts and sciences are continually explored and advanced. To this day, Radialsystem remains the home base of Sasha Waltz & Guests, with a studio on the fifth floor, and serves as an anchor institution for a wide variety of independent ensembles in contemporary dance, music and performance art. Radialsystem itself is a symbol of Berlin's enduring transformation. Art needs space to grow, and Radialsystem will continue to provide such a space – open, curious and always ready for the new. Today, the building belongs to the State of Berlin and is managed by the nonprofit Radial Foundation in collaboration with Radialsystem V GmbH.

Am 9. September 2006 wird das Radialsystem mit einer bewegenden Festrede von Prof. Ivan Nagel feierlich eröffnet: »Hier vor unseren Augen geschieht ein Wunder. Es ist kein mystisches Mirakel, sondern ein nüchternes und notwendiges Wunder. Dieses Haus wird gebraucht.« Die Gründung dieses Hauses ist tatsächlich ein Wunder, gegen jede ökonomische Vernunft. Niemand zweifelt an der Notwendigkeit, aber es wird ein langer, harter Weg.
Sasha Waltz & Guests ist die treibende Kraft hinter der Gründung des Radialsystems. Als »Space for Arts and Ideas« wird es über viele Jahre von Jochen Sandig und Folkert Uhde entwickelt und geleitet. Tacheles, Sophiensæle und Schaubühne am Lehniner Platz haben die innere Raumstruktur für eine maximale Nutzungsflexibilität mitgeprägt. Die Transformation des Raums führt zu einem Raum der Transformation, der die Offenheit und Kreativität der Stadt in doppeltem Sinne widerspiegelt – aufgrund seiner Lage am Spreeufer und der Nachbarschaft zum Holzmarkt, einem utopischen urbanen Dorf. Das Ergebnis ist ein in Berlin einzigartiger »Möglichkeitsraum« im ehemaligen Niemandsland zwischen Kreuzberg, Mitte und Friedrichshain. Das Gebäude wird zum Instrument, das immer wieder neu bespielt wird. Hier tanzt die Musik!
Der internationale Erfolg von »Dido & Aeneas« ist der Beginn einer neuen Ära und gleichzeitig die Initialzündung für das Radialsystem. Folkert Uhde ist Manager der Akademie für Alte Musik, mit der die erste Choreographische Oper von Sasha Waltz entwickelt wird, und Jochen Sandig findet in ihm den kongenialen Partner, um den gemeinsamen Traum eines eigenen Produktionshauses zu realisieren. Die Unternehmensgründer sind geleitet von der Idee, einen Ort zu schaffen, der sich nicht auf einzelne Kunstsparten beschränkt, sondern sich als offenes, grenzüberschreitendes und in alle Richtungen ausstrahlendes »radiales System« versteht.
1860 erfand James Hobrecht gemeinsam mit Rudolf Virchow in Berlin die nachhaltige Kreislaufwirtschaft der »Radialsysteme«, zwölf Pumpwerke einer Kanalisation mit landwirtschaftlich genutzten Rieselfeldern außerhalb der Stadt. Das »Dialogische Prinzip« zwischen Tradition und Innovation findet im denkmalgeschützten »Radialsystem V« die perfekte Bühne für künstlerische Kreationen, Zukunftskongresse und Konferenzen – ein Raum, in dem die Künste und Wissenschaften erforscht und stetig weiterentwickelt werden. Das Radialsystem ist bis heute Heimat von Sasha Waltz & Guests mit Studio im fünften Stock und darüber hinaus Ankerinstitution einer breiten Vielfalt freier Ensembles des zeitgenössischen Tanzes, der Musik und der Performancekunst. Das Radialsystem selbst ist Symbol des dauerhaften Wandels in Berlin. Kunst braucht Raum, um zu wachsen, und das Radialsystem wird auch in Zukunft ein solcher Raum bleiben – offen, neugierig und immer bereit für das Neue. Mittlerweile gehört das Gebäude dem Land Berlin und wird von der gemeinnützigen Radial Stiftung gemeinsam mit der Radialsystem V GmbH betrieben.

2006

Founding and opening of Radialsystem, festive event with artistic programme by Sasha Waltz & Guests. ↘p. **267**

Sasha Waltz continues her work with young dancers under the name **»Kindertanzcompany Sasha Waltz & Guests«.** ↘p. **299**

»Zweiland« is performed for the 100th time at Schaubühne am Lehniner Platz in Berlin.

REPERTOIRE

Dido & Aeneas Berlin, Ferrara, Amsterdam, St. Pölten
Fantasie Lyon
Gezeiten Berlin, Stuttgart, Paris, Reggio Emilia
Impromptus Berlin, Lille, Luxembourg
insideout Berlin
Körper Berlin, Athens, Taipei, Barcelona
Solo für Vladimir Malakhov Berlin
Zweiland Berlin, Metz, Seville

GUEST PRODUCTIONS

colours may fade… Leuven, Luxembourg
d'avant Berlin, Paris, Vienna
Don't we Berlin, Luxembourg
Frans Poelstra, his dramaturg and Bach *Frans Poelstra, Robert Steijn* Berlin
Friedrich Liechtenstein Concert, Berlin
lawn Stuttgart
Miss very Wagner *Charlotte Engelkes* Berlin
My dearest… My fairest Berlin
Soul Project *David Zambrano* Berlin
under Berlin, Milan, Urbino, Bremen
White Trash *Ben Anderson, Benoît Lachambre, Bruno Pocheron, Isabelle Schad* Berlin

FILM

Garten der Lüste Die Choreographin Sasha Waltz [59']
Direction Brigitte Kramer
Production nachtaktivfilm in collaboration with ZDFtheaterkanal and Arte Distribution DVD, goodmovies 2008

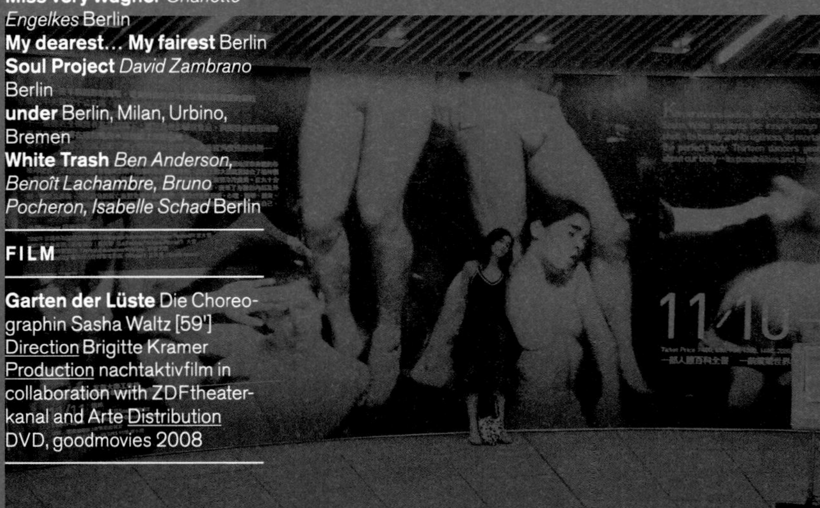

A

B

Fantasie
↘p. 199

Opéra de Lyon
12 Feb
Direction/Choreography
Sasha Waltz
Music
Franz Schubert
Dance
Bruno Cesario da Silva
Louis Clement da Costa
Sora Lee
Hongjun Li
Yu Otagaki
Kevin Quinaou
Antonio Ruz
Corey Scott-Gilbert
Piano
Aglaia Bätzner
Cristina Marton
Costume Design
Christine Birkle
Light Design
Martin Hauk
Production
Opéra de Lyon

Dialoge – Freiburg

E-Werk, Freiburg
19 Mar
Direction/Concept
Sasha Waltz
Dance/Choreography
Joanna Dudley
Edivaldo Ernesto
Eugénie Rebetez
László Sandig
Sasha Waltz
David Zambrano
Music/Performance
Robyn Schulkowsky

Solo für Vladimir Malakhov

Haus der Kulturen der Welt, Berlin
20 Apr
Direction/Choreography
Sasha Waltz
Music
Edgardo Rudnitzky
Dance
Vladimir Malakhov
Light Design
Martin Hauk
Production
Sasha Waltz & Guests
Staatsballett Berlin
Supported by
Kulturstiftung des Bundes

Dialoge – Bologna

Chiostro San Martino, Bologna
1 Jul
Direction/Concept
Sasha Waltz
Dance/Choreography
Gabriel Galindez Cruz
Peggy Grelat-Dupont
Michal Mualem
Antonio Ruz
Sasha Waltz
Music/Performance
Robyn Schulkowsky

Dialoge 06 – Radiale Systeme
↘pp. 40, 151, 176, 186, **269**

Radialsystem, Berlin
14 Sep
Direction/Concept
Sasha Waltz
Dance/Choreography
Liza Alpízar Aguilar
Diego Alberto Alvaroz Sanou
Emily Archer
Mikel Aristegui
Jiří Bartovanec
Davide Camplani
Johanna Chemnitz
Maria Marta Colusi
Lisa Densem
Juan Kruz Diaz de Garaio Esnaola
Luc Dunberry
Matija Ferlin
Gabriel Galindez Cruz
Vanessa Huber-Christen
Mamajeang Kim
Nicola Mascia
Grayson Millwood
Maria Öhman
Pinar Ömerbeyoglu
Ricardo de Paula
Manuel Alfonso Pérez Torres
Virgis Puodziunas
Sasa Queliz
Mata Sakka
Claudia de Serpa Soares
Xuan Shi
Laura Siegmund
Davide Sportelli
Takako Suzuki
Sasha Waltz
Music/Performance
Akademie für Alte Musik Berlin
Ensemble Musikfabrik
Vocalconsort Berlin
Production
Radialsystem
Sasha Waltz & Guests
Cooperation
Akademie für Alte Musik Berlin
Ensemble Musikfabrik
Vocalconsort Berlin

A **»Körper« tour to Taipei** B **»Dialoge 06 – Radiale Systeme«**

Dialoge 06 – Radiale Systeme

To celebrate the foundation and opening of Radialsystem V, Sasha Waltz expansively stages a production throughout Pumpwerk, a modified historical pump house on the banks of the Spree River. Twenty-two dancers and 25 musicians from the Akademie für Alte Musik Berlin and Ensemble Musikfabrik together with eight vocalists from the Vocalconsort Berlin participated in »Dialoge 06 – Radiale Systeme«. After the audience can freely explore the building and its various rooms, halls and studios during the performance, they gather at the end in the large, unseated hall as the Spree becomes a stage. The musicians of Ensemble Musikfabrik become part of the large-scale choreography, performing excerpts from Purcell's »King Arthur« while lying down. Elements from these dialogues serve as inspiration and preparation for works such as »Jagden und Formen (Zustand 2008)«, »Medea« and »Roméo et Juliette«.

Zur Gründung und Eröffnung des Radialsystem V bespielt Sasha Waltz weiträumig das umgebaute ehemalige Pumpwerk am Ufer der Spree. An »Dialoge 06 – Radiale Systeme« sind 22 Tänzer:innen und 25 Musiker:innen der Akademie für Alte Musik Berlin und des Ensemble Musikfabrik sowie acht Sänger:innen des Vocalconsort Berlin beteiligt. Nachdem das Publikum das Gebäude, die verschiedenen Räume, Säle und Studios während der Performance frei begangen hat und die Spree selbst zum Aufführungsort wird, ziehen die Zuschauer:innen zum Abschluss in die große, nicht bestuhlte Halle. Die Musiker:innen des Ensemble Musikfabrik werden Teil der großformatigen Choreographie und spielen im Liegen Auszüge aus »King Arthur« von Purcell. Elemente aus diesen Dialogen dienen als Inspiration und Vorbereitung für Stücke wie »Jagden und Formen (Zustand 2008)«, »Medea« und »Roméo et Juliette«.

Sasha Waltz is awarded **»Most Notable Artist« in the field of dance in the 2006/07 season** (critics survey by the magazine of the Deutscher Bühnenverein »Die Deutsche Bühne«) and **»Best Choreographer« of the 2006/07 season** (critics' survey by the »ballettanz« magazine).

Bronze at New York Festival in the category »Performing Arts« for the film adaptation of »Dido & Aeneas«.

»Cluster« is published by Henschel Verlag.

REPERTOIRE

Dido & Aeneas Lisbon, London
Fantasie Berlin
Gezeiten Berlin, Lille
Impromptus Berlin, Stockholm, Oslo, Ludwigshafen
insideout Luxembourg, Avignon
Körper Berlin, Tokyo, Otsu
Medea Berlin, Luxembourg
noBody New Delhi, Kolkata, Ferrara
Roméo et Juliette Paris
Travelogue I – Twenty to eight Berlin

GUEST PRODUCTIONS

4 Elemente – 4 Jahreszeiten *Akademie für Alte Musik Berlin, Midori Seiler, Juan Kruz Diaz de Garaio Esnaola* Berlin
Anything else Rovereto
colours may fade… Rovereto
Dance on Screen Dancefilm-festival *Karsten Liske* Berlin
d'avant Antwerp, Rouen, Bruges
Edgar *Claudia de Serpa Soares, Grayson Millwood* Berlin, Freiburg
Ladies First *matanicola* Berlin
lawn Berlin, Heilbronn
Mayim Mayim *Jiří Bartovanec* Fürth
medeamorphosen Ein Fest für die Künste, Berlin
My dearest… My fairest Paris
OmU *Laurie Young* Berlin
Péplum *Nasser Martin-Gousset* Berlin

FILM

Roméo et Juliette Hector Berlioz, Sasha Waltz [104']
TV-Direction Vincent Bataillon
Producer François Duplat, Antoine Perset, Xavier Dubois, Emma Enjalbert, Denis Morlière
Production Opéra national de Paris, Bel Air Media, telmondis, 3sat 2012

2007

A

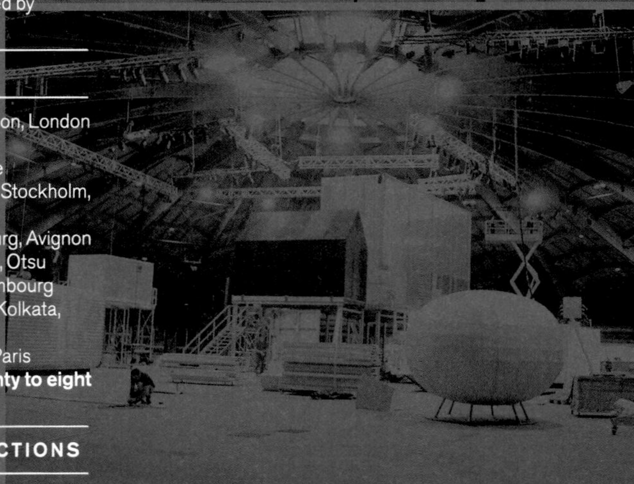

B

Dialoge – Bangalore

Ranga Shankara, Bangalore
10 Jan
Direction/Concept
Sasha Waltz
Music/Performance
Robyn Schulkowsky
Musicians of Karnataka College of Percussion
Dance/Choreography
Lisa Densem
Juan Kruz Diaz de Garaio Esnaola
Luc Dunberry
Grayson Millwood
Virgis Puodziunas
Claudia de Serpa Soares
Xuan Shi
Production
Sasha Waltz & Guests
Goethe-Institut Bangalore

Dialoge 07 – Pergamonmuseum

↘pp. 58, 62, 151, 152, 169, 175, 211, **272**

Pergamonmuseum, Berlin
24 Mar
Direction/Concept
Sasha Waltz
Dance/Choreography
Liza Alpízar Aguilar
Jiří Bartovanec
Davide Camplani
Maria Marta Colusi
Lisa Densem
Juan Kruz Diaz de Garaio Esnaola
Luc Dunberry
Gabriel Galindez Cruz
Mamajeang Kim
Pinar Ömerbeyoglu
Virgis Puodziunas
Sasa Queliz
Mata Sakka
Yael Schnell
Xuan Shi
Davide Sportelli
Music
Pascal Dusapin
Jakob Arcadelt
Giovanni Palestrina
Choir
Vocalconsort Berlin
Production
Sasha Waltz & Guests

Medea

↘pp. 37, 50, 62, 63, 76, 78, 88, 116, 134, 150, 151, 152, 188, 198, 210, 211, **273**

Grand Théâtre de la Ville de Luxembourg
23 May
Music
Pascal Dusapin
Text
Heiner Müller
Direction/Choreography
Sasha Waltz
Musical Direction
Marcus Creed
Dance/Choreography
Liza Alpízar Aguilar
Jiří Bartovanec
Davide Camplani
Maria Marta Colusi
Lisa Densem
Juan Kruz Diaz de Garaio Esnaola
Luc Dunberry
Gabriel Galindez Cruz
Mamajeang Kim
Pinar Ömerbeyoglu
Virgis Puodziunas
Sasa Queliz
Mata Sakka
Yael Schnell
Xuan Shi
Davide Sportelli
Children
László Sandig
Luna Zscharnt
Soloist
Caroline Stein (Medea)
Concept Stage Design/Video
Sasha Waltz
Stage Design
Pia Maier Schriever
Thomas Schenk
Heike Schuppelius
Costume Design
Christine Birkle
Light Design
Thilo Reuther
Dramaturgy
Jochen Sandig
Yoreme Waltz
Production
Sasha Waltz & Guests
Made in Radialsystem
Coproduction
Les Théâtres de la Ville de Luxembourg
Akademie für Alte Musik Berlin
Staatsoper Unter den Linden
Supported by
Hauptstadtkulturfonds

Roméo et Juliette

↘pp. 28, 44, 104, 105, 109, 110, 168, 177, 186, 201, **271**, 298

Opéra Bastille, Paris
5 Oct
Music
Hector Berlioz
Direction/Choreography
Sasha Waltz
Musical Direction
Valery Gergiev
Vello Pähn
Soloists Dance
Aurélie Dupont (Juliette)
Hervé Moreau (Roméo)
Wilfried Romoli (Frère Laurent)
Soloists Vocals
Ekaterina Gubanova
Yann Beuron
Mikhail Petrenko
Orchestra and Choir
Opéra national de Paris
Dance
Ballet de l'Opéra de Paris
Stage Design
Pia Maier Schriever
Thomas Schenk
Sasha Waltz
Costume Design
Bernd Skodzig
Light Design
David Finn
Production
Opéra national de Paris
Made in Radialsystem

C

A+B **»insideout« tour to Avignon** C **Sasha Waltz studying the score of »Medea«**

Roméo et Juliette

Commissioned by the Opéra national de Paris, Sasha Waltz creates her third choreographic opera, Hector Berlioz's »Roméo et Juliette«. Berlioz's symphonie dramatique does not follow Shakespeare's storyline word for word. While the narration provides a sequence of events, it is frequently interrupted by jumps in time. This structure, liberated from a strictly chronological narrative flow, offers Sasha Waltz an open framework to explore the deeper layers of the unconscious through dance. In this process, she combines three soloists and the 100 singers of the choir with dance, creating a choreographic-musical Gesamtkunstwerk.
The stage set plays a decisive role in imbuing the dramaturgy with a three-dimensional quality. A psychology of space is generated that represents in its transformations the different stages of the plot as it unfolds. The mobile sculpture of two planes, one over the other, opens up in the course of the story like a clam. These planes can vary in elevation and sometimes produce steep inclines – an instability, a real danger, which the figures in the drama also experience. We move in the mindset of a society that finds no path to peace. The families of the two young lovers, Juliette and Roméo, are sworn enemies. The couple rebel against this with their love and seek a solution, hoping to be able to live the way they want. Their vulnerable passion for one another presents a counterweight to the established powers of their families. However, the hopeful outcome of this story is thwarted by the unintentional suicide of the lovers. The traumatic loss must resolve the conflict between their families; their reconciliation means that the deaths of Roméo and Juliette are not in vain and fulfil a social purpose. The plot thus fits in with the classic logic of opera: the Dance Macabre, or Dance of Death, becomes a Dance of Life.

Mit Hector Berlioz' »Roméo et Juliette« erschafft Sasha Waltz im Auftrag der Opéra national de Paris ihre dritte Choreographische Oper. Berlioz' Symphonie dramatique folgt Shakespeares Handlungsverlauf nicht Wort für Wort. Die Narration gibt zwar eine Handlungskette vor, wird aber immer wieder durch Zeitsprünge durchbrochen. Diese Form, befreit von einem streng chronologischen Erzählstrom, bietet Sasha Waltz einen offenen Rahmen, um die tieferen Ebenen des Unbewussten tänzerisch freizulegen. Dabei fügt sie drei Solist:innen und die hundert Sänger:innen des Chores zusammen mit dem Tanz zu einem choreographisch-musikalischen Gesamtkunstwerk.
Das Bühnenbild spielt als Verräumlichung der Dramaturgie eine entscheidende Rolle. Es entsteht eine Psychologie des Raumes, der in seinen Verwandlungen die unterschiedlichen Stationen des Geschehens abbildet. Die bewegliche Skulptur zweier aufeinander gelagerter Ebenen öffnet sich im Laufe der Handlung wie eine Muschel. Sie ermöglichen verschiedene Höhen und teils steile Neigungen der Flächen – eine Instabilität, eine reale Gefahr, wie sie auch die Figuren des Dramas erleben. Wir bewegen uns in den Seelenlandschaften einer Gesellschaft, die keinen Weg in den Frieden findet. Die Familien zweier junger Liebender, Juliette und Roméo, sind tief verfeindet. Sie begehren mit ihrer Liebe auf und suchen Lösungsmöglichkeiten, um ihr eigenes, selbstbestimmtes Leben zu leben. Die zerbrechliche Leidenschaft des jungen Paares lässt ein Gegengewicht zu den etablierten Kräften der Familien entstehen. Doch endet die hoffnungsvolle Geschichte im unfreiwilligen Selbstmord der Liebenden. Dieser traumatische Verlust soll den Konflikt beider Familien heilen: Damit diese Tode nicht umsonst waren, bekommen sie durch die Versöhnung einen sozialen Sinn und werden damit in die klassische Opferlogik eingeschrieben – der Tanz des Todes wird zum Tanz des Lebens.

Sasha Waltz tackles the figure of Medea in the mythology of antiquity for the visit to the Pergamonmuseum for the »Europe Night of Beauty«. Sixteen dancers from Sasha Waltz & Guests and singers from the Vocalconsort Berlin meet the remarkable exhibits of this museum space and perform the first excerpts from their current project for the audience, which sits on the steps of the Pergamon Altar. A frieze like the one in the museum is projected onto the back wall of the stage at the beginning of »Medea«. An archaic vocabulary flows into the movements of the choreographic opera »Medea«, reflecting the encounter with the sculptures in the Pergamonmuseum. The fluttering garments rendered in stone inspire Sasha Waltz to make wind a central element in the piece alongside music of Pascal Dusapin.

In der Annäherung an den antiken Mythos von Medea besucht Sasha Waltz das Pergamonmuseum: 16 Tänzer:innen von Sasha Waltz & Guests sowie die Sänger:innen des Vocalconsort Berlin treffen zur »Nacht der Schönheit« auf die außergewöhnlichen Exponate dieses musealen Raumes und zeigen dem auf den Stufen des Pergamonaltars sitzenden Publikum erste Ausschnitte aus der aktuellen Arbeit. Ein Fries, wie jenes im Museum, wird zu Beginn von »Medea« als Projektion auf der Rückwand der Bühne zu sehen sein. Durch die Begegnung mit den Skulpturen des Pergamonmuseums fließt die archaische Bildsprache in das Bewegungsvokabular der Choreographischen Oper »Medea« ein. Der in Stein festgehaltene Faltenwurf der Kleider inspiriert Sasha Waltz, das Element des Windes in ihrer Inszenierung in den Mittelpunkt zu rücken und als Klanginstallation der Musik Dusapins gegenüberzustellen.

Medea

A frieze of a scene from antiquity fades in. Single bodies coloured like the marble of the frieze slowly begin to move. We catch a glimpse of an ancient mnemonic device; it is set into motion and disappears again. The dance takes bodies out of the mythological past into the present and creates the scene of an ancient world.
Pascal Dusapin's composition »Medeamaterial« (1991) for Heiner Müller's text provides the framework for this choreographic opera. Heiner Müller's text has three characters: Medea, her Nurse and Jason; Dusapin, however, restricts his composition to just Medea. Jason's and Nurse's passages come from off-stage; they are thrust out into the periphery of Medea's memories. Sasha Waltz investigates the figure of Medea in more ancient interpretations of the myth than in Euripides's tragedy and also researches contemporary feminist interpretations such as in Christa Wolf's novel, »Medea: A Modern Retelling«. The focus is on gender relations and the hierarchical exertion of authority. Jason, the male, after war and having fled, acquires social standing and influence in his new homeland. But Medea's presence reminds him of his origins and former helplessness.
On his adventure to steal the Golden Fleece, he only succeeds with Medea's assistance. She is the daughter of the king of Colchis and points out the way to Jason by means of her sorcery. He profits from her powers until they reach Corinth. No longer of any use to him, he discards her for a younger woman, the daughter of the king of Corinth, Glauce. Medea sacrifices and betrays her country out of love for Jason. She even cuts her brother to pieces when he pursues her after the robbery. In Euripides's version of the myth, she sacrifices her beloved children and murders Jason's new wife to take her revenge on him. The image that Euripides paints of Medea is that of a Fury, an avenger and child murderer; her powers as a woman, as a healer and mother reveal a very different side. The person of Medea personifies the conflicting forces of creation and destruction.

Ein Fries einer antiken Szene wird sichtbar. Die einzelnen Körper in der Farbe des Steins, aus dem das Fries geschlagen ist, beginnen, sich langsam zu regen. Eine alte Erinnerungsstruktur ist kurz zu sehen, wird in Bewegung versetzt und vergeht wieder. Der Tanz holt Körper aus mythologischer Vergangenheit in die Gegenwart und formt den Schauplatz einer antiken Welt.
Pascal Dusapins Komposition »Medeamaterial« (1991) zum Text von Heiner Müller ist das Grundgewebe dieser Choreographischen Oper. Hat der Ausgangstext bei Müller noch drei Figuren – Medea, deren Amme und Jason –, so beschränkt der Komponist sich auf die Figur der Medea. Jasons Passagen und die der Amme kommen aus dem Off, in die Peripherie der Erinnerung Medeas geschoben. Sasha Waltz erarbeitet Medeas Figur aus Auslegungen des Mythos, die älter sind als jene von Euripides, sowie aus zeitgenössischen feministischen Interpretationen wie unter anderem in Christa Wolfs Roman »Medea. Stimmen«. Zentral sind die Geschlechterverhältnisse und ihre Machtspiele. Der Mann, Jason, der nach Krieg und Flucht in der Gesellschaft aufsteigt, wird von Medea an seinen Ursprung und seine Hilflosigkeit erinnert. Jason war ausgezogen, das Goldene Vlies zu rauben, erhält es nur mit der Hilfe Medeas, die als Tochter des Königs von Kolchis mit Zauberkraft den Weg weist. Er nutzt ihre Macht, bis sie in Korinth ankommen und sie ihm nicht mehr von Nutzen ist, und verlässt sie für eine jüngere Frau, die Tochter des Königs von Korinth, Glauke. Medea opfert und verrät ihr Land aus Liebe zu Jason, zerstückelt sogar ihren Bruder, der sie nach dem Raub verfolgt.
In der Version von Euripides opfert sie ihre geliebten Kinder und ermordet seine neue Frau, um sich an Jason zu rächen. Das von Euripides gezeichnete Bild der Medea als Furie, Rächerin und Kindsmörderin wird kontrastiert mit der Perspektive auf ihre weibliche Macht. Sie ist Heilerin und Mutter – dabei gehen die kreativen und die zerstörerischen Kräfte der Figur ein Spannungsverhältnis ein.

15th anniversary of Sasha Waltz & Guests.

European theatre prize »New Theatrical Realities« for Sasha Waltz.

REPERTOIRE

Dido & Aeneas Berlin, Brussels, Tel Aviv, Barcelona, Aarhus
Gezeiten Berlin, Rennes, Groningen
Impromptus Rome
Jagden und Formen (Zustand 2008) Berlin, Frankfurt
Körper Berlin
Medea Berlin
noBody Berlin
Travelogue I – Twenty to eight Berlin, Vienna, Paris, Groningen, Seville
Zweiland Berlin

CHOREOGRAPHEN DER ZUKUNFT 2008

Solos and Duets by Sasha Waltz & Guests Berlin, Prague, Ludwigshafen
Aphasiadisiac (Work in progress) *Ted Stoffer, Les ballets C de la B*
Parallel/Moving *Xuan Shi, Niannian Zhou*
When my mind is rocking, I know it's 7 *Jiří Bartovanec*

GUEST PRODUCTIONS

Ars melancholiae *Juan Kruz Diaz de Garaio Esnaola* Berlin
Comédie *Nasser Martin-Gousset* Berlin, Montpellier
d'avant Berlin, Moscow
Edgar Luxembourg
My dearest… My fairest Moscow, Tel Aviv, Groningen
Teach me tonight *Friedrich Liechtenstein* Berlin

2008

A

B

Jagden und Formen (Zustand 2008)

↘p. **275**

Festival Frankfurter Positionen 2008, Schauspielhaus Frankfurt
7 May
Music
Wolfgang Rihm
Direction/Choreography
Sasha Waltz
Artistic Project Management
Juan Kruz Diaz de Garaio Esnaola
Musical Direction
Franck Ollu
Dance/Choreography
Liza Alpízar Aguilar
Jiří Bartovanec
Davide Camplani
Juan Kruz Diaz de Garaio Esnaola
Edivaldo Ernesto
Gabriel Galindez Cruz
Renate Graziadei
Mamajeang Kim
Nicola Mascia
Virgis Puodziunas
Zaratiana Randrianantenaina
Antonio Ruz
Mata Sakka
Yael Schnell
Orchestra
Ensemble Modern
Costume Design
Beate Borrmann
Light Design
Martin Hauk
Production
Sasha Waltz & Guests
Ensemble Modern
Made in Radialsystem
Initiated and funded in the frame of Frankfurter Positionen 2008 by
BHF-Bank-Stiftung
Kulturstiftung des Bundes

Dialoge 08 – Venedig

Palazzo Carlo Scarpa in the frame of Concordanze Venice
28 Nov
Concept/Choreography
Sasha Waltz
Costume Design
Beate Borrmann
Light Design
Martin Hauk
Dance/Choreography
Liza Alpízar Aguilar
Jiří Bartovanec
Davide Camplani
Juan Kruz Diaz de Garaio Esnaola
Luc Dunberry
Charlotte Engelkes
Mamajeang Kim
Nicola Mascia
Virgis Puodziunas
Sasa Queliz
Mata Sakka
Yael Schnell
Claudia de Serpa Soares
Orchestra
Solistenensemble Kaleidoskop
Production
Sasha Waltz & Guests
Supported by
La Fondazione Scientifica Querini Stampalia

A+B **»Dialoge 08 – Venedig«**

Jagden und Formen (Zustand 2008)

The composition »Jagden und Formen« (Hunting and Forms) meanders like a landscape artwork through Wolfgang Rihm's oeuvre. In this edition he names it »Zustand 2008« (Version 2008), because it is performed in a number of stages, spaces and constellations. After meeting Sasha Waltz, the composer adds new ideas to the score. This serves as the basis for Ensemble Modern and the Dance Company to engage in an intense artistic exchange. A violinist begins the piece with a solo, then moves onto the stage while still playing, traversing the space through the choreography as it unfolds. »Jagden und Formen (Zustand 2008)« is a premiere for musicians and dancers sitting and performing on the stage together: the musicians are integrated in the same choreographies, carried or lying on the stage where they continue to play their instruments.
Wolfgang Rihm's energy-laden and demanding music seems to take on greatly varying corporeal shapes and collective states and describes physical primaeval states. The choreography echoes this as the dance allows us to experience the music in its complexity and at the same time flows into the composition as an independent layer of musical movement. The last part of the composition, reminiscent of a modern rite, shapes the choreography of a sacrificial dance.

Die Komposition »Jagden und Formen« zieht sich als Werklandschaft mäandernd durch das Œuvre von Wolfgang Rihm. Er nennt sie in dieser Fassung »Zustand 2008«, da sie in unterschiedlichen Stadien, Räumen und Konstellationen auftritt. Nach der Begegnung mit Sasha Waltz denkt der Komponist die Partitur weiter, auf deren Grundlage das Ensemble Modern und die Tanzcompagnie in einen konzentrierten Austausch treten. Ein Violinist leitet das Stück ein mit einem Solo, abseits, betritt dann die Bühne, weiterhin spielend, und durchquert den Raum durch die sich entfaltende Choreographie. Mit »Jagden und Formen« sitzen und tanzen zum ersten Mal Musiker:innen zusammen mit den Tänzer:innen auf der Bühne: Integriert in gemeinsame Choreographien werden sie getragen oder liegen, weiterhin ihre Instrumente spielend, auf dem Boden. Die hochenergetische und anspruchsvolle Musik Wolfgang Rihms, die selbst unterschiedliche körperliche Gestalten, Aggregatzustände anzunehmen und physikalische Urzustände zu beschreiben scheint, findet ihre Resonanz in der Choreographie. Der Tanz macht die Musik in ihrer Komplexität erfahrbar, legt sich zugleich als eigene musikalisch-bewegte Schicht in die Komposition hinein. Der letzte Teil der Komposition, an einen modernen Sacre erinnernd, dient als choreographische Orientierung für einen Opfertanz.

Fellowship of Sasha Waltz at Deutsche Akademie Rom **Villa Massimo.**

Sasha Waltz is awarded **»Officier de l'Ordre des Arts et des Lettres«** by the French Ministry of Culture.

A fragment of **»Dialoge 09 – Neues Museum« is performed** on the occasion of a **visit by HM King Charles III** (in 2009 HRH Charles, Prince of Wales), at Neues Museum Berlin.

REPERTOIRE

Allee der Kosmonauten Berlin, Paris
Dido & Aeneas Lyon
Gezeiten Brussels, Seoul
Impromptus Berlin, Toulouse
Jagden und Formen (Zustand 2008) Berlin
Körper Santiago de Chile, Ottawa, Montreal, Melbourne, Zurich
Medea Amsterdam, Melbourne, Lille, Caen
Travelogue I – Twenty to eight Berlin, Berkeley, Hanoi, Lille
Zweiland Paris, Havana

KINDERTANZCOMPANY

Der kleine Mann *Gabriel Galindez Cruz* Berlin

CHOREOGRAPHEN DER ZUKUNFT 2009

Solos and Duets by Sasha Waltz & Guests Berlin, Prague, Luxembourg
Aliens! *Luc Dunberry*
Dialogue II *Shang-Shi Sun*
From… To *Davide Camplani*
Rückwärts *Renate Graziadei*

GUEST PRODUCTIONS

d'avant Berlin
My dearest… My fairest Berlin, Lille
Radiale Nächte *Sasha Waltz & Guests, Solistenensemble Kaleidoskop, Vocalconsort Berlin, Robyn Schulkowsky* Berlin
Shock *David Zambrano* Berlin
Tanja Liedtke Fellowship 2009 Showing *Antony Hamilton* Berlin

FILM

Dialoge 09 – Neues Museum [52'] A film by Sasha Waltz Co-Direction Brigitte Kramer, Jörg Jeshel Production Commissioned by ZDF in collaboration with Arte, Sasha Waltz & Guests

2009

A

Dialoge 09 – Neues Museum

↘pp. 34, 74, 97, 150, 179, **277**

Neues Museum, Berlin
18 Mar
Direction/Choreography
Sasha Waltz
Dance/Choreography
Liza Alpízar Aguilar
Ayaka Azechi
Jiří Bartovanec
Davide Camplani
Hervé Chaussard
Maria Marta Colusi
Lisa Densem
Juan Kruz Diaz de Garaio Esnaola
Luc Dunberry
Charlotte Engelkes
Delphine Gaborit
Gabriel Galindez Cruz
Renate Graziadei
Mamajeang Kim
Florencia Lamarca
Nicola Mascia
Sergiu Matis
Thomas Michaux
Jeroen Mosselman
Michal Mualem
Elena Murcia Pinto
Pinar Ömerbeyoglu
Francesca Pennini
Manuel Alfonso Pérez Torres
Jonathan Pranlas
Virgis Puodziunas
Sasa Queliz
Zaratiana Randrianantenaina
Orlando Rodriguez
Antonio Ruz
Mata Sakka
Yael Schnell
Xuan Shi
Shang-Chi Sun
Takako Suzuki
Niannian Zhou
Choir
Vocalconsort Berlin
Orchestra
Solistenensemble Kaleidoskop
Costume Design
Bernd Skodzig
Production
Sasha Waltz & Guests
Cooperation
Stiftung Preußischer Kulturbesitz
Staatliche Museen zu Berlin
David Chipperfield Architects
Radial Stiftung

Dialoge 09 – MAXXI

↘pp. 70, 89, 91, 93, 96, 107, 115, 139, 173, 175, 181, 204, 210, **278**

Museo nazionale delle arti del XXI secolo (MAXXI), Rome
13 Nov
Direction/Choreography
Sasha Waltz
Soundinstallation
Hans Peter Kuhn
Costume Design
Bernd Skodzig
Dance/Choreography
Liza Alpízar Aguilar
Ayaka Azechi
Jiří Bartovanec
Davide Camplani
Hervé Chaussard
Nadia Cusimano
Juan Kruz Diaz de Garaio Esnaola
Luc Dunberry
Charlotte Engelkes
Edivaldo Ernesto
Giannalberto de Filippis
Renate Graziadei
Mamajeang Kim
Florencia Lamarca
Nicola Mascia
Sergiu Matis
Todd McQuade
Thomas Michaux
Grayson Millwood
Michal Mualem
Francesca Noia
Pinar Ömerbeyoglu
Francesca Pennini
Virgis Puodziunas
Sasa Queliz
Zaratiana Randrianantenaina
Orlando Rodriguez
Antonio Ruz
Mata Sakka
Yael Schnell
Claudia de Serpa Soares
Xuan Shi
Davide Sportelli
Shang-Chi Sun
Takako Suzuki
Junko Wada
Laurie Young
Niannian Zhou
Music
Frances-Marie Uitti (Violoncello)
Sava Stoianov (Trumpet)
Valentín Garvie (Trumpet)
Michael Weilacher (Percussion)
String Quartet of Solistenensemble Kaleidoskop
Biliana Voutchkova (Violin)
Ayumi Paul (Violin)
Yair Lantner (Viola)
Augustin Maurs (Violoncello)
Production
MAXXI
Coproduction
Sasha Waltz & Guests
Project Organisation
Fondazione Romaeuropa
Supported by
Goethe-Institut Rom
Funded by
Hauptstadtkulturfonds

B

A **Atelier of Sasha Waltz at Villa Massimo** B **»Dialoge 09 – MAXXI«**

Neues Museum on Berlin's Museumsinsel is in a special moment of transition after being rebuilt according to the designs and under the supervision of David Chipperfield Architects. Immediately after the building's completion, and before the exhibits move into the restored spaces, Sasha Waltz, together with 70 dancers, musicians and singers, guides us through the still-empty rooms of the multi-level building. The audience, moving freely within the museum, encounters choreographies that respond to the spatial conditions, including stair railings, wall projections and steps, as well as the archaeological themes of the numerous halls. Burial rituals, mummifications and death cults of past civilisations provide a thematic backdrop for this exploration of the empty museum. Worship of femininity in early cultures and concepts of the magical woman and her power serve as central sources of inspiration. The image of women during the classical period of the museum's construction, alongside societal dances and attire, offers another reference point. The musical dramaturgy similarly traverses various periods. Works by Xenakis, Claude Vivier and other 20th-century composers are integrated into the performance with percussion, choir and the Solistenensemble Kaleidoskop Berlin string ensemble. For the grand finale, the audience converges from all rooms and floors into the vast, temple-like stairwell for the moment of inauguration, accompanied by the music of Xenakis's »Rebound« and Bruckner's String Quartet in F Major (WAB 112).

Das Neue Museum auf der Museumsinsel in Berlin befindet sich nach dem Wiederaufbau unter der Leitung von David Chipperfield Architects in einem besonderen Moment der Transition. Direkt nach der baulichen Fertigstellung des Gebäudes und bevor die Exponate in die restaurierten Räume einziehen, führt Sasha Waltz mit siebzig Tänzer:innen, Musiker:innen und Sänger:innen durch die noch leeren Räume des mehrgeschossigen Bauwerks. Das sich frei im Museum bewegende Publikum trifft auf Choreographien, die sich sowohl an den räumlichen Bedingungen, den Treppengeländern, Mauervorsprüngen, Stufen als auch an den archäologischen Themen der zahlreichen Säle orientieren. So bilden Begräbnisrituale, Mumifizierungen und Todeskulte vergangener Zivilisationen einen thematischen Hintergrund der Bespielung des leeren Museums. Anbetungen der Weiblichkeit in frühen Kulturen, Vorstellungen der magischen Frau und ihrer Kraft sind zentrale Inspirationsquellen. Auch das Bild der Frau zur klassizistischen Zeit des Baus des Museums, zusammen mit den Gesellschaftstänzen und Kleidern, setzt einen weiteren Referenzpunkt. Die musikalische Dramaturgie durchläuft in ähnlicher Weise verschiedene Zeiträume. Werke von Xenakis, Claude Vivier und anderen Komponist:innen des 20. Jahrhunderts sind mit einem Schlagwerk, dem Chor und dem Streicherensemble des Solistenensemble Kaleidoskop Berlin in die Raumbespielung integriert. Zum großen Finale fließt das Publikum zusammen aus allen Räumen und Etagen ins tempelartige Treppenhaus, zum Moment der Einweihung zur Musik von Xenakis' »Rebound« und Bruckners Streichquartett in F-Dur (WAB 112).

Zaha Hadid's architecture sets the tone of the rooms through which the dancers move. Levels that overlap and interflow open up long vistas on the choreographies staged simultaneously on different storeys. Interpreted by Solistenensemble Kaleidoskop, the music by Hans Peter Kuhn and others intermixes in these spaces as well, creating sound layers and echoing the impression of superimposed views of the dance taking place on the various levels and in the galleries.
At the invitation of Hou Hanru and Fabrizio Grifasi, Sasha Waltz stages the opening ceremony for MAXXI, the museum of contemporary art in Rome, in 2009. She interlinks the exploration of MAXXI with an exhibition of her own work and examines the oeuvre she has presented up to this time. Between what she has created to date and the spaces of the building, she discovers new cross-references and elements that directly refer to the architecture and history of the museum. One scene, for example, describes an account of the executions by firing squads on the grounds of the old barracks, the plot on which MAXXI is built. A significant new element is »Die Hängenden«, that is, bodies that are suspended in the air, hanging on thin ropes. They move so slowly that we hardly notice it, creating a dream-like landscape of bodies in elongated spaces. The black flights of stairs, seemingly free-hanging trails through the open spaces of the building, stand out starkly against the white of the walls and the light fittings in the museum: which Sasha Waltz reflects in the scenic imagery and Bernd Skodzig in his costume design. The sounds made by white porcelain plates pushed along the floor create a soundscape in which the dancers dressed in black stand out like silhouettes against the sterile white of the walls. Tallow and chalk in the corners seem to want to cover the space in dusty white. Once again, the inauguration culminates in extensive group choreography, visible from all sides and levels, like in a grand amphitheatre. Flowers are laid out, painting a yellow ribbon in the white room.

Die Architektur von Zaha Hadid prägt die Bewegungsräume der Tänzer:innen: Sich überlappende und ineinanderfließende Ebenen des Gebäudes erlauben lange Blickachsen auf die simultan auf verschiedenen Etagen stattfindenden Choreographien. Die Musik von unter anderem Hans Peter Kuhn oder dem Solistenensemble Kaleidoskop vermengt sich in diesen Räumen ebenso zu Klangschichten, wie sich der Tanz – sichtbar auf den unterschiedlichen Stockwerken und Galerien – überlagert.
Auf Einladung von Hou Hanru und Fabrizio Grifasi inszeniert Sasha Waltz 2009 die Einweihung des römischen Museums für zeitgenössische Kunst MAXXI. Sie verbindet die Auseinandersetzung mit dem MAXXI mit einer eigenen Werkschau und befragt ihre bisherigen Arbeiten. Sie findet zwischen ihrem bestehenden Werk und den Räumen neue Beziehungen und Elemente, die sich direkt auf die Architektur und Geschichte des Museums beziehen. So referiert eine Szene auf Erschießungen im alten Kasernenareal, auf dessen Boden das MAXXI errichtet wurde. Wichtiges neues Element sind »Die Hängenden«, an feinen Seilen befestigte schwebende Körper, die sich unmerklich langsam bewegen und in den lang gezogenen Räumen eine traumartige Körperlandschaft entstehen lassen. Die schwarzen Treppenläufe, die wie frei schwebende Bahnen durch die Lufträume des Gebäude ziehen, lassen einen Kontrast zum Weiß der Wände und Leuchtelemente des Museums entstehen, den Sasha Waltz in der szenischen Bildsprache und im Kostümbild von Bernd Skodzig widerspiegelt: Die Geräusche über den Boden geschobener weißer Porzellanteller erzeugen einen Klangraum, in dem sich die schwarz gekleideten Figuren der Tänzer:innen wie Schattenrisse von den klinisch weißen Wänden absetzen. Talg und Kalk in den Ecken scheinen den Raum mit staubigem Weiß überziehen zu wollen. Erneut kulminiert die Einweihung in einer großen Gruppenchoreographie, die von allen Seiten und Ebenen aus, wie in einem großen Amphitheater, sichtbar ist. Blumen werden ausgelegt, malen ein gelbes Band in den weißen Raum.

The Berlin Cultural Committee awards Sasha Waltz & Guests **its own budget item.**

»Caroline-Neuber-Preis« of the city Leipzig for Sasha Waltz.

Jochen Sandig is awarded **»Officier de l'Ordre des Arts et des Lettres«** by the French Ministry of Culture.

Fragment of **»Dialoge 09 – MAXXI«** (»Die Hängenden«) at Martin Gropius Bau, Berlin, in the frame of a show by Villa Massimo.

REPERTOIRE

Continu Berlin, Zurich
Gezeiten New York
Impromptus Barcelona, Dijon, Bonn, Bruges
Jagden und Formen (Zustand 2008) Hamburg, Cologne, Salzburg
Körper Berlin
Medea Brussels
Métamorphoses Berlin
Passion Paris
Travelogue I – Twenty to eight Berlin, Luxembourg, Heilbronn, Ferrara
Zweiland Berlin, Beirut, Damascus, Ramallah, Jerusalem, Cairo

KINDERTANZCOMPANY

Monster *Gabriel Galindez Cruz* Berlin

CHOREOGRAPHEN DER ZUKUNFT 2010

Solos and Duets by Sasha Waltz & Guests Ludwigshafen
Aného *Jiří Bartovanec*
The Sound of Qin *Xuan Shi, Niannian Zhou*

GUEST PRODUCTIONS

A Mary Wigman Dance Evening *Fabian Barba*
Casi *Juan Kruz Diaz de Garaio Esnaola* Havana
Composition with Twelve Windows Videoinstallation *Meggie Schneider, Sasha Waltz & Guests, Bernd Uhlig* Berlin
Curtain Calls *Charlotte Engelkes* Stockholm
d'avant Berlin, Budapest
Human Writes *Forsythe Company/William Forsythe and Kendall Thomas* Berlin
My dearest… My fairest Bruges
Synopsis *Florencia Lamarca, Edan Gorlicki* Berlin
Teach me tonight Berlin

2010

A

B

C

D

E

F

Continu
↘pp. 43, 73, 114, 142, 156, 171, 177, 187, **281**

Festspiele Zürich, Schauspielhaus Zürich
20 Jun
Direction/Choreography
Sasha Waltz
Dance/Choreography
Liza Alpízar Aguilar
Ayaka Azechi
Jiří Bartovanec
Justin John Billy
Davide Camplani
Maria Marta Colusi
Juan Kruz Diaz de Garaio Esnaola
Luc Dunberry
Edivaldo Ernesto
Delphine Gaborit
Mamajeang Kim
Florencia Lamarca
Sergiu Matis
Todd McQuade
Thomas Michaux
Virgis Puodziunas
Sasa Queliz
Zaratiana Randrianantenaina
Orlando Rodriguez
Mata Sakka
Yael Schnell
Xuan Shi
Shang-Shi Sun
Niannian Zhou
Percussion
Robyn Schulkowsky
Music
Edgar Varèse
Claude Vivier
Iannis Xenakis
Stage Design
Thomas Schenk
Pia Maier Schriever
Sasha Waltz
Costume Design
Bernd Skodzig
Light Design
Martin Hauk
Production
Sasha Waltz & Guests
Made in Radialsystem
Coproduction
Festspiele Zürich/Schauspielhaus Zürich
spielzeit'europa/Berliner Festspiele
Sadler's Wells, London

Zweiland Tour
↘pp. 121, 122

Shortly before the start of the Arab Spring, Sasha Waltz & Guests travels with the production »Zweiland« (1997) to Beirut, Damascus, Ramallah, Jerusalem and Cairo through a historically and politically charged area.

Passion
↘pp. 42, 88, 157, **282**

Théâtre des Champs-Elysées, Paris
6 Oct
Music
Pascal Dusapin
Libretto
Pascal Dusapin
Rita de Letteriis
Direction/Choreography
Sasha Waltz
Musical Direction
Franck Ollu
Dance/Choreography
Edivaldo Ernesto
Virgis Puodziunas
Zaratiana Randrianantenaina
Yael Schnell
Xuan Shi
Niannian Zhou
Soloists
Barbara Hannigan (Lei)
Georg Nigl (Lui)
Choir
Vocalconsort Berlin
Orchestra
Ensemble Modern
Stage Design
Thilo Reuther
Sasha Waltz
Costume Design
Hussein Chalayan
Light Design
Thilo Reuther
Electroacoustic System
Thierry Coduys
Production
Théâtre des Champs-Elysées
Sasha Waltz & Guests
Made in Radialsystem
Coproduction
Opéra de Lille

Métamorphoses

Radialsystem, Berlin
19 Nov
Direction/Choreography
Sasha Waltz
Dance/Choreography
Liza Alpízar Aguilar
Davide Camplani
Maria Marta Colusi
Edivaldo Ernesto
Delphine Gaborit
Gabriel Galindez Cruz
Renate Graziadei
Mamajeang Kim
Florencia Lamarca
Sergiu Matis
Sasa Queliz
Zaratiana Randrianantenaina
Orlando Rodriguez
Mata Sakka
Yael Schnell
Xuan Shi
Shang-Chi Sun
Niannian Zhou
Music
Georg Friedrich Haas
György Ligeti
Ruth Wiesenfeld
Iannis Xenakis
Percussion
Robyn Schulkowsky
Orchestra
Solistenensemble Kaleidoskop
Costume Design
Bernd Skodzig
Production
Sasha Waltz & Guests
Made in Radialsystem

A–F **»Continu«**

Continu

In »Continu«, Sasha Waltz consolidates key elements of her work from the past ten years, drawing on significant impulses from 2009. Together with 24 dancers, she creates a grand score centred around the epochal orchestral work »Arcana« by Edgar Varèse, surrounded by additional compositions by Iannis Xenakis and Claude Vivier. The contrast between black and white, which was already a defining feature at the inauguration of the MAXXI, now structures the dramatic framework of »Continu«: the first part of the piece takes place in an oversized black cubic space designed with Pia Maier Schriever, into which a white floor is introduced in the second part. To the cosmically contrasting music of Varèse, Sasha Waltz deepens her choreographic exploration of the beginnings of civilisation: a tightly knit group stands and moves in the space, united as one. First differences become visible, with parts of the group developing their rhythms and movement patterns multiplying. Centrifugal forces pull, and everything transforms quickly and incessantly – oscillating between chaos and order. Individual figures emerge, facing the violence of the mass, alone, rejected, exposed, spat out and swallowed again. Some lose their orientation in this existential threat, in the raw collision of bodies. Social structures reveal their instability.

Then, a new beginning. A massive blank sheet of white paper seems to have fallen onto the black floor during the pause. There is now space for delicate scenes and intricate constellations. Humanity reveals itself as a vulnerable, fragile being. Naked and peculiar. Movements leave traces on the white surface like prehistoric drawings: feet create pigment-coloured lines across the paper – testimonies of a moment, transformed into signs.

In »Continu« führt Sasha Waltz wesentliche Elemente ihrer Arbeit der vergangenen zehn Jahre zusammen und greift wichtige Impulse von 2009 auf. Gemeinsam mit 24 Tänzer:innen entwirft sie eine große Partitur, in deren Zentrum das epochale Orchesterwerk »Arcana« von Edgar Varèse steht, umgeben von weiteren Kompositionen von Iannis Xenakis und Claude Vivier. Der Kontrast zwischen Schwarz und Weiß, der schon bei der Einweihung des MAXXI prägend war, strukturiert nun in »Continu« den dramaturgischen Rahmen: Der erste Teil des Stücks findet in einem mit Pia Maier Schriever entworfenen schwarzen überdimensionalen kubischen Raum statt, in den sich im zweiten Teil ein weißer Boden legt. Zur kosmisch-kontrastreichen Musik von Varèse vertieft Sasha Waltz ihre choreographische Exploration des zivilisatorischen Beginns: Eine eng geschlossene Gruppe steht und bewegt sich im Raum, zusammengehörig, als Einheit. Erste Differenzen werden sichtbar, Teile innerhalb der Gruppe entwickeln eigene Rhythmen, Bewegungsmuster vervielfältigen sich. Zentrifugalkräfte ziehen, alles wandelt sich, schnell und immerzu. Oszillation zwischen Chaos und Ordnung. Einzelne Personen treten hervor, stehen der Gewalt der Masse gegenüber, allein, abgewiesen, ausgesetzt, ausgespuckt und wieder geschluckt. Manche verlieren ihre Orientierung in dieser existenziellen Bedrohung, im rohen Aneinandergeraten der Menschen. Soziale Strukturen entblößen ihre Instabilität.

Dann ein Neubeginn. Ein riesiges unbeschriebenes weißes Blatt Papier scheint in der Pause auf den schwarzen Boden gefallen zu sein. Nun ist Platz für filigrane Szenen, feingliedrige Konstellationen. Der Mensch zeigt sich als verletzlich-zartes Einzelwesen. Nackt und eigenartig. Bewegungen hinterlassen Spuren auf dem weißen Boden wie prähistorische Zeichnungen: Füße ziehen pigmentfarbene Linien über das Papier – Zeugnisse eines Augenblicks, zum Zeichen geworden.

Passion

The music for »Passion« by Pascal Dusapin is a contemporary exploration of the Orpheus myth, particularly engaging with Claudio Monteverdi's opera. The Festival d'Aix-en-Provence commissioned the music with a libretto in Italian in 2008. The first performance of Sasha Waltz's choreographic opera took place in Paris in October 2010. The myth is largely told through Eurydice's eyes. The stage and light design delineate the boundaries between the land of the living and the underworld while playing associatively with images of Hades. The two soloists Barbara Hannigan and Georg Nigl set the tone of the piece and are supported theatrically by a small group of dancers. The production continues the long-standing collaboration with the Vocalconsort Berlin as well as with Ensemble Modern.

Die Musik zu »Passion« von Pascal Dusapin ist eine zeitgenössische Beschäftigung mit dem Orpheus-Mythos, musikalisch insbesondere mit der Oper von Claudio Monteverdi. Die Komposition entstand als Auftragswerk des Festival d'Aix-en-Provence 2008 mit einem Libretto in italienischer Sprache, die Uraufführung von Sasha Waltz' Choreographischer Oper erfolgte im Oktober 2010 in Paris. Erzählt wird der Mythos weitgehend aus der Sicht von Eurydike. Mit dem Bühnenbild und Licht markiert Sasha Waltz die Grenze zwischen Oberwelt und Unterwelt und spielt assoziativ mit Bildern des Hades. Die Begegnung mit den beiden Solist:innen Barbara Hannigan und Georg Nigl prägt das Stück, darstellerisch begleitet von einer kleinen Gruppe Tänzer:innen. Die Produktion setzt die langjährige Kollaboration mit dem Vocalconsort Berlin sowie mit dem Ensemble Modern fort.

2011

Sasha Waltz is awarded the **»Bundesverdienstkreuz am Bande«** of the Federal Republic of Germany.

Vision Summit Award »Arts for Social Impacts« for Sasha Waltz.

»Impromptus« is performed for the 100th time at Radialsystem, Berlin.

REPERTOIRE

Continu Berlin, Paris, Barcelona, Salzburg
Dido & Aeneas Berlin
Impromptus Berlin, Zurich
Jagden und Formen (Zustand 2008) Amsterdam
Körper Madrid, Ludwigshafen
Matsukaze Berlin, Brussels, Warsaw, Luxembourg
Medea Toulouse
Métamorphoses Berlin, Cologne
Travelogue I – Twenty to eight Berlin, Cologne, Salvador, São Paulo

KINDERTANZCOMPANY

Davon *Gabriel Galindez Cruz* Berlin
no matter the size *Gabriel Galindez Cruz* Berlin

GUEST PRODUCTIONS

4 Elemente – 4 Jahreszeiten Ludwigsburg
5 Jahre Radialsystem *with Sasha Waltz & Guests a.o.* Berlin
Dance on Screen Dancefilmfestival, Berlin
Mahler Chamber Orchestra-Nacht *with Sasha Waltz & Guests a.o.* Berlin
My dearest… My fairest Paris
Natural Habitat *Laurie Young* Berlin
Why Not *David Zambrano* Berlin

FILM

Matsukaze Toshio Hosokawa, Sasha Waltz [81'] A film by Karsten Liske Production La Monnaie / De Munt Extra Muros 2016–17

Matsukaze
↘pp. 18, 36, 43, 89, 118, 124, 125, 177, 192, 193, **285**

Théâtre Royal de la Monnaie, Brussels
3 May
Music
Toshio Hosokawa
Libretto
Hannah Dübgen
Direction/Choreography
Sasha Waltz
Musical Direction
Pablo Heras-Casado
Dance/Choreography
Jiří Bartovanec
Davide Camplani
Juan Kruz Diaz de Garaio Esnaola
Delphine Gaborit
Mamajeang Kim
Florencia Lamarca
Sergiu Matis
Sasa Queliz
Zaratiana Randrianantenaina
Orlando Rodriguez
Mata Sakka
Xuan Shi
Junko Wada
Niannian Zhou
Soloists
Barbara Hannigan (Schwester Matsukaze)
Charlotte Hellekant (Schwester Murasame)
Frode Olsen (Mönch)
Kai-Uwe Fahnert (Fischer)
Choir
Vocalconsort Berlin
Orchestra
Orchestre Théâtre Royal de la Monnaie
Stage Design
Pia Maier Schriever
Chiharu Shiota
Costume Design
Christine Birkle
Light Design
Martin Hauk
Production
Sasha Waltz & Guests commissioned by Théâtre Royal de la Monnaie, Brussels
Made in Radialsystem
Coproduction
Les Théâtres de la Ville de Luxembourg
Theatre Wielki Opera Narodowa, Warsaw
Cooperation
Staatsoper Unter den Linden, Berlin
Supported by
Kulturstiftung des Bundes

A

B

A+B **»Dido & Aeneas« at Waldbühne, Berlin**

Matsukaze

»Matsukaze« explores the fates of two women and hence follows up on »Medea« and »Dido & Aeneas«. The contemporary Japanese composer Toshio Hosokawa wrote the original score for the libretto of Hannah Dübgen's reworking of this Noh theatre classic. On reaching the banks of a sea, a monk finds the spirits of two sisters who, although deceased, are still hopelessly in love with a prince. Their passion has entrapped them in karma. Love has chained them to the world of the living. They linger between this and the other world, seeking a way in which their souls can be released. In classical Noh theatre, the nuanced and reciprocal relationship between music, song, recitation and movement generates a state of trance, of drifting off to sleep on the threshold of dream and reality. Sasha Waltz comes close to evoking this ambience: she combines symbols of Japanese philosophy and aesthetic, such as the interaction of light and shadow and poetic images of nature. Like the two sisters, everything moves as if in a liminal realm, twofold, and at the same time as if in separate worlds. What is living and what lies in the past, what is real and what is reflected, what is a human voice and what is rustling pines, what is rain and what is the rush of falling bamboo twigs? The stage setting, designed with Chiharu Shiota and Pia Maier Schriever, spins a spiderweb of threads across the space. The enormous net marks the boundary between life and what lies beyond it. During the transition, the two spirits seem to be caught there. They are not free-flying spirits, unbound by the laws of the human world, but prisoners of their emotions. They twist and turn, fight their way through the air, search for an escape out of this gloomy web. Moonlight is mirrored in water. The wooden, skeletal structure of a house emerges between matter and void. Gutted, it is only the idea of a house. Shadows that draw lines in the space. By dancing, the figures transform into natural phenomena, turn into waves and wind, cranes and pine needles. It is a purifying rain that finally dissolves the chains holding the sisters in no man's land and liberates them from their prison.

»Matsukaze« bearbeitet zwei Frauenschicksale und schließt somit an »Medea« und »Dido & Aeneas« an. Der zeitgenössische japanische Komponist Toshio Hosokawa schrieb die Originalmusik zum Libretto des von Hannah Dübgen überarbeiteten Nō-Klassikers. Ein Mönch gelangt an ein Ufer und trifft die Geister zweier Schwestern, die bis über ihren Tod hinaus unsterblich in einen Prinzen verliebt sind. Ihre Leidenschaft hält sie im Karma gefangen. Die Liebe fesselt sie an die Welt der Lebenden. So schweben sie zwischen Dies- und Jenseits, suchen einen Weg, der ihre Seelen erlöst. Das Zusammenspiel aus Musik, Gesang, Rezitativ und Bewegung generiert im klassischen Nō-Theater einen Zustand der Trance, des Halbschlafs an der Schwelle von Traum und Wirklichkeit. Sasha Waltz nähert sich einer solchen Stimmung: Sie verknüpft Symbole der japanischen Philosophie und Ästhetik, wie dem Spiel von Licht und Schatten, und poetischen Naturbildern. Wie die zwei Schwestern bewegt sich alles in einer Zwischenwelt, verdoppelt sich, erscheint gleichzeitig in getrennten Welten. Was ist lebendig und was ist vergangen, was ist echt und was ist Spiegelung, was ist die Stimme eines Menschen und was ist das Rascheln der Kiefernzweige, was ist Regen und was ist das Rauschen fallender Bambuszweige? Das Bühnenbild, mit Chiharu Shiota und Pia Maier Schriever entworfen, spannt sich als Wand aus Fäden über die Rückseite des Raumes. Das riesige Netz markiert die Grenze des Lebens und dessen, was danach, dahinter kommt. Während des Übergangs scheinen die beiden Geister dort hängen geblieben zu sein. Es sind keine frei fliegenden Geister, für die die Gesetze der Menschenwelt nicht mehr gelten, sondern Gefangene ihrer Gefühle. Sie winden sich, kämpfen sich durch die Luft, suchen einen Ausweg aus diesem zwielichtigen Geflecht. Mondeslicht spiegelt sich im Wasser. Zwischen Materie und Leere erscheint auch eine hölzerne, skelettartige Struktur eines Hauses. Entkernt, auf eine Idee reduziert. Schatten, die Linien in den Raum zeichnen. Im Tanz verwandeln die Menschen sich in Naturphänomene, werden Wellengang und Wind, Kraniche und Kiefernadeln. Es ist ein reinigender Regen, der schließlich die Bindung der Schwestern an die Zwischenwelt löst und sie aus ihrer Gefangenschaft treten lässt.

La Scala in Milan adds **»Roméo et Juliette«** to its repertoire.

GöteborgsOperans Danskompani in Göteborg adds **»noBody«** to its repertoire.

Rebonds *Sasha Waltz* in the frame of the Edgar Degas exhibition at Fondation Beyeler, Basel.

»Nahaufnahme Sasha Waltz« by Michaela Schlagenwerth is published by Alexander Verlag, Berlin.

REPERTOIRE

Continu Luxembourg, Brussels, Athens, London
Dido & Aeneas Berlin
gefaltet Berlin, Salzburg, Zurich
human requiem Berlin
Impromptus Berlin, Marseille, Moscow
Jagden und Formen (Zustand 2008) Baden-Baden
Medea Paris
Métamorphoses Dresden
noBody Gothenburg
Passion Lille, Brussels
Roméo et Juliette Paris, Milan
Travelogue I – Twenty to eight Berlin, Rome
Zweiland Jakarta, Bandung, Surakarta

KINDERTANZCOMPANY

Davon Berlin
Der kleine Mann Berlin
Monster Berlin

GUEST PRODUCTIONS

4 Elemente – 4 Jahreszeiten Dijon, Brussels
d'avant Berlin
OJO *Antonio Ruz* Berlin
Radiale Nacht *with Mahler Chamber Orchestra, Sasha Waltz & Guests a.o.* Berlin

A

B

gefaltet
↘p. 288

Salzburger Landestheater
27 Jan
Direction/Choreography
Sasha Waltz
Music
Mark Andre
Wolfgang Amadeus Mozart
Dance/Choreography
Edivaldo Ernesto
Saju Hari
Todd McQuade
Virgis Puodziunas
Zaratiana Randrianantenaina
Judith Sánchez Ruíz
Yael Schnell
Violin
Carolin Widmann
Viola
Guy Ben-Ziony
Violoncello
Nicolas Altstaedt
Piano
Alexander Lonquich
Stage Design
Thomas Schenk
Costume Design
Beate Borrmann
Light Design
David Finn
Production
Sasha Waltz & Guests
Made in Radialsystem
Coproduction
Stiftung Mozarteum Salzburg
Théâtre Royal de La Monnaie, Brussels
MaerzMusik/Berliner Festspiele
Supported by
Radial Stiftung
Funded by
Hauptstadtkulturfonds

human requiem
↘p. 289

Johannes Brahms »Ein deutsches Requiem« für Soli, gemischten Chor und Klavier zu vier Händen
Radialsystem, Berlin
11 Feb
Concept/Direction
Jochen Sandig
Musical Direction
Simon Halsey
Choir
Rundfunkchor Berlin
Soloists
Marlis Petersen (Soprano)
Konrad Jarnot (Bariton)
Piano
Philip Mayers
Phillip Moll
Dramaturgy
Ilka Seifert
Sasha Waltz
Repetition
Davide Camplani
Claudia de Serpa Soares
Scenography
Brad Hwang
Light Design
Jörg Bittner
Production
Rundfunkchor Berlin
Cooperation
Sasha Waltz & Guests
Radialsystem

MusikTANZ – CARMEN
↘p. 287

A dance project of Berliner Philharmoniker with Sasha Waltz & Guests and students from Berlin
Arena Berlin
25 May
Musical Direction
Sir Simon Rattle
Direction/Choreography
Sasha Waltz
Music
Rodion Schtschedrin (Carmen-Suite)
Light Design
Martin Hauk
Costume Design
Beate Borrmann
Dance school groups
Klasse 8a, Caspar-David-Friedrich Oberschule, Berlin Hellersdorf
Klasse 11.3, Sophie-Scholl-Schule, Berlin Schöneberg
Klasse 11, Katholische Schule St. Marien, Berlin Neukölln
Klasse 9sf, Askanische Oberschule, Berlin Tempelhof
Dance/Choreography
Liza Alpízar Aguilar
Jiří Bartovanec
Edivaldo Ernesto
Gabriel Galindez Cruz
Hwanhee Hwang
Florencia Lamarca
Nicola Mascia
Sergiu Matis
Adalisa Menghini
Grayson Millwood
Virgis Puodziunas
Sasa Queliz
Zaratiana Randrianantenaina
Orlando Rodriguez
Mata Sakka
Judith Sánchez Ruíz
Yael Schnell
Claudia de Serpa Soares
Xuan Shi
Antonios Vais
Laurie Young
Niannian Zhou
Repetition
Davide Camplani
Orchestra
Berliner Philharmoniker
Production
Berliner Philharmoniker in the frame of the Education Programme 2012
Cooperation
Sasha Waltz & Guests
Education Programme supported by
Deutsche Bank

2012

C

A **Sir Simon Rattle and Sasha Waltz during rehearsals** B+C **»MusikTANZ – CARMEN« at Arena Berlin**

A packed Berlin bus arrives at the large arena. A colourful crowd of young people jumps out. They spread across the asphalt, sitting on scattered beer crates and casually lining up at a bar in the background. Some cycle in circles, passing a sweeping street cleaner. This scene of the streets of Berlin serves as the backdrop for the story of Carmen. As part of the Education Programme of the Berliner Philharmoniker, a choreography for Rodion Shchedrin's »Carmen Suite« is created during an intensive multi-week rehearsal phase with 120 young people from 12 schools across various districts of Berlin. Accompanied by dancers from the company and Sasha Waltz, the students develop their own dance material, which is woven together by Sasha Waltz into a large group choreography. The goal of the Education Programme of the Berliner Philharmoniker is to provide young people from diverse social and cultural backgrounds and with varying talents the opportunity to connect with the world of sound, musical forms and dance expression through collaborative creation.

Ein gefüllter Berliner Bus fährt in die große Arena. Heraus springt eine bunt gekleidete Menge junger Menschen. Sie verteilen sich auf der Asphaltfläche, setzen sich auf herumliegende Bierkästen, stellen sich lässig an eine Bar im Hintergrund. Manche drehen Kreise mit ihren Fahrrädern, an einem fegenden Müllmann vorbei. Szenerie der Straßen Berlins, in die sich die Geschichte der Carmen verlagert. Im Rahmen des Education-Programms der Berliner Philharmoniker entsteht während einer mehrwöchigen intensiven Probenphase zusammen mit 120 Jugendlichen aus zwölf Schulen verschiedener Bezirke Berlins die Choreographie zur »Carmen-Suite« von Rodion Schtschedrin. Begleitet von Tänzer:innen der Compagnie und Sasha Waltz, erarbeiten die Schüler:innen ihr eigenes tänzerisches Material, das von Sasha Waltz zur großen Gruppenchoreographie verbunden wird. Ziel des Education-Programms der Berliner Philharmoniker ist unter anderem im gemeinsamen Kreieren Jugendlichen unterschiedlicher sozialer und kultureller Herkunft und Begabung die Möglichkeit zu geben, einen Zugang zur Welt der Klänge, zu musikalischen Formen und tänzerischem Ausdruck zu finden.

gefaltet

The choreographic concert »gefaltet« is arranged at the invitation of the Mozarteum Salzburg and leads to a first collaboration between Sasha Waltz and Mark Andre. The world premiere opens the Mozartwoche 2012 at Salzburger Landestheater. Together with eight dancers and four soloists, the choreographer and the composer engage with interactions between classical and new music, sound, movement and silence. In electronic music, »convolution«, or here »folding«, refers to a procedure in which acoustic impulses produce acoustic responses. The bodies of the performers create impulses and resonances that compress the interstices and thresholds, voids and distance. Compositions by Wolfgang Amadeus Mozart together with scores by Mark Andre provide the basis for this musical experiment. The confrontation between the styles of music engenders new listening experiences. Fragments from Mozart's correspondence and situations described in his biography provide input for comic scenes. For the duration of Mozart's playful Gigue in G major, a dancer balances on one foot, her arms and raised leg swirling outwards, spiraling shapes into the air. Her upper body is unsettled by the asynchronous rotations of her limbs, while the supporting ankle is in constant search of balance. One of the tasks Sasha Waltz sets for herself and the dancers is to provide a counterpoint to musical virtuosity with a contemporary movement language.

Das choreographische Konzert »gefaltet« erfolgt auf Einladung des Mozarteum Salzburg und führt zu einer ersten Zusammenarbeit von Sasha Waltz mit Mark Andre. Das Werk wird zum Auftakt der Mozartwoche 2012 im Salzburger Landestheater uraufgeführt. Mit acht Tänzer:innen und vier Solist:innen imaginieren die Choreographin und der Komponist Wechselwirkungen zwischen klassischer und Neuer Musik, Klang, Bewegung und Stille. Eine »Faltung« bezeichnet in der elektronischen Musik ein Verfahren, das über akustische Impulse akustische Antworten erzeugt. Die Impulse und Resonanzen ihrer Körper im Raum verdichten Zwischenräume und Schwellen, Leere und Distanz. Das musikalische Experimentierfeld bilden Kompositionen von Wolfgang Amadeus Mozart im Zusammenhang mit Kompositionen von Mark Andre, die in der Gegenüberstellung zu neuen Hörerfahrungen anregen. Fragmente aus Mozarts Briefen und Situationen seiner Biographie geben humorvolle szenische Impulse. Für die Dauer von Mozarts spielerischer Gigue in G-Dur balanciert eine Tänzerin auf einem Fuß, die Arme und das erhobene Bein ausgestreckt in alle Richtungen wirbelnd, spiralförmige Zeichen in die Luft schraubend, der Oberkörper von den asynchronen Rotationen der Gliedmaßen in Unruhe gesetzt, das haltgebende Fußgelenk auf ständiger Suche nach dem Gleichgewicht. Der musikalischen Virtuosität ein Pendant in zeitgenössischer Bewegungssprache gegenüberzustellen, ist eine der Aufgaben, die Sasha Waltz für sich und die Tänzer:innen definiert.

In a letter from 1867, Johannes Brahms wrote to the conductor for the premiere of »A German Requiem«, Carl Reinthaler, that »I must admit, as far as the text is concerned, I'd be quite happy to leave out the word ›German‹ and replace it with ›human‹«. In conjunction with the series »Broadening the Scope of Choral Music«, the Rundfunkchor Berlin presents Johannes Brahms's »A German Requiem« (1867) in a new light. Under the title »human requiem«, Jochen Sandig and a team of artists from the dance company of Sasha Waltz & Guests develop a choreographed embodiment of Brahms's music by interlinking text, sound, bodies and space.

The choir is also part of the scene, the vocalists and audience move in the same way; there is no separation of stage and auditorium. The traditional concert experience dissolves. Brahms's composition is not a requiem mass, and the text does not follow Catholic liturgy. The requiem seeks to bring consolation to the living. Brahms wishes to make us aware of our mortality, the meaning of death and mourning, but also how to overcome this – it directs our focus towards life. In the community of singers and listeners, this message is transported as a space-filling and personal experience, as a »human requiem«. Jochen Sandig wishes »to create a first-hand experience, the expression of humility and unpretentiousness. We don't want anything grand. We want everyone, that is, the choir, the conductor and the audience to get involved«. Johannes Brahms's »German Requiem« is one of the favourite compositions in the Rundfunkchor Berlin's repertoire. The choir and Simon Halsey 2008 won a Grammy for the Best Choral Performance for the CD they recorded together with the Berliner Philharmoniker conducted by Sir Simon Rattle.

»Was den Text betrifft, will ich bekennen, dass ich recht gern das ›Deutsch‹ fortließe und einfach den ›Menschen‹ setzte.« (Johannes Brahms, 1867 in einem Brief an Carl Reinthaler, Dirigent der Uraufführung »Ein deutsches Requiem«.) Im Rahmen seiner Reihe »Broadening the Scope of Choral Music« präsentiert der Rundfunkchor Berlin Johannes Brahms' »Ein deutsches Requiem« (1867) in neuem Licht: Jochen Sandig und ein künstlerisches Team aus den Reihen der Compagnie Sasha Waltz & Guests entwickeln unter dem Titel »human requiem« eine choreographierte »Verkörperlichung« des Werkes, bei der Text, Klang, Körper und Raum miteinander in Beziehung gesetzt werden. Der Chor wird in den Raum inszeniert, Sänger:innen und Zuschauende gleichermaßen bewegt, die Trennung von Bühne und Zuschauerraum aufgehoben – das traditionelle Konzerterlebnis löst sich auf. Brahms' Requiem ist keine Totenmesse, der Text folgt daher nicht der katholischen Liturgie. Das Requiem will den Lebenden Trost spenden: Sein Thema ist die Vergegenwärtigung unserer Vergänglichkeit, die Bedeutung des Todes und der Trauer, aber auch deren Überwindung – der Blick bleibt dem Leben zugewandt. In der Gemeinschaft von Singenden und Hörenden wird diese Botschaft zu einem raumgreifenden und persönlichen Erlebnis – zu einem »human requiem«. Jochen Sandig geht es »um ein sehr unmittelbares Erlebnis, um eine Form von Demut und Bescheidenheit. Wir wollen nichts Großes. Wir wollen, dass sich die Menschen, und damit meine ich alle, den Chor, den Dirigenten, die Besucher:innen, darauf einlassen.« Brahms' »Ein deutsches Requiem« gehört zu den Herzstücken im Repertoire des Rundfunkchores Berlin. Für die gemeinsame CD-Einspielung mit den Berliner Philharmonikern unter Sir Simon Rattle gewannen der Chor und Simon Halsey 2008 einen Grammy für die »Beste Choreinspielung«.

Sasha Waltz becomes a **member of Akademie der Künste,** Berlin.

On the occasion of its 20th anniversary, Sasha Waltz & Guests is appointed **»Cultural Ambassador of the European Union«.**

REPERTOIRE

Continu Sibiu, Rome, Reggio Emilia, Rouen
gefaltet Berlin, Lisbon, Luxembourg, Oslo
human requiem Berlin
Impromptus Berlin
Jagden und Formen (Zustand 2008) Brussels
Körper Vilnius, Marseille, Helsinki
Roméo et Juliette Milan
Sacre Berlin, Saint Petersburg, Paris, Brussels
Travelogue I – Twenty to eight Berlin, Santiago de Chile, Geneva

KINDERTANZCOMPANY

The Wild Things *Gabriel Galindez Cruz* Berlin

GUEST PRODUCTIONS

Mahler Chamber Orchestra-Nacht *with Sasha Waltz & Guests a.o.* Berlin
Romances *Juan Kruz Diaz de Garaio Esnaola* Berlin

FILM

Sacre Igor Stravinsky, Sasha Waltz [41'] A film by Karsten Liske Production La Monnaie / De Munt 2013

Dialoge 2013 – Kolkata

↘pp. 57, 63, 160, 179, **293**

Jorasanko Rajbati, Kolkata
13 Jan
Direction/Choreography
Sasha Waltz
Dance/Choreography
Sasha Waltz & Guests
Liza Alpízar Aguilar
Jiří Bartovanec
Juan Kruz Diaz de Garaio Esnaola
Luc Dunberry
Hwanhee Hwang
Sergiu Matis
Virgis Puodziunas
Zaratiana Randrianantenaina
Orlando Rodriguez
Mata Sakka
Judith Sánchez Ruíz
Yael Schnell
Xuan Shi
László Sandig
Sophia Sandig
Dance/Choreography
Padmini Chettur
P. Akila
Preethi Athreya
Padmini Chettur
Aarabi Veeraraghavan
Music
Mahler Chamber Orchestra
Videoinstallation
Tapio Snellman
Light Design
Martin Hauk
Costume Design
Beate Borrmann
Margaretha Heller
Objects trouvées
Brad Hwang
Production
Sasha Waltz & Guests in the frame of »Deutschland – Indien 2011–2012«
Coproduction
Goethe-Institut/Max Mueller Bhavan Kolkata
Padmini Chettur
Mahler Chamber Orchestra

Sacre

↘pp. 20, 33, 60, 62, 83, 104, 107, 126, 153, **291**, 308

Mariinsky Theatre, Saint Petersburg (Mariinsky Ballet), 13 May
Théâtre Royal de La Monnaie, Brussels (Sasha Waltz & Guests), 13 Sep
Staatsoper im Schiller Theater, Berlin (Sasha Waltz & Guests), 26 Oct
Music
Igor Strawinsky
Direction/Choreography
Sasha Waltz
Musical Direction
Valery Gergiev (Saint Petersburg)
Frank Ollu (Brussels)
Daniel Barenboim (Berlin)
Costume Design
Bernd Skodzig
Stage Design
Pia Maier Schriever
Sasha Waltz
Light Design
Thilo Reuther
Dance Mariinsky Ballett
Alexander Belobodorov
Elena Chmil
Mikhail Degtyarev
Oleg Demchenko
Nadezhda Dvurechenskaya
Margarita Frolova
Yulia Kobzar
Yekaterina Kondaurova
Yevgeni Konovalov
Alexander Kusmin
Anna Lavrinenko
Maria Lebedeva
Nikita Lyashchenko
Trofim Malanin
Alexei Nedviga
Alexander Neff
Daria Pavlenko
Alexander Sergeyev
Maria Shevykova
Yuri Smekalov
Alisa Sodaleva
Irina Tolshilshchikova
Zlata Yalinich
Denis Zainetdinov
Valeria Zhuravleva
Boris Zhurilov
Dance/Choreography Sasha Waltz & Guests
Israel Aloni
Liza Alpízar Aguilar
Jiří Bartovanec
Davide Camplani
Maria Marta Colusi
Juan Kruz Diaz de Garaio Esnaola
Luc Dunberry
Edivaldo Ernesto
Delphine Gaborit
Peggy Grelat-Dupont
Hwanhee Hwang
Sergiu Matis
Michal Mualem
Virgis Puodziunas
Sasa Queliz
Zaratiana Randrianantenaina
Orlando Rodriguez
Mata Sakka
Judith Sánchez Ruíz
Yael Schnell
Corey Scott-Gilbert
Claudia de Serpa Soares
Xuan Shi
Joel Suárez Gómez
Antonios Vais
Niannian Zhou
László Sandig (child)
Sophia Sandig (child)
Production
Sasha Waltz & Guests
Coproduction
Mariinsky Theatre
Théâtre des Champs-Elysées
Théâtre Royal de la Monnaie
Staatsoper im Schiller Theater
Made in Radialsystem

L'Après-midi d'un faune

↘p. **326**

Staatsoper im Schiller Theater, Berlin – performed at the German premiere of »Sacre«
26 Oct
Music
Claude Debussy
Direction/Choreography
Sasha Waltz
Musical Direction
Daniel Barenboim
Costume Design/Stage Design
GIOM (Guillaume Bruère)
Light Design
Martin Hauk
Dance/Choreography
Jiří Bartovanec
Davide Camplani
Juan Kruz Diaz de Garaio Esnaola
Luc Dunberry
Hwanhee Hwang
Virgis Puodziunas
Sasa Queliz
Mata Sakka
Judith Sánchez Ruíz
Yael Schnell
Joel Suárez Gómez
Repetition
Jiří Bartovanec
Production
Sasha Waltz & Guests
Coproduction
Staatsoper im Schiller Theater, Berlin
Made in Radialsystem

Dialoge 2013 – Avignon

Opéra Grand Avignon, Festival d'Avignon
7 Jul
Dance/Choreography
Davide Camplani
Juan Kruz Diaz de Garaio Esnaola
Luc Dunberry
Nicola Mascia
Zaratiana Randrianantenaina
Yael Schnell
Claudia de Serpa Soares
Xuan Shi
Sasha Waltz
Niannian Zhou
László Sandig
Sophia Sandig
Paintings
GIOM (Guillaume Bruère)
Music
Burak Özdemir (Bassoon)
Light Design
Martin Hauk
Costume Design
Beate Borrmann
Production
Sasha Waltz & Guests

Sasha Waltz. Installations. Objects. Performances

↘pp. 38, 48, 49, 67, 68, 77, 82, 112, 115, 139, 153, 171, **292**

Exhibition at ZKM | Center for Art and Media Karlsruhe
27 Sep–2 Feb 2014
Curated by
Sasha Waltz
Peter Weibel
CEO Management
Christiane Riedel
Production Direction
Yoreme Waltz
Fabian Offert
Sibah Pomplun
Concept/Direction
Sasha Waltz
Dance/Performance Sasha Waltz & Guests
Davide Camplani
Lisa Densem
Juan Kruz Diaz de Garaio Esnaola
Luc Dunberry
Nicola Mascia
Sergiu Matis
Grayson Millwood
Michal Mualem
Virgis Puodziunas
Orlando Rodriguez
Yael Schnell
Claudia de Serpa Soares
Xuan Shi
Takako Suzuki
Laurie Young
Niannian Zhou
Dance/Performance external
Jadi Carboni
Claudia Catarzi
Emmanouela Dolianiti
Tina Gerken
Maya Gomez
Ageliki Gouvi
Sarah Herr
Claire Hurpeau
Sarah Jeannine Kiesecker
Katharina Klaßmann
Risa Kojima
Paula Kukawka
Margaux Marielle-Tréhoüart
Daniela Näger
Kyriaki Nasioula
Elik Niv
Andreas Rama
Alexandra Rogovska
Anna Romeo
Stephanie Roser
Kira Juliane Senkpiel
Wibke Storkan
Piotr Tomczyk
Lene Vollhardt
Tamara Weinzierl
Nadine Wermund
Repetition
Nicola Mascia
Music
Jonathan Bepler
Pascal Dusapin
Hans Peter Kuhn
Henry Purcell
Franz Schubert
Set Design
Thomas Schenk
Sasha Waltz
Construction
Hertzer & Partner
Technical Implementation Videoinstallations
Karl Wedemeyer
Sound
Lutz Nerger
Light Design
Martin Hauk
Hair/Make-up
Urte Kusserow
Costume Direction
Beate Borrmann
Technical Direction
Reinhard Wizisla
Assistance Technical Direction
Leonardo Bucalossi

A

B

2013

A **The archive room with scores, drafts and sketches at ZKM** B **Daniel Barenboim and Sasha Waltz during »Sacre« rehearsals in Berlin**

Sacre

A smooth pyramid of earth rises in the centre of the stage. Community members dance their way around this mound, this source of life, driven by the anticipation of the impending ritual. Light and agile, the women dance, attempting to evade every grasp and approach. They sidestep an invisible threat, the threat of tradition, which seeks to impose itself upon their bodies and assign them a role. The music cuts through the collective body mercilessly, like the long metallic tip of an oversized dagger of death, slowly, unnoticed, yet ever-present, approaching the ground. The rhythm forces the community into the ritual, binding people to the laws of time. The lashings of the rules they have created: the inevitable sacrifice must be sought. For the earth, for the spring, that is life. Someone must die for life to begin anew. The search for the »Chosen One« blankets the women with fear. Some are frozen in shock, while others break free from the thread of fate that seems to wrap around them: it is the man who chooses them, the wise man who appears to know which of the women must perform the sacrificial dance, who believes he understands how to make nature yield. The ritual scars the earth. It is plowed, trampled, grasped and dug up. Clods of earth scatter across the stage, torn apart by the violence of the community. Shaped by the active human, yet not controlled. Humanity is exposed to this ground; their lives hang upon it, and they know it. They cannot fully master it; they can only plow, sow and fertilise, but what will come is not their choice. Humanity can only hope that spring bears fruit and that the earth provides sustenance. As a rebellion against death, this hope leaves traces upon the earth.
One hundred years after Igor Stravinsky's »The Rite of Spring« was created, Sasha Waltz reinterprets this key work of dance and music history with the Mariinsky Ballet.

Eine glatte Pyramide aus Erde häuft sich in der Mitte der Bühne. Menschen einer Gemeinschaft bahnen sich tanzend ihre Wege um diesen Haufen, diesen Lebensquell, getrieben von der Vorahnung des bevorstehenden Ritus. Leicht und wendig tanzen die Frauen, wollen sich jedem Griff, jeder Annäherung entziehen. Sie weichen einer unsichtbaren Bedrohung aus, die Bedrohung der Tradition, die sich auf ihren Körpern erzählen will und ihnen eine Rolle zuschreibt. Unbarmherzig schneidet die Musik durch den kollektiven Körper wie die lange metallene Spitze eines überdimensionalen Todesdolches, der sich langsam, unbemerkt und zugleich allgegenwärtig dem Boden nähert. Der Rhythmus zwingt die Gemeinschaft zum Ritus, spannt den Menschen in die Gesetze der Zeit ein. Peitschenhiebe der Regeln, die sich die Menschen gegeben haben: Das unvermeidliche Opfer muss gesucht werden. Für die Erde, für den Frühling, der das Leben ist. Jemand muss sterben, damit das Leben wieder beginnt. Die Suche nach der »Auserwählten« überzieht die Frauen mit Angst. Manche in Schockstarre, manche reißen sich los vom Faden des Schicksals, der sich um sie zu wickeln scheint: Es ist der Mann, der sie auswählt, der weise Mann, der zu erkennen scheint, welche der Frauen den Opfertanz vollbringen muss, der zu wissen glaubt, wie sich die Natur verfügbar machen lässt. Der Ritus zerfurcht die Erde. Sie wird gepflügt, getreten, gegriffen, gegraben. Erdklumpen verteilen sich auf der Bühne, von der Gewalt der Gemeinschaft zerrissen. Vom tätigen Menschen bearbeitet und doch nicht beherrscht. Der Mensch ist diesem Boden ausgesetzt, sein Leben hängt an ihm und das weiß er. Beherrschen kann er nicht, nicht vollkommen, er kann nur pflügen, säen, düngen, aber was dann sein wird, ist nicht seine Wahl. Der Mensch kann nur hoffen, dass der Frühling Früchte trägt, dass die Erde Nahrung bringt. Dieses Hoffen, als Aufbegehren gegen den Tod, überzieht die Erde mit Spuren. Hundert Jahre nach der Entstehung von Igor Strawinskys »Le Sacre du Printemps« interpretiert Sasha Waltz mit dem Ballett des Mariinsky-Theaters dieses Schlüsselwerk der Tanz- und Musikgeschichte neu.

Sasha Waltz. Installations. Objects. Performances

The four-month exhibition at the ZKM | Center for Art and Media in Karlsruhe offers a comprehensive overview of Sasha Waltz's work for the first time. Invited by Peter Weibel, who coined the term »performative turn«, she intentionally places her works within the visual arts context, where she has continuously operated as a distinctly multidisciplinary artist. The exhibition is accompanied by a performance programme featuring Sasha Waltz & Guests, drawing around 60,000 visitors.

Objects, stage designs and videos are extracted from their original context within the pieces and presented as performatively framed objects throughout the museum's spaces. Frosted glass panels from »noBody« reveal body silhouettes that draw closer, gaining clarity as their hands touch the separating glass, momentarily becoming truly visible. Then, they retreat back into obscurity, disappearing. »Dissolution«. Circular rotors from »Medea« create a howling wind that drowns nearly any human sound. The massive black wall, the legendary stage set from »Körper«, stands in one of the airy halls. Many bodies slowly push into the vertically confined space of the »Vitrine«, multiplying as they squeeze against each other, press through the mass of limbs, and slide along the glass. On the wall's black exterior, various people's outlines are drawn in chalk.

Alongside the objects, various scenes are distributed throughout the spaces as animated sculptures. »Bodymountains« from »Körper« continually form silent group formations in different configurations, creating images of the anatomy of a collective organism. »Die Hängenden« figures from MAXXI also return: performers float in the air for extended periods. Gravity and weightlessness battle over their bodies, which change their postures in barely perceptible slowness. The opening and closing of the exhibition are accompanied by key excerpts from the works, such as the scene from the »Cloud« in »noBody«. For this exhibition, the archive room offers a glimpse into Sasha Waltz's notes, scores and drawings.

Die viermonatige Ausstellung des ZKM | Zentrum für Kunst und Medien Karlsruhe bietet erstmalig einen Überblick über Sasha Waltz' Schaffen. Auf Einladung von Peter Weibel, der den Begriff der »performativen Wende« prägte, setzt sie ihre Arbeiten mit großräumigen und umfassenden Präsentationen dabei bewusst in den Kontext der Bildenden Kunst, in dem sie sich als dezidiert multidisziplinäre Künstlerin immer schon bewegt. Die Ausstellung wird begleitet von einem Performance-Programm von Sasha Waltz & Guests. Rund 60.000 Menschen besuchen die Ausstellung.

Gegenstände, Bühnenbilder und Videos werden aus dem ursprünglichen Rahmen der Stücke herausgelöst und zeigen sich als performativ eingefasste Objekte in den Räumen des Museums. Milchglasscheiben aus »noBody«, hinter denen Körperschemen näher rücken, an Klarheit gewinnen, ihre Hände die trennende Scheibe berühren und sie nur für einen Moment wirklich erkennbar werden. Dann treten sie wieder zurück ins Unkenntliche, verschwinden. »Auflösung«. Kreisrunde Rotoren aus »Medea« erzeugen lärmenden Wind, gegen den kaum ein menschlicher Laut ankommen kann. Die riesige schwarze Wand, das legendäre Bühnenbild aus »Körper«, steht in einer der luftigen Hallen. In den vertikalen beengten Raum der »Vitrine« schieben sich langsam viele Körper. Es werden immer mehr. Sie quetschen sich übereinander, aneinander vorbei, drücken sich durch die Masse der Gliedmaßen, rutschen an der Scheibe entlang. An der schwarzen Außenseite der Wand werden mit Kreide die Umrisse verschiedener Menschen gezeichnet.

Neben den Objekten sind diverse Szenen als animierte Skulpturen in den Räumen verteilt. »Bodymountains« aus »Körper« sind immer wieder anders entstehende, stille Gruppenformationen. Sie erzeugen Bilder der Anatomie eines kollektiven Organismus. Ebenso kehren »Die Hängenden« aus dem MAXXI wieder: Performer:innen schweben für lange Perioden in der Luft. Schwerkraft und Schwerelosigkeit umkämpfen die Leiber, welche in kaum wahrnehmbarer Langsamkeit ihre Posturen verändern. Die Vernissage und Finissage der Ausstellung werden von zentralen Auszügen der Werke begleitet wie der Szene der »Cloud« aus »noBody«. Aus Anlass dieser Werkschau öffnet sich im Archivraum der Blick auf Notizen, Partituren und Zeichnungen von Sasha Waltz.

Dialoge 2013 – Kolkata

An old palace stands still in the noisy streets of Kolkata. The owning family moved into the small back section of the building decades ago; maintaining the main wing had become too costly. The furniture and belongings were left behind, locked away behind dozens of doors. Time stands still behind them. Everything rests untouched in the dark. Only dust slowly and quietly inhabits the rooms. In this »Dialogue« project, the old doors open, allowing the present to enter. Invited by the family and as part of the »Germany-India Year« in cooperation with the Goethe-Institut/Max Mueller Bhavan Kolkata, Sasha Waltz brings this villa in Kolkata's old quarter to life. Together with 13 dancers from Sasha Waltz & Guests, Indian choreographer Padmini Chettur and her ensemble, as well as four musicians from the Mahler Chamber Orchestra, Sasha Waltz animates the memories woven into the rooms. In the many spaces radiating from the two-story cloister, the audience discovers a variety of dance scenes. In the children's room, songs are sung. In the study of a desperate lawyer, crucial information disappears beneath piles of files. In the dining room, with its heavy black oak furniture, séances are held. However, the back hall is off-limits; only the ghosts dance there. Projections by Tapio Snellman reanimate the old portraits on the walls. Along the exterior facade of the palace, white shadows move along the house wall, merging with the bustling city life of the street. Chimes resonate from the corners of the palace. An old clockwork runs backwards. At the end of this surreal performance, all the dancers come together in the courtyard for a choreographic conclusion, surrounded by an audience looking down from the cloister.

Ein alter Palast steht still in den lärmenden Straßen Kalkuttas. Die besitzende Familie ist vor Jahrzehnten in den hinteren, kleinen Teil des Gebäudes gezogen. Zu teuer war die Instandhaltung des Haupttraktes. Die Möbel und Gegenstände wurden liegen gelassen und hinter Dutzenden Türen verschlossen. Hinter ihnen steht die Zeit still. Unberührt ruht alles da im Dunkel. Nur der Staub bewohnt langsam und leise die Räume. Die alten Türen öffnen sich in diesem »Dialoge«-Projekt und lassen die Gegenwart zum Besuch herein. Auf Einladung der Familie und im Rahmen des »Deutschland-Indien-Jahres« in Kooperation mit dem Goethe-Institut/Max Mueller Bhavan Kolkata erweckt Sasha Waltz diese Villa im alten Viertel Kalkuttas zum Leben. Zusammen mit 13 Tänzer:innen von Sasha Waltz & Guests, der indischen Choreographin Padmini Chettur, ihrem Ensemble sowie vier Musiker:innen vom Mahler Chamber Orchestra lässt Sasha Waltz die in den Zimmern gelagerten, eingesponnenen Erinnerungen lebendig werden. In den vielen Räumen, die vom zweigeschossigen Kreuzgang ausstrahlen, erschließen sich dem Publikum unterschiedlichste tänzerische Szenen. Im Kinderzimmer wird gesungen. Im Arbeitszimmer eines verzweifelten Anwalts verschwinden wichtige Informationen unter Bergen von Akten. Im Esszimmer mit schwarzen, schweren Eichenmöbeln werden Séancen gehalten. Der hintere Saal darf jedoch nicht betreten werden, dort tanzen nur die Geister. Projektionen von Tapio Snellman reanimieren die alten Porträts an den Wänden. An der Außenfassade des Palastes, in das verkehrsreiche Stadtleben der Straße hinein, wandern weiße Schatten an der Hauswand entlang. Glockenspiele erklingen aus Ecken des Palastes. Ein altes Uhrwerk läuft rückwärts. Zum Ende dieses surrealen Spiels kommen alle Tänzer:innen im Innenhof zum choreographischen Abschluss zusammen, umringt vom Publikum, das vom Kreuzgang herabschaut.

Sasha Waltz & Guests is awarded the **»George Tabori Preis«** of the Fonds Darstellende Künste.

»Travelogue I – Twenty to eight« is performed for the 150th time at the National Theatre Yangon in Myanmar (Birma).

The ZKM catalogue **»Sasha Waltz. Installations, Objects, Performances«** is published by Hatje Cantz.

REPERTOIRE

Dido & Aeneas Berlin, Sydney, Munich
gefaltet Lille
human requiem Rotterdam
Impromptus Berkeley
Jagden und Formen (Zustand 2008) Berlin
Matsukaze Lille
Métamorphoses Ferrara
Orfeo Amsterdam, Luxembourg
Sacre Berlin, Luxembourg, Moscow, Cologne
Tannhäuser Berlin
Travelogue I – Twenty to eight Berlin, Yangon
Zweiland Berlin

KINDERTANZCOMPANY

The Wild Things Berlin

GUEST PRODUCTIONS

4 Elemente – 4 Jahreszeiten Luxembourg, Donostia-San Sebastián
d'avant Antwerp
Dialogic Movement *Judith Sánchez Ruíz and Edivaldo Ernesto* Berlin
Mahler Chamber Orchestra-Nacht *with Sasha Waltz & Guests a.o.* Berlin

FILM

Sasha Waltz – A Portrait [72'+59' extra] A film by Brigitte Kramer Production nachtaktiv-film Distribution DVD, Arthaus Musik 2014
Tannhäuser Richard Wagner, Sasha Waltz [192'] TV-Direction Vincent Bataillon Producer François Duplat Production Staatsoper im Schiller Theater, Bel Air Media Distribution Naxos Distribution

Tannhäuser
↘pp. 59, 182, 192, **295**

Richard Wagner »Tannhäuser und der Sängerkrieg auf Wartburg«
Staatsoper im Schiller Theater, Berlin
12 Apr
Musical Direction
Daniel Barenboim
Direction/Choreography
Sasha Waltz
Stage Design
Pia Maier Schriever
Sasha Waltz
Costume Design
Bernd Skodzig
Light Design
David Finn
Dramaturgy
Jens Schroth
Jochen Sandig
Choir Direction
Martin Wright
Dance/Choreography
Liza Alpízar Aguilar
Davide Camplani
Gabriel Galindez Cruz
Peggy Grelat-Dupont
Hwanhee Hwang
Stephan Laks
Maureen López Lembo
Margaux Marielle-Tréhoüart
Nicola Mascia
Virgis Puodziunas
Kevin Quinaou
Orlando Rodriguez
Mata Sakka
Judith Sánchez Ruíz
Claudia de Serpa Soares
Joel Suárez Gómez
Antonios Vais
Soloists
Peter Seiffert (Tannhäuser)
Ann Petersen (Elisabeth)
Peter Mattei (Wolfram von Eschenbach)
Marina Prudenskaya (Venus)
René Pape (Landgraf Hermann)
Peter Sonn
Tobias Schnabel
Jürgen Sacher
Jan Martinik
Sonia Grané
Soloists Choir
Anna Charim
Konstanze Löwe
Julia Mencke
Hannah Wighardt
Choir
Staatsopernchor Berlin
Orchestra
Staatskapelle Berlin
Assistance Direction
Tristan Braun
Reyna Burns
Repetition
Juan Kruz Diaz de Garaio Esnaola
Luc Dunberry
Production
Staatsoper Unter den Linden, Berlin

Orfeo
↘pp. 90, 161, 181, 205, 206, **296**

Claudio Monteverdi »L'Orfeo«
Dutch National Opera & Ballet, Amsterdam
3 Sep
Direction/Choreography
Sasha Waltz
Libretto
Alessandro Striggio
Musical Direction
Pablo Heras-Casado
Stage Design
Alexander Schwarz
Costume Design
Beate Bormann (2014)
Bernd Skodzig (2022)
Light Design
Martin Hauk
Video
Tapio Snellman
Dance/Choreography
Davide Camplani
Juan Kruz Diaz de Garaio Esnaola
Luc Dunberry
Hwanhee Hwang
Michal Mualem
Virgis Puodziunas
Sasa Queliz
Zaratiana Randrianantenaina
Orlando Rodriguez
Judith Sánchez Ruíz
Yael Schnell
Joel Suárez Gómez
Soloists
Georg Nigl (Orfeo)
Anna Lucia Richter (Euridice/ La Musica)
Charlotte Hellekant (Messaggiera/La Speranza)
Douglas Williams (Caronte)
Konstantin Wolff (Plutone)
Luciana Mancini (Proserpina)
Soloists Choir
Julián Millán (Apollo/Eco/ Pastore 4)
Cécile Kempenaers (Ninfa/ Pastore 1)
Kaspar Kröner (Pastore 2/ Spirito)
Kevin Skelton (Pastore 3/ Spirito)
Hans Wijers (Pastore 5/Spirito)
Choir
Vocalconsort Berlin
Orchestra
Freiburger BarockConsort
Production
Sasha Waltz & Guests
Made in Radialsystem
Coproduction
Dutch National Opera & Ballet, Amsterdam
Les Théâtres de la Ville de Luxembourg
Bergen International Festival
Opéra de Lille

2014

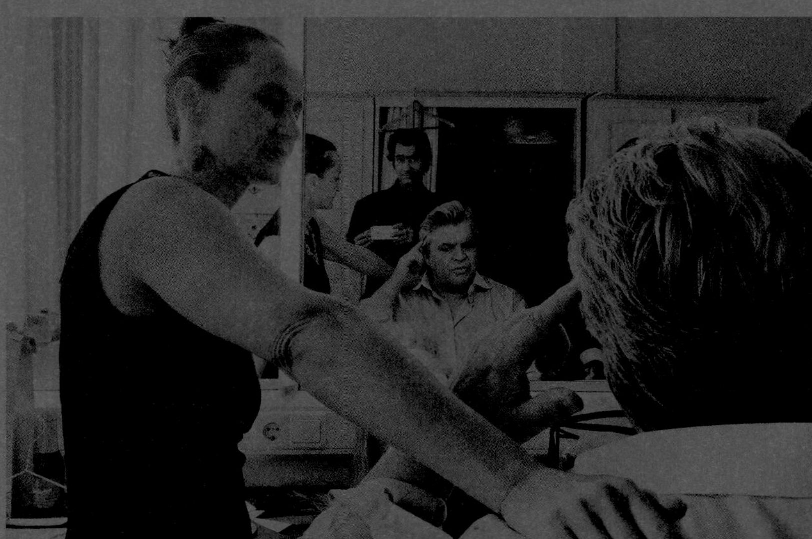

A **»Tannhäuser«, dressing room: Sasha Waltz, Jochen Sandig, Peter Seiffert**

Tannhäuser

A large, arched recess in the white backdrop of the stage. An opening in the ceiling of a baroque church? The pupil of one seeking knowledge? From the hole of this horizontally tilted dome, half-naked bodies glide and slide over the sensual curvature of steep slopes. The nymphs caress each other, with Tannhäuser in their midst. In their playful interactions, they repeatedly approach the front edge of the arch with daring proximity. The play with Eros is also a game on the edge of an abyss. Tannhäuser grows weary of the pleasures of sensual love and yearns for true love, which he hopes to find with Elisabeth. Venus attempts to persuade him to stay, but he leaves the world of the nymphs and seeks his fortune by competing in the song festival to win Elisabeth's hand – resulting in a tragic ending.
In 2014, Sasha Waltz was invited by the artistic direction of the Staatsoper im Schiller Theater, Berlin, to stage Richard Wagner's opera »Tannhäuser and the Minnesängers' Contest at Wartburg«. The musical direction is led by Daniel Barenboim, the renowned pianist, West-Eastern Divan Orchestra's founder, and Staatskapelle Berlin's longstanding General Music Director (1992–2023). Sasha Waltz connects Tannhäuser's suppression of bodily love as a sinner to the hostility towards pleasure inherent in fascist ideology, which was repressed in its ongoing impact in post-war Germany. Using costumes, the story is set in the 1950s, linking Tannhäuser's banishment and the social punishment for his forbidden physicality to the collective repression of that era. The society, dressed in cheerful colours, appears orderly and outwardly well-groomed, masking the abysses that open up within.

Eine große, gewölbte Vertiefung in der weißen Rückseite der Bühne. Eine Öffnung an der Decke einer barocken Kirche? Die Pupille eines nach Erkenntnis Suchenden? Aus dem Loch dieser in die Horizontale gekippten Kuppel gleiten halb nackte Körper und rutschen über die lustvolle Wölbung steiler Schrägen. Die Nymphen liebkosen sich und Tannhäuser in ihrer Mitte. Und kommen dabei in ihren Spielen immer wieder der vorderen Kante der Wölbung riskant nahe. Das Spiel mit Eros ist auch ein Spiel am Abgrund. Tannhäuser wird des Genusses der sinnlichen Liebe überdrüssig und sehnt sich nach der wahren Liebe, die er mit Elisabeth zu finden hofft. Venus versucht, ihn zum Bleiben zu überreden, doch er verlässt die Welt der Nymphen und versucht sein Glück, indem er beim Wettbewerb des Sängerfests die Hand von Elisabeth zu gewinnen sucht – mit tragischem Ende.
Im Jahr 2014 wird Sasha Waltz von der künstlerischen Leitung der Staatsoper im Schiller Theater, Berlin, eingeladen, Richard Wagners Oper »Tannhäuser und der Sängerkrieg auf Wartburg« zu inszenieren. Die musikalische Leitung hat Daniel Barenboim, der bekannte Pianist, Gründer des West-Eastern Divan Orchestra und langjährige Generalmusikdirektor der Staatskapelle Berlin (1992–2023). Sasha Waltz stellt aus der Suppression der Liebe des Leibes, die Tannhäuser als Sünder entgegentritt, eine Beziehung zur Lustfeindlichkeit der faschistischen Ideologie her, die in ihrem Fortwirken im Nachkriegsdeutschland verdrängt wurde. Mithilfe des Kostüms wird die Geschichte in die 1950er Jahre versetzt und somit Tannhäusers Verbannung und die soziale Strafe für seine verbotene Körperlichkeit mit der kollektiven Verdrängung dieser Zeit verknüpft. Die Gesellschaft, gekleidet in fröhlichen Farben, wirkt nach außen ordentlich und gepflegt und überdeckt die Abgründe, die sich im Innern auftun.

Orfeo

The frescoes of the Palazzo Schifanoia in Ferrara inspire Sasha Waltz to engage with the Orpheus myth. Once again, the choir, soloists and dance ensemble form a dynamic musical unit. The orchestra is also placed on both sides of the stage at the same level.
The stage design by Alexander Schwarz from David Chipperfield Architects, Berlin, begins as a baroque theatre and transforms into the gateway to the underworld: a freestanding wooden plate descends silently from above, resting like an island in shallow water. In the spirit of Claudio Monteverdi, Sasha Waltz largely forgoes props, instead blending a wealth of flowers, shrubs, fruits and vegetables with dance movements, referencing Arcimboldo's portraits. The connection to nature from the Orpheus mythology is highlighted as a central theme: the unstoppable cycle of life and death, the interplay between growth and decay, is expressed in the arrangement between the abducted Proserpina and Pluto. Once a year, she is permitted to visit the upper world, where she, as the goddess of fertility, can ensure humanity's survival before returning to the underworld. This fate, this arrangement with Pluto – to remain on Earth only for a limited time – is reaffirmed after Orpheus's failed attempt to bring Euridice back from the dead. After Euridice dies a violent death during her wedding to Orpheus, he, in his despair, decides to rescue her from the underworld. Through his singing, he puts Charon, the ferryman, to sleep and crosses into the realm of the dead with his boat. There, he asks Pluto to release Euridice. Proserpina appeals to Pluto, her husband, to grant Orpheus's request. Pluto agrees, but with the condition that Orpheus must not look back at Euridice on the way to the upper world. The couple begins their journey back, but a sudden thunderclap causes Orpheus to turn in fear to look at Euridice, and he loses her forever.

Die Fresken des Palazzo Schifanoia in Ferrara inspirieren Sasha Waltz, sich mit dem Orpheus-Mythos auseinanderzusetzen. Erneut bilden Chor, Solist:innen und Tanzensemble eine bewegt-musikalische Einheit. Auch das Orchester wird auf beiden Seiten der Bühne auf gleicher Ebene platziert.
Das Bühnenbild von Alexander Schwarz von David Chipperfield Architects beginnt als barockes Theater und transformiert sich in das Tor zur Unterwelt: Eine frei schwebende Holzplatte senkt sich in der Stille von oben herab und legt sich als Insel in flaches Wasser. Wie zu Zeiten Claudio Monteverdis verzichtet Sasha Waltz weitestgehend auf Requisiten, vermengt gleichwohl eine Fülle an Blumen, Sträuchern, Früchten und Gemüse mit den Bewegungen des Tanzes, in Referenz zu Arcimboldos Portraits. Der Naturbezug aus der Orpheus-Mythologie wird hier als zentrales Thema hervorgehoben: Der unbezwingliche Kreislauf aus Leben und Sterben, dem Wechsel zwischen Wachstum und Zerfall, drückt sich in der Abmachung zwischen der entführten Proserpina und Pluto aus. Ihr ist einmal im Jahr der Besuch der Oberwelt gestattet, wo sie als Fruchtbarkeitsgöttin das Überleben der Menschen sichern kann, bevor sie wieder in die Unterwelt zurückkehren muss. Dieses Schicksal, diese Abmachung mit Pluto, als Menschen nur begrenzte Zeit auf der Erde zu weilen, bestätigt sich auch nach Orfeos gescheitertem Versuch, Euridice von den Toten zurückzuholen. Denn nachdem Euridice während ihrer Vermählung mit Orfeo eines gewaltvollen Todes stirbt, beschließt Orfeo in seiner Verzweiflung, sie aus der Unterwelt zu befreien. Durch seinen Gesang schläfert er Caronte den Fährmann ein und setzt mit dessen Boot über ins Totenreich. Dort bittet er Pluto, Euridice freizugeben. Proserpina appelliert an Pluto, ihren Mann, der Bitte Orfeos nachzukommen. Pluto willigt ein, jedoch mit der Forderung an Orfeo, dass er sich auf dem Weg in die Oberwelt nicht nach Euridice umdrehen darf. Das Paar macht sich auf den Rückweg, doch ein plötzlicher Donner lässt Orfeo aus Angst nach Euridice blicken, und er verliert sie so für immer.

Fellowship of Sasha Waltz at **Villa Aurora/Thomas Mann House** in Los Angeles.

German Premiere of **»Roméo et Juliette«** with dancers of Sasha Waltz & Guests at Deutsche Oper Berlin.

REPERTOIRE

Continu St. Pölten, New York
human requiem Berlin, Paris
Impromptus Berlin, Brussels, Prague, Turin
Körper Clermont-Ferrand, Vienna
Matsukaze Berlin
Orfeo Berlin, Bergen, Baden-Baden
Roméo et Juliette Berlin
Sacre London
Tannhäuser Berlin
Travelogue I – Twenty to eight Plzeň, Tbilisi
Zweiland Berlin, Hanoi

KINDERTANZCOMPANY

Showing *Davide Camplani, Gabriel Galindez Cruz* Berlin
Feuerblume *Gabriel Galindez Cruz* Berlin, invited to the »Tanztreffen der Jugend«, the 10th anniversary of TanzZeit e.V. at Podewil and the cultural reception of the Social Democrats

GUEST PRODUCTIONS

40.000 centimetri quadrati *Claudia Catarzi* Berlin
d'avant London
precarity positions *Todd McQuade* Berlin
Radiale Nacht *Teodor Currentzis, MusicAeterna, Sasha Waltz & Guests* Berlin

A

B

Open Studio

On the initiative of Sasha Waltz together with the performer Rosabel Huguet, the project »Open Studio« is initiated. Sasha Waltz & Guests has opened the dance company's studio on the fifth floor of the Radialsystem in Berlin almost every month since January 2015 to artists of all disciplines for free improvisation. Experienced artists and new-comers from Berlin and outside, from the fields of dance, music, song, photography, video, visual arts and philosophy are invited and can join in and flexibly participate in a collective, open improvisation process. »Open Studio« is a space to meet – it offers a liberated framework for lived plurality and the exchange of various forms of artistic knowledge, joint research, brainstorming and the opening up of new perspectives.

C

2015

A+B **»Open Studio«** C **»Roméo et Juliette« rehearsals at Studio A, Radialsystem, Berlin**

Kinder- und Jugendtanzcompany Sasha Waltz & Guests

In 2004, at the initiative of »TanzZeit«, Sasha Waltz teaches dance once a week in a primary school. She continues that within her own company with a regular dance course for children, allowing them to train their movements and hone their talents. A playful way of practising movement and dance is central to the work of the Kinder- und Jugendtanzcompany, which grows year by year. Guided by dancers from Sasha Waltz & Guests – for many years significantly by Davide Camplani and Gabriel Galindez Cruz – the children and adolescents, now grouped into four age categories, discover themselves and each other through movement and develop their own stage pieces. Since 2010, the young dancers have also had the opportunity to show their resulting creations to the public under professional conditions at annual shows at Radialsystem. In 2015, the piece »Feuerblume« was invited to the 2nd »Tanztreffen der Jugend« festival at the Haus der Berliner Festspiele in Berlin, and for a guest performance in Oslo in 2016.

Auf Initiative von »TanzZeit« unterrichtet Sasha Waltz 2004 einmal wöchentlich Tanz in einer Grundschule. Dies führt sie innerhalb ihrer Compagnie weiter in einem regelmäßigen Tanzkurs für Kinder, die ihre Bewegungen schulen und ihre Talente weiter ausprägen können. Ein spielerischer Zugang zu Bewegung und Tanz ist Mittelpunkt der Arbeit der jährlich wachsenden Kinder- und Jugendtanzcompany. Angeleitet durch Tänzer:innen von Sasha Waltz & Guests – viele Jahre maßgeblich durch Davide Camplani und Gabriel Galindez Cruz –, entdecken die Kinder und Jugendlichen inzwischen in vier Altersgruppen sich selbst und einander in der Bewegung und erarbeiten eigene Stücke. Seit 2010 haben die jungen Tänzer:innen zudem in jährlichen Showings im Radialsystem die Möglichkeit, vor Publikum und unter professionellen Bedingungen die entstandenen Kreationen zu zeigen. 2015 wird das Stück »Feuerblume« zum 2. Tanztreffen der Jugend ins Haus der Berliner Festspiele, Berlin, und 2016 auf ein Gastspiel nach Oslo eingeladen.

2016

Sasha Waltz and Johannes Öhman are appointed **co-directors of Staatsballett Berlin.**

Dutch National Opera & Ballet Amsterdam adds **»Roméo et Juliette«** to its repertoire.

The Royal Swedish Ballet in Stockholm adds **»Körper«** to its repertoire.

REPERTOIRE

Allee der Kosmonauten Berlin
Continu Berlin
Dido & Aeneas Berlin, Buenos Aires, Rome
Fantasie New York
human requiem Hong Kong, Brussels, Athens, Berlin, New York
Körper Berlin, Stockholm, Luxembourg
Matsukaze Hong Kong
Orfeo Lille
Roméo et Juliette Berlin, Amsterdam
Sacre Berlin, Madrid, Donostia-San Sebastián, Pamplona, Hanover, Cardiff, St. Pölten
Travelogue I – Twenty to eight Berlin, Freiburg

KINDERTANZCOMPANY

Feuerblume is invited to the »International Conference of Teaching Artists« in Oslo
Genau so, aber anders *Gabriel Galindez Cruz* Berlin
Invités sur la terre *Davide Camplani* Berlin
Märchensonaten *Gabriel Galindez Cruz* Berlin

GUEST PRODUCTIONS

10 Jahre Radialsystem *with Sasha Waltz & Guests a.o.* Berlin
Amal *Medhat Aldaabal, Davide Camplani* Berlin
Un/Ruhe, Freispiel *Junge Deutsche Philharmonie, Jochen Sandig* Berlin

A

B

Zuhören #1: Continu und Gespräche
↘p. **301**

Radialsystem, Berlin
3–9 Feb
Concept/Artistic Direction
Sasha Waltz
Programme/Coordination
Emilie Guérin
Anja Schmalfuß
Continu ↘2010
Interventions, Conversations with
Aeham Ahmad
Mohammad Al Attar
Keti Dolidze
Carolin Emcke
Felix Gebauer
Nino Haratischwili
Tahera Hashemi
Salomé Jaschi
Herlinde Koelbl
Yasmine Nayef Merei
MICT Media in Cooperation and Transition
Stephan Talneau
Karim Wasfi
Lydia Ziemke
Moderation
Georg Diez
Christian Mihr
Jutta Schwengsbier
Live Music
Aeham Ahmad
Iddo Bar-Shai
Pharoah Chromium
Dorit Chrysler
Daniela Gubatz
Ipek Ipekçioğlu
Roni JOJO
Petra Nachtmanova
Orphe
Burak Özdemir
Acid Pauli
Mohammad Reza Mortazavi
Farhan Sabbagh
Cymin Samawatie
Gerhard Stäbler & Kunsu Shim
Biliana Voutchkova
Karim Wasfi
Film
»Not Who We Are« by Carol Mansour
Food/Multaqa-Meeting Place
Sharehaus Refugio
Installations Saal
Thomas Schenk
Production
Sasha Waltz & Guests

Zuhören #2: Improvisationen und Gespräche

Radialsystem, Berlin
18–19 Jun
Concept/Artistic Direction
Sasha Waltz
Dramaturgy/Moderation Talks
Yasmine Nayef Merei
Programme/Coordination
Emilie Guérin
Anja Schmalfuß
Improvisation Dance and Music
Edivaldo Ernesto
Hyaejin Lee
Burak Özdemir
Zaratiana Randrianantenaina
Michael Rauter
Aladino Rivera Blanca
Bob Rutman
László Sandig
Sophia Sandig
Robyn Schulkowsky
Claudia de Serpa Soares
Grégoire Simon
Sasha Waltz
Stage Design
Thomas Schenk
Pia Maier Schriever
Sasha Waltz
Showing AMAL
Medhat Aldaabal
Moufak Aldoabl
Firas Almassre
Davide Camplani
Nima Thiem
Fadi Waked
Conversations with
Duha Ashour
Emil Brechenmacher
Mazen Darwish
Deborah Feldmann
Daniel Gerlach
Ghatfan Ghanoum
Gordian Grüntuch
Majdoleen Hassan
Mohammad Mallak
Amer Matar
Mekonnen Mesghena
Marcel Mettelsiefen
Lara Quack
Christian Ruzicska
László Sandig
Jonathan Stolze
Masih Tajzai
Luna Watfa
Presentations Initiatives
Embassy of Arcadia/Peter Kees
Stone by Stone/Vilelmini Vilma Andrioti
The International Cities of Refuge Network (ICORN)/Helge Lunde
Concerts
Avi & Ahmed
Ipek Ipekçioğlu
Orphe
Petra Nachtmanova und Hogir Göregen
Filmprogramme Syria Mobile Film Festival
»4th floor«
»Barbed Wire«
»Buzkashi Boys«
»Haunted«
»I am here«
»ISIL in Aleppo«
»Moon in the Skype«
»Not Who We Are«
»one precious thing«
»Watani – my homeland«
Audiovisual Installations
»Freisein in the Labyrinth«
»Tierra Sin Males«
Hosts
Faces of Change & Chance
Gladt e.V.
Hotel Utopia Prinzip Heimat e.V.
»I am here«
Kiron University
Kreuzberg hilft
Terre de Femmes »Connect«
Welcome Dinner
Food/Bar
»Holzmarkt«
»Levante Gourmet Catering«
Installations Saal
Brad Hwang
Sasha Waltz
Production
Sasha Waltz & Guests

A **»Zuhören #1« Carolin Emcke and Yasmine Nayef Merei in conversation** B **»Zuhören #1« Multaqa – eating and exchanging**

Sasha Waltz & Guests has been working with people from all continents for over 20 years and has gained important intercultural experience on tours around the world. Against the background of the refugee crisis in 2015 and shaped by her personal encounter with the journalist Yasmine Nayef Merei from Syria, whom she met during a residency at the Villa Aurora, Sasha Waltz takes the shows of »Continu« in spring 2016 as an opportunity to give guests from the Middle East, the Mediterranean and Germany a platform for the first time to discuss urgent socio-political issues, and to design alternative visions for the future: in presentations, artistic interventions and open discussions on topics like »Women in Crisis Situations in the Middle East« and on opportunities for civic engagement in the arts, the media and everyday life. What are our artistic strategies to exert political influence? »Zuhören #1: Continu und Gespräche« gives rise to the event format »Zuhören – Dritter Raum für Kunst und Politik« which, in the years that follow, regularly stimulates an interdisciplinary exchange on pressing issues of our time, and brings together artistic and political perspectives.

Sasha Waltz & Guests arbeitet seit über zwanzig Jahren mit Menschen aus allen Kontinenten und sammelt auf weltweiten Tourneen wichtige interkulturelle Erfahrungen. Vor dem Hintergrund der Flüchtlingskrise 2015 und geprägt von der persönlichen Begegnung mit der Journalistin Yasmine Nayef Merei aus Syrien, die sie in der Villa Aurora im Rahmen einer Residenz kennengelernt hat, nimmt Sasha Waltz im Frühjahr 2016 die Vorstellungen von »Continu« zum Anlass, Gästen aus dem Nahen Osten, dem Mittelmeerraum und Deutschland erstmals eine Plattform zu geben, um dringende gesellschaftspolitische Fragen zu diskutieren und alternative Zukunftsvisionen zu entwerfen: in Präsentationen, künstlerischen Interventionen und offenen Gesprächen unter anderem zum Thema »Frauen in Krisensituationen im Nahen Osten« sowie zu Möglichkeiten zivilgesellschaftlichen Engagements in den Künsten, den Medien und im täglichen Leben. Was sind unsere künstlerischen Strategien, um politisch Einfluss zu nehmen? Aus »Zuhören #1: Continu und Gespräche« geht das Format »Zuhören – Dritter Raum für Kunst und Politik« hervor, das auch in den folgenden Jahren regelmäßig den interdisziplinären Austausch zu drängenden Fragen unserer Zeit sowie die Begegnung von künstlerischen und politischen Perspektiven anregt.

2017

Sasha Waltz takes over the honorary sponsorship of the festival **»RADIKAL – Contemporary Dance from Brussels«** at Radialsystem, Berlin.

REPERTOIRE

Allee der Kosmonauten Berlin, Weimar
Continu Tbilisi
human requiem Berlin
Körper Berlin
Kreatur Berlin, Rome, Barcelona, Lisbon
Matsukaze Brussels, Warsaw
Sacre Berlin
Tannhäuser Berlin
Women Berlin

KINDERTANZCOMPANY

Dance talk *Davide Camplani* Berlin
Genau so, aber anders Berlin
Märchensonate Berlin

GUEST PRODUCTIONS

Amal Berlin, Karlsruhe
From A to Z *Jeremy Nelson, Luis Lara Malvacias* Berlin
Nobody's Land & Fleeting Feathers *Blenard Azizaj, Maya Gomez* Berlin
RADIKAL – Contemporary Dance from Brussels Berlin
Soundwalk Collective Record Release Party, Berlin
The Trip *Charlotte Zerbey, Alessandro Certini* Berlin

FILM

Figure Humaine Sasha Waltz [59'] Direction Marcus Richardt Production Elbphilharmonie, Hamburg, in coproduction with Sasha Waltz & Guests Broadcaster ZDF/Arte
Kreatur Sasha Waltz [90'] Direction Bettina Borgfeld, Jochen Sandig Production Sasha Waltz & Guests in coproduction with Festspielhaus St. Pölten, Les Théâtres de la Ville de Luxembourg and Opéra de Dijon Broadcaster ZDF/Arte

A

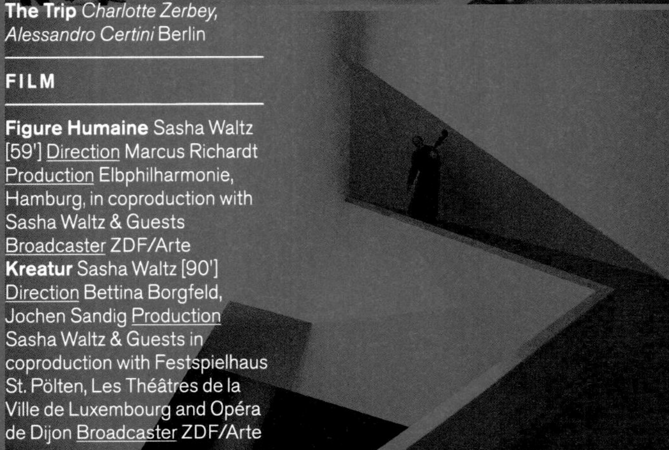
B

C

D

Figure Humaine
↘pp. 40, 114, 154, 164, 169, **303**

Elbphilharmonie, Hamburg
1 Jan
Concept/Choreography
Sasha Waltz
Costume Design
Margaretha Heller
Federico Polucci
Light Design
Martin Hauk
Dramaturgy
Jochen Sandig
Musical Concept (in collaboration with the musicians)
Michael Rauter
Sasha Waltz
Dance/Choreography
Liza Alpízar Aguilar
Blenard Azizaj
Jiří Bartovanec
Davide Camplani
Claudia Catarzi
Clémentine Deluy
Davide Di Pretoro
Juan Kruz Diaz de Garaio Esnaola
Iyar El-Ezra
Edivaldo Ernesto
Peggy Grelat-Dupont
Hwanhee Hwang
Lorena Justribó Manion
Gyung Moo Kim
Hyajin Lee
Annapaola Leso
Anthony Lomuljo
Maureen López Lembo
Margaux Marielle-Tréhoüart
Nicola Mascia
Sergiu Matis
Thusnelda Mercy
Michal Mualem
Virgis Puodziunas
Sasa Queliz
Zaratiana Randrianantenaina
Kristian Refslund
Aladino Rivera Blanca
Orlando Rodriguez
Corey Scott-Gilbert
Claudia de Serpa Soares
Gil Shachar
Joel Suárez Gómez
Takako Suzuki
Stylianos Tsatsos
Idan Yoav
Repetition
Antonio Ruz
Choir
Vocalconsort Berlin
Choir Direction
Nicolas Fink
Soloists
Luciana Mancini (Mezzo-soprano)
Carolin Widmann (Violin)
Annette Walther (Violin)
Pauline Sachse (Viola)
Michael Rauter (Violoncello)
Gunārs Upatnieks (Double Bass)
Sava Stoianov (Trumpet)
Uwe Dierksen (Trombone)
Krisztián Palágyi (Accordion)
Alexej Gerassimez (Percussion)
Production
Elbphilharmonie, Hamburg
Coproduction
Sasha Waltz & Guests
Made in Radialsystem
Funded by
Förderkreis Elbphilharmonie + Laeiszhalle e.V.

Kreatur
↘pp. 32, 33, 45, 66, 71, 81, 86, 90, 92, 100, 102, 104, 109, 140, 141, 148, 149, 160, 165, 178, 200, 201, **305**

Radialsystem, Berlin
9 Jun
Direction/Choreography
Sasha Waltz
Costume Design
Iris van Herpen
Music
Soundwalk Collective
Light Design
Urs Schönebaum
Dramaturgy
Jochen Sandig
Dance/Choreography
Liza Alpízar Aguilar
Jiří Bartovanec
Davide Camplani
Clémentine Deluy
Peggy Grelat-Dupont
Hwanhee Hwang
Annapaola Leso
Nicola Mascia
Thusnelda Mercy
Virgis Puodziunas
Zaratiana Randrianantenaina
Yael Schnell
Corey Scott-Gilbert
Claudia de Serpa Soares
Repetition
Davide Di Pretoro
Production
Sasha Waltz & Guests
Coproduction
Festspielhaus St. Pölten
Les Théatres de la Ville de Luxembourg
Opéra de Dijon
Made in Radialsystem

Women
↘pp. 46, 47, 57, 61, 138, 144, **304**

St. Elisabeth-Kirche, Berlin
30 Aug
Direction/Choreography
Sasha Waltz
Music
Soundwalk Collective
Stage Design
Sasha Waltz
Thomas Schenk
Costume Design
Christine Birkle
Light Design
Martin Hauk
Dramaturgy
Jochen Sandig
Dance/Performance
Liza Alpízar Aguilar
Claudia Catarzi
Maria Marta Colusi
Clémentine Deluy
Lisa Densem
Lorena Justribó Manion
Florencia Lamarca
Annapaola Leso
Maureen López Lembo
Margaux Marielle-Tréhoüart
Thusnelda Mercy
Michal Mualem
Sasa Queliz
Zaratiana Randrianantenaina
Yael Schnell
Claudia de Serpa Soares
Wibke Storkan
Takako Suzuki
Charlotte Zerbey
Repetition
Michal Mualem
Production
Sasha Waltz & Guests
Made in Radialsystem
Cooperation
Kultur Büro Elisabeth
Presented by Tanz im August – Internationales Festival Berlin
Funded by
Schering Stiftung

Zuhören #3: The Art of Resistance & Empowerment of Communities

Radialsystem, Berlin
24–26 Nov
Concept/Artistic Direction
Sasha Waltz
Programme Curation
Emilie Guérin
Anja Schmalfuß
Excerpt from »Women«
↘above
Improvisation Dance and Music
Medhat Aldaabal
Moufak Aldoabl
Davide Camplani
Juan Kruz Diaz de Garaio Esnaola
Alexej Gerassimez (Percussion)
Modjgan Hashemian
Hwanhee Hwang
Elik Niv
Yael Schnell
Sasha Waltz
Dabke Community Dancing
AMAL Project
Conversations with
Gina Belafonte
Modjgan Hashemian
Gal Hurvitz
Hiwa K
Muna Khalidi
Rick Lowe
Carol Mansour
Itay Mautner
Elik Niv
Lia Rodrigues
Izhak Schnell
Alya Sebti
Floris White Bull
Michal Yaakobi
Moderation
Andreas Görgen
Anja Schmalfuß
Presentations Initiatives
»Etty Hillesum Youth Theatre«
Ines Kappert for »Weiter Schreiben« and »Baynetna – Between us – Deutsch-arabische Bibliothek«
»Mekudeshet«
»The Poetry Project« presentation by Susanne Koelbl and performance with the Teens of Kindertanzcompany of Sasha Waltz & Guests (concept and choreography: Davide Camplani and Gabriel Galindez Cruz)
Yasmine Nayef Merei for »Women for Common Spaces«
»Women Wage Peace«
Concerts
Boulanger Trio
DJ Parole Emil!
Ibrahim Keivo
Jamila & The Other Heroes
Karmatürji – Anadolu Electronics
Matar
Filmprogramme
»Awake. A Dream From Standing Rock« by Josh Fox, James Spirone and Myron Dewey with Floris White Bull (co author)
»Sing Your Song« by Susanne Rosteck with Harry Belafonte
»Stitching Palestine« by Carol Mansour and Muna Khalidi
Audiovisual Installations
Hiwa K: »The Bell Project«
»Pre-Image (Blind as the mother tongue)«
VR-360° Filminstallation by Sasha Waltz & Guests with INVR Space
Installations Saal
Thomas Schenk
Sasha Waltz
Food/Bar
»The Space Berlin«
Production
Sasha Waltz & Guests
Supported by
Robert Bosch Stiftung

A–D **»Figure Humaine«**

At the beginning of 2017, Sasha Waltz, together with 80 musicians and dancers, inaugurates the expansive foyers and stairways of the recently completed Elbphilharmonie with the project »Figure Humaine« shortly before the official opening of the building. The musical-choreographic site-specific exploration takes place at the invitation of the general director Christoph Lieben-Seutter. The musical centrepiece is the polyphonic a cappella choral work »Figure Humaine« composed by Francis Poulenc on poems by Paul Éluard. Works are heard by composers including Johann Sebastian Bach, Béla Bartók, György Ligeti, Cathy Milliken, Dmitri Shostakovich, Pēteris Vasks, Eugène Ysaÿe and Hildegard von Bingen. A special surprise awaits the audience in the large concert hall – here, eight musicians perform John Cage's piece »4' 33''«, thus inaugurating this hall with silence – and the sounds of the dancers' bodies from the ensemble.

Kurz vor der offiziellen Eröffnung des Hauses weiht Sasha Waltz gemeinsam mit achtzig Musiker:innen und Tänzer:innen unter dem Titel »Figure Humaine« zu Beginn des Jahres 2017 die weiträumigen Foyers und Treppenaufgänge der frisch fertiggestellten Elbphilharmonie in Hamburg ein. Die musikalisch-choreographische Raumerkundung erfolgt auf Einladung des Generalintendanten Christoph Lieben-Seutter. Das musikalische Herzstück bildet das vielstimmige A-cappella-Chorwerk »Figure Humaine« von Francis Poulenc zu Gedichten von Paul Éluard. Es erklingen Werke von Johann Sebastian Bach, Béla Bartók, György Ligeti, Cathy Milliken, Dmitri Schostakowitsch, Pēteris Vasks, Eugène Ysaÿe, Hildegard von Bingen und weiteren Komponist:innen. Eine besondere Überraschung erlebt das Publikum im großen Konzertsaal – hier bringen die acht Musiker:innen das Werk »4' 33''« von John Cage zur Aufführung –, somit wird dieser Saal ausgerechnet mit Stille eröffnet – und den Geräuschen der Körper der Tänzer:innen des Ensembles.

Inspired by Judy Chicago's iconic work »The Dinner Party« (1979, Brooklyn Museum, New York), Sasha Waltz works for the first time with an all-women ensemble. Twenty women sit at tables arranged in a triangle, practice rituals of femininity and explore the forces of destruction and creation as embodied in the Indian goddess Kali. Plates form the tableware of a dramatised sacrificial banquet: bodies are dissected and opened, organs are removed to the sound of chanting and one of the women is ritually eaten. This human sacrifice also refers to the film »Suspiria«, for whose remake the choreography was initially requested but which did not come to fruition due to production difficulties. In that horror classic, the headmistress of a girls' school regularly sacrifices young women to extend her own life. In Karl Friedrich Schinkel's St Elisabeth Church, the live performance for »Tanz im August – 29. Internationales Festival Berlin« interacts with one of Berlin's architectural icons, as do the dancers with the audience to create an immersive experience of space.

Inspiriert von Judy Chicagos ikonischer Arbeit »The Dinner Party« (1979, Brooklyn Museum, New York), arbeitet Sasha Waltz in »Women« erstmals mit einem reinen Frauenensemble. An einem zum Dreieck gestellten Tisch sitzen zwanzig Tänzerinnen, exerzieren Rituale der Weiblichkeit und untersuchen die Kräfte der Zerstörung und der Kreation, wie sie in der indischen Göttin Kali versinnbildlicht sind. Teller sind das Geschirr eines inszenierten Opfermahls: Körper werden seziert, geöffnet, Organe entnommen und besungen und eine der Frauen rituell verspeist. Dieses Menschenopfer bezieht sich auch auf den Film »Suspiria«, für dessen Neuverfilmung die Choreographie ursprünglich gefragt war, jedoch wegen Produktionsschwierigkeiten nicht zustande kam. In diesem Horrorklassiker opfert die Leiterin eines Fraueninternats regelmäßig junge Frauen, um ihr eigenes Leben zu verlängern. In Karl Friedrich Schinkels St. Elisabeth-Kirche verbinden sich die Liveperformance im Rahmen von »Tanz im August – 29. Internationales Festival Berlin« mit einer Architekturikone der Stadt und die Tänzerinnen mit dem Publikum in einem immersiven Raumerlebnis.

Beings appear, wrapped in grey-silver cocoons. A soft mesh of fine wire protects their naked, vulnerable skin. The enclosed beings slowly search for paths through the space. They seek and approach, even before escaping their shells. They are humans, becoming visible in the light. One body leaves its shell and intertwines into another's cocoon, finding a tender, close connection. Blackout. A group stands together, shimmering in dark, light clothing. An impulse emanates from those in the foreground, sending a shockwave through the human mass in a lightning-like resonance. All follow in uncontrolled agreement. An organism. Eventually, it disintegrates into individual parts, which become threats to one another.
Sasha Waltz once again questions the nature of humanity as a social being, as life, as a loving-tender and brutally destructive species. She examines phenomena of existence against the backdrop of a fractured society: power and powerlessness, dominance and weakness, freedom and control, community and isolation. The production is a collaboration of artistic voices that connect through an interdisciplinary approach: the sculptural costumes, which appear both organic and technoid, were designed by Dutch fashion designer Iris van Herpen; lighting designer Urs Schönebaum creates lighting concepts for theatres, operas, exhibitions, performances and installations worldwide; and the musicians of the Soundwalk Collective incorporate methods from anthropology, ethnography and psychogeography into their genre-crossing sound compositions.

Wesen erscheinen in grau-silbrige Kokons gehüllt. Ein weiches Geflecht feinmaschigen Drahtes, unter dem nackt-verletzliche Haut Schutz findet. Die eingehüllten Wesen suchen langsam Wege durch den Raum. Sie suchen und nähern sich, noch bevor sie ihren Schalen entkommen. Es sind Menschen, die im Licht nun erkennbar werden. Ein Körper verlässt die eigene Hülle und windet sich in den Kokon eines anderen hinein, findet in ein zärtlich-enges Zusammensein. Blackout. Eine Gruppe steht zusammen, in dunkel schimmernd leichter Bekleidung. Ein Impuls geht von den im Vordergrund Stehenden aus und durchzuckt die menschliche Masse in blitzartiger Resonanz. Alle folgen in unkontrollierter Zustimmung. Ein Organismus. Irgendwann zerfällt er in Einzelteile, die sich gegenseitig zur Bedrohung werden.
Sasha Waltz befragt ein weiteres Mal den Menschen nach seiner Beschaffenheit als soziales Wesen, als Leben, als liebend-zärtliche und brutal-zerstörerische Spezie. Sie untersucht Phänomene des Seins vor dem Hintergrund einer zerrissenen Gesellschaft: Macht und Ohnmacht, Dominanz und Schwäche, Freiheit und Kontrolle, Gemeinschaft und Isolation. Die Produktion ist ein Zusammenspiel künstlerischer Stimmen, die eine interdisziplinäre Haltung verbindet: Die skulpturalen, zugleich organisch und technoid anmutenden Kostüme wurden von der niederländischen Modedesignerin Iris van Herpen entworfen, Lichtdesigner Urs Schönebaum gestaltet mit seinen Lichtkonzepten weltweit Räume für Theater- und Operninszenierungen, Ausstellungen, Performances und Installationen, und die Musiker des Soundwalk Collective lassen in ihre genreübergreifenden Klangkompositionen Methoden der Anthropologie, Ethnographie und Psychogeographie einfließen.

2018

The state of Berlin **buys the Radialsystem.**

Sasha Waltz & Guests celebrates **25th anniversary** – ceremony and premiere of the movie »Kreatur« at Kino International, Berlin.

Companhia Nacional de Bailado adds **»Impromptus«** to its repertoire.

»Körper« is performed for the 200th time in Berkeley during a USA tour.

REPERTOIRE

Allee der Kosmonauten Berlin, Cologne, Seville
ΕΞΟΔΟΣ | Exodos Berlin, Bochum
human requiem Adelaide
Impromptus Lisbon
Körper Berlin, London, Hanover, Lille, Berkeley
Kreatur Berlin, Dijon, Brussels, Essen, Athens, Avignon, New York, St. Pölten, Luxembourg
Matsukaze Tokyo
Orfeo Berlin
Roméo et Juliette Berlin, Paris
Travelogue I – Twenty to eight Berlin

KINDERTANZCOMPANY

Check out your mate *Gabriel Galindez Cruz* Berlin
TANZ *Davide Camplani* Berlin
Teqsi muyu marq'ay – eine warme Umarmung für die Erde *Gabriel Galindez Cruz* Berlin

GUEST PRODUCTIONS

Amal Berlin, Erfurt
Dabke Community Dancing *Medhat Aldaabal, Ali Hasan* Berlin
From A to Z Berlin
Hunted Territories *Alex Nowitz, Florencia Lamarca* Berlin
Live *Omar Rajeh* Berlin
My dearest… My fairest Helsinki
»Still/Life« at C/O Berlin *Dancers of Sasha Waltz & Guests* Berlin
SWG25Y Soundinstallation with performance *Hanno Leichtmann, dancers of Sasha Waltz & Guests* Berlin
The truth has changed *Josh Fox* Berlin

A

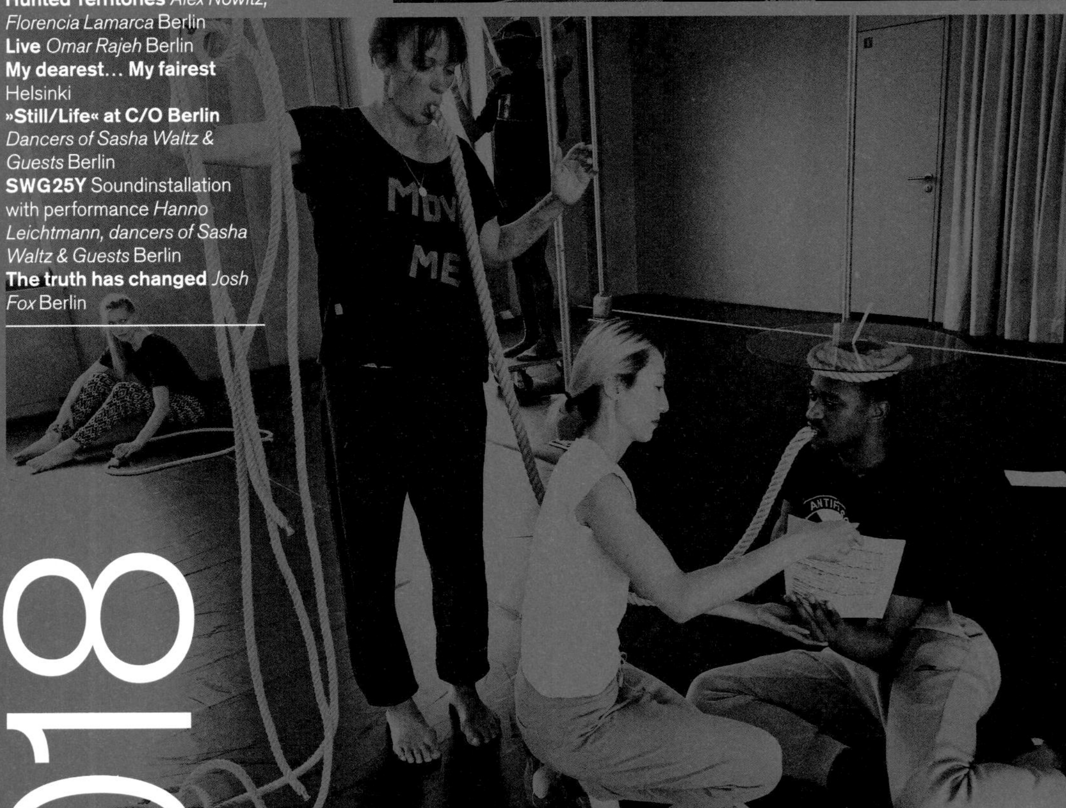

B

Dialoge 2018 – Wirbel
↘pp. 113, 124, 198, 199, 205

Radialsystem, Berlin
Idea/Concept
Sasha Waltz
Costume Design
Jasmin Lepore
Production
Sasha Waltz & Guests
I
7 Apr
Dance
Davide Camplani
Inga Huld Hakonardottir
Hwanhee Hwang
Enad Marouf
Sergiu Matis
Virgis Puodziunas
Sophia Sandig
Takako Suzuki
Sasha Waltz
Music
Jonathan Bepler
Rachel Maio
Andrea Parkins
Video
Lillevan
Light Design
Martin Hauk
II
8 Apr
Dance
Davide Camplani
Yoshiko Chuma
Edivaldo Ernesto
Annapaola Leso
Virgis Puodziunas
Zaratiana Randrianantenaina
Meg Stuart
Takako Suzuki
Sasha Waltz
Music
Brendan Dougherty
Light Design
Martin Hauk
III
14 Apr
Dance
Juan Kruz Diaz de Garaio Esnaola
Julyen Hamilton
Hwanhee Hwang
Annapaola Leso
Nicola Mascia
Sergiu Matis
Sasa Queliz
Zaratiana Randrianantenaina
Sasha Waltz
Music
Francesco Donadello
Ayumi Paul
Michael Rauter
Light Design
André Pronk
Stage Design
Brad Hwang
IV
15 Apr
Dance
Davide Camplani
Maria Marta Colusi
Luc Dunberry
Annapaola Leso
Enad Marouf
Virgis Puodziunas
Orlando Rodriguez
Sigal Zouk
Music
Hanno Leichtmann (Curator)
Sabine Erklentz
Morten J. Olsen
Magda Mayas
Stage Design
Brad Hwang
Light Design
André Pronk

ΕΞΟΔΟΣ | Exodos
↘pp. 35, 44, 52, 53, 54, 59, 61, 62, 70, 80, 98, 115, 126, 127, 143, 147, 174, 184, 194, 197, **307**

Radialsystem, Berlin
23 Aug
Direction/Choreography
Sasha Waltz
Music
Soundwalk Collective
Costume Design
Federico Polucci
Sasha Waltz & Guests
Light Design
Urs Schönebaum
Stage Design
Heike Schuppelius
Sasha Waltz
Music Dramaturgy
Steffen Döring
Dramaturgy
Jochen Sandig
Agnes Scherer
Dance/Choreography
Liza Alpízar Aguilar
Blenard Azizaj
Jiří Bartovanec
Davide Camplani
Clémentine Deluy
Davide Di Pretoro
Luc Dunberry
Charlotte Engelkes
Tian Gao
Peggy Grelat-Dupont
Hwanhee Hwang
Josh Johnson
Lorena Justribó Manion
Annapaola Leso
Margaux Marielle-Tréhoüart
Nicola Mascia
Thusnelda Mercy
Michal Mualem
Virgis Puodziunas
Sasa Queliz
Zaratiana Randrianantenaina
Aladino Rivera Blanca
Yael Schnell
Corey Scott-Gilbert
Claudia de Serpa Soares
Stylianos Tsatsos
Repetition
Sergiu Matis
Production
Sasha Waltz & Guests
Coproduction
Ruhrtriennale 2018
Made in Radialsystem

A **25th anniversary at Kino International, Berlin** B **»ΕΞΟΔΟΣ | Exodos« rehearsal**

In »Exodos«, Sasha Waltz connects with the existential questions of her earlier works, illuminating how people and their collective movements are driven by the longing to break free from the here to the there, to escape, to flee, from the self into the we, from the material space into realms of sound and light. In modern Greek, »exodos« means »exodus« or »way out«, and metaphorically, it also refers to going out into nightlife. The significant migration movements and the personal fates of the 26 dancers form the core of this work. Throughout the journey through these various layers of meaning, the ensemble experiences many collective and emotional states: like living exhibits captured in plexiglass vitrines, confronted with their dark and light selves, they stand in narrow columns of light. Mass panic erupts, where only individual survival matters. Those who fall and cannot breathe are overlooked. A large transparent box changes its face with the phenomena of the masses: at times, it is a prison for many, then a refuge. Sometimes, it is a memory of a stolen home, the beginning of an escape. Then, it transforms into a club, where sweat, breath and bodies are driven to ecstasy and slam against the transparent panes. In the large hall, a moshpit forms like at heavy metal concerts, dissolving boundaries as electrified bodies collide: they run, leap towards each other in the beat, throw themselves into one another, shoving away any approaching body, swirling in euphoric loss of control. Similarly, they later toss words together into a repetitive mantra, words of a contemporary prayer, words of the longed-for, phrases of a playful demonstration in physically manifesting repetitions. The separation between stage and audience is abolished from the very beginning; the paths of dance flow through and move the spectators, allowing them to become part of the performance.

In »Exodos« knüpft Sasha Waltz an die existenziellen Fragen ihrer früheren Werke an und beleuchtet, wie Menschen und ihre kollektiven Bewegungen durch die Sehnsucht bestimmt werden, aus dem Hier in ein Dort auszubrechen, zu fliehen, zu flüchten, aus dem Selbst ins Wir, aus dem materiellen Raum heraus in Räume aus Klang und Licht. Im Neugriechischen bedeutet »Exodos« »Auszug«, »Ausweg« sowie im übertragenen Sinn das Ausgehen ins Nachtleben. Die großen Migrationsbewegungen und die persönlichen Schicksale der 26 Tänzer:innen bilden das Herzstück dieser Arbeit. Während der Reise durch diese verschiedenen Bedeutungsebenen durchläuft das Ensemble eine Vielzahl an kollektiven und emotionalen Zuständen: Wie lebendige Exponate einer Ausstellung eingefangen in Plexiglas-Vitrinen, konfrontiert mit ihrem dunklen und hellen Selbst, stehen sie in schmalen Säulen aus Licht. Massenpanik bricht aus, nur das eigene Überleben zählt. Übersehen werden diejenigen, die fallen und keine Luft mehr bekommen. Eine große transparente Box wechselt mit den Massenphänomenen ihr Gesicht: Mal ist sie ein Gefängnis vieler, dann ein Zufluchtsort. Mal eine Erinnerung an ein geraubtes Haus, der Beginn einer Flucht. Dann ein Club, in dem Schweiß, Atem und zur Ekstase getriebene Körper an die transparenten Scheiben schlagen. In der großen Halle bildet sich ein Moshpit wie auf Heavy-Metal-Konzerten. Zur Entgrenzung im Aufeinandertreffen elektrisierter Körper: Sie rennen, springen im Beat aufeinander zu, werfen sich ineinander, schubsen jeden Körper, der sich nähert, herumgewirbelt im euphorisierenden Kontrollverlust. In ähnlicher Weise werfen sie später Worte zu einem repetitiven Mantra zusammen, Worte eines zeitgenössischen Gebets, Worte des Ersehnten, Sprüche einer spielerischen Demonstration in physisch werdenden Wiederholungen. Die Trennung zwischen Bühne und Publikum ist von Anfang an aufgehoben, die Wege des Tanzes durchströmen und bewegen die Zuschauer:innen, lassen sie Teil der Inszenierung werden.

2019

Sasha Waltz and Johannes Öhman start the **co-direction of Staatsballett Berlin.**

»Allee der Kosmonauten« is performed for the 150th time at Volksbühne Berlin.

Painting from »Impromptus« at exhibition »Tanz. Bewegung. Geste. Bild« at Kunsthalle Göppingen.

REPERTOIRE

Allee der Kosmonauten Berlin
Continu Berlin, Tel Aviv
Dido & Aeneas Berlin, Madrid
human requiem Berlin, Istanbul
Impromptus Berlin, Venice
Körper Singapore, Portland, Cannes
Kreatur Bilbao, Paris, Hamburg, Cologne, Dresden
rauschen Berlin
Sacre Berlin

KINDERTANZCOMPANY

Check out your mate is invited to »Tanztreffen der Jugend« Berlin
Hindernis *Davide Camplani* Berlin
Teqsi muyu marq'ay – eine warme Umarmung für die Erde Berlin, the piece is also invited to the festival »Rampenlichter« Munich

GUEST PRODUCTIONS

Dabke Community Dancing Berlin
From A to Z Berlin
Zoomorphic bodies *Jonathan Osborn and Orlando Rodriguez* Berlin

A

B

rauschen
↘pp. 8, 16, 61, 84, 119, 133, 150, 157, 158, 170, 172, 199, 220, **309**

Volksbühne Berlin
7 Mar
Direction/Choreography
Sasha Waltz
Stage Design
Thomas Schenk
Sasha Waltz
Costume Design
Bernd Skodzig
Light Design
David Finn
Dramaturgy
Jochen Sandig
Agnes Scherer
Dance/Choreography
Blenard Azizaj
Davide Camplani
Clémentine Deluy
Edivaldo Ernesto
Hwanhee Hwang
Lorena Justribó Manion
Annapaola Leso
Zaratiana Randrianantenaina
Aladino Rivera Blanca
László Sandig
Yael Schnell
Stylianos Tsatsos
Repetition
Claudia de Serpa Soares
Production
Sasha Waltz & Guests
Coproduction
Volksbühne Berlin
Made in Radialsystem

Zuhören #4: Climate change & democracy. From complexity to action
↘p. 222

Radialsystem, Berlin
13–15 Dec
Concept/Artistic Direction
Sasha Waltz
Programme Direction
Emilie Guérin
Anja Schmalfuß
Performances
»Extinction Room« Sergiu Matis, Lisa Densem
»Future Leaks – The recruiting«, immersive parcours by Anna de Carlo
»Teqsi muyu marq'ay – Eine warme Umarmung für die Erde« Gabriel Galindez Cruz with the teens of Kindertanz-company of Sasha Waltz & Guests
»The Truth Has Changed« Josh Fox
Workshops
Medhat Aldaabal (Dance), Ali Hasan (Music)
Angela Baldini, Presencing Institute
Paola Bascón, Jorge Villaseca (Live Music) Amazonas Solidarity Berlin
Julia Dalmadi, Marie Populus, SuperCoop
Josh Fox, Lucy Martens
Gabriel Galindez Cruz
Pedro Jardim, Morris Clay, Revision
Kathrin Petz, urgewald
Restlos Glücklich
Bernard le Roux, School of Collective Intelligence
Kate Sagovsky, Jonas Marx, Extinction Rebellion
Jochen Sandig, World Human Forum
Impulses and Conversations with
Antje Boetius
Maria Exner
Maja Göpel
Solveig Klier
Isabel Knauf
Grace Mbungu
Quang Paasch
Lex Paulson
Hannah Pirot
Janis Prinz
Bernard le Roux
Andreas Weber
Luz Zenaida Hualpa Garcia
Concerts
Ali Hasan (Musical Intervention)
Cymin Samawatie with Ralf Schwarz and Milan Vogel
Diego Noguera
DJ SeSe aka The sleeping Phoenix
Final Jam with Samar Habibi, all musicians and audience warm up
Sarah Saviet (Violin) and Joseph Houston (Piano)
Filmprogramme
»How to let go of the world and love the things climate can't change«, Josh Fox
»Rede von Sebastião Salgado«
»The Twelve« Le ciel Fondation, Lucy Martens
Live Design
Olaf Baldini
Installations Saal
Thomas Schenk
Food/Bar
»Restlos Glücklich«
Production
Sasha Waltz & Guests
Supported by
Radial Stiftung
Cooperation
Berlin Mondiale
Allianz Kulturstiftung

C

A **»Impromptus« stage set transport in Venice** B **»Dido & Aeneas« water tank backstage** C **»Sacre« circle time before the performance**

»rauschen« explores the life embedded within the artificial structures of contemporary existence and a society that has lost touch with the world behind the facade of its perfect living environment. A reference point is George Lucas's dystopian film classic »THX 1138«. The central directive forbids physical contact, gaining new significance against social distancing during the COVID-19 pandemic. Sasha Waltz shapes a language of movement that arises from states in which body and mind are inseparably intertwined with technology. Artificial voices evoke the innermost feelings, desires and dreams of humanity. They confess to machines, revealing vulnerabilities before these new gods. The cold yet affirmative responses of the androids numb and alleviate the pressure of alienation, neutralising emotions and disempowering them. This illumination and calming of emotional turmoil maintain the illusion of safety while further entrenching individuals in the ego of an atomised society. The androids appear to have replaced all roles in social relationships: they serve as caregivers, therapists and partners.
At the same time, humans draw closer to machines, embarking on a journey into the post-human age. Over everything looms a clinical white, cloaking the rounded backdrop of the stage. For moments, it washes away, revealing the darkness hidden beneath concealed traumas, memories of alternative humanity, unfulfilled human rights and an old belief in different gods. As if by instinct, the white, bleached layer settles back in place. Yet fears cannot be completely bleached away by therapies involving artificial intelligence. They break free, finding their way back into consciousness. The piece moves towards a process of revelation in which visual language transforms through a subversive force. Delicate, white garments made of artificial skin dissolve under a cleansing wash, rendering the individuals in their nakedness accessible to the world's touch once more. In the rhythm of their steps and breaths, they rewrite the composition of their coexistence. They scream, crying out for what resides within them and must not be suppressed.

»rauschen« beschäftigt sich mit dem in künstliche Strukturen eingebetteten Leben der Gegenwart und einer Gesellschaft, der in den Kulissen ihres perfekten Lebensraumes die Welt abhandengekommen ist. Eine Referenz ist George Lucas' dystopischer Filmklassiker »THX 1138«. Die zentrale Bewegungsanleitung erlaubt keine Berührung und erhält vor dem Hintergrund sozialer Distanz während der Coronapandemie eine neue Dimension. Sasha Waltz formt eine Bewegungssprache, die aus Zuständen hervorgeht, in denen Körper und Geist von Technologie unabgrenzbar durchdrungen sind. Es sind künstliche Stimmen, die den Menschen ihre innersten Gefühle, Wünsche und Träume entlocken. Sie öffnen sich zur Buße vor den Maschinen, zu Konfessionen vor den neuen Göttern. Die kalten, doch affirmativen Antworten der Androiden betäuben. Sie entlasten den Druck der Entfremdung, neutralisieren Emotionen und entmachten sie. Diese Durchleuchtung und Beruhigung der Gefühlsregungen erhält die Illusion von Sicherheit aufrecht und schließt die Menschen weiter im Ego einer atomisierten Gesellschaft ein. Die Androiden scheinen alle Rollen sozialer Beziehungen ersetzt zu haben: Sie treten auf als Pfleger:innen, als Therapeut:innen, als Partner:innen. Gleichzeitig nähern sich die Menschen den Maschinen an. Der Mensch auf dem Weg ins posthumane Zeitalter. Verdrängendes klinisches Weiß schichtet sich über alles und überzieht die gerundete Rückwand der Bühne. Für Momente wird sie weggewaschen, das Dunkle, das versteckt darunterliegt, wird kurz sichtbar: verdeckte Traumata, Erinnerungen eines anderen Menschseins, an unerfüllte Menschenrechte, alter Glaube an andere Götter. Wie von selbst legt sich das Weiße, Bleiche wieder darüber. Doch Ängste lassen sich nicht vollkommen durch Therapien künstlicher Intelligenzen ausbleichen. Sie brechen heraus, finden einen Weg zurück ins Bewusstsein. Das Stück steuert auf einen Enthüllungsprozess zu, in dem die bildliche Sprache durch eine subversive Kraft verwandelt wird. Weiße, hauchdünne Kleider aus künstlicher Haut lösen sich unter einer Waschung, die Menschen werden in ihrer Nacktheit der Berührung der Welt wieder zugänglich. Im Rhythmus der Schritte und ihres Atems schreiben sie die Komposition ihres Zusammenlebens neu. Sie schreien, schreien für das, was in ihnen ruht und nicht unterdrückt werden darf.

2020

REPERTOIRE

Allee der Kosmonauten Strasbourg
rauschen Hamburg

GUEST PRODUCTIONS

Lohengrin Dreams *Charlotte Engelkes* Berlin
SCULPTURE Project *Hanno Leichtmann* Berlin

remains
by Andrew Schneider

Radialsystem, Berlin
12 Mar
Direction/Choreography/ Concept Stage, Sound & Video
Andrew Schneider
Costume Design
Jasmin Lepore
Light Design
Yi Zhao
Andrew Schneider
Dance/Choreography
Juan Kruz Diaz de Garaio Esnaola
Luc Dunberry
Ageliki Gouvi
Margaux Marielle-Tréhoüart
Sasa Queliz
Orlando Rodriguez
Joel Suárez Gómez
Takako Suzuki
Stylianos Tsatsos
Production
Sasha Waltz & Guests
Made in Radialsystem

Tanztagebuch
↘p. **311**

»We stay at home – but keep on dancing« Home recorded videoclips published on YouTube
30 Mar–30 Jun
Choreography
Sasha Waltz
With contributions by
Ayaka Azechi
Blenard Azizaj
Zaida Ballesteros Parejo
Fernando Balsera Pita
Jiří Bartovanec
Davide Camplani
Yoshiko Chuma
Alessandra Defazio
Davide Di Pretoro
Juan Kruz Diaz de Garaio Esnaola
Luc Dunberry
Edivaldo Ernesto
Yuya Fujinami
Tian Gao
Eva Georgitsopoulou
Maya Gomez
Dmytro Grynov
Hwanhee Hwang
Lorena Justribó Manion
Annapaola Leso
Maureen López Lembo
Margaux Marielle-Tréhoüart
Nicola Mascia
Gyung Moo Kim
Michal Mualem
Sean Nederlof
Francesca Noia
Sofia Pintzou
Virgis Puodziunas
Zaratiana Randrianantenaina
Aladino Rivera Blanca
Orlando Rodriguez
Mata Sakka
Andrew Schneider
Yael Schnell
Claudia de Serpa Soares
Xuan Shi
Wibke Storkan
Joel Suárez Gómez
Stylianos Tsatsos
Junko Wada
Niannian Zhou

Dialoge 2020 – Relevante Systeme
↘pp. 94, 116, 128, 129, 146, 147, 161, 180, 186, 187, 194, 210, **312**

Radialsystem, Berlin
20 Aug
Direction/Choreography
Sasha Waltz
Costume Design
Jasmin Lepore
Bernd Skodzig (»Sacre«)
Light Design
Martin Hauk
Dramaturgy
Jochen Sandig
Solo Trumpet
Marco Blaauw
Dance/Choreography
Ayaka Azechi
Blenard Azizaj
Jiří Bartovanec
Anne Brinon
Davide Camplani
Maria Marta Colusi
Juan Kruz Diaz de Garaio Esnaola
Davide Di Pretoro
Luc Dunberry
Yuya Fujinami
Tian Gao
Hwanhee Hwang
Annapaola Leso
Margaux Marielle-Tréhoüart
Sergiu Matis
Sean Nederlof
Virgis Puodziunas
Sasa Queliz
Zaratiana Randrianantenaina
Aladino Rivera Blanca
Orlando Rodriguez
Mata Sakka
Yael Schnell
Claudia de Serpa Soares
Wibke Storkan
Joel Suárez Gómez
Stylianos Tsatsos
Repetition
Antonio Ruz
Production
Sasha Waltz & Guests
Cooperation
Radialsystem, Berlin
Supported by
Radial Stiftung

Dialoge Roma 2020 – Terra Sacra

Festival Romaeuropa, Auditorium Parco della Musica – Cavea, Rome
18 Sep
Direction/Choreography
Sasha Waltz
Costume Design
Jasmin Lepore (»Boléro«)
Bernd Skodzig (»Sacre«)
Light Design
Martin Hauk
Dramaturgy
Jochen Sandig
Dance/Choreography
Jiří Bartovanec
Davide Camplani
Maria Marta Colusi
Juan Kruz Diaz de Garaio Esnaola
Davide Di Pretoro
Luc Dunberry
Edivaldo Ernesto
Yuya Fujinami
Tian Gao
Hwanhee Hwang
Annapaola Leso
Margaux Marielle-Tréhoüart
Sergiu Matis
Sean Nederlof
Virgis Puodziunas
Zaratiana Randrianantenaina
Orlando Rodriguez
Mata Sakka
Yael Schnell
Claudia de Serpa Soares
Joel Suárez Gómez
Repetition
Antonio Ruz
Production
Sasha Waltz & Guests

Dialoge 2020 – Strandbad Tegelsee
↘pp. 129, 193, **313**

Strandbad Tegelsee, Berlin
3 Oct
Choreography
Sasha Waltz
Dance/Choreography
Jiří Bartovanec
Davide Camplani
Maria Marta Colusi
Juan Kruz Diaz de Garaio Esnaola
Davide Di Pretoro
Luc Dunberry
Yuya Fujinami
Tian Gao
Annapaola Leso
Nicola Mascia
Sergiu Matis
Sean Nederlof
Virgis Puodziunas
Zaratiana Randrianantenaina
Aladino Rivera Blanca
Orlando Rodriguez
Mata Sakka
Yael Schnell
Claudia de Serpa Soares
Production
Sasha Waltz & Guests

Dialoge 2020 – Relevante Systeme II
↘pp. 57, 188

Radialsystem, Berlin – Livestream
3 Dec
Idea
Sasha Waltz
Costume Design
Jasmin Lepore
Light Design
Olaf Danilsen
Music
Lucrecia Dalt (6 Dec)
Diego Noguera (5 Dec)
Acid Pauli (3+4 Dec)
Dance/Choreography
Edivaldo Ernesto
Hwanhee Hwang
Annapaola Leso
Nicola Mascia
Zaratiana Randrianantenaina
Aladino Rivera Blanca
Claudia de Serpa Soares
Meg Stuart (5+6 Dec)
Joel Suárez Gómez
Takako Suzuki
Sasha Waltz
Production
Sasha Waltz & Guests

A

A **»Dialoge 2020 – Strandbad Tegelsee«**

Tanztagebuch

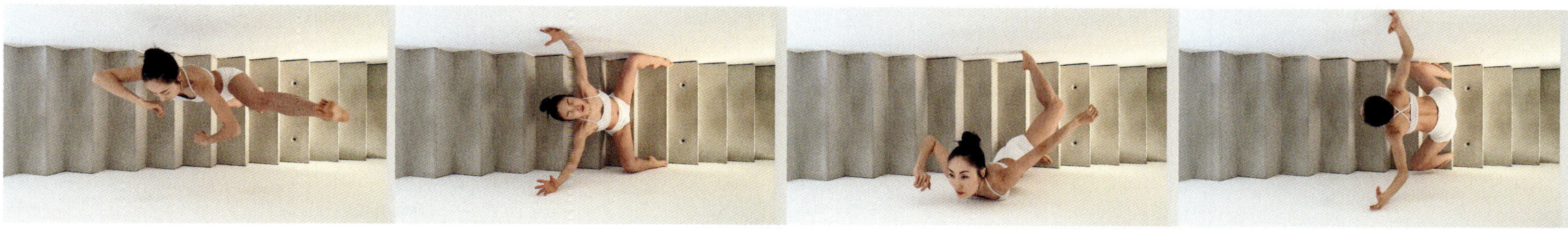

From 30 March to 30 June 2020, Sasha Waltz & Guests spontaneously responds to the first lockdown of the COVID-19 pandemic with a digital dance diary comprising 50 chapters. The dance company regularly sends video greetings to the audience via its website, YouTube channel and social media. Dancers from Sasha Waltz & Guests perform creative short solo or group sequences from various choreographies by Sasha Waltz in their own homes, showcasing their personal interpretations. This initiative allows the dancers to remain artistically active during the lockdown, regardless of location.

Vom 30. März bis 30. Juni 2020 reagiert Sasha Waltz & Guests auf den ersten Lockdown der Coronapandemie spontan mit einem digitalen Tanztagebuch, das fünfzig Kapitel umfassen wird. In regelmäßigen Abständen schickt die Tanzcompagnie dem Publikum über ihre Website, den YouTube-Kanal und die sozialen Medien getanzte Videogrüße nach Hause. Tänzer:innen von Sasha Waltz & Guests zeigen hier jeweils kreative kurze Solo- oder Gruppensequenzen aus diversen Choreographien von Sasha Waltz in ihren eigenen vier Wänden und Interpretationen. Auf diesem Weg können die Tänzer:innen auch während des Lockdowns künstlerisch tätig sein, egal in welchem Land sie sich befinden.

Dialoge 2020 – Relevante Systeme

After the first lockdown due to COVID-19, Sasha Waltz & Guests return with a project that navigates the intersection of music, choreography and architecture. »Dialoge 2020 – Relevante Systeme« features 27 dancers at the Radialsystem and its expansive outdoor area. The evening begins with individual dance solos addressing the theme of discrimination, set to Georg Friedrich Haas's trumpet solo »I Can't Breathe« (2014), followed by an adaptation of Sasha Waltz's »Sacre« choreography, which creatively responds to the restrictive circumstances of the pandemic. The event concludes with a life-affirming interpretation of Maurice Ravel's »Boléro«. For the last two pieces, the audience and dance ensemble are divided into three groups at three locations within and around the Radialsystem, allowing for a live dance experience despite health regulations. Through this »Dialogue« project, Sasha Waltz emphasises the relevance of the arts and the necessity for direct encounters with the audience.

Nach dem ersten coronabedingten Lockdown kehren Sasha Waltz & Guests mit einem Projekt zurück, das sich im Spannungsfeld zwischen Musik, Choreographie und Architektur bewegt. »Dialoge 2020 – Relevante Systeme« bespielt mit 27 Tänzer:innen das Radialsystem und seinen weiträumigen Außenbereich. Nach individuellen tänzerischen Soli zum Thema »Diskriminierung« zu Georg Friedrich Haas' Trompetensolo »I can't breathe« (2014) sowie der Bearbeitung von Sasha Waltz' »Sacre«-Choreographie, die mit den einschränkenden Gegebenheiten der pandemischen Situation kreativ umgeht, schließt der Abend mit der lebensbejahenden Interpretation von Maurice Ravels »Boléro«. Publikum und Tanzensemble sind für die letzten beiden Stücke parallel an drei verschiedenen Orten in und um das Radialsystem in drei Gruppen geteilt, um so trotz der gesundheitspolitischen Maßnahmen die Möglichkeit zu finden, Tanz wieder live erleben zu können. Sasha Waltz unterstreicht mit diesem »Dialoge«-Projekt die Systemrelevanz der Kunst und die Notwendigkeit unmittelbarer Begegnungen mit dem Publikum.

Dialoge 2020 – Strandbad Tegelsee

Following an encounter between the artists Marina Naprushkina and Sasha Waltz at Lake Tegel in Berlin, Sasha Waltz & Guests collaborates with the non-profit operators of the lake's lido, the community organisation »Neue Nachbarschaft Moabit«. As part of an open house event in October 2020, dancers from the company make artistic interventions across the entire area to music by Nino Rota, engaging with an audience that explores the site with curiosity, all while adhering to pandemic conditions. The choreographies occur on the lawns, in the water and on the piers leading out into the lake, culminating under a large tree with Maurice Ravel's »Boléro«.

Nach einer Begegnung zwischen den beiden Künstlerinnen Marina Naprushkina und Sasha Waltz am Tegeler See kooperiert Sasha Waltz & Guests mit den gemeinnützigen Betreibern des Strandbads und der »Neuen Nachbarschaft Moabit«. Im Rahmen des Tages der offenen Tür im Oktober 2020 intervenieren Tänzer:innen der Compagnie unter den Bedingungen der Pandemie zur Musik von Nino Rota künstlerisch auf dem gesamten Gelände für das neugierig den Ort entdeckende Publikum. Die Choreographien auf den Wiesen, im Wasser, auf den in den See hinaus führenden Stegen kulminieren zum Ende unter einem großen Baum mit Maurice Ravels »Boléro«.

Sasha Waltz is awarded **»Commandeur de l'Ordre des Arts et des Lettres«** by the French Ministry of Culture.

Sasha Waltz is awarded a **star on the Sibiu Walk of Fame.**

REPERTOIRE

Allee der Kosmonauten Hamburg, Leipzig, Sofia
Impromptus (duet) Stockholm, Saint Petersburg, Moscow, Oslo, Paris
In C Berlin, Cologne, Munich
Kreatur Sibiu

GUEST PRODUCTIONS

Bang on a Can Concert, Berlin
remains Berlin

2021

A

B

C

Chiharu Shiota – I Hope

»I Hope… in performance with Sasha Waltz & Guests and Lucrecia Dalt«
König Galerie – streamed via social media
27 Feb
Choreography
Sasha Waltz
Music
Lucrecia Dalt
Costume Design
Jasmin Lepore
Dance/Choreography
Davide Camplani
Juan Kruz Diaz de Garaio Esnaola
Luc Dunberry
Hwanhee Hwang
Annapaola Leso
Virgis Puodziunas
Zaratiana Randrianantenaina
Takako Suzuki

In C
↘pp. 22, 32, 34, 43, 178, 201, **315**, 318, 321

Radialsystem, Berlin – Arte Livestream
6 Mar
Concept/Light/Choreography
Sasha Waltz
Music
Terry Riley
Costume Design
Jasmin Lepore
Light Design
Olaf Danilsen
Concept/Dramaturgy
Jochen Sandig
Dance/Choreography
Davide Di Pretoro
Edivaldo Ernesto
Melissa Figueiredo
Hwanhee Hwang
Annapaola Leso
Michal Mualem
Zaratiana Randrianantenaina
Aladino Rivera Blanca
Orlando Rodriguez
Joel Suárez Gómez
Production
Sasha Waltz & Guests
Made in Radialsystem

Zuhören #5: In B

digital format
22 Apr
Eine künstlerische Begegnung Berlin/Belarus
Gespräch Berlin/Belarus/ Cooking with …
Vitali Alekseenok
Vitali Appow
Marina Naprushkina
Olga Podgaiskaya
Jochen Sandig
Performance »In B« (recorded & live)
Concept/Performance
Vitali Appow
Olga Podgaiskaya
Virgis Puodziunas
Igor Shugaleev
Composition
Olga Podgaiskaya
Vitali Appow
Organ
Olga Podgaiskaya
Choreographic Assistance
Davide Camplani
Production
Sasha Waltz & Guests
Cooperation
Kultur Büro Elisabeth
Sophienkirche, Berlin

Beethoven 7 in Delphi
↘pp. 73, 169

Ludwig van Beethoven Symphony no. 7 broadcast by Arte
»Beethoven – The European Tour: 9 Symphonies, 9 Cities«
6 Jun
Choreography
Sasha Waltz
Conductor
Teodor Currentzis
Orchestra
MusicAeterna
Dance/Choreography
Davide Camplani
Clémentine Deluy
Emmanouela Dolianiti
Edivaldo Ernesto
Tian Gao
Ageliki Gouvi
Sean Nederlof
Virgis Puodziunas
Sasa Queliz
Zaratiana Randrianantenaina
Orlando Rodriguez
Stylianos Tsatsos
Coproduction
Megaron
Unitel
ZDF in collaboration with Arte

Dialoge 2021 – Ludwigsburg
↘pp. 183, **316**

Ludwigsburger Schlossfestspiele, Residenzschloss Ludwigsburg, Blühendes Barock, Ehrenhof
25 Jun
Direction/Choreography
Sasha Waltz
Costume Design
Jasmin Lepore
Light Design
Olaf Danilsen
Dramaturgy
Jochen Sandig
Dance/Choreography
Blenard Azizaj
Jiří Bartovanec
Anne Brinon
Davide Camplani
Clémentine Deluy
Juan Kruz Diaz de Garaio Esnaola
Luc Dunberry
Edivaldo Ernesto
Melissa Figueiredo
Yuya Fujinami
Tian Gao
Agnieszka Jachym
Lorena Justribó Manion
Annapaola Leso
Sergiu Matis
Michal Mualem
Sean Nederlof
Gabriele Oechsle
Sasa Queliz
Aladino Rivera Blanca
Orlando Rodriguez
Claudia de Serpa Soares
Repetition
Michal Mualem
Yael Schnell
Production
Sasha Waltz & Guests
Coproduction
Ludwigsburger Schlossfestspiele

A–C **»Beethoven 7 in Delphi«**

With »In C« an artistic process begins that results in a growing number of new formats. Terry Riley's »In C« (1964) forms the musical foundation of this, a revolutionary composition consisting of 53 musical figures that is considered the first piece of minimalist music. Sasha Waltz writes a dance score with ten dancers that follows a similar structure, expanding the music with the dimension of space: a playful system of 53 choreographic figures with clear rules which enables encounters of any number of dancers. Within this set of rules, the individual performer is given creative freedom, similar to our democratic society, where limits apply to personal freedom to ensure no harm comes to the group. All bear the same degree of responsibility, freely switching between the roles of leading and following, until this oscillation attains a state in which the roles combine and decisions emerge from the attentive listening of one body to another. Yet »In C« is more than a probing dialectic between individual and collective freedom: the composition works like the grammar of a dance language with a vocabulary of 53 phrases of motion. Parts of these moving phrases can be detached, repeated, paused, mirrored and articulated in reverse. This language makes it possible to »say« something truly new in improvisation, to which innumerable responses are possible. »In C« is thinking together to negotiate the space and to fill it with the will of the many. In the arising of what has never been, in the articulation of what has never been said, in the exchange of communicated intention, the choreography transforms into an act in the fullest sense of the word. »In C« is digitally accessible by means of video tutorials and is being passed on to a steadily growing international dance community, becoming a large-scale collective construct.

Mit »In C« beginnt ein künstlerischer Prozess, aus dem kontinuierlich neue Formate hervorgehen. Musikalische Grundlage ist Terry Rileys »In C« (1964), eine revolutionäre Komposition, bestehend aus 53 musikalischen Figuren, die als Beginn der Minimal Music gilt. Sasha Waltz schreibt mit zehn Tänzer:innen eine Tanzpartitur, die einer ähnlichen Struktur folgt und die Musik mit der Dimension des Raumes erweitert: ein Spielsystem aus 53 Bewegungsfiguren mit klaren Regeln, die eine Begegnung einer beliebigen Anzahl an Tänzer:innen erlaubt. Innerhalb dieses Regelwerks wird den Performenden Gestaltungsraum gegeben, ähnlich unserer demokratischen Gesellschaft, in der die Grenzen der persönlichen Freiheit dort verlaufen, wo die Gruppe nicht verletzt wird. Alle tragen zu gleichen Teilen Verantwortung, wechseln frei zwischen Rollen des Führens und Folgens, bis diese Oszillation einen Zustand erreicht, in dem sich die Rollen vereinen und Entscheidungen aus dem aufmerksamen Zuhören zwischen Körpern emergieren. Doch »In C« ist mehr als das dialektische Ausloten zwischen individueller und kollektiver Freiheit: Die Komposition wirkt wie die Grammatik einer tänzerischen Sprache mit 53 Sätzen bewegten Vokabulars. Teile dieser bewegten Sätze können herausgelöst, wiederholt, pausiert, gespiegelt und rückwärts artikuliert werden. Diese Sprache ermöglicht in der Improvisation wahrhaft Neuartiges zu »sagen«, auf das unzählige Antworten möglich sind. »In C« ist gemeinsames Denken, den Raum zu verhandeln und mit dem Willen der Vielen zu füllen. Im Auftauchen des niemals Gewesenen, im Artikulieren des nie Gesagten, im Austausch kommunizierter Intention wandelt sich die Choreographie zur wahrhaften Handlung. »In C« ist über Video-Tutorials digital zugänglich, wird an eine stetig wachsende internationale und generationsübergreifende Tanz-Community weitergegeben und wird zur großformatigen sozialen Plastik.

As part of the Ludwigsburg Festival, Sasha Waltz dedicates herself to one of Europe's largest well-preserved baroque palaces and its garden. Accompanied by the music of Jean-Philippe Rameau and Henry Purcell, the audience is guided through the baroque setting, from the sea of blossoms in the north garden into the cour d'honneur of the Ludwigsburg Residential Palace. The danced parcours creates picturesque scenes and culminates at sunset in the palace courtyard with Sasha Waltz's new choreography »In C«, set to the music by Terry Riley.

Im Rahmen der Ludwigsburger Schlossfestspiele widmet sich Sasha Waltz einem der größten original erhaltenen Schlösser Europas und seinem Garten. Begleitet von den Klängen Jean-Philippe Rameaus und Henry Purcells, wird das Publikum durch die barocke Kulisse aus dem Blütenmeer des Nordgartens bis in den Ehrenhof des Ludwigsburger Residenzschlosses geführt. Der getanzte Parcours erschafft malerische Szenen und endet bei untergehender Sonne im Schlosshof mit der neuen Choreographie von Sasha Waltz »In C« zur Musik von Terry Riley.

2022

REPERTOIRE

Dido & Aeneas Berlin, Ludwigsburg
human requiem Stuttgart
In C Berlin, Barcelona, New York, Rome, Strasbourg, Rotterdam, Karlsruhe
In C projects Sofia, Marl, Essen, Guadalajara, Tbilisi, Mexico City
Kreatur Berlin, Sibiu
Orfeo Madrid
SYM-PHONIE MMXX Berlin, Łódź

KINDER- UND JUGEND-TANZCOMPANY

Hin & Zurück *Davide Camplani* Berlin
In C – nächste Generation *Sasha Waltz, Alessandra Defazio, Annapaola Leso, Wibke Storkan, Orlando Rodriguez, Jiří Bartovanec* Berlin
TEXERE *Gabriel Galindez Cruz* Berlin, Cottbus

GUEST PRODUCTIONS

remains Berlin

A

B

A **»In C«, advertisement in front of BAM – Brooklyn Academy of Music, New York** B **»In C – Marler Partitur«**

SYM-PHONIE MMXX

↘pp. 37, 42, 44, 51, 101, 120, 121, 126, 129, 142, 146, 160, 176, 190, 193, 200, **319**

Staatsoper Unter den Linden, Berlin
13 Mar
Concept/Direction/Choreography
Sasha Waltz
Music
Georg Friedrich Haas
Stage Design
Pia Maier Schriever
Costume Design
Bernd Skodzig
Light Design
David Finn
Musical Direction
Ilan Volkov
Orchestra
Staatskapelle Berlin
Dance/Choreography
Sebastian Abarbanell
Blenard Azizaj
Jiří Bartovanec
Anne Brinon
Rosa Dicuonzo
Edivaldo Ernesto
Melissa Figueiredo
Yuya Fujinami
Tian Gao
Eva Georgitsopoulou
Hwanhee Hwang
Agnieszka Jachym
Lorena Justribó Manion
Kelvin Kilonzo
Annapaola Leso
Jaan Männima
Sean Nederlof
Virgis Puodziunas
Zaratiana Randrianantenaina
Joel Suárez Gómez
Ichiro Sugae
Repetition
Michal Mualem
Production
Staatsballett Berlin
Coproduction
Sasha Waltz & Guests
Made in Radialsystem

Ira – Zorn – Wrath

↘pp. 143, **320**

Theaterhaus Stuttgart
7 May
Choreography
Sasha Waltz
Music
Diego Noguera
Costume Design
Sasha Waltz
Light Design
Arnaud Poumerat
Dance
Mark Sampson (UA)
Shori Yamamoto (UA)
Louiza Avraam
Sidney Elisabeth Turtschi
Repetition
Cesar Locsin
Zaratiana Randrianantenaina
Production
Gauthier Dance, Theaterhaus Stuttgart

In C – Marler Partitur

↘p. **321**

a community project with 100 citizens of Marl
open-air in the city of Marl
11 Sep
Choreography/Concept
Sasha Waltz
Music
Terry Riley
Commissioning Group
Hannelore Apitzsch
Werner Eisbrenner
Monika Kaczerowski
Kurt Langer
Heidi Pfeifer
Irene Rasch-Erb
Rolf Schumann
Brigitte Schumann-Knauff
Dr. Ulrich Spies
Karin Wagner
Paul Wagner
Project Management and Mediation
Lea Schleiffenbaum
Project Guidance
Gerrit Gohlke
Head of Artistic Production Sasha Waltz & Guests
Bärbel Kern
Artistic Assistance
Thusnelda Mercy
Tutors
Alessandra Defazio
Lorena Justribó Manion
Annapaola Leso
Claudia de Serpa Soares
Production Marl
Katharina Scheidtmann
Local Dancers
Chrystel Guillebeaud
Josephine Kalies
Sara Koluchova
Annika Kompart
Frederico Mendes Teixeira
Sophia Otto
Dancers Sasha Waltz & Guests
Sebastian Abarbanell
Alessandra Defazio
Tian Gao
Annapaola Leso
Jaan Männima
Dominique McDougal
Orlando Rodriguez
Claudia de Serpa Soares
Wibke Storkan
Joel Suárez Gómez
Local Participants
AkzepTanz with Sandra Müller
Albert-Schweitzer-Geschwister-Scholl-Gymnasium Marl with Kornelia Langer
Gymnasium im Loekamp with Andrea Möller and Theresia Riekert
Hans-Böckler-Berufskolleg with Frauke Arnold
Martin-Luther-King Schule Marl with Andreas Becker, Anna-Lena Besten, Dustin Gashi, Ulrike Höpfner, Emine Karakaya and Alexa Kubiak
Musikschule Marl with Günther Braunstein
TanzKreativ with Melanie Drüke
Tanzschule Klein with Kirsten Klein
Willy-Brandt-Gesamtschule with Silvia Frechen and Janine Langer
Production
Sasha Waltz & Guests
Skulpturenmuseum Marl

SYM-PHONIE MMXX

Elegant human configurations and harmonious articulations of joints blend with the disruption of order, transforming their appearance into a crowd's revolutionary or violent gestures. Embedded dissonances can be found in the multi-layered soundscape and in the fabric of the choreography. The extremes of music, silence and the darkness of dance collide, much like a particle accelerator, revealing the macroscopic nature of the world in fleeting moments of pure energy meeting matter. The interplay between order and chaos is also a play of time: music and dance grapple with the flow of time, resisting it while striving to reflect it, seeking to undo what has been. A slow flow of bodies subtly brushes against the boundary of immobility, the cessation of time, death and nothingness. This slowness compels a close examination.
»SYM-PHONIE MMXX« is a work by Georg Friedrich Haas commissioned by Sasha Waltz, written for a symphonic ensemble of the Staatskapelle Berlin, and marks his first stage work for ballet. The piece was created before the COVID-19 pandemic but premiered only after the second lockdown, coinciding with the onset of the Ukraine war. This apocalyptic work serves as a seismograph for the contrasts and contradictions of our reality. The inevitability – of time, of death – emerges as a golden boundary, a threatening wall that fills the stage, separating some from others and pushing them to the limits of their possibilities. The material manifestation of inevitability slowly and steadily descends from above, granting those below a few moments in the golden glow of an impending end.
In the final moments, an individual seizes the last seconds to explore the freedom that remains, filling the space with the volume of possible movements, and then, at the last moment when the possibility of continuing fades, surrenders and exits the closing gap, bringing the movement of time to a halt.

Elegante menschliche Konfigurationen, harmonische Artikulationen der Gelenke vermengen sich mit dem Zerbrechen der Ordnung, verändern ihr Gesicht im revolutionären oder gewalttätigen Gestus einer Masse. Eingewebte Dissonanzen finden sich im vielschichtigen Klangteppich ebenso wie im Stoffmuster der Choreographie. Die Extreme der Musik, der Stille, der Dunkelheit des Tanzes prallen aufeinander, wie ein Teilchenbeschleuniger die makroskopische Beschaffenheit der Welt sichtbar macht, in winzigen Momenten des Aufeinandertreffens von purer Energie und Materie. Das Spiel zwischen Ordnung und Chaos ist auch ein Spiel der Zeit: Musik und Tanz kämpfen mit der Bewegung der Zeit, sie werfen sich dagegen und wollen sie spiegeln, wollen rückgängig machen, was war.
Ein langsames Fließen von Körpern reibt unmerklich an der Grenze zur Regungslosigkeit, dem Anhalten der Zeit, dem Tod, dem Nichts. Die Langsamkeit zwingt zum genauen Hinsehen.
Die Komposition »SYM-PHONIE MMXX« ist ein Auftragswerk von Sasha Waltz an den Komponisten Georg Friedrich Haas – für eine sinfonische Besetzung der Staatskapelle Berlin geschrieben – und sein erstes Bühnenwerk für Ballett. Die Produktion »SYM-PHONIE MMXX« von Sasha Waltz ist vor der Pandemie entstanden, kam aber erst nach dem zweiten Lockdown in Premiere, zeitgleich mit dem Beginn des Ukraine-Krieges. Das apokalyptische Werk zeichnet wie ein Seismograph Gegensätze und Widersprüche unserer Lebensrealität auf. Unbedingtheit – der Zeit, des Todes – schiebt sich als goldene Grenze, als raumfüllende bedrohliche Wand über die Bühne, trennt die einen von den anderen, drängt sie an die Grenze ihrer Möglichkeiten. Auch von oben kommt zuletzt die Materie gewordene Unaufhaltsamkeit, langsam und beständig, den Menschen darunter noch einige Augenblicke im goldenen Schimmer eines nahenden Endes gebend, bevor zuletzt ein Einzelner die letzten Minuten den Raum unter der sich absenkenden Fläche nutzt, die Freiheit auskostet, in den noch verbliebenen Sekunden das Volumen der möglichen Bewegungen ausfüllt und sich dann, im letzten Augenblick der Unmöglichkeit des Weitermachens, ergibt und die sich schließende Lücke verlässt, dass die Bewegung der Zeit zum Halt kommt.

Ira – Zorn – Wrath

In 2022, Sasha Waltz explores the deadly sin of wrath for the evening »The Seven Sins« by Gauthier Dance and transforms it into a duet. Together with the dancers, she examines the meaning of »wrath« and »sin« in a wide variety of traditions and languages: »Wrath is one of the oldest words of all; it is written in 47 ancient languages. This condition seems to be core to humanity. Even one of our greatest literary works, the ›Iliad‹, begins with wrath.« Together they find meanings for wrath such as »misdeed« or »going astray«. Important to the choreographer in her search for movement are the verbs associated with wrath, such as turning, bending, bowing. »A basic element is also the scream, as an expression and as an energy state – wrath as heat, fire or snorting,« says Sasha Waltz. »People enter an extreme space where one looses oneself.«

Im Jahr 2022 beschäftigt sich Sasha Waltz für den Abend »The Seven Sins« von Gauthier Dance mit der Todsünde Zorn und verwandelt diese in ein Duett. Gemeinsam mit den Tänzer:innen untersucht sie die Bedeutung von »Zorn« und »Sünde« in den verschiedensten Traditionen und Sprachen: »Zorn gehört zu den ältesten Wörtern überhaupt, es ist in 47 alten Sprachen verschriftlicht. Dieser Zustand ist scheinbar ein Kernwort der Menschheit. Selbst die ›Ilias‹ beginnt mit Zorn, eines unserer größten literarischen Werke.« Gemeinsam finden sie für Zorn Bedeutungen wie »Verfehlung« oder »in die Irre gehen«, wichtig sind der Choreographin für ihre Bewegungssuche die mit Zorn assoziierten Verben wie etwa drehen, krümmen, verbeugen. »Ein Grundelement ist auch der Schrei, als Ausdruck und als Energiezustand – Zorn als Hitze, Feuer oder Schnauben«, so Sasha Waltz: »Der Mensch gelangt in einen extremen Raum, wo er außer sich gerät.«

In C – Marler Partitur

In September 2022, the town of Marl in North Rhine-Westphalia itself becomes a stage for a unique event. With »In C – Marler Partitur«, Sasha Waltz develops a project that incorporates broad swathes of the town's population. About 120 non-professional dancers together with professional dancers from the region spend months studying and rehearsing the choreographic figures of »In C«, which they then present in a guided tour through the town. The dancers and the audience form a procession with bells and flags, slowly spiralling into the town centre, where this movement ends in a performance together with the dancers of Sasha Waltz & Guests on the Marl Forum. Since then, the project has kept evolving with new facets every year.
The project is initiated by a group of citizens of Marl who for years have been committed to the preservation of Marl's outstanding architecture. They turn to the New Patrons network, through which they are able to engage the choreographer Sasha Waltz for their project of using art and dance to revive the democratic spirit of renewal of the post-war years.

Die Stadt Marl in Nordrhein-Westfalen wird im September 2022 Schauplatz eines einzigartigen Ereignisses. Sasha Waltz baut mit »In C – Marler Partitur« ein Projekt auf, das weite Teile der Stadtbevölkerung einbezieht. Rund 120 Laien und professionelle Tänzer:innen aus der Region erlernen die choreographischen Figuren von »In C« in einem mehrmonatigen Probenprozess und präsentieren diese in einem geführten Rundgang durch die Stadt. Tanzende und Publikum bilden dabei eine Prozession mit Glocken und Fahnen und bewegen sich spiralförmig auf das Stadtzentrum zu. Die Bewegung endet in einer gemeinsamen Aufführung mit den Tänzer:innen von Sasha Waltz & Guests auf dem Forum Marl. Das Projekt entwickelt sich seither jedes Jahr mit neuen Facetten weiter.
Initiiert wurde das Projekt von einer Gruppe Marler Bürger:innen, die sich seit vielen Jahren für den Erhalt herausragender Bauwerke in ihrer Stadt engagieren. Die Marler Initiative wandte sich an das Netzwerk der Neuen Auftraggeber und konnte Sasha Waltz für das Vorhaben gewinnen, den demokratischen Aufbruchsgeist der Nachkriegsjahre mit künstlerischen Mitteln zu neuem Leben zu erwecken.

30th anniversary of Sasha Waltz & Guests.

Jochen Sandig is awarded the **»Bundesverdienstkreuz am Bande«** of the Federal Republic of Germany.

Nagelhus Schia Productions adds **»In C«** to its repertoire.

REPERTOIRE

Beethoven 7 Berlin, Barcelona, St. Pölten
human requiem Elefsina
In C Berlin, Hamburg, Oslo, Reggio Emilia, Brescia, Copenhagen, Bonn, Marl, Madrid
In C projects Berlin, Reggio Emilia, Guadalajara, Geneva, Recklinghausen, Kharkiv, London, Caracas, Palermo, Pesaro, Pune
Kreatur Kraków, Karlsruhe
SYM-PHONIE MMXX Berlin, Brno
Tannhäuser Berlin

KINDER- UND JUGEND-TANZCOMPANY

In C – nächste Generation Berlin
LINEA *Gabriel Galindez Cruz* Berlin
stimmen *Davide Camplani, Alessandra Defazio, Annapaola Leso with Fernando Balsera Pita* Berlin
TEXERE is invited to »Tanztreffen der Jugend« Berlin

GUEST PRODUCTIONS

Diego Noguera Record Release Concert, Berlin

A

Beethoven 7
↘pp. 1, 30, 161, 173, 210, **323**, 324

Radialsystem, Berlin
11 Mar
Choreography/Concept
Sasha Waltz
Music
Diego Noguera (live)
Ludwig van Beethoven
Costume Design
Bernd Skodzig
Federico Polucci
Light Design
Martin Hauk
Jörg Bittner
Dramaturgy
Jochen Sandig
Christopher Drum
Dance/Choreography
Clémentine Deluy
Rosa Dicuonzo
Edivaldo Ernesto
Tian Gao
Eva Georgitsopoulou
Hwanhee Hwang
Annapaola Leso
Jaan Männima
Sean Nederlof
Virgis Puodziunas
Sasa Queliz
Zaratiana Randrianantenaina / Lorena Justribó Manion
Orlando Rodriguez
Repetition
Yael Schnell
Production
Sasha Waltz & Guests
Made in Radialsystem

Mystery 14 Human Requiem in Eleusis

A site-specific ritualistic performance at the Eleusis archaeological site with the Rundfunkchor Berlin
29 Sep
Concept/Direction
Jochen Sandig
Dramaturgy/Choreography
Sasha Waltz
Scenography
Brad Hwang
Light Design
Jörg Bittner
André Pronk
Sound Design
Holger Schwark
Film Documentation
Stephan Talneau
Choir
Rundfunkchor Berlin
Conductor
Gijs Leenaars
Co-Conductor
Justus Barleben
Soloists
Marlis Petersen (Soprano)
Benjamin Appl (Baritone)
Angela Gassenhuber (Piano)
Philip Mayers (Piano)
Dancers
Clémentine Deluy (Demeter)
Virgis Puodziunas (Hades)
Claudia de Serpa Soares (Persephone)
Artistic Collaboration/ Repetition
Claudia de Serpa Soares
Ilka Seifert
Production
European Capital of Culture 2023 – Elefsina
World Human Forum
Made in Radialsystem

Sasha Waltz im Dialog mit Wolfgang Laib

Kunstmuseum Stuttgart
4 Nov
Concept/Choreography
Sasha Waltz
Dance/Choreography
Rosa Dicuonzo
Tian Gao
Hwanhee Hwang
Annapaola Leso
Virgis Puodziunas
Claudia de Serpa Soares
Sasha Waltz
Music
Ayumi Paul (Violin & Vocals)
Cooperation
Sasha Waltz & Guests
Ludwigsburger Schlossfestspiele

2023

B

C

A **»Sasha Waltz im Dialog mit Wolfgang Laib«** B+C **»Mystery 14 Human Requiem in Eleusis«**

Beethoven 7

In »Beethoven 7«, Sasha Waltz, together with an ensemble of 14 dancers, delves into Ludwig van Beethoven's complete »Symphony No. 7 in A Major (op. 92)«. This remarkable music, composed in 1812 during the later years of the composer's life as he was losing his hearing, resonates with questions of his time that remain relevant today: the failure of a revolution, the forced return to old traditions, the tension between the desire for social transformation and restoration, and the accompanying loss of freedom and future prospects. To the live electronic sounds of »Freiheit/Extasis«, a work commissioned and developed during the creation process and played on a modular synthesiser by artist Diego Noguera, Sasha Waltz revisits these themes at the start of the evening and interprets them from a contemporary perspective: How do personal freedom and societal constraints relate to one another?

In »Beethoven 7« widmet sich Sasha Waltz gemeinsam mit einem Ensemble von 14 Tänzer:innen der kompletten »Sinfonie Nr. 7 in A-Dur (op. 92)« von Ludwig van Beethoven. In dieser besonderen Musik, entstanden 1812 am Lebensende des Komponisten, als er bereits taub wurde, schwingen Fragen seiner Zeit mit, die für uns auch heute noch eine Rolle spielen: das Scheitern einer Revolution, die erzwungene Rückkehr zu alten Traditionen, die Reibung zwischen dem Wunsch nach gesellschaftlicher Transformation und Restauration und der damit einhergehende Verlust von Freiheit und Zukunftsperspektiven. Zu den live auf einem Modular Synthesizer gespielten elektronischen Klängen von Diego Noguera mit dem Titel »Freiheit/Extasis«, die während des Kreationsprozesses als Auftragswerk entstanden, greift Sasha Waltz diese Themen zu Beginn des Abends auf und interpretiert sie aus zeitgenössischer Perspektive neu: Wie verhalten sich persönliche Freiheit und gesellschaftliche Zwänge zueinander?

The Ballet of the Grand Theatre Łódź adds **»Roméo et Juliette«** to its repertoire.

Sasha Waltz is honoured with the **»German Dance Award«.**

REPERTOIRE

Beethoven 7 Berlin, Hamburg, Helsinki, Ludwigsburg, Rome
human requiem Berlin
In C Berlin, Hamburg, Weimar, Oslo, Paris, Thessaloniki, Guimarães, Essen, Lisbon
In C – Marler Partitur Marl
In C projects Ludwigsburg, Athens, London, Oslo, Beijing, Berlin, Havana, New York, Prague
Johannes-Passion Salzburg, Dijon, Paris
Roméo et Juliette Łódź
Sacre Berlin, Barcelona

KINDER- UND JUGEND-TANZCOMPANY

Constantly becoming *Alessandra Defazio, Wibke Storkan* Berlin
NEXUS *Wibke Storkan* Berlin
Wasser Tanz *Fernando Balsera Pita, Mata Sakka, Neslihan Schmidt* Berlin
Welleneffekt *Fernando Balsera Pita, Alessandra Defazio, Annapaola Leso* Berlin

GUEST PRODUCTIONS

Spiegelneuronen Berlin, Salzburg, Cologne, Hamburg, Kraków

FILM

Mystery 14 Human Requiem in Eleusis [70'] Direction Stephan Talneau, Jochen Sandig Coproduction Eleusis 2023 – Culture Capital of Europe, World Human Forum, Rundfunkchor Berlin, Sasha Waltz & Guests
La Passion selon saint Jean Sasha Waltz [130'] TV-Direction Corentin Leconte Production Arte France, Ozango, Opéra de Dijon, Sasha Waltz & Guests Broadcaster Arte France
In C [75'] Direction David Daurier Production Futur Antérieur Broadcaster Mezzo/ Philharmonie de Paris

2024

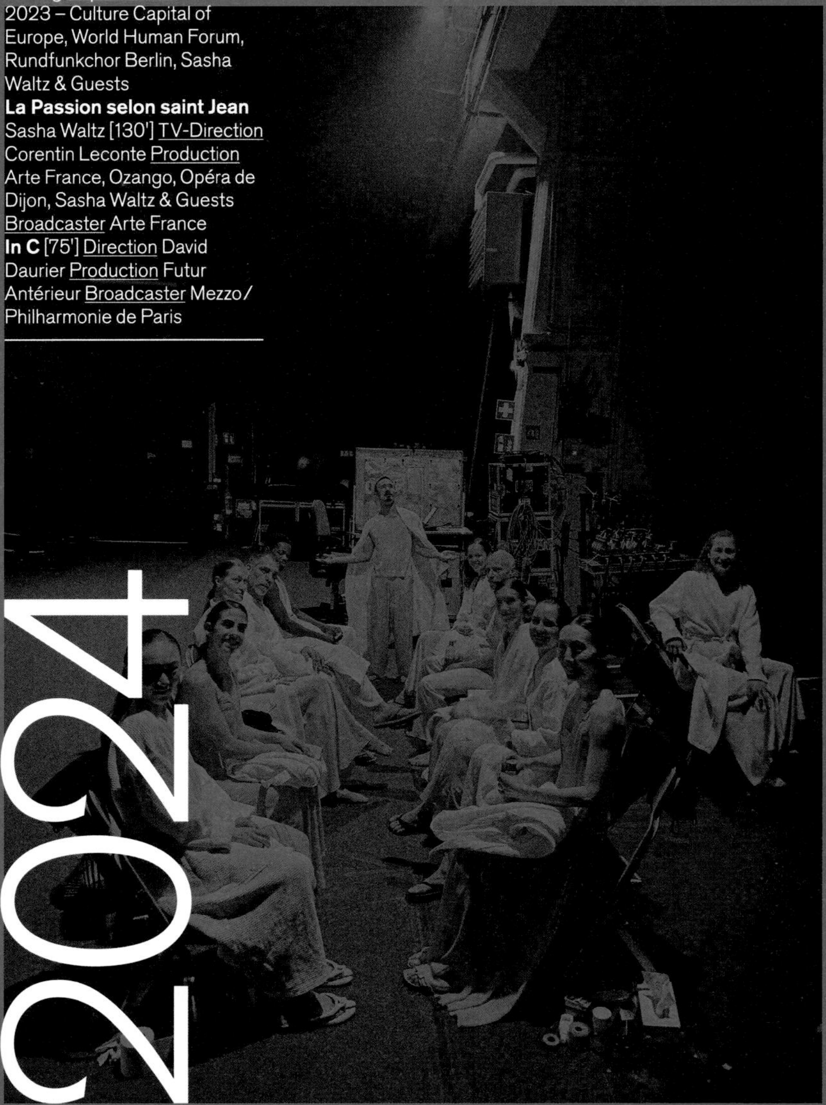

A

Johannes-Passion
↘pp. 28, 63, 132, 178, 180, 181, 212, 214, **325**

Johann Sebastian Bach
Osterfestspiele Salzburg, Felsenreitschule
22 Mar
Direction/Choreography
Sasha Waltz
Musical Direction
Leonardo García Alarcón
Costume Design
Bernd Skodzig
Stage Design
Heike Schuppelius
Light Design
David Finn
Dance/Choreography
Rosa Dicuonzo
Yuya Fujinami
Tian Gao
Eva Georgitsopoulou
Hwanhee Hwang
Annapaola Leso
Jaan Männima
Margaux Marielle-Tréhoüart
Virgis Puodziunas
Orlando Rodriguez
Joel Suárez Gómez
Sound Intervention
Diego Noguera
Soloists
Valerio Contaldo (Evangelist)
Georg Nigl (Pilate)
Christian Immler (Jesus)
Benno Schachtner (Countertenor)
Sophie Junker (Soprano)
Mark Milhofer (Tenor)
Estelle Lefort* (Ancilla)
Augustin Laudet* (Servus)
Rafael Galaz Ramirez* (Pierre)
Logan Lopez Gonzalez* (Countertenor)
Ensembles
Sasha Waltz & Guests
Chœur de Chambre de Namur*
Cappella Mediterranea
Chœur de l'Opéra de Dijon
Assistance Direction
Steffen Döring
Musical Dramaturgy
Tristan Braun
Repetition Dance
Yael Schnell
Repetition Dance Choir
Tristan Braun
Alessandra Defazio
Assistance Musical Direction
Rodrigo Calvevra
Choir Director
Anass Ismat
Production
Opéra de Dijon
Coproduction
Sasha Waltz & Guests
Théâtre des Champs-Elysées
Made in Radialsystem
Supported by
Aline Foriel-Destezet

L'Après-midi d'un faune
(Restaging)
↘pp. 128, 130, 132, **326**

Haus der Berliner Festspiele
27 Jun
Music
Claude Debussy
Direction/Choreography
Sasha Waltz
Video
Tapio Snellman
Light Design
Olaf Danilsen
Dance/Choreography
Rosa Dicuonzo
Eva Georgitsopoulou
Hwanhee Hwang
Annapaola Leso
Jaan Männima
Margaux Marielle-Tréhoüart
Joel Suárez Gómez
Repetition
Jiří Bartovanec
Production
Sasha Waltz & Guests
Made in Radialsystem

Spiegelneuronen
by Stefan Kaegi

A documentary dance evening Sasha Waltz & Guests with Rimini Protokoll
Salzburger Festspiele, Szene Salzburg
14 Aug
Concept/Direction
Stefan Kaegi (Rimini Protokoll)
Dramaturgy
Silke Bake
Music
Tobias Koch
Scenography
Dominic Huber
Video
Mikko Gaestel
Light Design
Martin Hauk
Costume Design
Sandra Tiersch
Rehearsal Direction
Claudia de Serpa Soares
Dance/Choreography
Melissa Kieffer
Francisco Martínez
Dominique McDougal
Orlando Rodriguez
László Sandig
Claudia de Serpa Soares
Wibke Storkan
With the voices of
Christina von Braun, Professor emerita, cultural history, gender theory, filmmaker
John-Dylan Haynes, Professor of Brain Research at the Charité Berlin
Sarah Karim, Sociologist and Lecturer at the Institute for Rehabilitation Sciences, Humboldt-University Berlin
Tim Landgraf, Professor of Artificial and Collective Intelligence
Nora Schultz, Research Officer at the German Ethics Council, freelance science journalist
Tania Singer, Professor of Psychology and Social Neuroscience
Production
Sasha Waltz & Guests
Made in Radialsystem
Cooperation
Rimini Protokoll
Coproduction
Salzburger Festspiele
Tanz Köln
Kampnagel – Internationales Zentrum für Schönere Künste

A **»Beethoven 7« backstage in Hamburg**

Eleven dancers sit naked at a long table, pulling fabrics through rattling sewing machines. They are stitching the dress of their lives, which will accompany them as the first cloth for baptism and the last shirt on their deathbed. Holding the white fabrics in their arms, they stand in the dim light of the stage horizon. Under the impact of the powerful opening movement and the choir's voices, the dancers approach the audience in slow vulnerability. They move closely together, yet each remains alone. Small before the great and simultaneously elevated by a will to live. A smile. An imperceptible tightening of the torso as it clings to the fabric, seeking protection. Throughout the piece, each will wear this dress at some point on their journey of suffering. This is a human passion in which Jesus appears in all bodies, transcending gender. They face a frenzied, discriminatory mob that mockingly laughs at Peter's suffering after he denies his discipleship. This group becomes a hateful assembly, ostracising the individual for divergent beliefs. Bach's »St John Passion« emphasises tenderness and sensuality despite despair, opening spaces for dance to explore states of the soul and transcend the narrative. The dramatic driving force of the turba choruses intensifies the work, shifting it from the liturgical to the operatic. Wooden staffs held by soldiers, as extended limbs of a murderous will, cut through the air in jagged movements of an agitated crowd, pointing towards the victim. The frame of a triptych, also made of thin wood, unfolds a living painting, referencing the Isenheim Altarpiece. Round mirrors render the human body visible at the moment of crucifixion, then reflect a fragmented image of a large painting that hangs just out of sight in the stage's heavens.

Elf Tänzer:innen sitzen nackt an einem langen Tisch und ziehen Stoffe durch ratternde Nähmaschinen. Sie nähen das Kleid ihres Lebens, das sie begleiten wird, als erstes Tuch zur Taufe, als letztes Hemd auf dem Totenbett. Sie halten die weißen Stoffe in ihren Armen und stehen im Halbdunkel des Bühnenhorizonts. Unter der Erschütterung des gewaltigen ersten Satzes und den Stimmen des Chores beginnen die Tänzer:innen, sich nackt, in langsamer Verletzlichkeit dem Publikum zu nähern. Sie gehen zusammen in nächster Nähe und doch alle für sich. Allein. Klein vor dem Großen. Und zugleich erhaben, von Lebenswillen getragen. Ein Lächeln. Ein unmerkliches Zusammenziehen eines Oberkörpers, der sich festklammert am Stoff und Schutz sucht. Im Laufe des Stückes werden alle einmal dieses Kleid tragen, auf ihrem persönlichen Leidensweg. Es ist eine menschliche Passion, in der Jesus in den Körpern aller auftritt, jenseits der Geschlechter. Sie sehen sich einer hetzenden, diskriminierenden Meute gegenüber, die hämisch über Petrus' Leiden lacht, nachdem er seine Jüngerschaft verleugnet. Sie wird zur hasserfüllten Gruppe, die das Individuum für einen abweichenden Glauben ausstößt. Bachs »Johannes-Passion« betont Zärtlichkeit, Sinnlichkeit trotz Verzweiflung, wodurch sich Räume für den Tanz eröffnen, Seelenzustände zu durchwandern und über die Narration hinauszugehen. Die dramaturgisch treibende Kraft der Turba-Chöre, die sich immer weiter zuspitzt, bewegt das Werk vom Liturgischen hin zur Oper. Hölzerne Stäbe der Soldaten, als verlängerte Körperglieder eines mordenden Willens, durchfahren mit den Bewegungen eines aufgebrachten Volkes in kantigen Zeichen die Luft, auf das Opfer deutend. Aus dünnem Holz ist auch der Rahmen eines Triptychons, in dem sich ein lebendiges Gemälde ausbreitet, eine Referenz auf den Isenheimer Altar. Runde Spiegel machen im Moment der Kreuzigung erst den menschlichen Körper sichtbar, reflektieren dann fragmentarisch ein großes Gemälde, das dem Blick entzogen am Bühnenhimmel hängt.

L'Après-midi d'un faune

Eleven years after the first version, Sasha Waltz reinterprets the piece »L'Après-midi d'un faune« by Debussy. She envisions a video work and invites visual artist Tapio Snelman to film with her. For the shoot, the dancers immerse themselves in untouched nature – an ancient landscape, a riverbank, purple lupines and a clearing covered with silvery leaves from the previous year. The touches of our naked skin, the scents and sun-dappled shadows, the rustling of branches and the caress of leaves against our legs give rise to a physical vocabulary and a dramaturgy of the faun. We are nature, diving in, becoming enchanted. The sensation of freedom in the body, naked, without social status or guilt. How does a body move that is not constrained by the prohibition of shame? Is innocence conceivable to hallucinate a pure erotic field? Is this paradise or an illusion? In this space of freedom, no gender exists; attraction is infinite. On the heat of a summer afternoon, surrounded by buzzing insects and crackling air, a childlike simplicity reigns in the meadows, and the primal state of unbridled desire transports us into the realm of fauna and flora. This contemporary interpretation, set to Debussy's impressionistic music, is a painting that reveals a hint of beauty. The dramatic structure follows the experience of a day in nature and is contrapuntally and ironically disrupted by a fragmentary classical ballet vocabulary. It evokes images of Nijinsky's dance without directly referencing it. The images reflect from the deep, subconscious waters, revealing the ever-challenging form of the faun.

Elf Jahre nach der ersten Version schreibt Sasha Waltz das Stück »L'Après-midi d'un faune« von Debussy neu. Sie denkt an eine Videoarbeit und bittet den Bildenden Künstler Tapio Snelman, mit ihr zu filmen. Für die Dreharbeiten begeben sich die Tänzer:innen in unberührte Natur – eine vorzeitliche Landschaft, ein Flussufer, lila Lupinen, eine Lichtung, die Erde bedeckt mit silbrigen Blättern des vergangenen Jahres. Die Berührungen unserer nackten Haut, die Gerüche und sonnenbeschienenen Schatten, das Rauschen der Äste und das Streicheln der Blätter an den Beinen führen zu einem körperlichen Vokabular und einer Dramaturgie des Fauns. Wir sind die Natur, tauchen ein, werden verführt. Das Gefühl von Freiheit im Körper, nackt, ohne gesellschaftlichen Status oder Schuld. Wie bewegt sich ein Körper, der nicht durch das Verbot der Scham eingeschränkt ist? Ist Unschuld vorstellbar, um ein reines erotisches Feld zu halluzinieren? Ist das das Paradies oder Täuschung? In diesem Freiheitsraum existiert kein Geschlecht, die Anziehung ist unendlich. In der Hitze eines Sommernachmittags, umgeben von summenden Insekten und knisternder Luft, herrscht kindliche Einfachheit auf den Wiesen, und der animalische Zustand ungebundener Sehnsucht entführt uns in die Vorstellung einer Fauna und Flora. Eine zeitgenössische Interpretation zur impressionistischen Musik von Debussy, ein Gemälde, das uns einen Hauch von Schönheit offenbart. Die dramatische Struktur folgt der Erfahrung eines Tages in der Natur und wird durch ein fragmentarisches klassisches Ballettvokabular kontrapunktiert und ironisch gebrochen. Sie evoziert Bilder von Nijinskys Tanz, ohne sich direkt darauf zu beziehen. Die Bilder spiegeln sich in den tiefen, unterbewussten Gewässern wider und enthüllen die immer wieder herausfordernde Gestalt des Fauns.

Appendix

Anhang

List of Figures
Abbildungsverzeichnis

47 H »The Medici Venus, female whole body model with removable internal organs«, workshop La Specola, Florence, 1781–86. Photo: Josephinum – Ethics, Collections and History of Medicine, MedUni Vienna

47 I »Körper«, study for the costume design, 2000 © Bernd Skodzig

47 J »Women«, St. Elisabeth-Kirche, Berlin, 2016, premiere © Ute Zscharnt

48 A »Dialoge '99/II – Jüdisches Museum«, Jüdisches Museum, Berlin, 1999 © Bernd Uhlig

48 B »Körper« at Center for Art and Media Karlsruhe (ZKM), 2013 © Martin Wagenhan

48 C Francisco de Goya, »Muertos recogido« from »Desastres de la guerra«, 1810–23. Photo: bpk / Herzog Anton Ulrich-Museum

49 D Louise Bourgeois, »Seven in Bed«, 2001. Photo: Christopher Burke © The Easton Foundation / VG Bild-Kunst, Bonn 2024

49 E »Körper« at Center for Art and Media Karlsruhe (ZKM), 2013, rehearsal © Sasha Waltz & Guests

49 F »Körper«, State Theatre at the Art Centre, Melbourne, 2009 © Ute Zscharnt

50 A »Körper«, Schaubühne am Lehniner Platz, Berlin, 2000, premiere © Bernd Uhlig

50 B »Medea«, Grand Théâtre de la Ville de Luxembourg, 2007, premiere © Sebastian Bolesch

51 C Abraham Bosse, ink drawing on the manuscript of Thomas Hobbes' »Leviathan«, 1651, offered by Thomas Hobbes to Charles II. Photo: British Library, London, UK / From the British Library archive / Bridgeman Images

51 D »SYM-PHONIE MMXX«, Radialsystem, Berlin, 2022, rehearsal © Bernd Uhlig

52 A »Allee der Kosmonauten«, sketchbook, 1995–96 © Sasha Waltz Photo: farbanalyse, Köln

52 B »ΕΞΟΔΟΣ | Exodos«, Radialsystem, Berlin, 2018, premiere © Carolin Saage

52 C »Körper«, State Theatre at the Art Centre, Melbourne, 2009 © Ute Zscharnt

52 D »insideout«, Radialsystem, Berlin, 2006 © David Baltzer

53 E »ΕΞΟΔΟΣ | Exodos«, Radialsystem, Berlin, 2018, premiere © Carolin Saage

53 F »Zweiland«, Berlin, 1996–97, research for the set design © Thomas Schenk

53 G »Zweiland«, Sophiensæle, Berlin, 1998 © Achille Le Pera

53 H »insideout«, Radialsystem, Berlin, 2006 © Angela Kröll

53 I »Dialoge – Künstlerhaus Bethanien (Showing I–V)«, Künstlerhaus Bethanien, Berlin, 1993 © David Brandt

53 J »Allee der Kosmonauten«, Radialsystem, Berlin, 2009 © Sebastian Bolesch

54 »ΕΞΟΔΟΣ | Exodos«, Radialsystem, Berlin, 2018, premiere © Carolin Saage

56 A »Gezeiten«, Schaubühne am Lehniner Platz, Berlin, 2005, premiere © Gert Weigelt

56 B »Zweiland«, Sophiensæle, Berlin, 2006 © Sebastian Bolesch

56 C »Travelogue II – Tears break fast«, Podewil, Berlin, 1994, premiere © Dirk Bleicker

56 D »insideout«, Radialsystem, Berlin, 2006 © André Rival

57 E »Gezeiten«, Schaubühne am Lehniner Platz, Berlin, 2005, premiere © Sebastian Bolesch

57 F »Women«, St. Elisabeth-Kirche, Berlin, 2016, rehearsal © Jochen Sandig

57 G »Dialoge 2020 – Relevante Systeme II«, film stills, Radialsystem, Berlin, 2020 © Christina Voigt

57 H »Travelogue I – Twenty to eight«, Rustaveli National Theatre, Tbilisi, 2015 © Gia Gogatishvili

57 I »Dialoge 2013 – Kolkata«, Jorasanko Rajbati, Kolkata, 2013 © Martin Wälde

58 A »Dialoge 07 – Pergamonmuseum«, Pergamonmuseum, Berlin, 2007 © Sebastian Bolesch

58 B Radegast Station – Łódź Ghetto Holocaust Memorial, research, 2022 © Sasha Waltz

58 C »Na Zemlje«, Sophiensæle, Berlin, 1998, premiere © David Baltzer

59 D »ΕΞΟΔΟΣ | Exodos«, Radialsystem, Berlin, 2018, premiere © Carolin Saage

59 E Hieronymus Bosch, »Ascent of the Blessed«, c. 1505–15, detail. Photo: bpk | Scala – courtesy of the Ministero Beni e Att. Culturali

59 F Sketchbook, c. 2001–08 © Sasha Waltz

59 G »Tannhäuser«, Staatsoper Unter den Linden, Berlin, 2023 © Bernd Uhlig

60 A »Sacre«, study, 2012–13 © Sasha Waltz

60 B »Sacre«, Staatsoper Unter den Linden, Berlin, 2013 © Bernd Uhlig

60 C Hieronymus Bosch, »The Garden of Earthly Delights«, 1490–1500, detail. Photo: Bridgeman Images

61 D »Women«, St. Elisabeth-Kirche, Berlin, 2016, premiere © Ute Zscharnt

61 E »insideout«, Radialsystem, Berlin, 2006 © Stephanie Pilick

61 F »ΕΞΟΔΟΣ | Exodos«, Radialsystem, Berlin, 2018, premiere © Carolin Saage

61 G »Dialoge '99/I – Sophiensæle«, Sophiensæle, Berlin, 1999 © Heike Schuppelius

61 H »rauschen«, Volksbühne Berlin, 2018, premiere © Oliver Look

62 A »Dialoge 07 – Pergamonmuseum«, Pergamonmuseum, Berlin, 2007 © Sebastian Bolesch

62 B »ΕΞΟΔΟΣ | Exodos«, Radialsystem, Berlin, 2018, premiere © Carolin Saage

62 C »Sacre«, study, 2012–13 © Sasha Waltz. Photo: Martin Wagenhan and ZKM | Karlsruhe

62 D »Medea«, Grand Théâtre de la Ville de Luxembourg, 2007, premiere © Sebastian Bolesch

63 E »Dialoge 2013 – Kolkata«, Jorasanko Rajbati, Kolkata, 2013 © Martin Wälde

63 F »Johannes-Passion«, film still, Opéra de Dijon, 2024 © Arte France, Ozango, Opéra de Dijon, Sasha Waltz & Guests

63 G »Medea«, Grand Théâtre de la Ville de Luxembourg, 2007, premiere © Sebastian Bolesch

64 »Körper«, Schaubühne am Lehniner Platz, Berlin, 2000, premiere © Bernd Uhlig

66 A »Kreatur«, photo shoot, Radialsystem, Berlin, 2017 © Ute Zscharnt

66 B »noBody«, Avignon, 2002 © Jochen Sandig

67 C »noBody« at Center for Art and Media Karlsruhe (ZKM), 2013 © Bernd Hentschel

68 »noBody« at Center for Art and Media Karlsruhe (ZKM), 2013 © Felix Grünschloss

70 A »Dialoge 09 – MAXXI«, Museo nazionale delle arti del XXI secolo (MAXXI), Rome, 2009 © Achille Le Pera

70 B »ΕΞΟΔΟΣ | Exodos«, Radialsystem, Berlin, 2018, premiere © Carolin Saage

70 C Sketchbook, 2008 © Sasha Waltz. Photo: farbanalyse, Köln

70 D Leonardo da Vinci, study of the fetus in the womb, c. 1511 © Royal Collection Trust / © His Majesty King Charles III, 2025 / Bridgeman Images

70 E Newspaper clipping from Sasha Waltz's sketchbook, undated

70 F »ΕΞΟΔΟΣ | Exodos«, Radialsystem, Berlin, 2018, rehearsal © Carolin Saage

71 G »noBody«, film stills, Schaubühne am Lehniner Platz, Berlin, 2000, premiere © Jörg Jeshel, Brigitte Kramer (nachtaktivfilm) ZDF/Arte

71 H »Kreatur«, Radialsystem, Berlin, 2017, rehearsal © Sasha Waltz. Edited for »Zusammenhalten«, poster campaign, 2020

71 I Rachel Kneebone, »Balance«, 2017 © Rachel Kneebone. Photo © Stephen White. Courtesy White Cube

71 J »noBody«, Schaubühne am Lehniner Platz, Berlin, 2000, premiere © Bernd Uhlig

72 A Drawing from sketchbook, undated © Sasha Waltz

72 B »Na Zemlje«, Sophiensæle, Berlin, 1998, premiere. Photo: Matthias Zölle © VG Bild-Kunst, Bonn 2024

72 C »Gezeiten«, Schaubühne am Lehniner Platz, Berlin, 2005, premiere © Gert Weigelt

73 D »Beethoven 7 in Delphi«, Ancient theatre of Delphi, 2021, contribution to »Beethoven – The European Tour: 9 Symphonies, 9 Cities« © Stephan Talneau

73 E »Continu«, notes, 2010 © Sasha Waltz

74 »Dialoge 09 – Neues Museum«, Neues Museum, Berlin, 2009 © Bernd Uhlig

76 A »Medea«, Grand Théâtre de la Ville de Luxembourg, 2007, premiere © Sebastian Bolesch

76 B Sasha Waltz, Karlsruhe-Rüppur, 1967 © Michael Voormann

76 C »Medea«, Grand Théâtre de la Ville de Luxembourg, 2007, premiere © Sebastian Bolesch

76 D »Körper«, film still, Schaubühne am Lehniner Platz, Berlin, 2000 © Jörg Jeshel, Brigitte Kramer (nachtaktivfilm) ZDF/Arte

77 E »S«, Schaubühne am Lehniner Platz, Berlin, 2000, premiere © Bernd Uhlig

77 F Hieronymus Bosch, »The Garden of Earthly Delights«, 1490–1500, detail. Photo: Bridgeman Images

77 G »Körper« at Center for Art and Media Karlsruhe (ZKM), 2013 © Bernd Hentschel

78 A »Medea«, Grand Théâtre de la Ville de Luxembourg, 2007, premiere © Sebastian Bolesch

80 A Théodore Géricault, »The Raft of the Medusa«, 1818–19. Photo: bpk | GrandPalaisRmn | Michel Urtado

80 B »ΕΞΟΔΟΣ | Exodos«, Jahrhunderthalle, Bochum, 2018 © Ursula Kaufmann

80 C »Dido & Aeneas«, Grand Théâtre de la Ville de Luxembourg, 2005, premiere © Sebastian Bolesch

81 D »Kreatur«, Haus der Berliner Festspiele, 2017 © Sebastian Bolesch

82 A »insideout«, sketchbook, 2003 © Sasha Waltz. Photo: Martin Wagenhan and ZKM | Karlsruhe

82 B+C »insideout«, Radialsystem, Berlin, 2006 © Stephanie Pilick

82 D »insideout«, Schaubühne am Lehniner Platz, Berlin, 2003, premiere © David Baltzer

82 E »insideout« at Center for Art and Media Karlsruhe (ZKM), 2013 © Martin Wagenhan

83 F »Allee der Kosmonauten«, photo shoot, Allee der Kosmonauten 81, Berlin, 1996. Photo: Matthias Zölle © VG Bild-Kunst, Bonn 2024

83 G »Dido & Aeneas«, Grand Théâtre de la Ville de Luxembourg, 2005, premiere © Sebastian Bolesch

83 H Federico Barocci, »Aeneas Carrying His Father Out of Troy«, before 1598. Photo: © GrandPalaisRmn (musée du Louvre) / Gérard Blot

83 I »Sacre«, Théâtre Royal de la Monnaie, Brussels, 2013, premiere © Bernd Uhlig

84 A »rauschen«, Volksbühne Berlin, 2019, premiere © Oliver Look

86 »Kreatur«, Radialsystem, Berlin, 2017, premiere © Luna Zscharnt

88 A Sketchbook, c. 2001–08 © Sasha Waltz

88 B »Passion«, film stills, Théâtre Royal de la Monnaie, Brussels, 2010 © Karsten Liske

88 C »Medea«, Grand Théâtre de la Ville de Luxembourg, 2007, premiere © Sebastian Bolesch

88 D »Dialoge – 17-25/4«, video installation, Schaubühne am Lehniner Platz, Berlin, 2001 © Heike Schuppelius

89 E »Dialoge 09 – MAXXI«, Museo nazionale delle arti del XXI secolo (MAXXI), Rome, 2009 © Bernd Uhlig

89 F »Matsukaze«, Théâtre Royal de la Monnaie, Brussels, 2011, premiere © Bernd Uhlig

90 A Notebook, 2020 © Sasha Waltz. Photo: farbanalyse, Köln

90 B »Orfeo«, Grand Théâtre de la Ville de Luxembourg, 2014 © Sebastian Bolesch

90 C Joos van Cleve, »Madonna and Child«, 1530–35, detail. Photo: Sailko / Wikimedia Commons

90 D »Kreatur«, Megaron, Athens, 2018 © Stylianos Tsatsos

91 E Watercolour, c. 2002–04 © Sasha Waltz

91 F Cosimo Tura, Dean from »Month of August«, Palazzo Schifanoia, c. 1470, detail. Photo: Musei Civici di Arte Antica, Museo Schifanoia and Palazzo Schifanoia, Ferrara Italy © NPL – DeA Picture Library / Bridgeman Images

91 G »Dialoge 09 – MAXXI«, Museo nazionale delle arti del XXI secolo (MAXXI), Rome, 2009 © Ute Zscharnt

91 H »Dialoge 09 – MAXXI«, Museo nazionale delle arti del XXI secolo (MAXXI), Rome, 2009 © Bernd Uhlig

92 A »Travelogue I – Twenty to eight«, Teatro Eliseo, Rome, 2012 © Achille Le Pera

92 B »Dido & Aeneas«, studio Saalmannstraße, Berlin, rehearsal © Sasha Waltz & Guests

92 C »Kreatur«, Opera Krakowska, Krakow, 2023 © Anna Kaczmarz

93 D »Dialoge 09 – MAXXI«, Museo nazionale delle arti del XXI secolo (MAXXI), Rome, 2009 © Bernd Uhlig

94 A »Gezeiten«, Schaubühne am Lehniner Platz, Berlin, 2005, rehearsal © Sebastian Bolesch

94 B »Dialoge 2020 – Relevante Systeme«, Radialsystem, Berlin, 2020 © Luna Zscharnt

94 C Francisco de Goya, »The Duchess of Alba Arranging Her Hair«, 1795 © Biblioteca Nacional de España

94 D »Zweiland«, Sophiensæle, Berlin, 1997, premiere © David Baltzer

95 E »Körper«, Schaubühne am Lehniner Platz, Berlin, 2000, premiere © Bernd Uhlig

96 A Drawing, undated © Sasha Waltz

96 B Andrea del Sarto, two studies of a man suspended by his left leg, 1530. Photo: The Devonshire Collections, Chatsworth / Reproduced by permission of Chatsworth Settlement Trustees / Bridgeman Images

96 C »Dialoge 09 – MAXXI«, Museo nazionale delle arti del XXI secolo (MAXXI), Rome, 2009 © Bernd Uhlig

96 D »Dialoge – Künstlerhaus Bethanien (Showing I–V)«, Künstlerhaus Bethanien, Berlin, 1993 © David Brandt

97 E »Dialoge 09 – Neues Museum«, Neues Museum, Berlin, 2009 © Bernd Uhlig

98 »ΕΞΟΔΟΣ | Exodos«, Radialsystem, Berlin, 2018, premiere © Phil Dera

100 A »Kreatur«, Radialsystem, Berlin, 2017, premiere © Ute Zscharnt

101 B »SYM-PHONIE MMXX«, Radialsystem, Berlin, 2021, rehearsal © Bernd Uhlig

101 C »SYM-PHONIE MMXX«, Teatr Wielki, Łódź, 2022 © Joanna Miklaszewskadz

102 »Kreatur«, Radialsystem, Berlin, 2017, premiere © Sebastian Bolesch

104 A »Roméo et Juliette«, Radialsystem, Berlin, 2017, rehearsal © Sebastian Bolesch

104 B »Kreatur«, film stills, Radialsystem, Berlin, 2017 © Bettina Borgfeld, Jochen Sandig

104 C »Kreatur«, Megaron, Athens, 2018 © Stylianos Tsatsos

104 D »Sacre«, Staatsoper im Schiller Theater, Berlin, 2013 © Bernd Uhlig

105 E »Roméo et Juliette«, Radialsystem, Berlin, 2007, photo shoot © Sebastian Bolesch

106 A »Dialoge '99/II – Jüdisches Museum«, Jüdisches Museum, Berlin, 1999 © Bernd Uhlig

106 B »Pomnik Willy'ego Brandta w Warszawie, główna tablica«. Photo: Cybularny / Wikimedia Commons

106 C Hieronymus Bosch, »The Garden of Earthly Delights«, 1490–1500, detail. Photo: Bridgeman Images

107 D »A woman kneeling down to pray«, collotype after Eadweard Muybridge, 1887. Public Domain Mark Photo: Wellcome Collection

107 E »Dialoge 09 – MAXXI«, Museo nazionale delle arti del XXI secolo (MAXXI), Rome, 2009 © Achille Le Pera

107 F »Sacre«, Haus der Berliner Festspiele, 2024 © Bernd Uhlig

108 A »Travelogue I – Twenty to eight«, Radialsystem, Berlin, 2007 © Sebastian Bolesch

108 B »Zweiland«, Sophiensæle, Berlin, 1997, premiere. Photo: Matthias Zölle © VG Bild-Kunst, Bonn 2024

108 C »Travelogue I – Twenty to eight«, Grand Theatre Groningen, 1993, premiere © Dirk Bleicker

109 D »Roméo et Juliette«, drawings, premiere gifts, 2018 © Sasha Waltz

109 E »Roméo et Juliette«, Opéra national de Paris, 2007, premiere © Bernd Uhlig

109 F »Travelogue II – Tears break fast«, Podewil, Berlin, 1994, premiere © David Baltzer

109 G »Dido & Aeneas«, Staatsoper Unter den Linden, Berlin, 2008 © Sebastian Bolesch

109 H »Kreatur«, Haus der Berliner Festspiele, 2017 © Ute & Luna Zscharnt

110 »Roméo et Juliette«, Opéra national de Paris, 2007, premiere © Bernd Uhlig

112 A »Körper« at Center for Art and Media Karlsruhe (ZKM), 2013 © Felix Grünschloss

113 B »Dialoge 2018 – Wirbel«, Radialsystem, Berlin © Eva Radünzel

114 A »Figure Humaine«, Elbphilharmonie, Hamburg, 2017, premiere © Bernd Uhlig

114 B Étienne-Jules Marey, »Cheval au trot, tenu par la bride«, Meudon Station physiologique, 1886. Photo: Collège de France. Archives. Fonds Marey (3 PV 1243)

114 C »Continu«, Haus der Berliner Festspiele, 2019 © Sebastian Bolesch

115 D »Dialoge 09 – MAXXI«, Museo nazionale delle arti del XXI secolo (MAXXI), Rome, 2009 © Bernd Uhlig

115 E »Körper« at Center for Art and Media Karlsruhe (ZKM), 2013, rehearsal © Sasha Waltz & Guests

115 F »ΕΞΟΔΟΣ | Exodos«, Radialsystem, Berlin, 2013, premiere © Carolin Saage

116 A »Dialoge 2020 – Relevante Systeme«, Radialsystem, Berlin, 2020 © Luna Zscharnt

116 B »Medea«, study, 2006–07 © Sasha Waltz

116 C Hans Namuth, untitled (Jackson Pollock), 1950. Photo: National Portrait Gallery, Smithsonian Institution; gift of the Estate of Hans Namuth. © 1991 Hans Namuth Estate, Courtesy Center for Creative Photography, University of Arizona

116 D »Impromptus«, BAM – Brooklyn Academy of Music, New York, 2005 © Julieta Cervantes

117 E »Körper«, Schaubühne am Lehniner Platz, Berlin, 2000, premiere © Bernd Uhlig

118 A Katsushika Hokusai, »Denshin kaishu: Hokusai manga« (Transmitting the Spirit, Revealing the Form of Things), vol. 7, 1819, detail. Photo: The Metropolitan Museum of Art, New York. Purchase, Mary and James G. Wallach Foundation Gift, 2013. Rogers Fund 1931

118 B »Matsukaze«, Théâtre Royal de la Monnaie, Brussels, 2011, premiere © Bernd Uhlig

119 C »rauschen«, Volksbühne Berlin, 2019, premiere © Julian Röder

119 D »S«, film stills, Schaubühne am Lehniner Platz, Berlin, 2011 © Jörg Jeshel, Brigitte Kramer (nachtaktivfilm) ZDF/Arte

120 A »SYM-PHONIE MMXX«, Staatsoper Unter den Linden, Berlin, 2022, premiere © Carolin Saage

120 B »SYM-PHONIE MMXX«, Staatsoper Unter den Linden, Berlin, 2022, premiere, rehearsal © Otello Annigoni

120 C »Impromptus«, Schaubühne am Lehniner Platz, Berlin, 2007 © Sebastian Bolesch

121 D »Zweiland Tour«, photo shoot, Damascus, 2010 © Sebastian Bolesch

121 E »SYM-PHONIE MMXX«, film still, Radialsystem, Berlin, 2021, rehearsal © Michael Ackermann

122 »Zweiland Tour«, photo shoot, Beirut, 2010 © Sebastian Bolesch

124 A »Matsukaze«, Théâtre Royal de la Monnaie, Brussels, 2011, premiere © Bernd Uhlig

124 B+C »Dialoge 2018 – Wirbel«, Radialsystem, Berlin © Eva Radünzel

125 D »Impromptus«, film stills, Radialsystem, Berlin, 2013 © MimeCenter Berlin

125 E Galileo Galilei, »Sidereus Nuncius«, 1610. Photo: bpk / DeAgostini / New Picture Library

125 F »Matsukaze«, sketchbook, 2011 © Sasha Waltz, pasted photograph: »Dialoge '99/I – Sophiensæle«, Sophiensæle, Berlin, 1999 © Heike Schuppelius

125 G »Impromptus«, BAM – Brooklyn Academy of Music, New York, 2005 © Julieta Cervantes

126 A »Sacre«, sketchbook, 2013 © Sasha Waltz. Photo: farbanalyse, Köln

126 B »SYM-PHONIE MMXX«, film stills, Staatsoper Unter den Linden, Berlin, 2022, premiere © Sasha Waltz & Guests

126 C »ΕΞΟΔΟΣ | Exodos«, film stills, Radialsystem, Berlin, 2018, premiere © Boiling Head Media, Sasha Waltz & Guests

126 D »ΕΞΟΔΟΣ | Exodos«, study, 2018 © Sasha Waltz

127 E »ΕΞΟΔΟΣ | Exodos«, Radialsystem, Berlin, 2018, premiere © Carolin Saage

128 A »L'Après-midi d'un faune«, video shoot, 2024, research © Steffen Döring

128 B »Dialoge 2020 – Relevante Systeme«, Radialsystem, Berlin, 2020 © Luna Zscharnt

129 C »Dialoge 2020 – Relevante Systeme«, Radialsystem, Berlin, 2020 © Luna Zscharnt

129 D »Dialoge 2020 – Strandbad Tegelsee«, Berlin, 2020 © Jochen Sandig

129 E »SYM-PHONIE MMXX«, Teatr Wielki, Łódź, 2022 © Joanna Miklaszewskadz

130 »L'Après-midi d'un faune«, Haus der Berliner Festspiele, 2024, premiere © Bernd Uhlig

132 A Matthias Grünewald, »Isenheim Altarpiece«, 1512–16. Photo: bpk / Grand PalaisRmn / image Société Schongauer

132 B »L'Après-midi d'un faune«, Haus der Berliner Festspiele, 2024, premiere © Bernd Uhlig

132 C »Johannes-Passion«, Felsenreitschule, Salzburg, 2024, premiere © Bernd Uhlig

133 D »Dido & Aeneas«, Staatsoper Unter den Linden, Berlin, 2005 © David Baltzer

133 E »rauschen«, Volksbühne Berlin, 2019, premiere © Julian Röder

134 »Medea Fries«, film stills, 2007, rehearsal © Hans Rombach Montage © Daniel Wiesmann

136 A »Körper«, State Theatre at the Art Centre, Melbourne, 2009 © Ute Zscharnt

136 B Lucas Cranach the Elder, »Hercules and Antaeus (?)«, H62/B1315, after 1505. Photo: Friedrich-Alexander-Universität Erlangen-Nürnberg, Graphische Sammlung

136 C+D »Körper«, Schaubühne am Lehniner Platz, Berlin, 2000, premiere © Bernd Uhlig

136 E Hans Bellmer, »La poupée«, 1934. Photo: bpk / Nationalgalerie, SMB, Sammlung Scharf-Gerstenberg / Hans Bellmer © VG Bild-Kunst, Bonn 2024

137 F »Zweiland«, Beirut International Platform of Dance, 2010 © Sebastian Bolesch

137 G Dirck Volkertszoon Coornhert, »Seditio (Rebellion), or the Separation of the Netherlands«, after Adriaan de Weerdt, 1604. Photo: Rijksmuseum, Amsterdam

137 H »Zweiland«, drawings, 1997–98 © Sasha Waltz

137 I Hieronymus Bosch, »The Garden of Earthly Delights«, 1490–1500, detail. Photo: Bridgeman Images

138 A »Women«, St. Elisabeth-Kirche, Berlin, 2017, premiere © Ute Zscharnt

138 B »Körper«, film stills, Schaubühne am Lehniner Platz, Berlin, 2000, premiere © Jörg Jeshel, Brigitte Kramer (nachtaktivfilm) ZDF/Arte

138 C Judy Chicago, »Boadaceia«, from: »The Dinner Party«, 1974–79 © VG Bild-Kunst, Bonn 2024

138 D Judy Chicago, »Eleanor of Aquitaine«, from: »The Dinner Party«, 1974–79 © VG Bild-Kunst, Bonn 2024

139 E »Dialoge 09 – MAXXI«, Museo nazionale delle arti del XXI secolo (MAXXI), Rome, 2009 © Bernd Uhlig

139 F »Körper« at Center for Art and Media Karlsruhe (ZKM), 2013 © Bernd Uhlig

139 G Photograph of detail of the Oval Dining Room of Palazzo Cini. Photo: Sasha Waltz

139 H »Körper«, Royal Swedish Opera, Stockholm, 2016 © Carl Thorborg

140 A »Kreatur«, Radialsystem, Berlin, 2017, premiere © Sebastian Bolesch

141 B »Allee der Kosmonauten«, Radialsystem, Berlin, 2009 © Sebastian Bolesch

141 C »Kreatur«, Radialsystem, Berlin, 2017, premiere © Sebastian Bolesch

141 D Sketchbook, c. 2001–08 © Sasha Waltz

141 E »Kreatur«, Radialsystem, Berlin, 2017, premiere © Sebastian Bolesch

142 A Hans Thalhofer, »Gerichtskampf Mann gegen Frau« aus »Fechtbuch von 1467 (BSB Cod.icon. 394a)«, 1467. Photo: Bayerische Staatsbibliothek, München

142 B »Continu«, Haus der Berliner Festspiele, 2010 © Sebastian Bolesch

142 C »SYM-PHONIE MMXX«, Staatsoper Unter den Linden, Berlin, 2022, premiere © Bernd Uhlig

143 D »ΕΞΟΔΟΣ | Exodos«, Radialsystem, Berlin, 2018, premiere © Carolin Saage

143 E Giotto di Bondone, »Ira (Allegory of Wrath)«, 1303–05. Photo: Mondadori Portfolio / Archivio Antonio Quattrone / Bridgeman Images

143 F »Ira – Zorn – Wrath«, Theaterhaus Stuttgart, 2022, premiere © Jeanette Bak

144 »Women«, St. Elisabeth-Kirche, Berlin, 2017, premiere © Ute Zscharnt

146 A »Dialoge 2020 – Relevante Systeme«, Radialsystem, Berlin, 2020 © Stylianos Tsatsos

146 B »Dialoge 2020 – Relevante Systeme«, Radialsystem, Berlin, 2020 © Luna Zscharnt

146 C Demonstration in Valparaiso, Chile, 8 March 2023, research © Sophia Sandig

146 D »Körper«, Schaubühne am Lehniner Platz, Berlin, 2000, premiere © Bernd Uhlig

146 E Newspaper clipping of X González at the »March for Our Lives«, 2018, research

146 F »SYM-PHONIE MMXX«, Teatr Wielki, Łódź, 2022 © Joanna Miklaszewskadz

147 G+H »Dialoge 2020 – Relevante Systeme«, Radialsystem, Berlin, 2020 © Luna Zscharnt

147 I »ΕΞΟΔΟΣ | Exodos«, film still, Radialsystem, Berlin, 2018, premiere © Boiling Head Media, Sasha Waltz & Guests

147 J »ΕΞΟΔΟΣ | Exodos«, Radialsystem, Berlin, 2018, premiere © Phil Dera

148 A »Kreatur«, film stills, Radialsystem, Berlin, 2017 © Bettina Borgfeld, Jochen Sandig

148 B »Kreatur«, Radialsystem, Berlin, 2017, premiere © Sebastian Bolesch

149 C »Kreatur«, study, 2016–17 © Sasha Waltz

149 D »Kreatur«, film stills, Radialsystem, Berlin, 2017 © Bettina Borgfeld, Jochen Sandig

149 E »Kreatur«, Haus der Berliner Festspiele, 2017 © Ute & Luna Zscharnt

150 A »rauschen«, Volksbühne Berlin, 2019, premiere © Oliver Look

150 B »Dialoge 09 – Neues Museum«, Neues Museum, Berlin, 2009 © Jochen Sandig
150 C »Medea Fries«, 2007, research © Sebastian Bolesch
150 D »insideout«, Radialsystem, Berlin, 2006 © Stephanie Pilick
151 E »Dialoge 06 – Radiale Systeme«, Radialsystem, Berlin, 2006 © Sebastian Bolesch
151 F »Medea Fries«, 2007, research © Sebastian Bolesch
151 G »Dialoge 07 – Pergamonmuseum«, Pergamonmuseum, Berlin, 2007 © Sebastian Bolesch
152 A »Dialoge 07 – Pergamonmuseum«, Pergamonmuseum, Berlin, 2007 © Sebastian Bolesch
152 B »Medea«, film stills, Staatsoper Unter den Linden, Berlin, 2007 © Karsten Liske
152 C »Medea«, study, undated © Sasha Waltz
153 D »Sacre«, film stills, Théâtre Royal de la Monnaie, Brussels, 2013 © Karsten Liske
153 E »Flower growing machine« from »Na Zemlje«, interactive object, Center for Art and Media Karlsruhe (ZKM), 2013 © Bernd Uhlig
154 »Figure Humaine«, Elbphilharmonie, Hamburg, 2017, premiere © Bernd Uhlig
156 A »noBody«, drawing, 2001 © Sasha Waltz
156 B Sasha Stone, Nelson-Revue, »Lichter von Berlin«, 1927
156 C »Continu«, Haus der Berliner Festspiele, 2010 © Sebastian Bolesch
156 D »Dialoge – Les Grandes Traversées«, Bordeaux, 2003 © Rodolphe Escher
157 E »rauschen«, Volksbühne Berlin, 2019, premiere © Julian Röder
157 F »Passion«, film stills, Opera de Lille, 2012 © Karsten Liske
158 »rauschen«, Volksbühne Berlin, 2019, premiere © Julian Röder
160 A »Kreatur«, Haus der Berliner Festspiele, 2017 © Sebastian Bolesch
160 B »Gezeiten«, Schaubühne am Lehniner Platz, Berlin, 2005, premiere © Gert Weigelt
160 C »Dialoge 2013 – Kolkata«, Jorasanko Rajbati, Kolkata, 2013 © Anubha Fatehpuria
160 D »SYM-PHONIE MMXX«, film stills, Staatsoper Unter den Linden, Berlin, 2022, premiere © Sasha Waltz & Guests
160 E »insideout«, Schaubühne am Lehniner Platz, Berlin, 2003, premiere © André Rival
161 F »Dialoge 2020 – Relevante Systeme«, Radialsystem, Berlin, 2020 © Luna Zscharnt
161 G »Orfeo«, photo shoot, Valentinswerder, Berlin, 2014 © Bo Madvig
161 H »Beethoven 7«, Radialsystem, Berlin, 2023, premiere © Sebastian Bolesch
162 A »Körper«, Schaubühne am Lehniner Platz, Berlin, 2000, premiere © Bernd Uhlig
162 B Titian, »Flaying of Marsyas«, 1570–76 © Derek Bayes. All rights reserved 2025 / Bridgeman Images
163 C »Körper«, Schaubühne am Lehniner Platz, Berlin, 2000, premiere © Bernd Uhlig
164 A–D »Figure Humaine«, film stills, Elbphilharmonie, Hamburg, 2017 © FAVO Film, Sasha Waltz & Guests, ZDF/Arte/Marcus Richardt
165 E »Kreatur«, Haus der Berliner Festspiele, 2017 © Sebastian Bolesch
166 »S«, Schaubühne am Lehniner Platz, Berlin, 2000, premiere © David Baltzer
168 A »S«, photo shoot, Schaubühne am Lehniner Platz, Berlin, 2000 © David Baltzer
168 B »Roméo et Juliette«, Opéra national de Paris, 2007, premiere © Bernd Uhlig
169 C »Figure Humaine«, Elbphilharmonie, Hamburg, 2017, premiere © Bernd Uhlig
169 D »Beethoven 7 in Delphi«, Ancient theatre of Delphi, 2021, contribution to »Beethoven – The European Tour: 9 Symphonies, 9 Cities« © Stephan Talneau
169 E Sketchbook, c. 2001–08 © Sasha Waltz
169 F »Dialoge 07 – Pergamonmuseum«, Radialsystem, Berlin, 2007, rehearsal © Sebastian Bolesch
170 A »THX 1138«, 1971, directed by George Lucas, film still © Warner Brothers/Getty Images / Michael Ochs Archives
170 B »rauschen«, Volksbühne Berlin, 2019, premiere © Julian Röder
171 C »Continu«, Haus der Berliner Festspiele, 2019 © Sebastian Bolesch
171 D »Continu« at Center for Art and Media Karlsruhe (ZKM), 2013 © Bernd Uhlig
172 A »rauschen«, Volksbühne Berlin, 2019, premiere © Julian Röder
173 B »Dialoge 09 – MAXXI«, Museo nazionale delle arti del XXI secolo (MAXXI), Rome, 2009 © Ute Zscharnt
173 C »Beethoven 7«, Radialsystem, Berlin, 2023, premiere © Sebastian Bolesch
174 A »Impromptus«, study, 2004 © Sasha Waltz
174 B »ΕΞΟΔΟΣ | Exodos«, Jahrhunderthalle, Bochum, 2018 © Ursula Kaufmann
175 C »Dialoge 09 – MAXXI«, Museo nazionale delle arti del XXI secolo (MAXXI), Rome, 2009 © Achille Le Pera
175 D »Dialoge 07 – Pergamonmuseum«, Pergamonmuseum, Berlin, 2007 © Sebastian Bolesch
175 E »Impromptus«, film stills, Radialsystem, Berlin, 2019 © Boiling Head Media, Sasha Waltz & Guests
176 A Wilhelm Eduard Weber, »A skeleton in motion«, lithograph, after 1836. Photo: Wellcome Collection
176 B »Dialoge 06 – Radiale Systeme«, Radialsystem, Berlin, 2006 © Sebastian Bolesch
176 C »Gezeiten«, film stills, Schaubühne am Lehniner Platz, Berlin, 2005, premiere © Sasha Waltz & Guests
176 D »SYM-PHONIE MMXX«, film stills, Radialsystem, Berlin, 2021, rehearsal © Michael Ackermann
177 E »Continu«, Radialsystem, Berlin, 2010 © David Baltzer
177 F »Roméo et Juliette«, Opéra national de Paris, 2007, premiere © Bernd Uhlig
177 G »Matsukaze«, Théâtre Royal de la Monnaie, Brussels, 2011, premiere © Bernd Uhlig
178 A »Johannes-Passion«, Felsenreitschule, Salzburg, 2024, premiere © Bernd Uhlig
178 B »Kreatur«, Megaron, Athens, 2018 © Stylianos Tsatsos
178 C »Kreatur«, Radialsystem, Berlin, 2017, premiere © Sebastian Bolesch
178 D »In C«, Berliner Dom, 2021 © Sebastian Bolesch
179 E »Dialoge 09 – Neues Museum«, Neues Museum, Berlin, 2009 © Bernd Uhlig
179 F »Dialoge '99/II – Jüdisches Museum«, Jüdisches Museum, Berlin, 1999 © Bernd Uhlig
179 G »Dialoge 2013 – Kolkata«, Jorasanko Rajbati, Kolkata, 2013 © Emilie Guérin
179 H »Dialoge – 17-25/4«, Schaubühne am Lehniner Platz, Berlin, 2001 © Jochen Sandig
180 A »Dialoge 2020 – Relevante Systeme«, Radialsystem, Berlin, 2020, premiere © Bernd Uhlig
180 B Andrea Mantegna, »St Sebastian«, c. 1470–80. Photo: bpk | GrandPalais Rmn | René-Gabriel Ojéda
180 C »Johannes-Passion«, Felsenreitschule, Salzburg, 2024, premiere © Bernd Uhlig
181 D »Johannes-Passion«, Felsenreitschule, Salzburg, 2024, premiere © Bernd Uhlig
181 E »Orfeo«, Teatro Real Madrid, 2019 © Sebastian Bolesch
181 F »Dialoge 09 – MAXXI«, Museo nazionale delle arti del XXI secolo (MAXXI), Rome, 2009 © Bernd Uhlig
182 A »Travelogue III – All ways six steps«, Theater am Halleschen Ufer, Berlin, 1995, premiere © Dirk Bleicker
182 B »Gezeiten«, Schaubühne am Lehniner Platz, Berlin, 2005, premiere © Sebastian Bolesch
182 C »Tannhäuser«, Staatsoper Unter den Linden, Berlin, 2014, premiere © Bernd Uhlig
182 D Lucas Cranach the Elder, »The Tournament with Lances«, 1509. Photo: The Metropolitan Museum of Art, New York. Gift of Alberta M. Welch, in memory of Alexander McMillan Welch, 1945
183 E+F »Dialoge 2021 – Ludwigsburg«, Blühendes Barock, Ludwigsburg, 2021 © Sebastian Bolesch
184 »ΕΞΟΔΟΣ | Exodos«, Radialsystem, Berlin, 2018, premiere © Carolin Saage
186 A »Dialoge 06 – Radiale Systeme«, Radialsystem, Berlin, 2006 © Jochen Sandig
186 B Drawing, undated © Sasha Waltz
186 C »Dialoge 2020 – Relevante Systeme«, Radialsystem, Berlin, 2020 © Stylianos Tsatsos
186 D »Roméo et Juliette«, Opéra national de Paris, 2007, premiere © Bernd Uhlig
187 E »Impromptus«, film still, Radialsystem, Berlin, 2019 © Boiling Head Media, Sasha Waltz & Guests
187 F+G »Dialoge 2020 – Relevante Systeme«, Radialsystem, Berlin, 2020 © Sebastian Bolesch
187 H »Dialoge 2020 – Relevante Systeme«, Radialsystem, Berlin, 2020 © Luna Zscharnt
188 A »Dialoge 2020 – Relevante Systeme II«, Radialsystem, Berlin, 2020 © Carolin Saage
188 B »insideout«, Radialsystem, Berlin, 2006 © Stephanie Pilick
188 C »Medea«, study, 2007 © Sasha Waltz
188 D »S«, Schaubühne am Lehniner Platz, Berlin, 2000, premiere © Bernd Uhlig
189 E »S«, Schaubühne am Lehniner Platz, Berlin, 2000, premiere © Bernd Uhlig
189 F Giovanni Battista Bracelli, »Bizarrie de varie figure«, 1624, detail. Photo: National Gallery of Art, Rosenwald Collection
189 G »Gezeiten«, Schaubühne am Lehniner Platz, Berlin, 2005, premiere © Gert Weigelt
190 A »SYM-PHONIE MMXX«, poster motif, 2023 © Daniel Wiesmann; film stills: »SYM-PHONIE MMXX« Radialsystem, Berlin, 2021 © Michael Ackermann
192 A »Tannhäuser«, Staatsoper Unter den Linden, Berlin, 2014, premiere © Bernd Uhlig
192 B »Matsukaze«, study, 2010/11 © Sasha Waltz
192 C Piero del Pollaiuolo, »Apollo and Daphne«, 1470–80 © The National Gallery, London, Wynn Ellis Bequest, 1876
192 D »Dido & Aeneas«, Grand Théâtre de la Ville de Luxembourg, 2005, premiere © Sebastian Bolesch
192 E Abraham Jamnitzer, statuette of Daphne, 1580–86. Photo: bpk / Staatliche Kunstsammlungen Dresden / Jürgen Karpinski
193 F »Matsukaze«, Théâtre Royal de la Monnaie, Brussels, 2011, premiere © Bernd Uhlig
193 G »Dialoge 2020 – Strandbad Tegelsee«, Strandbad Tegelsee, Berlin, 2020 © Philipp Dümcke
193 H »SYM-PHONIE MMXX«, Teatr Wielki, Łódź, 2022 © Joanna Miklaszewskadz
194 A »Dialoge '99/I – Sophiensæle«, Sophiensæle, Berlin, 1999 © Bernd Uhlig
194 B »ΕΞΟΔΟΣ | Exodos«, Radialsystem, Berlin, 2018, premiere © Phil Dera
194 C Hieronymus Bosch, »The Garden of Earthly Delights«, 1490–1500, detail. Photo: Bridgeman Images
194 D »Dialoge 2020 – Relevante Systeme«, Radialsystem, Berlin, 2020 © Stylianos Tsatsos
195 E »Körper«, Schaubühne am Lehniner Platz, Berlin, 2000, premiere © Bernd Uhlig
196 A »Körper«, film stills, Schaubühne am Lehniner Platz, Berlin, 2000, premiere © Jörg Jeshel, Brigitte Kramer (nachtaktivfilm) ZDF/Arte
197 B »ΕΞΟΔΟΣ | Exodos«, Radialsystem, Berlin, 2018, premiere © Carolin Saage
197 C »insideout«, Radialsystem, Berlin, 2006 © David Baltzer
197 D Christoph Angermair, Table clock (»Little Death Clock«), 1624 © KHM-Museumsverband
197 E »ΕΞΟΔΟΣ | Exodos«, Radialsystem, Berlin, 2018, premiere © Carolin Saage
197 F »insideout«, Radialsystem, Berlin, 2006 © Angela Kröll
198 A Margaret (Megan) Watts Hughes, »Untitled Voice Figure«, date unknown. Photo: Courtesy of Cyfarthfa Castle Museum & Art Gallery, Merthyr Tydfil
198 B »Dialoge 2018 – Wirbel«, Radialsystem, Berlin, 2018 © Eva Radünzel
198 C »insideout«, Radialsystem, Berlin, 2006 © Jochen Sandig
198 D »Dialoge – Künstlerhaus Bethanien (Showing I–V)«, Künstlerhaus Bethanien, Berlin, 1993 © David Brandt
198 E »Medea«, study, 2006 © Sasha Waltz
199 F »rauschen« Volksbühne Berlin, 2019, premiere © Julian Röder
199 G »Fantasie«, film stills, Opéra national de Lyon, 2006, premiere © Sasha Waltz & Guests
199 H+I »Dialoge 2018 – Wirbel«, Radialsystem, Berlin, 2018 © Eva Radünzel
200 A »SYM-PHONIE MMXX«, Staatsoper Unter den Linden, Berlin, 2022, premiere © Bernd Uhlig
200 B »SYM-PHONIE MMXX«, study, 2019 © Sasha Waltz. Photo: cyan/hausstætter herstellung
200 C »Körper«, Schaubühne am Lehniner Platz, Berlin, 2000, premiere © Bernd Uhlig
200 D »Kreatur«, Radialsystem, Berlin, 2017, premiere © Sebastian Bolesch
201 E »In C«, Berliner Dom, 2021 © Sebastian Bolesch
201 F »Kreatur«, Megaron, Athens, 2018 © Stylianos Tsatsos
201 G »Roméo et Juliette«, Opéra national de Paris, 2007, premiere © Bernd Uhlig
202 »Körper«, Schaubühne am Lehniner Platz, Berlin, 2000, premiere © Bernd Uhlig

204 A »Dialoge 09 – MAXXI«, Museo nazionale delle arti del XXI secolo (MAXXI), Rome, 2009 © Bernd Uhlig
205 B »Orfeo«, Teatro Real, Madrid, 2022 © Sebastian Bolesch
205 C »Dialoge 2018 – Wirbel«, Radialsystem, Berlin, 2018 © Eva Radünzel
205 D Writing, undated © Sasha Waltz
205 E »Körper«, sketchbook, 1999 © Sasha Waltz. Photo: farbanalyse, Köln
205 F »Impromptus«, Schaubühne am Lehniner Platz, Berlin, 2004, premiere © Jirka Jansch
206 A »Orfeo«, Grand Théâtre de la Ville de Luxembourg, 2014 © Sebastian Bolesch
206 B »Zweiland«, Beirut International Platform of Dance, 2010 © Sebastian Bolesch
206 C »Gezeiten«, Schaubühne am Lehniner Platz, Berlin, 2005, premiere © Gert Weigelt
207 D »Dido & Aeneas«, Staatsoper Unter den Linden, Berlin, 2019 © Carolin Saage
208 »Dido & Aeneas«, film stills, Staatsoper Unter den Linden, Berlin, 2005 © ZDF, Arte, ZDF theaterkanal, Sasha Waltz & Guests
210 A »Medea«, Grand Théâtre de la Ville de Luxembourg, 2007, premiere © Sebastian Bolesch
210 B »Beethoven 7«, Radialsystem, Berlin, 2023, premiere © Sebastian Bolesch
210 C »Dialoge 2020 – Relevante Systeme«, Radialsystem, Berlin, 2020 © Stylianos Tsatsos
210 D »Dialoge 09 – MAXXI«, Museo nazionale delle arti del XXI secolo (MAXXI), Rome, 2009 © Bernd Uhlig
211 E »Dialoge 07 – Pergamonmuseum«, Pergamonmuseum, Berlin, 2007 © Sebastian Bolesch
211 F »Medea«, Grand Théâtre de la Ville de Luxembourg, 2007, premiere © Sebastian Bolesch
212 »Johannes-Passion«, Felsenreitschule, Salzburg, 2024, premiere © Bernd Uhlig
214 A »Johannes-Passion«, Felsenreitschule, Salzburg, 2024, premiere © Bernd Uhlig
214 B »Gezeiten«, Schaubühne am Lehniner Platz, Berlin, 2005, premiere © Gert Weigelt
215 C »Allee der Kosmonauten«, Radialsystem, Berlin, 2017 © Eva Radünzel
215 D »Dialoge '99/I – Sophiensæle«, study, 1999 © Sasha Waltz
215 E »Gezeiten«, Schaubühne am Lehniner Platz, Berlin, 2005, premiere © Gert Weigelt
215 F »noBody«, Schaubühne am Lehniner Platz, Berlin, 2002, premiere © David Baltzer
215 G »Na Zemlje«, Sophiensæle, Berlin, 1998, premiere © David Baltzer
217 A »Körper«, film stills, Schaubühne am Lehniner Platz, Berlin, 2000, premiere © Jörg Jeshel, Brigitte Kramer (nachtaktivfilm) ZDF/Arte
217 B »Körper«, Schaubühne am Lehniner Platz, Berlin, 2000, premiere © Bernd Uhlig
218 Portrait of Sasha Waltz, Schaubühne am Lehniner Platz, Berlin, 2000 © André Rival
220 »rauschen«, Volksbühne Berlin, 2019, premiere © Oliver Look
222 »Zuhören #4: Climate change & democracy. From complexity to action«, Radialsystem, Berlin, 2019 © Eva Radünzel
226 A »Bungalow«, Hackesche Höfe, Berlin, 1993, premiere © David Baltzer
226 B Künstlerhaus Bethanien, Berlin, 2012 © Jörg Zägel / Wikimedia Commons
227 »Dialoge – Künstlerhaus Bethanien (Showing I–V)«, Künstlerhaus Bethanien, Berlin, 1993 © David Brandt
228 »Travelogue I – Twenty to eight«, Grand Theatre Groningen, 1993, premiere. Photo: Matthias Zölle © VG Bild-Kunst, Bonn 2024
230 A »Travelogue II – Tears break fast«, Podewil, Berlin, 1994, premiere © Dirk Bleicker
231 »Travelogue II – Tears break fast«, Podewil, Berlin, 1994, premiere. Photo: Matthias Zölle © VG Bild-Kunst, Bonn 2024
232 A+B »Travelogue III – All ways six steps«, Theater am Halleschen Ufer, Berlin, 1995, premiere. Photo: Matthias Zölle © VG Bild-Kunst, Bonn 2024
233 »Travelogue III – All ways six steps«, Theater am Halleschen Ufer, Berlin, 1995, premiere © Dirk Bleicker
234 »Dialoge '99/I – Sophiensæle«, Sophiensæle, Berlin, 1999 © Bernd Uhlig
236 A+B »Allee der Kosmonauten«, photo shoot, Allee der Kosmonauten 81, Berlin, 1996. Photo: Matthias Zölle © VG Bild-Kunst, Bonn 2024
237 »Allee der Kosmonauten«, Sophiensæle, Berlin, 1996, premiere. Photo: Matthias Zölle © VG Bild-Kunst, Bonn 2024
238 A Sasha Waltz and son László, Berlin, 1997 © Jochen Sandig
238 B »Travelogue I – Twenty to eight«, stage set with László, Bordeaux, 1997 © Jochen Sandig
238 C »Travelogue I – Twenty to eight«, Jochen Sandig and son László, Bordeaux, 1997 © Sasha Waltz
239 »Zweiland«, Sophiensæle, Berlin, 1997, premiere. Photo: Matthias Zölle © VG Bild-Kunst, Bonn 2024
240 A »Na Zemlje«, Sophiensæle, Berlin, 1998, premiere © Gerhard F. Ludwig
241 »Na Zemlje«, Sophiensæle, Berlin, 1998, premiere © David Baltzer
242 A »Dialoge '99/II – Jüdisches Museum«, Jüdisches Museum, Berlin, 1999 © Bernd Uhlig
242 B »Dialoge '99/I – Sophiensæle«, Sophiensæle, Berlin, 1999 © Bernd Uhlig
243 »Dialoge '99/I – Sophiensæle«, Sophiensæle, Berlin, 1999 © Bernd Uhlig
244 »Dialoge '99/II – Jüdisches Museum«, Jüdisches Museum, Berlin, 1999 © Bernd Uhlig
246 »Schaubühne am Lehniner Platz« © picture-alliance, ZB, Hubert Link
248 A Artistic direction of Schaubühne am Lehniner Platz (f.l.t.r.): Jochen Sandig, Sasha Waltz, Thomas Ostermeier, Jens Hillje, Berlin, 2000 © André Rival
248 B »Körper«, Schaubühne am Lehniner Platz, Berlin, 2000, rehearsal © Bernd Uhlig
249 »Körper«, Schaubühne am Lehniner Platz, Berlin, 2000, premiere © Bernd Uhlig
250 »S«, Schaubühne am Lehniner Platz, Berlin, 2000, premiere © Bernd Uhlig
252 A Artistic team of »noBody«, 2001 © André Rival
252 B »Dialoge – 17-25/4«, Schaubühne am Lehniner Platz, Berlin, 2001 © Jochen Sandig
253 »Dialoge – 17-25/4«, Schaubühne am Lehniner Platz, Berlin, 2001 © Jochen Sandig
254 A+B »noBody«, Schaubühne am Lehniner Platz, Berlin, 2002, premiere © Bernd Uhlig
255 »noBody«, Schaubühne am Lehniner Platz, Berlin, 2002, premiere © Bernd Uhlig
256 A »insideout«, Sasha Waltz with daughter Sophia and Thomas Schenk working on the stage design, Berlin, 2003 © Jochen Sandig
256 B »insideout«, stage model, Helmut-List-Halle, Graz, 2003 © Thomas Schenk
257 »insideout«, Helmut-List-Halle, Graz, 2003, premiere © André Rival
258 A+B »Dialoge 04 – Palast der Republik«, Palast der Republik, Berlin, 2004 © Bernd Uhlig
258 C »Dialoge 04 – St. Elisabeth I–IV«, St. Elisabeth-Kirche, Berlin, 2004 © Sasha Waltz & Guests
259 »Impromptus«, Schaubühne am Lehniner Platz, Berlin, 2004, premiere © Jochen Sandig
260 »Dialoge 04 – St. Elisabeth I–IV«, St. Elisabeth-Kirche, Berlin, 2004 © Sasha Waltz & Guests
261 »Dialoge 04 – Palast der Republik«, Palast der Republik, Berlin, 2004 © Bernd Uhlig
262 A First movement group for children by Sasha Waltz, 2005 © Sebastian Bolesch
263 »Dido & Aeneas«, Grand Théâtre de la Ville de Luxembourg, 2005, premiere © Sebastian Bolesch
264 »Gezeiten«, Schaubühne am Lehniner Platz, Berlin, 2005, premiere © Gert Weigelt
266 »Radialsystem«, Berlin, 2006 © Sebastian Bolesch
268 A »Körper«, poster in front of venue, Taipei, 2006 © Sasha Waltz & Guests
268 B »Dialoge 06 – Radiale Systeme«, Radialsystem, Berlin, 2006 © Sebastian Bolesch
269 »Dialoge 06 – Radiale Systeme«, Radialsystem, Berlin, 2006 © Sebastian Bolesch
270 A+B »insideout«, Festival d'Avignon, Espace St Louis, 2007, set up stage © Thomas Schenk
270 C »Medea«, Sasha Waltz studying the score, Berlin, 2006–07 © Jochen Sandig
271 »Roméo et Juliette«, Opéra national de Paris, 2007, premiere © Bernd Uhlig
272 »Dialoge 07 – Pergamonmuseum«, Pergamonmuseum, Berlin, 2007 © David Baltzer
273 »Medea«, Grand Théâtre de la Ville de Luxembourg, 2007, premiere © Sebastian Bolesch
274 A+B »Dialoge 08 – Venedig«, Palazzo Carlo Scarpa, Venice, 2008 © Luca Giarbardo
275 »Jagden und Formen (Zustand 2008)«, Schauspielhaus Frankfurt, 2008, premiere © Dominik Mentzos
276 A Sasha Waltz' Atelier at Villa Massimo, Rome, 2009 © Sasha Waltz
276 B »Dialoge 09 – MAXXI«, Museo nazionale delle arti del XXI secolo (MAXXI), Rome, 2009 © Ute Zscharnt
277 »Dialoge 09 – Neues Museum«, Neues Museum, Berlin, 2009 © Sebastian Bolesch
278 »Dialoge 09 – MAXXI«, Museo nazionale delle arti del XXI secolo (MAXXI), Rome, 2009 © Ute Zscharnt
280 A–F »Continu«, Schauspielhaus Zürich, 2010, premiere © Sebastian Bolesch
281 »Continu«, Schauspielhaus Zürich, 2010, premiere © Sebastian Bolesch
282 »Passion«, Théâtre des Champs-Elysées, Paris, 2010, premiere © Bernd Uhlig
284 A Sasha Waltz at Waldbühne, Berlin, 2011 © David Baltzer
284 B »Dido & Aeneas« at Waldbühne, Berlin, 2011 © Bernd Uhlig
285 »Matsukaze«, Théâtre Royal de la Monnaie, Brussels, 2011, premiere © Bernd Uhlig
286 A »MusikTANZ – CARMEN«, Sir Simon Rattle and Sasha Waltz during the rehearsal, Arena Berlin, 2012 © Monika Rittershaus
286 B »MusikTANZ – CARMEN«, Arena Berlin, 2012, premiere © Monika Rittershaus
286 C »MusikTANZ – CARMEN«, film still from a 180-degree shot, Arena Berlin, 2012, premiere © Heinrich Hertz Institut and Berliner Philharmoniker
287 »MusikTANZ – CARMEN«, Arena Berlin, 2012, premiere © Monika Rittershaus
288 »gefaltet«, Salzburger Landestheater, 2012, premiere © Bernd Uhlig
289 »human requiem«, Radialsystem, Berlin, 2012, premiere © Phil Dera
290 A Archive room with scores, drafts and sketches at Center for Art and Media Karlsruhe (ZKM), 2013 © Martin Wagenhan
290 B »Sacre«, Daniel Barenboim and Sasha Waltz during the rehearsal, Staatsoper im Schiller Theater, Berlin, 2013 © Bernd Uhlig
291 »Sacre«, Haus der Berliner Festspiele, 2024 © Bernd Uhlig
292 »noBody« at Center for Art and Media Karlsruhe (ZKM), 2013 © Martin Wagenhan
293 »Dialoge 2013 – Kolkata«, Jorasanko Rajbati, Kolkata, 2013 © Julieta Cervantes
294 A »Tannhäuser«, Sasha Waltz, Jochen Sandig, Peter Seiffert, dressing room, Staatsoper Unter den Linden, Berlin, 2014 © Jochen Sandig
295 »Tannhäuser«, Staatsoper Unter den Linden, Berlin, 2014, premiere © Bernd Uhlig
296 »Orfeo«, Teatro Real, Madrid, 2022 © Elena & Javier del Real
298 A Drawing for »Open Studio«, Radialsystem, Berlin, 2015 © Natascha Roy
298 B »Open Studio«, Radialsystem, Berlin, 2015 © Natascha Roy
298 C »Roméo et Juliette«, Radialsystem, Berlin, 2007, rehearsal © Emilie Guérin
299 »Feuerblume«, Radialsystem, Berlin, 2015, premiere © Sebastian Bolesch
300 A »Zuhören #1 – Continu und Gespräche«, Carolin Emcke and Yasmine Nayef Merei in conversation, Radialsystem, Berlin, 2016 © Stephanie Pilick
300 B »Zuhören #1 – Continu und Gespräche«, Multaqa – eating and exchanging, Radialsystem, Berlin, 2016 © Stephanie Pilick
301 »Zuhören #1 – Continu und Gespräche«, Radialsystem, Berlin, 2016 © Stephanie Pilick
302 A–D »Figure Humaine«, Elbphilharmonie, Hamburg, 2017, premiere © Bernd Uhlig
303 »Figure Humaine«, Elbphilharmonie, Hamburg, 2017, premiere © Bernd Uhlig
304 »Women«, St. Elisabeth-Kirche, Berlin, 2017, premiere © Ute Zscharnt
305 »Kreatur«, Radialsystem, Berlin, 2017, premiere © Sebastian Bolesch
306 A 25th anniversary of Sasha Waltz & Guests, Kino International, Berlin, 2018 © Jason Krüger
306 B »ΕΞΟΔΟΣ | Exodos«, Radialsystem, Berlin, 2018, rehearsal © Sasha Waltz

307 »ΕΞΟΔΟΣ | Exodos«, Radialsystem, Berlin, 2018, rehearsal © Carolin Saage
308 A »Impromptus«, stage set transport in Venice, 2019 © Martin Hauk
308 B »Dido & Aeneas«, water tank heating, backstage, Staatsoper Unter den Linden, Berlin, 2019 © Reinhard Wizisla
308 C »Sacre«, circle time before the performance, Staatsoper Unter den Linden, Berlin, 2019 © Reinhard Wizisla
309 »rauschen«, Volksbühne Berlin, 2019, premiere © Julian Röder
310 A »Dialoge 2020 – Strandbad Tegelsee«, Strandbad Tegelsee, Berlin, 2020 © Dieter Hartwig
311 »Tanztagebuch«, on YouTube, video stills, 2020 © Zaratiana Randrianantenaina, Hwanhee Hwang, Joel Suárez Gómez, Edivaldo Ernesto, Yael Schnell, Eva Georgitsopoulou
312 »Dialoge 2020 – Relevante Systeme«, Radialsystem, Berlin, 2020 © Stylianos Tsatsos
313 »Dialoge 2020 – Strandbad Tegelsee«, Strandbad Tegelsee, Berlin, 2020 © Philipp Dümcke
314 A–C »Beethoven 7 in Delphi«, ancient theatre of Delphi, 2021, contribution to Arte production »Beethoven – The European Tour: 9 Symphonies, 9 Cities« © Stephan Talneau
315 »In C«, Radialsystem, Berlin, 2020, premiere on a livestream © Yanina Isla
316 »Dialoge 2021 – Ludwigsburg«, Blühendes Barock, Ludwigsburg, 2021 © Reiner Pfisterer
318 A »In C«, advertisement in front of venue, New York, 2022 © Reinhard Wizisla
318 B »In C – Marler Partitur«, open-air in the city of Marl, 2022, premiere © Sebastian Bolesch
319 »SYM-PHONIE MMXX«, Staatsoper Unter den Linden, Berlin, 2022, premiere © Bernd Uhlig
320 »Ira – Zorn – Wrath«, Theaterhaus Stuttgart, 2022, premiere © Jeanette Bak
321 »In C – Marler Partitur«, open-air in the city of Marl, 2022, premiere © Florian Wagner
322 A »Sasha Waltz im Dialog mit Wolfgang Laib«. Wolfgang Laib, Not here, 1996, Installationsansicht: »Wolfgang Laib. The Beginning of Something Else«, 17.06.–05.11.2023, Kunstmuseum Stuttgart, © Wolfgang Laib / Photo: Gerald Ulmann, Stuttgart
322 B+C »Mystery 14 Human Requiem in Eleusis«, Eleusis archaeologial site, 2023, premiere © John Kouskoutis
323 »Beethoven 7«, Radialsystem, Berlin, 2023, premiere © Sebastian Bolesch
324 A »Beethoven 7«, backstage during the break, Kampnagel, Hamburg, 2024 © Francisco Martínez
325 »Johannes-Passion«, Felsenreitschule, Salzburg, 2024, premiere © Bernd Uhlig
326 »L'Après-midi d'un faune«, Haus der Berliner Festspiele, 2024, premiere © Bernd Uhlig
339 Team of Sasha Waltz & Guests, Berlin, 2024 © Jochen Sandig
344 »Körper«, photo shoot with Sasha Waltz and ensemble, Schaubühne am Lehniner Platz, Berlin, 2000 © André Rival

Text Credits
Textnachweise

28 Excerpt from »Nahaufnahme Sasha Waltz: Gespräche mit Michaela Schlagenwerth«, second extended and updated edition, Alexander Verlag Berlin, 2012, p. 123.
30 Text of dancer Clémentine Deluy in »rauschen«, 2019.
42 Claudio Monteverdi, »Orfeo: Favola in Musica / A Tale in Music«, Italian libretto by Alessandro Striggio and English translation by Gilbert Blin, 2012. https://monteverdi.co.uk/downloads/Monteverdis_Orfeo_-_Libretto_and_translation.pdf. Claudio Monteverdi, »Orfeo: Favola in Musica«, libretto by Alessandro Striggio, German translation by Liesel Bachem Sayre, printed in the programme booklet for »Orfeo«, 2014.
47 Texts of dancers Sigal Zouk and Claudia de Serpa Soares in »Körper«, 2000.
52/53 Words recited in »ΕΞΟΔΟΣ | Exodos«, put into text form by Simon Schmalhorst, printed in the programme booklet for the production, 2018, pp. 45–76.
78 Excerpt from Christian Ruzicska, »Medea, ihre Kinder sind wir: Zehn Angebote«, printed in the programme booklet for »Medea«, 2007, p. 63.
80 Yasmine Nayef Merei, foreword from »Female Voices in Exile«, no. 1, November 2017.
83 Excerpt from Heiner Müller, »Hamletmachine and other texts for the stage«. © 1984 PAJ Publications. Translation © 1984 by Carl Weber. Excerpt from Heiner Müller, »verkommenes ufer medeamaterial landschaft mit argonauten«, aus ders., Werke Bd. 5: Die Stücke 3. © Suhrkamp Verlag Frankfurt am Main 2002. Alle Rechte bei und vorbehalten durch Suhrkamp Verlag AG, Berlin.
85 Text of dancer Clémentine Deluy in »rauschen«, 2019.
92 Excerpt from the programme booklet »Dialoge: Künstlerhaus Bethanien, Showings I bis V« by Sasha Waltz.
101 Excerpt from T. S. Eliot, Vier Quartette. Übertragung und Nachwort von Norbert Hummelt. © Suhrkamp Verlag Berlin 2015.
108 Excerpt from the programme booklet »Dialoge: Künstlerhaus Bethanien, Showings I bis V« by Sasha Waltz.
120 Excerpt from »Nahaufnahme Sasha Waltz: Gespräche mit Michaela Schlagenwerth«, second extended and updated edition, Alexander Verlag Berlin, 2012, pp. 63/64.
126 Excerpt from Agnes Scherer, »Angstlust in der Enge: Moshpits, Drogenlabyrinthe, das Techno-Geisterhaus«, printed in the programme booklet for »SYM-PHONIE MMXX«, 2022, p. 28.
128 Excerpt from an original text contribution by Julia Franck for the programme booklet for »SYM-PHONIE MMXX«, 2022, pp. 34/35.
142 Yang Lian, »BUTTERFLY OF REVENGE«, in »Concentric Circles«, Bloodaxe Books, 2005, translated by Brian Holton. Reproduced with permission of Bloodaxe Books. www.bloodaxebooks.com
152 Excerpt from Christian Ruzicska, »Medea, ihre Kinder sind wir: Zehn Angebote«, printed in the programme booklet for »Medea«, 2007, p. 73.
157 Text of dancer Clémentine Deluy in »rauschen«, 2019.
162 Excerpt from an original text contribution by Julia Franck for the programme booklet for »Kreatur«, 2017, pp. 41–103, English translation by Katy Derbyshire.
168 Excerpt from Heiner Müller, »Hamletmachine and other texts for the stage«. © 1984 PAJ Publications. Translation © 1984 by Carl Weber. Excerpt from Heiner Müller, »verkommenes ufer medeamaterial landschaft mit argonauten«, aus ders., Werke Bd. 5: Die Stücke 3. © Suhrkamp Verlag Frankfurt am Main 2002. Alle Rechte bei und vorbehalten durch Suhrkamp Verlag AG, Berlin.
187 Yang Lian, »(1)«, in »Concentric Circles«, Bloodaxe Books, 2005, translated by Brian Holton. Reproduced with permission of Bloodaxe Books. www.bloodaxebooks.com
191 Excerpt from »Nahaufnahme Sasha Waltz: Gespräche mit Michaela Schlagenwerth«, second extended and updated edition, Alexander Verlag Berlin, 2012, pp. 81/82.
211 Excerpt from Virgil, »The Aeneid«, translated by A. S. Kline © 2002 Excerpt from Vergil, Aeneis: Studienausgabe Lateinisch – Deutsch (Sammlung Tusculum), De Gruyter, 1994, Buch I, S. 6.

Thank you for the kind permission to reprint. / Wir danken für die freundliche Erteilung der Abdruckrechte.

Original Text Contributions
Originaltextbeiträge

7 Sasha Waltz, Jochen Sandig
10–14 Senthuran Varatharajah
24 Stephanie Bender, Daniel Wiesmann
35 Undine Eberlein
36 Hannah Dübgen
40 Hannah Jonas
49 László Sandig
56 Friedrich von Borries
58 Candice Breitz
60 Jan Assmann
66 Volha Hapeyeva, English translation by Annie Rutherford
73 Undine Eberlein
101 Undine Eberlein
104 Senthuran Varatharajah
106 Senthuran Varatharajah
113 Christian Ruzicska
116 László Sandig
124 Hannah Dübgen
136 Katja Petrowskaja
140 Undine Eberlein
149 Robert Eikmeyer
150 Robert Eikmeyer
160 Yasmine Nayef Merei
170 Friedrich von Borries
173 Behzad Karim Khani
174 Aleida Assmann
178 Heinrich Kirschbaum
189 Hannah Jonas
193 Christian Ruzicska
194 Robert Eikmeyer
198 Hannah Dübgen
201 Hartmut Rosa
216 László Sandig
227–33 Jochen Sandig, László Sandig, Sasha Waltz
235 Jochen Sandig
237–44 Jochen Sandig, László Sandig, Sasha Waltz
247 Katrin Bettina Müller
249–64 Jochen Sandig, László Sandig, Sasha Waltz
267 Jochen Sandig
269–326 László Sandig, Sasha Waltz

With a few exceptions, the original texts are written in German and translated into English. / Mit wenigen Ausnahmen sind die Originaltextbeiträge auf Deutsch geschrieben und ins Englische übersetzt worden.

In this publication, gender-neutral language has been used wherever possible. In some cases, however, the authors have opted for the generic masculine. Unless otherwise indicated, the corresponding personal pronouns refer to all genders. / In dieser Publikation wurde, wo immer möglich, eine geschlechterneutrale Sprache verwendet. In einigen Fällen haben sich die Autor:innen für das generische Maskulinum entschieden. Sofern nicht anders angegeben, beziehen sich die entsprechenden Personalpronomen auf alle Geschlechter.

Sasha Waltz is a choreographer, dancer and director. After her initial studies at the School for New Dance Development in Amsterdam, in 1986 and 1987, she joins the postmodern-oriented dance scene in New York City that worked interdisciplinarily with other arts. Following her return to Europe in 1988, she begins an intensive phase of collaboration with choreographers, artists and musicians. In 1992, she comes to Berlin with a grant by the Künstlerhaus Bethanien, where she develops the improvisational format »Dialogue« driven by the spirit of her interdisciplinary and international work. She chooses the young German capital as the centre of her activities, where she practices new choreographic approaches in self-developed infrastructures. Together with Jochen Sandig, she founds the dance company Sasha Waltz & Guests in 1993, and in 1996 the Sophiensæle as a venue for dance and theatre – today it is a centre for the independent performing arts scene not only in Germany. From 1999–2004, she is one of the directors of the Schaubühne am Lehniner Platz. In 2006 she co-founded the Radialsystem, which up until today is the artistic home of Sasha Waltz & Guests. For the season 2019–20, Sasha Waltz is director of Staatsballett Berlin together with Johannes Öhman.
During her first decade in Berlin, Sasha Waltz creates internationally renowned and influential dance pieces, such as the »Travelogue« and »Körper« trilogies, as well as the immersive dance installation »insideout«. In the following years, she applies the language and strategies of contemporary dance to vitalise and explore historical and new operas and ballets. With »Dido & Aeneas« (2005), »Medea« (2007) and »Matsukaze« (2011), she realises three pieces about women and at the same time establishes the genre of the choreographic opera. In 2007, she directs »Roméo et Juliette«, interpreting the dramatic symphony of Hector Berlioz, for the Opéra national de Paris. After this follows »Sacre« in 2013, which is set to the music of Igor Stravinsky and commissioned by the Mariinsky Theatre in Saint Petersburg, and in 2014 »Tannhäuser« at the Staatsoper Unter den Linden in Berlin, which is conducted by Daniel Barenboim. Simultaneously, Sasha Waltz has been pursuing the sharing and teaching of dance knowledge and promoting dance as a medium of social and socio-political communication. As part of this endeavour, she founds the Berlin-based »Kindertanzcompany« (Children's Dance Company) in 2006 and, following an invitation from the Berliner Philharmoniker, develops a choreography with over 100 pupils to dance Rodion Shchedrin's »Carmen Suite«. In 2016, she founds the format »Zuhören« with which she opens a »third space for art and politics«. She expands the »Dialogue« concept to incorporate danced responses to architecture wherein the audience is invited to act as an equal part of the choreographic happening. Examples of this are »Dialoge '99/II – Jüdisches Museum« in the new construction of the Jewish Museum in Berlin by Daniel Libeskind, »Dialoge 09 – Neues Museum« performed in the still-vacant interior of the Neues Museum in Berlin after the renovation by David Chipperfield (2009) and the choreographic installation »Figure Humaine« for the inauguration of the Hamburg Elbphilharmonie (2017). In her present choreographic work, Sasha Waltz is focussing on the intensification of collaborative processes and the synchronic development of choreography and music. In collaboration with Soundwalk Collective and the costume designer Iris van Herpen (among others), she creates the choreography »Kreatur« (2017) followed by »ΕΞΟΔΟΣ | Exodos« (2018), both premiered at Radialsystem in Berlin. In early 2019, the project »rauschen« receives its world premiere at the Volksbühne Berlin. In March 2022, »SYM-PHONIE MMXX«, a piece for dance, light and orchestra by Sasha Waltz and Georg Friedrich Haas, receives its world premiere at Staatsoper Unter den Linden in Berlin, followed by »Beethoven 7« at Radialsystem, Berlin in March 2023. To mark the 300th anniversary of its world premiere, Sasha Waltz stages Johann Sebastian Bach's »St John Passion« (BWV 245) in spring 2024 as a timeless tale about the human search for truth and justice beyond its original religious implications. The production opens the Salzburg Easter Festival in 2024.
In 2020, Sasha Waltz reacts to the challenges of the COVID-19 pandemic with different projects on- and offline. From March to June 2020, she publishes an online »dance diary«, in August she develops the open-air project »Dialoge 2020 – Relevante Systeme«, premiering a choreography to Maurice Ravel's »Boléro« as well as solos to Georg Friedrich Haas' »I can't breathe« and in December streams a series of improvisations with the title »Dialoge 2020 – Relevante Systeme II« live from the Radialsystem in Berlin. In 2021, Sasha Waltz creates the choreography »In C«, which has since toured successfully nationally and internationally and has been passed on to a growing community worldwide. In June 2021, a choreography by Sasha Waltz to Ludwig van Beethoven's Symphony No. 7 receives its world premiere in the frame of the Franco-German television channel Arte's production »Beethoven – The European Tour: 9 Symphonies, 9 Cities«, broadcast live from the ancient Apollo temple in Delphi together with musicAeterna under the baton of Teodor Currentzis.
In 2011, Sasha Waltz is awarded the »Bundesverdienstkreuz am Bande« of the Federal Republic of Germany for her special services to the cultural field. Since 2013, she is a member of the Akademie der Künste Berlin. In 2021, Sasha Waltz is awarded a »Commandeur de l'Ordre des Arts et des Lettres« by the French Ministry of Culture and in 2024 she is honoured with the »German Dance Award«. In May 2025, Sasha Waltz is awarded the »Helmut-Schmidt-Zukunftspreis«; this award honours international personalities who, through their significant work, stand for democracy and the common good.

Jochen Sandig is born in Esslingen, Germany. In 1990 he moves to Berlin to study psychology and philosophy. Following the founding of the Tacheles Art Centre in 1990, in 1993, together with Sasha Waltz, he founds Sasha Waltz & Guests. In 1996 he co-founds Sophiensæle, an independent venue for dance and theatre in Berlin-Mitte, which he directs until 1999. From 1999 to 2004 Jochen Sandig is a member of the artistic direction of the Schaubühne am Lehniner Platz. Since 2004 he has been the director of the independent Sasha Waltz & Guests GmbH. In 2006, together with Folkert Uhde, Jochen Sandig founds Radialsystem in Berlin. In 2010, he is awarded a »Chevalier de l'Ordre des Arts et des Lettres« by the French Ministry of Culture. In February 2012, he celebrates his first direction work with »human requiem«, a staging of Johannes Brahms's »Ein Deutsches Requiem« in cooperation with the Rundfunkchor in Berlin and Simon Halsey. Since its premiere, the production has travelled to Hamburg, Amsterdam, Paris, Granada, Rotterdam, Athens, Hong Kong, Adelaide and New York. The production is awarded with the »Classical Next Innovation Award 2016«. As a social and political activist he becomes one of the three co-founders of the World Human Forum in Delphi, Greece. From 2019 to 2024, Jochen Sandig is artistic and executive director of the Ludwigsburger Schlossfestspiele. In the year 2023, Jochen Sandig is awarded the »Bundesverdienstkreuz am Bande« of the Federal Republic of Germany.

Sasha Waltz ist Choreographin, Tänzerin und Regisseurin. Nach ersten Studienjahren an der School for New Dance Development in Amsterdam schließt die gebürtige Karlsruherin sich in den Jahren 1986 und 1987 der postmodern geprägten, im interdisziplinären Austausch arbeitenden New Yorker Tanzszene an. Auf ihre Rückkehr nach Europa 1988 folgt eine intensive Zusammenarbeit mit Choreograph:innen, Bildenden Künstler:innen und Musiker:innen. Nach Berlin kommt sie 1992 durch ein Stipendium des Künstlerhauses Bethanien, wo sie aus dem Geiste des interdisziplinären, internationalen Arbeitens heraus das Improvisationsformat »Dialoge« entwickelt. Sie erwählt die junge Hauptstadt zum Zentrum ihres Wirkens und praktiziert dort neue choreographische Arbeitsweisen in selbst aufgebauten Infrastrukturen. Zusammen mit Jochen Sandig gründet sie 1993 die Compagnie Sasha Waltz & Guests und 1996 die Sophiensæle als eine Spielstätte für Tanz und Theater, die heute über Berlin hinaus ein Mittelpunkt der freien Szene ist. Von 1999 bis 2004 ist sie Mitglied der Leitung der Schaubühne am Lehniner Platz. 2006 ist sie Mitbegründerin des Radialsystems, wo bis heute die künstlerische Heimat von Sasha Waltz & Guests liegt. Für die Spielzeit 2019/20 übernimmt Sasha Waltz gemeinsam mit Johannes Öhman die Intendanz des Staatsballetts Berlin.
Während des ersten Jahrzehnts in Berlin schafft sie international maßgebliche Tanzstücke wie unter anderem die Trilogien »Travelogue«, »Körper« und die immersive Tanzinstallation »insideout«. In den darauffolgenden Jahren befasst sie sich mit der Mobilisierung des zeitgenössischen Tanzes für belebende und forschende Zugänge zu historischen und neuen Opern und Balletten. Mit »Dido & Aeneas« (2005), »Medea« (2007) und »Matsukaze« (2011) behandelt sie drei Werke über Frauen und prägt dabei das Genre der Choreographischen Oper. 2007 inszeniert sie außerdem für die Opéra national de Paris »Roméo et Juliette« zur dramatischen Sinfonie von Hector Berlioz. Es folgen 2013 »Sacre« zur Musik Igor Strawinskys im Auftrag des Mariinsky Theaters St. Petersburg und 2014 »Tannhäuser« in der Staatsoper Unter den Linden in Berlin unter der musikalischen Leitung von Daniel Barenboim. Parallel engagiert Sasha Waltz sich für den Transfer tänzerischen Wissens und den Tanz als Medium der sozialen und gesellschaftspolitischen Verständigung. Im Zuge dessen initiiert sie 2006 in Berlin die »Kindertanzcompany« und choreographiert 2012 auf Einladung der Berliner Philharmoniker mit über hundert Schüler:innen Rodion Schtschedrins Carmen-Suite. 2016 entwickelt sie das neue Format »Zuhören« und eröffnet damit einen »dritten Raum für Kunst und Politik«. Das »Dialoge«-Konzept erweitert sie um tänzerische Verhandlungen von Architektur, in denen das Publikum als gleichwertiger Teil des choreographischen Geschehens agiert. Zu diesen gehören »Dialoge '99/II – Jüdisches Museum« im damals noch leeren Neubau des Jüdischen Museums von Daniel Libeskind, »Dialoge 09 – Neues Museum« in den noch leeren Räumen des unter der Leitung von David Chipperfield wiederaufgebauten Neuen Museums in Berlin (2009) und die choreographische Installation »Figure Humaine« zur Einweihung der Elbphilharmonie (2017). In ihrer gegenwärtigen choreographischen Arbeit konzentriert Sasha Waltz sich auf die Verdichtung kollaborativer Prozesse und die synchrone Entwicklung von Choreographie und Musik. In Zusammenarbeit mit Soundwalk Collective und der Designerin Iris van Herpen (unter anderem) entsteht 2017 die Choreographie »Kreatur«, im Sommer 2018 folgt ihre Arbeit »ΕΞΟΔΟΣ | Exodos« (beide im Berliner Radialsystem), im Frühjahr 2019 feiert die Produktion »rauschen« an der Volksbühne Berlin Premiere. Im März 2022 kommt »SYM-PHONIE MMXX«, ein Werk für Tanz, Licht und Orchester von Sasha Waltz und Georg Friedrich Haas, an der Staatsoper Unter den Linden in Berlin zur Uraufführung, gefolgt von »Beethoven 7« im März 2023 im Radialsystem, Berlin. Zum 300. Jubiläum der Uraufführung inszeniert sie die »Johannes-Passion« (BWV 245) von Johann Sebastian Bach als eine universelle, zeitlose Erzählung über die menschliche Suche nach Wahrheit, Gerechtigkeit und Hoffnung auch jenseits seines religiösen Ursprungs. Die Produktion eröffnet 2024 die Osterfestspiele Salzburg.
Den besonderen Herausforderungen der Coronapandemie begegnet Sasha Waltz 2020/21 mit unterschiedlichen Projekten sowohl im digitalen Raum wie auch live vor Publikum: Es entsteht ein digitales »Tanztagebuch« auf YouTube, der Open-Air-Abend »Dialoge 2020 – Relevante Systeme«, in dessen Rahmen eine Choreographie zu Maurice Ravels »Boléro« und Soli zu Georg Friedrich Haas' »I can't breathe« zur Uraufführung kommen sowie eine Reihe von Improvisationen im Livestream aus dem Radialsystem unter dem Titel »Dialoge 2020 – Relevante Systeme II«. Im Jahr 2021 entwickelt Sasha Waltz die Arbeit »In C« zur Musik von Terry Riley, die seither erfolgreich national und international aufgeführt und an eine weltweit wachsende Community weitergegeben wird. Im Sommer 2021 entsteht eine Choreographie zu Ludwig van Beethovens 7. Sinfonie, gespielt von musicAeterna unter dem Dirigat von Teodor Currentzis, die im Rahmen des Projekts »Mit Beethoven durch Europa – 9 Sinfonien, 9 Städte« auf Arte in den Ruinen des Apollotempels in Delphi zur Uraufführung kommt.
Für ihre besonderen Leistungen erhält die Choreographin 2011 das »Bundesverdienstkreuz am Bande« der Bundesrepublik Deutschland. Seit Juni 2013 ist sie Mitglied der Akademie der Künste Berlin. Im Jahr 2021 wird Sasha Waltz vom französischen Kulturministerium zum »Commandeur de l'Ordre des Arts et des Lettres« ernannt. 2024 wird sie mit dem »Deutschen Tanzpreis« geehrt. Im Mai 2025 wird Sasha Waltz der »Helmut-Schmidt-Zukunftspreis« verliehen; diese Auszeichnung ehrt international Persönlichkeiten, die mit ihrem bedeutenden Wirken für Demokratie und Gemeinwohl stehen.

Jochen Sandig ist in Esslingen am Neckar geboren. 1990 kommt er zum Studium der Psychologie und Philosophie nach Berlin. Nach Gründung des Kunsthauses Tacheles 1990 gründet er gemeinsam mit Sasha Waltz 1993 Sasha Waltz & Guests. 1996 folgen die Sophiensæle in Berlin-Mitte als freie Produktionsstätte für Tanz und Theater, die er bis Ende 1999 leitet. Von 1999 bis 2004 ist Jochen Sandig Mitglied der Künstlerischen Leitung an der Schaubühne am Lehniner Platz in Berlin. Seit 2004 ist er Direktor der Sasha Waltz & Guests GmbH. Gemeinsam mit Folkert Uhde gründet er 2006 das Radialsystem am Spreeufer als »space for arts and ideas«. 2010 wird er vom französischen Kulturministerium zum »Chevalier de l'Ordre des Arts et des Lettres« ernannt. Mit »human requiem«, einer Inszenierung von »Ein deutsches Requiem« von Johannes Brahms mit dem Rundfunkchor Berlin unter Leitung von Simon Halsey, feiert Jochen Sandig im Februar 2012 sein Regiedebüt. Die Produktion gastiert seit ihrer Premiere im Radialsystem in Hamburg, Amsterdam, Paris, Granada, Rotterdam, Athen, Hongkong, Adelaide und New York. Sie wird mit dem renommierten »Classical Next Innovation Award 2016« ausgezeichnet. Im Rahmen seines gesellschaftspolitischen Engagements ist Jochen Sandig einer der drei Mitbegründer:innen des World Human Forums in Delphi, Griechenland. Von 2019 bis 2024 ist er Intendant der Ludwigsburger Schlossfestspiele. Im Jahr 2023 wird Jochen Sandig mit dem »Bundesverdienstkreuz am Bande« der Bundesrepublik Deutschland ausgezeichnet.

The dance company Sasha Waltz & Guests is founded in Berlin in 1993 by Sasha Waltz and Jochen Sandig and celebrates its 30th anniversary in 2023. To date, numerous artists and ensembles from the fields of architecture, visual arts, choreography, film, design, literature, fashion and music from more than 60 countries have collaborated as »Guests« on over 100 productions, »Dialogue« projects and films. Sasha Waltz & Guests works in a constantly evolving international and national network of production and guest performance partners, and since its foundation in 1993 has performed at over 300 venues and festivals in more than 50 countries and 180 cities. Today, the company is showing its current repertoire of 12 active pieces in about 80 performances each year. In Berlin, the company cooperates with a wide range of municipal theatres, opera houses and museums and has contributed to the founding of several new cultural institutions, including Sophiensæle (1996), St. Elisabeth-Kirche (2004) and Radialsystem (2006). In 2013, the company is named »European Cultural Ambassador« by the European Union. In 2014, Sasha Waltz & Guests is awarded the »George Tabori Preis« by the Fonds Darstellende Künste. Apart from Berlin stagings, national and international guest performances and the continual work on the repertoire, Sasha Waltz & Guests has been increasingly committed to educational and social projects. In 2006, the »Kindertanzcompany« (Children's Dance Company) is founded and since 2016 the interdisciplinary and open exchange platform titled »Zuhören« has served as a »third space for art and politics«. Alongside these initiatives, the company continues to propose diverse offers in the field of knowledge transfer. With the work »In C«, based on Terry Riley's open composition of the same name and consisting of 53 choreographic figures, a system with an internationally growing community has been developing since spring 2021: the choreographic material is recorded in video tutorials to enable the easy transfer of knowledge. As a result, participatory, diverse, international and sustainable »In C« projects, workshop formats and ever-new structures have emerged worldwide. Sasha Waltz & Guests is funded by the Senate Department for Culture and Social Cohesion.

Die Tanzcompagnie Sasha Waltz & Guests wird 1993 von Sasha Waltz und Jochen Sandig in Berlin gegründet und feierte im Jahr 2023 das 30-jährige Bestehen. Bis heute haben zahlreiche Künstler:innen und Ensembles aus Architektur, Bildender Kunst, Choreographie, Film, Design, Literatur, Mode und Musik aus mehr als sechzig Ländern in über hundert Produktionen, »Dialoge«-Projekten und Filmen als »Guests« mitgewirkt. Sasha Waltz & Guests arbeitet in einem internationalen und nationalen, sich ständig weiterentwickelnden Netz von Produktions- und Gastspielpartnern und war seit ihrer Gründung bereits an über dreihundert internationalen Aufführungsorten und Festivals in über fünfzig Ländern und 180 Städten zu erleben. Aus dem derzeit 12 aktive Produktionen umfassenden Repertoire zeigt die Compagnie ca. achtzig Vorstellungen pro Jahr. In Berlin kooperiert die Compagnie mit einer großen Bandbreite von Einrichtungen wie Stadttheatern, Opernhäusern und Museen und hat zur Gründung einiger neuer Kulturinstitutionen beigetragen, darunter die Sophiensæle (1996), die St. Elisabeth-Kirche (2004) und das Radialsystem (2006). 2013 wird die Compagnie zum »Kulturbotschafter der Europäischen Union« ernannt. 2014 ehrt der Fonds Darstellende Künste Sasha Waltz & Guests mit dem »George Tabori Preis«. Neben dem Berliner Spielbetrieb, nationalen wie internationalen Gastspielen und der Repertoirepflege ist Sasha Waltz & Guests auch sehr aktiv im Bereich »Education & Community« – ausgehend von der 2006 gegründeten Kindertanzcompany, der seit 2016 aktiven Plattform »Zuhören – Dritter Raum für Kunst und Politik« und verschiedenen Angeboten im Bereich Wissenstransfer. Mit der Arbeit »In C«, basierend auf Terry Rileys gleichnamiger und offener Komposition, bestehend aus 53 choreographischen Figuren, entwickelt sich seit Frühjahr 2021 ein eigenes System mit international wachsender Community: Das choreographische Material ist in Video-Tutorials festgehalten, um einen einfachen Wissenstransfer zu ermöglichen. Dadurch entstehen weltweit partizipative, diverse, internationale und nachhaltige »In C«-Projekte, Workshop-Formate und immer neue Strukturen. Sasha Waltz & Guests wird gefördert von der Senatsverwaltung für Kultur und Gesellschaftlichen Zusammenhalt.

1994 Prize for »Travelogue I – Twenty to eight« at the International Choreographer's Competition in Groningen.

»Berliner Zeitung« Critics' Prize for Sasha Waltz.

1997 »Allee der Kosmonauten« is invited to the 34th Theatertreffen, Berlin.

2000 »Körper« is invited to the 37th Theatertreffen, Berlin, and in addition to other international prizes, is awarded the »Grand Prix« at the Belgrade BITEF Festival.

The film »Körper« is nominated for the »Emmy Award«.

»Grimme-Preis« for the film »Allee der Kosmonauten«.

Critics' Prize from the Association of German Critics for Sasha Waltz.

2001 »Grand Prix Scènes d'Ecran« for the film »Körper« in Brussels.

2004 »OPUS-Preis« for the best set design of the year to »insideout« (Thomas Schenk and Sasha Waltz).

2007 Sasha Waltz is awarded »Most notable artist« in the field of dance in the 2006/07 season (critics survey by the magazine of the Deutscher Bühnenverein »Die Deutsche Bühne«) and »Best Choreographer« of the 2006/07 season (critics' survey by the »ballettanz« magazine).

Bronze at New York Festival in the category »Performing Arts« for the film adaptation of »Dido & Aeneas«.

2008 European theatre prize »New Theatrical Realities« for Sasha Waltz.

2009 Sasha Waltz is awarded »Officier de l'Ordre des Arts et des Lettres« by the French Ministry of Culture.

2010 »Caroline-Neuber-Preis« of the city Leipzig for Sasha Waltz.

Jochen Sandig is awarded »Officier de l'Ordre des Arts et des Lettres« by the French Ministry of Culture.

2011 Sasha Waltz is awarded the »Bundesverdienstkreuz am Bande« of the Federal Republic of Germany.

Vision Summit Award »Arts for Social Impacts« for Sasha Waltz.

2013 Sasha Waltz becomes a member of Akademie der Künste, Berlin.

On the occasion of its 20th anniversary, Sasha Waltz & Guests is appointed »Cultural Ambassador of the European Union«.

2014 Sasha Waltz & Guests is awarded the »George Tabori Preis« of the Fonds Darstellende Künste.

2021 Sasha Waltz is awarded »Commandeur de l'Ordre des Arts et des Lettres« by the French Ministry of Culture, and a star on the Sibiu Walk of Fame.

2023 Jochen Sandig is awarded the »Bundesverdienstkreuz am Bande« of the Federal Republic of Germany.

2024 Sasha Waltz is honoured with the »German Dance Award«.

2025 Sasha Waltz is awarded the »Helmut-Schmidt-Zukunftspreis«.

MONOGRAPHS, CATALOGUES (CHRONOLOGICAL) MONOGRAPHIEN, AUSSTELLUNGS-KATALOGE (CHRONOLOGISCH)

Waltz, S. and Künstlerhaus Bethanien (eds.) (1993) Dialoge: Fotodokumentation der Showings I bis V im Künstlerhaus Bethanien, mit Texten von Katrin Bettina Müller und Monika Stolina. Berlin: Künstlerhaus Bethanien.

Sasha Waltz & Guests (ed.) (2007) Cluster. Berlin: Henschel.

Sasha Waltz & Guests (ed.) (2010) Dialoge 09 – MAXXI. Berlin: Selfpublishing.

Waltz, S. and Schlagenwerth, M. (2012) Nahaufnahme Sasha Waltz: Gespräche. Second complete and revised new edition. Berlin: Alexander (Nahaufnahme).

Riedel, C., Waltz, Y. and Weibel, P. (2014) Sasha Waltz. Objekte, Installationen, Performances [Exhibition, Centre for Art and Media Technology Karlsruhe, 28 September 2013–2 February 2014]. Ostfildern: Hatje Cantz.

Uhlig, Bernd (2019) Bernd Uhlig fotografiert Sasha Waltz. Berlin: Selfpublishing.

Campanelli, N. (2023) Sasha Waltz & Guests: 30 Years of Creativity in Dance. Florence: Smith Editore.

PROGRAMME BOOKLETS (CHRONOLOGICAL) PROGRAMMBÜCHER (CHRONOLOGISCH)

Staatsoper Unter den Linden (ed.) (2005) Dido & Aeneas: Oper in drei Akten. Berlin: Selfpublishing.

Sasha Waltz & Guests (ed.) (2006) Gezeiten: Sasha Waltz. Berlin: Henschel.

Sasha Waltz & Guests (ed.) (2007) Medea. Berlin: Selfpublishing.

Sasha Waltz & Guests (ed.) (2011) Matsukaze. Berlin: Selfpublishing.

Sasha Waltz & Guests (ed.) (2014) Orfeo. Berlin: Selfpublishing.

Sasha Waltz & Guests (2016) Zuhören: Continu und Gespräche. Berlin: Selfpublishing.

Sasha Waltz & Guests (2016) Zuhören: Improvisationen und Gespräche. Berlin: Selfpublishing.

Sasha Waltz & Guests (ed.) (2017) Kreatur. Selfpublishing.

Sasha Waltz & Guests (2017) Zuhören: The Art of Resistance & Empowerment of Communities. Berlin: Selfpublishing.

Sasha Waltz & Guests (ed.) (2018) ΕΞΟΔΟΣ I Exodos. Berlin: Selfpublishing.

Sasha Waltz & Guests (2019) Zuhören: Climate Change & Democracy. From Complexity to Action. Berlin: Selfpublishing.

Sasha Waltz & Guests (2022) SYM-PHONIE MMXX. Berlin: Selfpublishing.

MONOGRAPHS/ ANTHOLOGIES WITH MENTIONS MONOGRAPHIEN MIT ERWÄHNUNGEN

Aimo, L. (2018) Corpo, danza, creazione: Sasha Waltz & Guests. Milan: Mimesis (Filosofie del teatro, 33).

Bätzner, N. and Brandstetter, G. (2010) Medeamorphosen: Mythos und ästhetische Transformationen. Munich: Wilhelm Fink.

Birkle, C. (2018) How I Felt. J. Kochs (ed.). Berlin: Revolver Publishing.

Bleeker, M. (2008) Anatomy Live: Performance and the Operating Theatre. Amsterdam: Amsterdam University Press.

Blüher, J. (2010) Villa Massimo Jahresbericht 2010. Rome: Deutsche Akademie Rom.

Bögner, H.-G. and Deutsches Tanzarchiv Köln (eds.) (2000) TanzGespräche: Zeitgenössischer Tanz im Dialog. First edition. Cologne: M7-Verlag.

Boisseau, R., Gattinoni, C. and Philippe, L. (2011) Danse et art contemporain. Paris: Nouvelles éditions Scala (Sentiers d'art).

Brandstätter, U. (2013) Erkenntnis durch Kunst: Theorie und Praxis der ästhetischen Transformation. Vienna, Cologne and Weimar: Böhlau Verlag.

Bredekamp, H. (2010) Theorie des Bildakts. First edition. Frankfurt: Suhrkamp.

Caleo, I. (2021) Performance, materia, affetti: una cartografia femminista. Roma: Bulzoni editore (Biblioteca teatrale, Estetica e politica della performance).

Cervantes, J. (2006) Sasha Waltz & Guests: Photographs by Julieta Cervantes. New York.

Fensch, A. (2024) Portraits aus dem neuen Deutschland: Leben ist Veränderung. First edition. Kieve.

Fesel, A. and Keller, C. (2014) Berlin Wonderland: Wild Years Revisited 1990–1996. Berlin: bobsairport.

Fesel, A. and Keller, C. (2017) Berlin Heartbeats: Stories from the Wild Years, 1990–present. First edition. Berlin: Suhrkamp nova (Suhrkamp Taschenbuch, 4768).

Fischer, D. E. (2019) Eine kurze Geschichte des Tanzes. Leipzig: Henschel.

Foelmer, S. (2009) Am Rand der Körper: Inventuren des Unabgeschlossenen im Zeitgenössischen Tanz. Bielefeld: Transcript (Tanz Scripte, 18).

Fondazione I Teatri (2007) Identità e memoria: La generazione di mezzo. Valli di Reggio Emilia: Edizioni del Teatro Municipale Valli di Reggio Emilia.

Garde, U. and Severn, J. R. (eds.) (2020) Theatre and Internationalization: Perspectives from Australia, Germany, and Beyond. London: Routledge.

Haitzinger, N. and Kollinger, F. (eds.) (2016) Überschreitungen: Beiträge zur Theoretisierung von Inszenierungs- und Aufführungspraxis. Munich: epodium.

Hinzmann, J. and Merschmeier, M. (eds.) (1998) Tanztheater heute: Dreissig Jahre Deutsche Tanzgeschichte. Der Katalog zur Fotoausstellung des Goethe-Instituts. Seelze/Hannover: Kallmeyersche.

Holleben, J. von (2008) Snowbed, Ars Melancholia. London: Photographer's Office.

Kellermann, J. (2022) Dramaturgies of Love in Romeo and Juliet: Word, Music, and Dance. New York: Routledge.

Meyer, W. and Kunsthalle Göppingen (eds.) (2019) Tanz, Bewegung, Geste, Bild. Göppingen: Kunsthalle Göppingen.

Mohs, D. (2021) Kinästhetische Interferenzen: Körpertechnik und Tanznotation im Entwurfsprozess architektonischer Räume. Bielefeld: transcript (Architekturen, 65).

No author (2016) Überschreitungen: Beiträge zur Theoretisierung von Inszenierungs- und Aufführungspraxis. Munich: epodium.

Noisette, P. (2019) Couturiers de la danse: De Chanel à Versace. Milan: Silvana Editoriale.

Schouten, S. (2007) Sinnliches Spüren: Wahrnehmung und Erzeugung von Atmosphären im Theater. Berlin: Theater der Zeit (Recherchen, 46).

Schulze, J. (1999) Dancing Bodies, Dancing Gender: Tanz im 20. Jahrhundert aus der Perspektive der Gender-Theorie. First edition. Dortmund: Ed. Ebersbach.

Serafin, S. and Yung, S. (eds.) (2018) BAM: The Next Wave Festival. New York: BAM: The Brooklyn Academy of Music.

Sörgel, S. (2015) Dance and the Body in Western Theatre: 1948 to the Present. London: Palgrave Macmillan.

Stocker, K., Cusimano, N. and Schurl, K. (eds.) (2003) Insideout. Vienna, New York: Springer.

Traub, U. (2010) Theater der Nacktheit: zum Bedeutungswandel entblößter Körper auf der Bühne seit 1900. Bielefeld: transcript Verlag (Theater, Bd. 24).

Uhlig, B. (2000) Tanzbilder: Fotografien; fotografiert mit der Leica und Leica-Objektiven. Berlin: Alexander Verlag.

Voigt, K. (2020) Sterbeorte: Über eine neue Sichtbarkeit des Sterbens in der Architektur. Bielefeld: transcript (Architekturen, 52).

Werner, F., Kalu, J. K. and Kirchner, A. (eds.) (2021) OPENINGS – Sophiensæle 2011–2021. Berlin: Alexander Verlag.

ACADEMIC PAPERS/ ARTICLES AKADEMISCHE AUFSÄTZE

Avanzini, S. (2022) »Choreografie, Kartographie oder Malerei?«, kunsttexte.de – Journal für Kunst- und Bildgeschichte, pp. 1–7.

Avanzini, S. (2023) »Insideout: Eine begehbare Installation von Sasha Waltz mit Musik von Rebecca Saunders«, Kieler Beiträge zur Filmmusikforschung, 11, pp. 249–77.

Becker, S. and Ngo, A.-L. (2006) »Innenleben des Städtischen: Insideout: Ein Tanzstück von Sasha Waltz«, Arch+: Zeitschrift für Architektur und Städtebau, 180.

Boxberger, E. (2001) »Planquadrat Schaubühne: Sasha Waltz erforscht das Innen und Außen des Mendelsohn-Baus am Lehniner Platz«, Theater heute, 42, pp. 34f.

Brandl-Risi, B. (2012) »Das Leben des Bildes und die Dauer der Pose: Überlegungen zum Paradox des ›tableau vivant‹«, in S. Diekmann, B. Brandl-Risi and G. Brandstetter (eds.) Hold it! Zur Pose zwischen Bild und Performance. Berlin: Theater der Zeit (Recherchen 89), pp. 52–67.

Brug, M. (2006) »Sasha Waltz«, in Opernregisseure heute: mit ausführlichem Lexikonteil. Leipzig: E. A. Seemann Henschel Verlagsgruppe, pp. 160–99.

Brüstle, C. and Waltz, S. (2017) »Körper – Musik – Performance: Sasha Waltz im Gespräch mit Christa Brüstle«, in J. P. Hiekel (ed.) Body Sounds: Aspekte des Körperlichen in der Musik der Gegenwart. Mainz (u.a.): Schott (Veröffentlichungen des Instituts für Neue Musik und Musikerziehung, 57), pp. 190–98.

Butler, J. (2002) »Body: recognizable/unrecognizable. Über das Stück Körper von Sasha Waltz«, in S. Sasse and S. Wenner (eds.) Kollektivkörper. transcript Verlag, pp. 165–88.

Butterworth, J. and Sanders, L. (eds.) (2020) »Sasha Waltz«, in Fifty Contemporary Choreographers. Third edition. Abingdon, UK, and New York: Routledge (Routledge Key Guides).

Cramer, F. A. (2002) »Abstraktion und Atemzug: ›noBody‹ von Sasha Waltz an der Berliner Schaubühne«, Theater heute, 43, pp. 14–15.

Cramer, F. A. (2000) »Ein Streifzug durch Körperlandschaften: Reflexionen über Literatur, Bild und Bedeutung«, Theater heute, 4, pp. 28–31.

Custodis, M. (2006) »Begrenzung der künstlerischen Mittel als Dialog von Musik und Tanz«, in Sonderforschungsbereich 626 (ed.): Grenzgänge der Kunst(wissenschaften): Sasha Waltz' Choreographie Dido & Aeneas. Berlin.

Eberlein, U. (2011) »Leibliche Resonanz: Phänomenologische und andere Annäherungen«, in K. Andermann and U. Eberlein (eds.) Gefühle als Atmosphären. AKADEMIE VERLAG (Deutsche Zeitschrift für Philosophie/Sonderband 29), pp. 141–52.

Eberlein, U. (2016) »Sasha Waltz«, in Zwischenleiblichkeit und bewegtes Verstehen – Intercorporeity, Movement and Tacit Knowledge. Bielefeld: Transcript (Körperkulturen), pp. 389–402.

Emcke, C. (2005) »Körper & Stimme: Sasha Waltz und Attilio Cremonesi zu Purcells Dido & Aeneas«, Vivace, 3, pp. 5–7.

Fielding, H. A. (2015) »Filming Dance: Embodied Syntax in Sasha Waltz's ›S‹«, Paragraph, 38(0), pp. 69–85.

Giersdorf, J. R. (2003) »Border Crossings and Intra-National Trespasses: East German Bodies in Sasha Waltz's and Jo Fabian's Choreographies«, Theatre Journal, 55(3), pp. 413–32.

Giersdorf, J. R. (2013) The Body of the People: East German Dance since 1945. Madison: University of Wisconsin Press (Studies in Dance History), pp. 143–49.

Hardt, Y. (2007) Sasha Waltz. Palermo: L'epos (Dance for word/dance forward: Interviste sulla coreografia contemporanea, 6).

Hardt, Y. (2010) »Insideout: Spatial Turn in der Tanzwissenschaft und die Choreographien von Sasha Waltz«, in F. Lampert (ed.) Choreographieren reflektieren: Choreographie-Tagung an der Hochschule für Musik und Tanz Köln. Berlin: Lit-Verlag (Tanzwissenschaft, 3), pp. 141–56.

Hartmann, A. and Woitas, M. (eds.) (2016) »Sasha Waltz«, in Das grosse Tanz Lexikon: Tanzkulturen, Epochen, Personen, Werke. Laaber: Laaber.

Jackob, A. (2017) »Gehen in der Schwebe begriffen: Dido & Aeneas von Sasha Waltz zwischen Sprache, Bild und Tod«, in D. Hahn, A. Mohnkern, and R. Parr (eds.) Kulturelle Anatomien: Gehen. Heidelberg: Synchron, pp. 161–80.

Jacobshagen, A. (2021) »The Role of Dance in Opera: Historical Perspectives from Claudio Monteverdi to Sasha Waltz«, in I. Schmid-Reiter and A. Cahn (eds.) Music Theatre in Motion: Reflections on Dance in Opera. Regensburg: ConBrio, pp. 11–31.

Kadivar, P. (2010) »Sasha Waltz, trilogie du corps: une interrogation politique«, Études théâtrales, 49(3), pp. 129–35.

Kellermann, J. (2020) »A Breach of Silence: Affective Soundscapes in Sasha Waltz's Roméo et Juliette«, Cahiers Élisabéthains: A Journal of English Renaissance Studies, 102(1), pp. 38–53.

Klein, G. and Cramer, F. A. (2024) Materialities in Dance and Performance: Writing, Documenting, Archiving. Bielefeld: Transcript (Critical Dance Studies, 70), pp. 104–17.

Knoll, Katie (2006) »I dialoghi di Sasha Waltz: Un cammino della prospettiva dei Dialoge«. Bologna: Culture Teatrali. Studi, interventi e scritture sullo spettacolo, Danza/900. Testimonianze e riflessioni intorno al processo creativo, pp. 171–87.

Lim, W. (2021) »Bodies in Color, Black and White, and in Piles: The Dichotomy of Concentration Camp Aesthetics and Somatic Dance Practices in Sasha Waltz's Screendance Körper (2000)«, German Studies Review, 44(2), pp. 335–58.

Maar, K. (2006) »Die doppelte Flüchtigkeit des Fließenden«, in Sonderforschungsbereich 626 (ed.) Berlin. Grenzgänge der Kunst(wissenschaften): Sasha Waltz' Choreographie Dido & Aeneas, p. 6.

Mannoni, G. (2015) Les grands chorégraphes du XXe siècle. Paris: Buchet-Chastel (Série Les Grands interprètes).

Rentsch, S. (no date) »Fließende Über-Setzungen«, in Sonderforschungsbereich 626 (ed.) Grenzgänge der Kunst(wissenschaften): Sasha Waltz' Choreographie Dido & Aeneas. Berlin.

»Sasha Waltz« (2007) in Theaterlexikon: Begriffe und Epochen, Bühnen und Ensembles. Fifth complete and revised new edition. Hamburg: Rowohlt (Rororo Rowohlts Enzyklopädie, 55673).

Schaper, R. (2005) »Lokale Globalisierung. … über das Modell der Sasha Waltz in Berlin«, in J. Odenthal (ed.) Tanz.de: zeitgenössischer Tanz in Deutschland – Strukturen im Wandel – eine neue Wissenschaft (Theater der Zeit Arbeitsbuch), pp. 114–20.

Schenck, C. (2016) »Les chœurs dansants de Sasha Waltz: Medea, d'après l'opéra Medeamaterial de Pascal Dusapin«, in C. Lechevalier and R. Piana (eds.) Médée à l'opéra: Emmanuelle Haïm, Pierre Audi, Marc-Antoine Charpentier, Sasha Waltz, Heiner Müller, Pascal Dusapin, Krysztof Warlikowski, Luigi Cherubini, Constantin Bogomolov, Gilles Laubert, Abilio Estévez. Besançon: Presses Universitaires de Franche-Comté (968), Annales littéraires de l'Université de Franche-Comté, 968, pp. 83–92.

Schmidt, J. (2002) »Sasha Waltz«, in Tanzgeschichte des 20. Jahrhunderts in einem Band: mit 101 Choreographenporträts. Berlin: Henschel (Arte-Edition), pp. 338–41.

Schouten, S. (2009) »Verlockungen der Dreidimensionalität. Neues Museum: ›Dialoge 09‹ von Sasha Waltz«, Theater der Zeit: Zeitschrift für Politik und Theater, 1/6.

Schulze, J. (1997) »Komische Geschlechtsdifferenz: Sasha Waltz' Post-Tanztheater«, in Jahrbuch Tanzforschung, pp. 175–94.

Shaw, B. (no date) »Phantom Limbs and the Weight of Grief in Sasha Waltz's ›noBody‹«, Theatre Journal, 67(1), pp. 21–42.

Sörgel, S. (2007) »Tanz-Genealogien. Tanz(Ge) schichte(n) von Kurt Jooss zu Sasha Waltz«, in Theaterhistoriographie. Kontinuitäten und Brüche in Diskurs und Praxis [= Mainzer Forschungen zu Drama und Theater. Tübingen: Francke.

Trappmann, V. (2010) »Widerspenstige Körper. Kapitalismuskritik im Tanz«, in K. Becker (ed.) Grenzverschiebungen des Kapitalismus: umkämpfte Räume und Orte des Widerstands. Frankfurt am Main: Campus Verl.

Varney, D. (2008) »Scenographies of the Everyday in Contemporary German Theatre – Anna Langhoff and Sasha Waltz Restage the Family Drama«, Contemporary Theatre Review, 18(1), pp. 56–68.

Vöhler, M. (2006) »Operninszenierung als Choreographie: Dido & Aeneas von Sasha Waltz«, in Sonderforschungsbereich 626 (ed.) Grenzgänge der Kunst(wissenschaften): Sasha Waltz' Choreographie Dido & Aeneas. Berlin, p. 6.

Voigt, K. (2019) »Reciprocity and Interaction«, in C. Leopold, C. Robeller and U. Weber (eds.) Research Culture in Architecture: Cross-Disciplinary Collaboration. Basel: De Gruyter, pp. 321–30.

Volkmann, A. (2003) »Körper und choreographisches Verfahren im Tanztheater von Pina Bausch und Sasha Waltz«, in F. Weltzien (ed.) Modell künstlerischer Produktion: Architektur, Kunst, Literatur, Philosophie, Tanz. Berlin: Reimer, pp. 91–98.

Voss, C. (2006) »Zur Intermedialität des Erzählens am Beispiel der Tanztheater-Opernaufführung Dido & Aeneas«, in Sonderforschungsbereich 626 (ed.) Grenzgänge der Kunst(wissenschaften): Sasha Waltz' Choreographie Dido & Aeneas. Berlin.

Waltz, S. and Emcke, C. (2009) »insideout: Sasha Waltz interviewed by Carolin Emcke«, in J. Fabius (ed.) Talk, 1982–2006. School for New Dance Development Publication: Dancers talking about Dance: 15 Interviews and Articles from 3 Decades of Dance Research in Amsterdam. Amsterdam: Internat. Theatre & Film Books.

Waltz, S. et al. (2015) »Space and Architecture in the Artistic Process: Panel Discussion with Ute Meta Bauer, Marjetica Potrc, and Sasha Waltz, Moderated by Lukas Feireiss«, in S. Hauser and J. Weber (eds.) Architektur in transdisziplinärer Perspektive: Von Philosophie bis Tanz: Aktuelle Zugänge und Positionen. Bielefeld: transcript (Architekturen).

Wessels, A. (2006) »Distanzierte Emotionen: Vergilrezeption in Sasha Waltz' Inszenierung von Purcells Dido and Aeneas«, in Sonderforschungsbereich 626 (ed.) Grenzgänge der Kunst(wissenschaften): Sasha Waltz' Choreographie Dido & Aeneas. Berlin.

Wiens, B. (2022) »Interdependenzen zwischen Choreographie und Szenographie in der Gegenwartskunst«, in S. Huschka and G. Siegmund (eds.) Choreographie als Kulturtechnik. Berlin: Neofelis Verlag GmbH, pp. 167–188.

Zenck, M. (2009) »Intermedialität von Performance, Improvisation und Choreografie im Neuen Musiktheater: Drei Modelle von Sasha Waltz: Dido and Aneas – Körper – noBody«, in M. Demuth (ed.) Freiräume und Spannungsfelder. Reflexionen zur Musik heute: Kolloquium im Rahmen der 20. Dresdner Tage der zeitgenössischen Musik. Mainz: Schott, pp. 195–206.

Filmography (in Extracts)
Filmographie (in Auszügen)

Allee der Kosmonauten [58'] Director Sasha Waltz Collaboration Elliot Caplan Director of Photography Jörg Jeshel Director of Editing Brigitte Kramer Sound Ulla Kösterke Producers Jochen Sandig, Sasha Waltz Executive Producer Peter Zach Editor Wolfgang Bergmann Production kosmonaut films for Arte/ZDF First Broadcast 7 Apr 1999

Körper [57'] Sasha Waltz, Hans Peter Kuhn A film by Jörg Jeshel and Brigitte Kramer Director of Photography Jörg Jeschel Additional Photography Konstantin Kröning, Hans Rombach Sound Oliver Lumpe, Michael Junge Mix Sven Piesker Producer Brigitte Kramer Editor Xina Graff Commissioning Editor Wolfgang Bergmann Production Schaubühne am Lehniner Platz, nachtaktivfilm commissioned by ZDF/Arte/ZDFtheaterkanal Cooperation Goethe-Institut First Broadcast 11 Apr 2000 Distribution DVD, Arthaus Musik 2011

S [66'] Sasha Waltz Filmed by Jörg Jeshel and Brigitte Kramer Director of Photography Jörg Jeschel Additional Photography Nico Felden Sound Oliver Lumpe Editor Gabriele Degener Production Schaubühne am Lehniner Platz, nachtaktivfilm Distribution DVD, Arthaus Musik 2011

noBody [85'] Sasha Waltz, Hans Peter Kuhn A film by Sasha Waltz Director of Photography Jörg Jeshel Additional Photography Ralf Klingelhöfer, Hans Rombach Sound Paul Oberle Mix/Sound Design Arpad Bondy Producer Brigitte Kramer Editor Xina Graff Commissioning Editor Wolfgang Bergmann Production Schaubühne am Lehniner Platz, nachtaktivfilm commissioned by ZDF Cooperation Arte and ZDFtheaterkanal First Broadcast 5 Dec 2002 Distribution DVD, Arthaus Musik 2011

Dido & Aeneas [90'] Henry Purcell, Sasha Waltz. Live Recording Staatsoper Unter den Linden, Berlin. Director for TV and Video Peter Schönhofer Camera Volker Schmidt, Christian Behrendt, Natascha Engel, Beate Häring, Kerstin Luxenhofer, Michael Pötzsch, Jens Schwarzkopf, Stefan Themann Sound Andreas Kremer Production Christian Schwalbe TV Editors Wolfgang Bergmann, Dieter Schneider Production ZDF in collaboration with Arte Coproduction ZDFtheaterkanal, Sasha Waltz & Guests First Broadcast 25 Jun 2005 Distribution DVD, Arthaus Musik 2008

Garten der Lüste – Die Choreographin Sasha Waltz [59'] Direction Brigitte Kramer Camera Jörg Jeshel Sound Stephan Köthe, Michaela Jordan Editing Michaela Jordan Editor Wolfgang Bergmann, ZDF/Arte Production nachtaktivfilm in collaboration with ZDFtheaterkanal and Arte First Broadcast 19 May 2007 Distribution DVD, goodmovies 2008

Roméo et Juliette [104'] Hector Berlioz, Sasha Waltz TV-Direction Vincent Bataillon Producer François Duplat, Antoine Perset, Xavier Dubois, Emma Enjalbert, Denis Morlière Production Opéra national de Paris, Bel Air Media, telmondis, 3sat 2012, with participation of France Télévisions

Dialoge 09 – Neues Museum [52'] A film by Sasha Waltz Co-Direction Brigitte Kramer, Jörg Jeshel Cinematography Jörg Jeshel, Hans Rombach Sound Recording and Mix Titus Maderlechner Editing Director Brigitte Kramer Editor Stephan Talneau Commissioning Editors Wolfgang Bergmann, Dieter Schneider Production Commissioned by ZDF in collaboration with Arte, Sasha Waltz & Guests First Broadcast 19 Oct 2009

Matsukaze [81'] Toshio Hosokawa, Sasha Waltz A film by Karsten Liske Production La Monnaie/De Munt Extra Muros 2016–17 With the Support of MM Channel First Broadcast Apr 2017

Sacre [41'] Igor Stravinsky, Sasha Waltz A film by Karsten Liske Production La Monnaie/De Munt 2013 First Broadcast Sep 2013

Sasha Waltz – A Portrait [72'+59' extra] A film by Brigitte Kramer Cinematography Jörg Jeshel, Christian Möller Sound and Mix Sven Junge Editing Stephan Talneau Music Hans Peter Kuhn Production nachtaktivfilm Distribution DVD, Arthaus Musik 2014

Tannhäuser [192'] Richard Wagner, Sasha Waltz TV-Direction Vincent Bataillon Producer François Duplat Production Staatsoper im Schiller Theater, Bel Air Media Distribution Naxos Distribution Release Date 4 Dec 2015

Figure Humaine [59'] Sasha Waltz Direction Marcus Richardt Camera Mark Liedtke, Jakob Süß, Eduard Ebel, Torben Asmussen Sound Miguel Murrieta Editing Mark Liedtke Postproduction Klaus Flemming Production Elbphilharmonie, Hamburg, in coproduction with Sasha Waltz & Guests Broadcaster ZDF/Arte First Broadcast 11 May 2017

Kreatur [90'] Sasha Waltz Direction Bettina Borgfeld, Jochen Sandig Camera Daniel Koppelkamm, Bettina Borgfeld, Jörg Jeshel, Matthias Biber, Martin Schlicht, Thomas Frischhut Sound Florian Niederleithinger Editing Jamin Benazzouz Postproduction Sergej Jurisdizkij, Jurij Tschbanow Production Sasha Waltz & Guests in coproduction with Festspielhaus St. Pölten, Les Théâtres de la Ville de Luxembourg and Opéra de Dijon Broadcaster ZDF/Arte First Broadcast 30 Sep 2018

Mystery 14 Human Requiem in Eleusis [70'] Jochen Sandig Direction Stephan Talneau, Jochen Sandig Coproduction Eleusis 2023 – Culture Capital of Europe, World Human Forum, Rundfunkchor Berlin, Sasha Waltz & Guests With the Support of Federal Foreign Office of the Federal Republic of Germany First Broadcast 24 Feb 2025

La Passion selon saint Jean [130'] Johann Sebastian Bach, Sasha Waltz TV-Direction Corentin Leconte Production Arte France, Ozango, Opéra de Dijon, Sasha Waltz & Guests Broadcaster Arte France First Broadcast 28 Apr 2025

In C [75'] Sasha Waltz, Terry Riley Direction David Daurier Production Futur Antérieur Broadcaster Mezzo/Philharmonie de Paris First Broadcast 29 Oct 2024

DANCE
TANZ

Abarbanell, Sebastian
A.C. MM Contemporary Dance Company
Albert, Albert
Aldaabal, Medhat
Aldoabl, Moufak
Almassre, Firas
Aloni, Israel
Alpízar Aguilar, Liza
Alvaroz Sanou, Diego Alberto
Annis, Lindy
Aozane Bilibio, Rita
Archer, Clyde Emmanuel
Archer, Emily
Aristegui, Mikel
Athreya, Preethi
Avraam, Louiza
Azechi, Ayaka
Azizaj, Blenard
Bachzetsis, Alexandra
Ballesteros, Zaida
Ballet Company of the Opéra de Lyon
Ballet Company of the Opéra national de Paris
Ballet Company of the Teatro alla Scala
Ballet Company of the Teatr Wielki w Łodzi
Ballet Junior de Genève
Balsera Pita, Fernando
Bartovanec, Jiří
Belobodorov, Alexander
Bencina, Giulia
Beyer, Robert
Billy, Justin John
Bitterli, Milli
Blanco Nuñez, Javier
Bock, Dagmar
Booth, Laurie
Bougard, Julie
Brinon, Anne
Camelin, Joris
Camplani, Davide
Carbone, Alessio
Carboni, Jadi
Catarzi, Claudia
Ceccarelli, Matteo
Charmatz, Boris
Chaussard, Hervé
Chemnitz, Johanna
Cheng, Hsuan
Cherkaoui, Sidi Larbi
Chettur, Padmini
Chmil, Elena
Chuma, Yoshiko
Codarts
Colusi, Maria Marta
Costa, Louis Clement da
Companhia National de Bailando
Cusimano, Nadia
Danielis, Tomas
De Preter, Koen
Defazio, Alessandra
Defazio, Viviana
Degtyarev, Mikhail
Deluy, Clémentine
Demchenko, Oleg
Densem, Lisa
Di Pretoro, Davide
Diaz de Garaio Esnaola, Juan Kruz
Dicuonzo, Rosa
Dolianiti, Emmanouela
Dunberry, Luc
Dupont, Aurélie
Dutch National Ballet
Dvurechenskaya, Nadezhda
Ebbert-Scholl, Andreas
El-Ezra, Iyar
Elliot Norell, Strinnö
Engelkes, Charlotte
Ernesto, Edivaldo
Estarás, Lisi
Evran, Joséphine
Ferlin, Matija
Figueiredo, Melissa
Filippis, Giannalberto de
Folkwang Universität der Künste, IZT
Forsythe Company
Forti, Simone
Frolova, Margarita
Fujinami, Yuya
Gaborit, Delphine
Galindez Cruz, Gabriel
Gao, Tian
Gauthier Dance
Georgitsopoulou, Eva
Gerken, Tina
Godder, Yasmeen
Golovašova, Elena
Gomez, Maya
Gontovaja, Irina
Gonzales Crespo, Iris
Good, Alan
GöteborgsOperans Danskompani
Gouvi, Ageliki
Graziadei, Renate
Grelat-Dupont, Peggy
Grynov, Dmytro
Guillebeaud, Chrystel
Hamilton, Julyen
Hargitai, Ákos
Hari, Saju
Hashemian, Modjgan
Hauert, Thomas
Henke, Swantje
Herr, Sarah
Huber-Christen, Vanessa
Huld Hakonardottir, Inga
Hurpeau, Claire
Hwang, Hwanhee
Ikeda, Kazue
Jachym, Agnieszka
Jalet, Damien
Jang, Su-Mi
Jasperse, John
Johnson, Josh
Johnson, Kitt
Jürgens, Klaus
Juščenko, Vasilij
Justribó Manion, Lorena
Kalies, Josephine
Kamondo, Nikos
Keil, Siggi
Kieffer, Melissa
Kiesecker, Sarah Jeannine
Kilonzo, Kelvin
Kim, Gyung Moo
Kim, Mamajeang
Klar, Annette
Klaßmann, Katharina
Kliesch, Norbert
Klohe, Hans-Werner
Kobzar, Yulia
Koch, Anna
Kojima, Risa
Koluchova, Sara
Kompart, Annika
Kondaurova, Yekaterina
Konnikova, Alexandra
Konovalov, Yevgeni
Kovac, Iztok
Kukawka, Paula
Kusmin, Alexander
Lachambre, Benoît
Laks, Stephan
Lamarca, Florencia
Lavrinenko, Anna
Lebedeva, Maria
Lee, Hyaejin
Lee, Sora
Legge, Joshua
Lehmen, Thomas
Les ballets C de la B
Leso, Annapaola
Li, Hongjun
Linke, Susanne
Lomuljo, Anthony
Lopez, Elia
López Lembo, Maureen
Louvet, Germain
Lyashchenko, Nikita
Macías, Constanza
Madvig, Bo
Malakhov, Vladimir
Malanin, Trofim
Männima, Jaan
Marchand, Jérôme
Marielle-Tréhoüart, Margaux
Mariinsky Ballet
Marks, Jared
Marouf, Enad
Martin-Gousset, Nasser
Martínez, Francisco
Martinson, Ross
Mascia, Nicola
Matis, Sergiu
McDougal, Dominique
McMillan, Johnny
McQuade, Todd
Meilleur, Robert
Mendes Teixeira, Frederico
Menghini, Adalisa
Mercy, Thusnelda
Mertens, Cécile
Michaux, Thomas
Millwood, Grayson
Miranda, Fatima
Mišin, Konstantin
Moalem, Ofek
Montanari, Emanuela
Montané, Neus
Moreau, Hervé
Morro, Jorge
Mosselman, Jeroen
Mualem, Michal
Murcia Pinto, Elena
NaBi Olsson, Joakim
Nagelhus Schia, Guro
Nagelhus Schia Productions
Näger, Daniela
Nasioula, Kyriaki
Nederlof, Sean
Necviga, Alexei
Neff, Alexander
Niv, Elik
Noia, Francesca
Norell Strinnö, Elliot
NYU Tisch School of the Arts, Department of Dance
Oechsle, Gabriele
Öhman, Maria
Ómarsdóttir, Erna
Ömerbeyoglu, Pinar
Otagaki, Yu
Otto, Sophia
Ouamba, Andréya
P., Akila
Pagliero, Ludmilla
Parker, Shaun
Paula, Ricardo de
Pavlenko, Daria
Pawar, Hrishikesh
Pennini, Francesca
Pérez Torres, Manuel Alfonso
Pintzou, Sofia
Plafki, Friederike
Poelstra, Frans
Pranlas, Jonathan
Puodziunas, Virgis
Quattrone, Giuseppina
Queliz, Sasa
Quinaou, Kevin
Rama, Andreas
Randrianantenaina, Zaratiana
Rebetez, Eugénie
Refslund, Kristian
Renalias, Carme
Rivas Medina, Maria Eugenia
Rivera Blanca, Aladino
Robertis, Davide de
Rodrigues, Lia
Rodrigues de Brito, Vivianne
Rodriguez, Orlando
Rogovska, Alexandra
Roman, Christopher
Romeo, Anna
Romoli, Wilfried
Roser, Stephanie
Royal Swedish Ballet
Ruz, Antonio
Sailo, Joshua
Sakka, Mata
Sampson, Mark
Sánchez Ruíz, Judith
Sandig, László
Sandig, Sophia
Santos, Paolo dos
Scandale, Alessio
Scheidtmann, Katharina
Schnell, Yael
Scott-Gilbert, Corey
Senkpiel, Kira Juliane
Sergeyev, Alexander
Serpa Soares, Claudia de
Seurat, Indalecio
Shachar, Gil
Shevykova, Maria
Shi, Xuan
Shugaleev, Igor
Siegmund, Laura
Silva, Bruno Cesario da
Simson, Kirstie
Smekalov, Yuri
Sodaleva, Alisa
Sportelli, Davide
Staatsballett Berlin
Steinwarz, Norbert
Sternenfels, Pablo von
Storkan, Wibke
Stuart, Meg
Suárez Gómez, Joel
Sugae, Ichiro
Sun, Shang-Shi
Sundby, Vebjørn
Sutera, Antonino
Suzuki, Takako
Szymanski, André
Tamir, Nir
tanzmainz
Thomas, Mohan C.
Thrull, Vanessa
Tiepold, Michael
Tolshilshchikova, Irina
Tomczyk, Piotr
Tompkins, Mark
Tsatsos, Stylianos
Tsur, Ygal
Turtschi, Sidney Elisabeth
UNEARTE Universidad Nacional Experimental de las Artes
Urbaniak, Karolina
Vais, Antonios
Varava, Roman
Veeraraghavan, Aarabi
Villa-Lobos, Maria Clara
Vollhardt, Lene
Voorter, Mat
Wada, Junko
Waked, Fadi
Waltz, Sasha
Weinzierl, Tamara
Wermund, Nadine
Yalinich, Zlata
Yamamoto, Shori
Yoav, Idan
Young, Laurie
Zainetdinov, Denis
Zambrano, David
Zamir, Matan
Zerbey, Charlotte
Zhou, Niannian
Zhuravleva, Valeria
Zhurilov, Boris
Zouk, Sigal

MUSIC
MUSIK

Acid Pauli
Akademie für Alte Musik Berlin
Akiki, Bassem
Alekseenok, Vitali
Altstaedt, Nicolas
Andre, Mark
Appl, Benjamin
Appow, Vitali
Arcadelt, Jakob
Athelas Sinfonietta Copenhagen
Bang On A Can All Stars
Barenboim, Daniel
Barleben, Justus
Bätzner, Aglaia
Ben-Ziony, Guy
Bennett, Michael
Bepler, Jonathan
Berliner Philharmoniker
Beuron, Yann
Blaauw, Marco
Blondelle, Thomas
Borchev, Nikolay
Bukahara
Bush, James
Bussmann, Nicholas
Cappella Mediterranea
Chappuis, Marie-Claude
Charim, Anna
Chœur de Chambre de Namur
Chœur de l'Opéra de Dijon
Chor der Deutschen Oper Berlin
Coduys, Thierry
Cohen, Jonathan
Coleman, Robert David
Contaldo, Valerio
Creed, Marcus
Cremonesi, Attilio
Currentzis, Teodor
Dalt, Lucrecia
Dierksen, Uwe
Diesner, Dietmar
DoelenEnsemble
Donadello, Francesco
Dörner, Axel
Dougherty, Brendan
Dudley, Joanna
Dusapin, Pascal
Dutch Ballet Orchestra
Eerens, Ilse
Engel, Titus
Ensemble Casella
Ensemble Lemur and Friends
Ensemble intercontemporaine
Ensemble Modern
Ensemble Musikfabrik
Escola Superior de Música de Lisboa
Erklentz, Sabine
Fahnert, Kai-Uwe
Feth, Florian
Fink, Nicolas
François, Yannis
Freiburger BarockConsort
Friedl, Reinhold
Galaz Ramirez, Rafael
Garcia Alarcon, Leonardo
Garvie, Valentín
Gassenhuber, Angela
Gerassimez, Alexej
Gergiev, Valery
Gouldian Finch/Martin Horntveth
Grané, Sonia
Gubanova, Ekaterina
Haas, Georg Friedrich
Halsey, Simon
Hanayo
Hannigan, Barbara
Hasan, Ali
Hautzinger, Franz
Hellekant, Charlotte
Heras-Casado, Pablo
Hindoyan, Domingo
Hollinger, Peter
Honsinger, Tristan
Hosokawa, Toshio
Ich schwitze nie
Immler, Christian
Ipekçioğlu, Ipek
Jarnot, Konrad
Johann, Torsten
Johansson, Sven-Åke
Joven Orquesta de la Communidad de Madrid
Junge Deutsche Philharmonie
Junges Blasorchester Marl
Junker, Sophie
Kammerloher, Katharina
Kehrer, Tobias
Kempenaers, Cécile
Kern, Andreas
Keser, Arnold
Kim, Byung Gil
Koch, Tobias
Kröner, Kaspar
Kuhn, Hans Peter
Lantner, Yair
Laudet, Augustin
Lee, Tammin J
Leenaars, Gijs
Lefort, Estelle
Leichtmann, Hanno
Liechtenstein, Friedrich
Lipp, Sebastian
Löffler, Ulrich
London Sinfonietta
Lonquich, Alexander
Lopez Gonzalez, Logan
Lorenz, Eberhard Francesco
Löwe, Konstanze
Lukoszevieze, Anton
Mahler Chamber Orchestra
Maio, Rachel
Mancini, Luciana
Mantegna, Fabrice
Martin, Maurice de
Martinik, Jan
Marton, Cristina
Marziotte, Leandro
Mattei, Peter
Maurs, Augustin
Mayas, Magda
Mayers, Philip
Mehta, Rajesh
Mencke, Julia
Milhofer, Mark
Millán, Julián
Miller, Ronnita
Moll, Phillip
Moss, David
Moulds, Christopher
MusicAeterna
Musicians of Karnataka College of Percussion
Musikschule Marl with Günther Braunstein
Nickmann, Alexander
Nigl, Georg
Noguera, Diego
Oesterdiekhoff, Thomas
Ollu, Franck
Olsen, Frode
Olsen, Morten J.
Orchester der Deutschen Oper Berlin
Orchestra of Mariinsky Theatre
Orchestre de l'Opéra national de Paris
Orchestre du Théâtre Royal de la Monnaie
Özdemir, Burak
Pähn, Vello
Palágyi, Krisztián
Pape, René
Parkins, Andrea
Patoulidou, Aphrodite

Paul, Ayumi
Pereyra, Adrian
Petersen, Ann
Petersen, Marlis
Petrenko, Mikhail
Philipp, Uli
Philharmonisches Staatsorchester Mainz
Podgaiskaya, Olga
Pomorin, Sibylle
Poore, Melvyn
Prudenskaya, Marina
Rattle, Simon, Sir
Rauter, Michael
Ricci, Céline
Richter, Anna Lucia
Rihm, Wolfgang
Riley, Terry
Rosen, Alex
Rosenius, Erik
Roset, Julie
Rosman, Carl
Rowe, Hahn
Rudnitzky, Edgardo
Rudolph, Lars
Rundfunkchor Berlin
Runnicles, Donald, Sir
Rutman, Bob
Sacher, Jürgen
Sachse, Pauline
Sandhoff, Ruth
Saunders, Rebecca
Schachtner, Benno
Schlothauer, Burkhard
Schmidt, Neslihan
Schnabel, Tobias
Schulkowsky, Robyn
Schwark, Holger
Seemann, Martin
Seiffert, Peter
Shkapura, Grigory
Simon, Grégoire
Simonis, Judith
Skelton, Kevin
Smallwood, Michael
Soddy, Alexander
Solistenensemble Kaleidoskop
Søndergard, Thomas
Sonn, Peter
Soundwalk Collective
Spaulding, William
Staatskapelle Berlin
Staatskapelle Weimar
Staatsopernchor Berlin
Stahler, Eva
Stein, Caroline
Stoianov, Sava
Sylla, Mola
Teige, Daniel
The Young Gods
Tokyo Symphony Orchestra
Tonkünstler-Orchester Niederösterreich
Tristan Honsinger Quintett
Tristan Honsinger Sextett
Trümpy, Fabio
Tuvia, Zoe
Ugolin, Aurore
Uitti, Frances-Marie
Upatnieks, Gunārs
Vocalconsort Berlin
Volkov, Ilan
Vorfeld, Michael
Voutchkova, Biliana
Walther, Annette
Way, James
Weigle, Sebastian
Weilacher, Michael
Wey, Terry
Widmann, Carolin
Wiesenfeld, Ruth
Wighardt, Hannah
Wijers, Hans
Willcox, Reuben
Williams, Douglas
Wolff, Konstantin
Wright, Martin
Yeghiyan, Narine
York, Deborah
Young, Simone
zeitkratzer
Zelwer, Jean-Marc

ARTISTIC CAST (DIRECTION, STAGE, COSTUME, LIGHT, VIDEO, DRAMATURGY, FILM, CONCEPT ETC.)
KÜNSTLERISCH BETEILIGTE (REGIE, BÜHNE, KOSTÜM, LICHT, VIDEO, DRAMATURGIE, FILM, KONZEPT ETC.)

Badet, Jean-Louis
Bake, Silke
Bätz, Annette
Bergsteinsdóttir, Thora Sólveig
Binsert, Tomski
Birkle, Christine
Bittner, Jörg
Borgfeld, Bettina
Borrmann, Beate
Böwe, Jule
Braun, Tristan
Bussmann, Philip
Calveyra, Rodrigo
Caplan, Elliot
Chalayan, Hussein
Coduys, Thierry
Danilsen, Olaf
Didwiszius, Rufus
Döring, Steffen
Drum, Christopher
Dübgen, Hannah
Emcke, Carolin
Finn, David
Frank, Regina
Gaestel, Mikko
Gallé, Valentin
GIOM (Guillaume Bruère)
Guérin, Emilie
Hagen-Schäfer, Sylvia
Harder, Andreas
Hauk, Martin
Heller, Margaretha
Herklotz, Nadja
Huber, Dominic
Huguet, Rosabel
Hwang, Brad
InForm – Platform for Inclusive Minds
Jeshel, Jörg
Kaegi, Stefan
Kapica, Nick
Kern, Bärbel
Koppelkamm, Daniel
Kramer, Brigitte
Lepore, Jasmin
Letteriis, Rita de
Lillevan
Liske, Karsten
Maier Schriever, Pia
Merei, Yasmine Nayef
Möller, Christian
MOVES Producción, Gestión Y Promoción Escénica
Offert, Fabian
Polucci, Federico
Pomplun, Sibah
Poumarat, Arnaud
Pronk, André
Reuther, Thilo
Rimini Protokoll
Rombach, Hans
Sandig, Jochen
Schenk, Thomas
Scherer, Agnes
Schmalfuß, Anja
Schneider, Andrew
Schneider, Maggie
Schönebaum, Urs
Schönhofer, Peter
Schroth, Jens
Schuppelius, Heike
Schwarz, Alexander
Seifert, Ilka
Shibata, Chiharu
Skodzig, Bernd
Snellman, Tapio
Steppe, Barbara
Stocker, Karl
Sussman, Eve
Talneau, Stephan
Tiersch, Sandra
Tolaas, Sissel
Uhde, Folkert
van der Werve, Erwin
van Herpen, Iris
Voigt, Christina
Waltz, Sasha
Waltz, Yoreme
Weibel, Peter
Wiesmann, Daniel
World Human Forum
Zhao, Yi

TEAM MEMBERS
TEAMMITGLIEDER

Albrink, Mika
Bender, Stephanie
Danilsen, Olaf
Döring, Steffen
Falk, Jasmin
Guérin, Emilie
Hauk, Martin
Hauptvogel, Moritz
Herklotz, Nadja
Heth, Patrick
Ishii, Kei
Kea, Vivian
Kern, Bärbel
Liske, Karsten
Martínez, Francisco
Pomplun, Sibah
Potrafke, Sarah
Sandig, Jochen
Schmidt, Stephan E.
Schmitz, Kira
Sziedat, Lisa
Tiersch, Sandra
Waltz, Sasha
Wizisla, Reinhard

FORMER TEAM MEMBERS
EHEMALIGE TEAMMITGLIEDER

Amat-Marwi, Damian
Bae, Cheong Uck
Bazin, Piere Yves
Bittencourt, Aline
Boock, Theresa
Borrmann, Beate
Bucalossi, Leonardo
Castillo, Irina
Dahmen, Rhea
Dehner, Alice
Drum, Christopher
Friedrich, Holger
Froreich, Harriet von
Grigo, Carsten
Heller, Margaretha
Jansen, Sara
Juschka, Tina
Kastler, Carina
Keysers, Verena
Kleinknecht, Janna
Klier, Nadja
Laudenbach, Karin
Leirich, Mona
Lepore, Jasmin
Margiotta, Chantal
Merei, Yasmine Nayef
Noia, Francesca
Ott, Stephanie
Perrone, Luisa
Salter, Eleanor
Schenk, Thomas
Scherer, Agnes
Schmalfuß, Anja
Schmökel, Ann Marie
Schneider, Franca
Schneider, Silke
Simon, Mira
Wagner, Anne
Waltz, Yoreme

STAFF
MITARBEIT

Abel, Emily
Adhikaril, Ranav
Bartels, Gabi
Bauer, Boris
Bauer, Joe
Beneke, Manja
Biber, Matthias
Bousselmi, Nessrin-Alia
Bozek, Vincent
Brehmer, Gesche
Bujack, Gabriela
Criqui, Jean-Michel
de Fries, Lukas
De Santis, Giorgio
Ebbing, Miriam
Eckert, Joscha
Fantin, Arianna
Felden, Nico
Förster, Nicole
Franco, Maayan
Freschi, Jonathan
Giabando, Paolo
Gieseke, Jan
Gmitrzuk, Justyna
Grippa, Carlo
Harder, Andreas
Heimann, Kati
Herrmann, Daniel
Hertzer, Boris
Hille, Lena
Hoffmann, Ellen
Hualpa Garcia, Luz Zenaida
Ismati, Anass
Janßen-Braje, Nina
Judica, Salvatore Giuseppe
Kiener, Sebastian
Kinzel, Stefanie
Klette, Tobias
Kovács, Ludovít
Krause, Sophie
Kruschel, Mathilda
Kuck, Cordula
Kusserow, Urte
Kwiatkowska, Katarzyna
Loy, Lena
Maderlechner, Titus
Martins, César
Nerger, Lutz
Podraza, Torsten
Rosin, Claudia
Schie, Gabriele
Schleiffenbaum, Lea
Schmidthals, Maximilian
Schüler, Anja
Schulz, Friederike
Schwark, Rebekka
Stürzl, Clara Fee
Trillhaas, Mareike
Tsantekidou, Athena
Vannini, Sofia
Wedemeyer, Karl
Weinhold, Katja
Weixler, Wolfgang

Team of Sasha Waltz & Guests, September 2024

ARGENTINA
ARGENTINIEN

Buenos Aires
Centro Cultural de la Cooperación
El cultural San Martín
Sala Martín Coronado
Teatro Colón

AUSTRALIA
AUSTRALIEN

Adelaide
Ridley Centre Wayville
Melbourne
State Theatre at the Arts Centre Melbourne
Sydney
Sydney Lyric Theatre

AUSTRIA
ÖSTERREICH

Gmunden
Stadttheater Gmunden
Graz
Helmut List Halle
Salzburg
Felsenreitschule
Perner-Insel
Salzburger Landestheater
Szene Salzburg
St. Pölten
Festspielhaus St. Pölten
Vienna
Burgtheater
Tanzquartier Wien
Volkstheater Wien

BELGIUM
BELGIEN

Antwerp
deSingel
Toneelhuis
Bruges
Concertgebouw Brugge
Brussels
Les Halles de Schaerbeek
Les Tanneurs
Théâtre National Wallonie – Bruxelles
Théâtre Royal de la Monnaie
Charleroi
Les Écuries de Charleroi Danse
Leuven
STUK Kunstencentrum vzw

BOSNIA AND HERZEGOVINA
BOSINEN UND HERZEGOWINA

Sarajevo
Narodno pozorište Sarajevo

BRAZIL
BRASILIEN

Belo Horizonte
Teatro Sesiminas / FID – Fórum Internacional de Dança
Porto Alegre
Teatro do Sesi
Salvador
Teatro Castro Alves
São Paulo
FID São Paulo
Teatro Alfa

BULGARIA
BULGARIEN

Sofia
Toplocentrala

CANADA
KANADA

Montreal
Agora de la danse
Place des Arts
Ottawa
National Arts Centre

CHILE
CHILE

Santiago de Chile
Teatro Municipal de Santiago

CHINA
CHINA

Beijing
Goethe-Institut Beijing

CROATIA
KROATIEN

Zagreb
HNK – Hrvatsko narodno kazalište

CUBA
KUBA

Havana
Gran Teatro de La Habana

CZECH REPUBLIC
TSCHECHIEN

Brno
Janáček Theatre
Plzeň
Divadlo Josefa Kajetána Tyla
Prague
Divadlo pod Palmovkou
Forum Karlín

DENMARK
DÄNEMARK

Aarhus
Musikhuset Aarhus
Ridehuset
Copenhagen
Dancescenen København
Det Kongelige Teater
Kanonhallen

EGYPT
ÄGYPTEN

Cairo
El Gomhouria Theatre

FINLAND
FINNLAND

Helsinki
Helsingin Kaupungin Teatteri
Musiikki Teatteri Kapsäkki
Tanssin Talo

FRANCE
FRANKREICH

Avignon
Cour d'honneur du Palais des papes
Cour du lycée Saint-Joseph
Gymnase du lycée Aubanel
La chapelle des Pénitents blancs
Opéra éphémère du Grand Avignon Confluence
Opéra Grand Avignon
Parc des Exposition
Bordeaux
Café des Arts
Le Cuvier de Feydeau
Opéra National de Bordeaux
Palais Rohan
Théâtre Femina
TnBA – Théâtre national de Bordeaux en Aquitaine
Caen
Théâtre de Caen
Cannes
Palais des Festivals et des Congrès de Cannes
Chalon-sur-Saône
Espace des Arts, Scène national Chalon-sur-Saône
Clermont-Ferrand
La Comédie de Clermont-Ferrand scène national
Dijon
Opéra de Dijon
Forbach
Le Carreau – Scène nationale de Forbach
Lille
Opéra de Lille
Lyon
Maison de la Danse
Opéra de Lyon
Théâtre National Populaire de Villeurbanne
Théâtres Romains de Lyon
Marseille
Centre de la Vieille Charité
CEPAC Silo
Metz
Arsenal
Montpellier
ICI – centre chorégraphique national de Montpellier
Opéra national de Montpellier
Mulhouse
La Filature
Nancy
CCAM – Centre Culturel André Malraux, Scène Nationale de Vandoeuvre Nancy
Paris
Centre Pompidou
La Ferme du Buisson
Opéra national de Paris, Opéra Bastille
Philharmonie de Paris – Cité de la musique
Théâtre de la Ville
Théâtre des Abbesses
Théâtre des Bouffes du Nord
Théâtre des Champs-Elysées
Théâtre Paris-Villette
Rennes
Théâtre National de Bretagne
Rouen
Opéra de Rouen Haute-Normandie – Théâtre des Arts
Théâtre de la Foudre – CND de Normandie – Rouen
Strasbourg
Maillon – Théâtre de Strasbourg
Toulouse
Théâtre du Capitole Toulouse
Théâtre national de Toulouse

GEORGIA
GEORGIEN

Tbilisi
Paliashvili Opera and Ballett Theatre of Tblisi
Royal District Theatre
Rustaveli National Theatre

GERMANY
DEUTSCHLAND

Baden-Baden
Festspielhaus Baden-Baden
Berlin
Alexanderplatz
Allee der Kosmonauten
Arena Berlin
Berlin Dance Institute
Berliner Dom
Bode-Museum
Brandenburger Tor
Charité Berlin
C/O Berlin
Deutsche Oper Berlin
Experimentierort »Bei-Wilhelm«
Georg Kolbe Museum
Hackesche Höfe
Haus der Berliner Festspiele
Haus der Kulturen der Welt
ICC Berlin
Jüdisches Museum Berlin
König Galerie
Kraftwerk
Kunsthaus Tacheles
Künstlerhaus Bethanien
Martin Gropius Bau
Museum für Naturkunde
Nachbarschaftscampus Dammweg
Neues Museum
Neue Nationalgalerie
Palast der Republik
Pergamonmuseum
Pfefferberg Theater
Podewil
Radialsystem
Schaubühne am Lehniner Platz
Schiller Theater
Sophienkirche
Sophiensæle
Spreepark
St. Elisabeth-Kirche
St. Johannes-Evangelist-Kirche
Staatsoper im Schiller Theater
Staatsoper Unter den Linden
Strandbad Tegelsee
Tanzfabrik
Tempelhofer Feld
Theater am Halleschen Ufer
Theater Aufbau Kreuzberg TAK
Volksbühne am Rosa-Luxemburg-Platz
Waldbühne
Bochum
Jahrhunderthalle Bochum
Bonn
Bundeskunsthalle
Theater Bonn – Opernhaus
Bremen
Schwankhalle
Cologne
AHK
Kölner Philharmonie
Oper Köln
Oper Köln im Staatenhaus
Palladium Köln
Schauspiel Köln
Cottbus
Piccolo Theater Cottbus
Dresden
Hellerau – Europäisches Zentrum der Künste
Staatsschauspiel Dresden
Düsseldorf
Düsseldorfer Schauspielhaus
Tanzhaus NRW
Erfurt
Theater Erfurt
Erlangen
Markgrafentheater
Essen
Aalto-Theater Essen
PACT Zollverein
Frankfurt
Künstlerhaus Mousonturm
Oper Frankfurt
Schauspiel Frankfurt
Schirn Kunsthalle Frankfurt
Freiburg
E-Werk Freiburg
Theater Freiburg
Fürth
Stadttheater Fürth
Göppingen
Kunsthalle Göppingen
Hamburg
Deutsches Schauspielhaus
Elbphilharmonie
Kampnagel
Hanover
Hochschule für Musik, Theater und Medien Hannover
Staatsoper Hannover
Heidelberg
Klingenteichhalle
Heilbronn
Theater Heilbronn
Karlsruhe
Tollhaus
ZKM: Zentrum für Kunst und Medien/Centre for Art and Media
Kassel
Staatstheater Kassel
Leipzig
Schauspiel Leipzig
Lörrach
Burghof Lörrach
Ludwigsburg
Forum am Schlosspark Ludwigsburg
Kunstzentrum Karlskaserne
Ludwigsburger Schloss, Ehrenhof and Blühendes Barock
Ludwigshafen
Corso-Filmtheater
Friedrich-Ebert-Halle
Theater im Pfalzbau
Mainz
Staatstheater Mainz
Marl
Forum, Grimme-Institut, Hügelhäuser, Planeten-siedlung, Skulpturenpark, Willy-Brandt-Gesamtschule
Scharounschule
Theater Marl
Munich
Bayerische Staatsoper
Muffatwerk
Prinzregententheater
Schauburg München
Theater Schwere Reiter
Münster
Theater im Pumpenhaus
Oldenburg
Kulturetage
Oldenburgisches Staatstheater
Pforzheim
CongressCentrum Pforzheim (CCP)
Potsdam
SAP Innovation Center
Recklinghausen
Ruhrfestspielhaus
Remscheid
Teo Otto Theater der Stadt Remscheid
Stuttgart
Kunstmuseum Stuttgart
Liederhalle Stuttgart
Theaterhaus Stuttgart
Weimar
Deutsches Nationaltheater Weimar
Wilhelmshaven
LBNN – Landesbühne Niedersachsen Nord
Wuppertal
Tanztheater Wuppertal Pina Bausch

GREECE
GRIECHENLAND

Athens
Megaron – Athens Concert Hall
Odeon of Herodes Atticus
Delphi
Temple of Apollo
Elefsina
Archaeological site of Eleusis
Thessaloniki
Helexpo – Thessaloniki International Trade Fair
Megaron

HONG KONG
HONGKONG

Drama Theatre Hong Kong
Loke Yew Hall, University of Hong Kong
National Centre for the Performing Arts

HUNGARY
UNGARN

Budapest
Madách Színház
Petőfi Csarnok
Trafó Kortárs Művészetek Háza

ICELAND
ISLAND

Reykjavik
Reykjavik City Theatre (Borgarleikhus)

INDIA
INDIEN

Bangalore
Ranga Shankara
Kolkata
Calcutta Music Academy
Jorasanko Rajbati
Rabindra Sadan
Mumbai
Dr. Homi Bhabha Auditorium
New Delhi
National School of Drama
Theatre Utsav Delhi
Pune
Centre of Contemporary Dance
The Box Hub Pune

INDONESIA
INDONESIEN

Bandung
Taman Budaya Bandung
Jakarta
Gedung Kesenian Jakarta
Teater Besar Jakarta
Surakarta
ISI Surakarta

ISRAEL
ISRAEL

Jerusalem
El-Hakawati
Tel Aviv
The Israeli Opera

ITALY
ITALIEN

Bologna
Chiostro San Martino

Brescia
Il Teatro Grande di Brescia
Ferrara
Teatro Comunale di Ferrara
Genoa
Il Teatro dell'Archivolto
Milan
MTM – Teatro Litta
Teatro alla Scala
Palermo
Spazio Tre Navate
Pesaro
Cortile di Palazzo Montani Antaldi
Reggio Emilia
Fondazione Nazionale della Danza /Aterballetto
Teatro Municipale Valli
Rome
Auditorium della Conciliazione
Auditorium Parco della Musica
MAXXI – Museo nazionale delle arti del XXI secolo
Teatro Argentina
Teatro dell' Opera di Roma
Teatro Eliseo
Teatro Quirino
Rovereto
Auditorium Fausto Melotti di Rovereto
Turin
Teatro Regio di Torino
Urbino
Teatro Raffaello Sanzio
Venice
Palazzo Carlo Scarpa Venezia
Teatro alle Tese
Teatro Palafenice Venezia

JAPAN
JAPAN

Osaka
Cultural Centre Osaka
Otsu
Biwako Hall
Tokyo
Kameari Lirio Hall
New National Theatre
Saitama Arts Theatre

LEBANON
LIBANON

Beirut
Al Madina Theatre

LITHUANIA
LITAUEN

Vilnius
Lietuvos nacionalinis dramos teatras

LUXEMBOURG
LUXEMBURG

Luxembourg
Grand Théâtre de la Ville de Luxembourg

MADAGASCAR
MADAGASKAR

Antananarivo
Institut Français de Madagascar

MEXICO
MEXIKO

Guadalajara
Esplanade of the Museo Cabañas
FIL – Guadalajara International Book Fair
Guanajuato
State Auditorium
Teatro Principal Guanajuato
Mexico City
Palacio de Bellas Artes
Zapopan
Conjunto Santander de Artes Escénicas

MYANMAR
MYANMAR

Yangon
National Theatre of Yangon

NETHERLANDS
NIEDERLANDE

Amsterdam
Dutch National Opera & Ballet
Felix Meritis
Koninklijk Theater Carré
NDSM – Docklands
Stadsschouwburg Amsterdam
Westergasfabriek
Zuiveringshal
Groningen
De Oosterpoort
Grand Theatre Groningen
Stadsschouwburg Groningen
Leeuwarden
Stadsschouwburg De Harmonie
Leiden
Leidse Schouwburg
Rotterdam
LantarenVenster
RDM – Onderzeebootloods
Theater Rotterdamse Schouwburg
The Hague
Lucent Dans Theater
Utrecht
De Utrechtse School
Veilinghuis

NORWAY
NORWEGEN

Bergen
Grieghallen
Oslo
Bærum Kulturhus
Dansens Hus
Den Norske Opera & Ballett
Det Norske Teatret
Sentralen

PALESTINE
PALÄSTINA

Ramallah
Al-Kasaba Theatre

PHILIPPINES
PHILIPPINEN

City of Manila
Teatro Aguinaldo Manila

POLAND
POLEN

Kraków
Kraków Opera
Łódź
Teatr Wielki w Lódzi
Toruń
Theatre of Wilam Horzyca
Warsaw
Teatr Wielki Opera Narodowa

PORTUGAL
PORTUGAL

Guimarães
Centro Cultural Vila Flor (CCVF)
Lisbon
Centro Cultural de Belém
Fundação Calouste Gulbenkian
Teatro Camões
Porto
Teatro Municipal do Porto – Rivoli

ROMANIA
RUMÄNIEN

Sibiu
Centrul Cultural Ion Besoiu

RUSSIA
RUSSLAND

Moscow
Central Academic Theatre of the Russian Army
Mossovet Theatre
Stanislavski and Nemirovich-Danchenko Theatre
State Academic Bolshoi Theatre of Russia
State Theatre of Nations
Teatr »škola dramatičeskogo iskusstva«
The State Academic Maly Theatre
Novosibirsk
Teatr Krasnyi Fackel
Omsk
Omsk Academic Dramatheatre
Saint Petersburg
Alexandrinsky Theatre
Baltic House Festival Theatre
Mariinsky Theatre II

SERBIA
SERBIEN

Belgrade
Sava Centar

SINGAPORE
SINGAPUR

Esplanade – Theatres on the Bay
Victoria Theatre and Concert Hall

SLOVENIA
SLOWENIEN

Lubljana
Cankarjev Dom – Kulturni in Kongresni Center

SOUTH KOREA
SÜDKOREA

Seoul
LG Arts Centre Seoul
Sejong Centre

SPAIN
SPANIEN

Barcelona
CCCB – Pati de les Dones
Gran Teatre del Liceu
Mercat de les Flors
Teatre Grec
Teatre Lliure de Barcelona
Teatre Nacional de Catalunya
Bilbao
Teatro Arriaga
Donostia-San Sebastián
Palacio de Congresos y Auditorio Kursaal
Madrid
Teatro Real
Teatros del Canal
Pamplona
Baluarte – Palacio de Congresos y Auditorio de Navarra
Salamanca
CAEM – Centro de las Artes Escénicas y de la Música
Seville
Teatro Central

SRI LANKA
SRI LANKA

Colombo
Bishop's College Auditorium

SWEDEN
SCHWEDEN

Gothenburg
GöteborgsOperan
Pustervik
Stockholm
Dansens Hus
Kungliga Operan
MDT – Moderna Dansteatern

SWITZERLAND
SCHWEIZ

Basel
Fondation Beyeler
Kaserne Basel
Klingenthalhalle
Bern
Dampfzentrale Bern
Geneva
Bâtiment des Forces Motrices
Forum Meyrin
Salle du Lignon-Vernier
Lugano
LAC Lugano Arte e Cultura
Zurich
Gessnerallee Zürich
Rote Fabrik
Schauspielhaus Zürich, Schiffbau

SYRIA
SYRIEN

Damascus
Opera Syria

TAIWAN
TAIWAN

Taipei
National Theatre and Concert Hall

THAILAND
THAILAND

Bangkok
Thailand Cultural Centre

TURKEY
TÜRKEI

Istanbul
Atatürk Cultural Centre
Zorlu Center Beşiktaş

UKRAINE
UKRAINE

Kharkiv
Kharkiv Theatre and Concert Centre

UNITED KINGDOM
GROSSBRITANNIEN

Cardiff
Wales Millennium Centre
Edinburgh
Edinburgh Playhouse
London
Barbican
Laban Theatre
Sadler's Wells
Southbank Centre
The Place
Trinity Laban Conservatoire of Music and Dance

USA
USA

Atlanta
14th Street Playhouse
Berkeley
Cal Performances – Zellerbach Hall
Chicago
Harold Washington Library Centre
Houston
Kaplan Theatre
Irvine
Irvine Barclay Theatre
Los Angeles
Occidental College, Thorne Hall
The Theatre at ACE Hotel
New York
BAM – Brooklyn Academy of Music
Columbia University
Jack Crystal Theatre
La MaMa
NYLA (New York Live Arts)
Synod House
Portland
Newmark Theatre

VENEZUELA
VENEZUELA

Caracas
Sala Anna Julia Rojas

VIETNAM
VIETNAM

Hanoi
Hanoi Opera House

Festivals Where Sasha Waltz & Guests Have Performed
Festivals, auf denen Sasha Waltz & Guests zu sehen war

Adelaide Festival AU
Athens Epidaurus Festival GR
AURA – International Dance Festival, Vilnius LT
Ballettfestwoche, Munich DE
Barocktage, Berlin DE
Beethovenfest Bonn DE
Bergen International Festival NO
Big Idea #2, Rotterdam NL
BIPOD – Beirut International Platform of Dance LB
BITEF – Belgrade International Theatre Festival RS
Body/Mind Festival, Warsaw PL
CODA Oslo International Dance Festival NO
CPH Stage, Copenhagen DK
December Dance, Brugge BE
Divine Comedy Festival, Krakow PL
Drei Wochen mit Pina Bausch, Düsseldorf DE
Dresdner Musikfestspiele DE
Drodesera Fies – Performing Art Festival, Dro IT
Edinburgh International Festival GB
euro-scene Leipzig DE
European Capital of Culture 2002 – Salamanca ES
European Capital of Culture 2003 – Graz, steirischer herbst AT
European Capital of Culture 2023 – Elefsina GR
Festival d'Avignon FR
Festival de Danse Cannes FR
Festival de Danse et des Arts multiples de Marseille F/D/Am/M* FR
Festival de Otoño ES
Festival Grec de Barcelona ES
Festival Internazionale di Danza, Messina IT
Festival Les Presqu'îles de Danse, Paris FR
Festival Perspectives, Saarbrücken DE
Festspiele Ludwigshafen DE
Festspiele Zürich CH
FIAC – Festival Internacional de Artes Cênicas da Bahia BR
FIBA – Festival Internacional de Buenos Aires AR
FIDPOA – Festival Internacional de Dança de Porto Alegre BR
forkortet KIT – Københavns Internationale Teater DK
Frankfurter Positionen DE
FTA – Festival TransAmériques, Montreal CA
GIFT – Georgian International Festival of Arts in Tbilisi GE
Golden Mask Theatre Festival, Moskow RU
Hangartfest – Festival di Danza Contemporanea, Pesaro IT
Helsingin juhlaviikot – Helsinki Festival FI
Holland Festival, Amsterdam NL
ImPulsTanz Festival, Vienna AT
INFEKTION! Festival für Neues Musiktheater DE
Istanbul Dance Festival TR
Julidans, Amsterdam NL
Kharkiv Music Fest UA
Kunstfest Weimar DE
La Bâtie – Festival de Genève CH
La Biennale di Venezia IT
Les Grandes Traversées, Bordeaux FR
Les Nuits de Fourvière, Lyon FR
Ludwigsburger Schlossfestspiele DE
MaerzMusik, Berlin DE
Materia Prima, Krakow PL
Melbourne International Arts Festival AU
Mercurio Festival, Palermo IT
Montpellier Danse FR
Mozartwoche, Salzburg AT
Multitudes, London GB
NET – The New European Theatre Festival, Moscow RU
New Vision Arts Festival HK
Next Wave Festival, New York US
Oriente Occidente, Rovereto IT
Osterfestspiele Salzburg AT
OsterTanzTage, Hanover DE
Ramallah Contemporary Dance Festival PS
Rampenlichter-Festival DE
Reggio Emilia in Danza IT
Reykjavík Arts Festival IS
Romaeuropa, Rome IT
Ruhrtriennale, Bochum DE
Salzburger Festspiele AT
Santiago a Mil – International Theatre Festival CL
SFIAF – San Francisco International Arts Festival US
Sibiu International Theater Festival RO
SIFA – Singapore International Festival of Arts SG
Singapore International Festival of Arts SG
SPIELART Festival, Munich DE
spielzeit'europa, Berlin DE
Sydney Festival AU
Tanec Praha festival CZ
Tanz im August – Internationales Festival Berlin DE
Tanz Karlsruhe DE
tanzmainz festival DE
Tanzplattform DE
Tanztreffen der Jugend, Berlin DE
Tbilisi International Festival of Theatre GE
Theaterfestival Basel CH
Theatertreffen, Berlin DE
Theatre World Brno festival CZ
Torinodanza Festival IT
White Bird Festival, Portland US
zürich moves! CH

Works
Werke

Allee der Kosmonauten ↘1996
Beethoven 7 ↘2023
Beethoven 7 in Delphi ↘2021
Bungalow ↘1993
Chiharu Shiota – I Hope ↘2021
Continu ↘2010
Dialoge – Künstlerhaus Bethanien (Showing I–V) ↘1993
Dialoge '99/I – Sophiensæle ↘1999
Dialoge '99/II – Jüdisches Museum ↘1999
Dialoge – La chapelle des Pénitents blancs ↘2000
Dialoge – Schaubühne am Lehniner Platz ↘2000
Dialoge – Mumbai ↘2001
Dialoge – 17-25/4 ↘2001
Dialoge – Les Grandes Traversées ↘2003
Dialoge – Paris ↘2004
Dialoge – Passages ↘2004
Dialoge 04 – St. Elisabeth I–IV ↘2004
Dialoge 04 – Palast der Republik ↘2004
Dialoge – Happy Day ↘2005
Dialoge 2005 – Open Church ↘2005
Dialoge – Freiburg ↘2006
Dialoge – Bologna ↘2006
Dialoge 06 – Radiale Systeme ↘2006
Dialoge – Bangalore ↘2007
Dialoge 07 – Pergamonmuseum ↘2007
Dialoge 08 – Venedig ↘2008
Dialoge 09 – Neues Museum ↘2009
Dialoge 09 – MAXXI ↘2009
Dialoge 2013 – Kolkata ↘2013
Dialoge 2013 – Avignon ↘2013
Dialoge 2018 – Wirbel ↘2018
Dialoge 2020 – Relevante Systeme ↘2020
Dialoge Roma 2020 – Terra Sacra ↘2020
Dialoge 2020 – Strandbad Tegelsee ↘2020
Dialoge 2020 – Relevante Systeme II ↘2020
Dialoge 2021 – Ludwigsburg ↘2021
Dido & Aeneas ↘2005
ΕΞΟΔΟΣ | Exodos ↘2018
Fantasie ↘2006
Figure Humaine ↘2017
gefaltet ↘2012
Gezeiten ↘2005
human requiem ↘2012
Impromptus ↘2004
In C ↘2021
In C – Marler Partitur ↘2022
insideout ↘2003
Ira – Zorn – Wrath ↘2022
Jagden und Formen (Zustand 2008) ↘2008
Johannes-Passion ↘2024
Körper ↘2000
Kreatur ↘2017
L'Après-midi d'un faune ↘2013 ↘2024
Matsukaze ↘2011
Medea ↘2007
Métamorphoses ↘2010
MusikTANZ – CARMEN ↘2012
Mystery 14 Human Requiem in Eleusis ↘2023
Na Zemlje ↘1998
noBody ↘2002
Orfeo ↘2014
Passion ↘2010
Paulinchen allein zu Haus ↘1994
rauschen ↘2019
remains ↘2020
Rötung (work in progress) ↘1998
Roméo et Juliette ↘2007
S ↘2000
Sacre ↘2013
Sasha Waltz im Dialog mit Wolfgang Laib ↘2023
Sasha Waltz. Installations. Objects. Performances ↘2013
Solo für Vladimir Malakhov ↘2006
Spiegelneuronen ↘2024
SYM-PHONIE MMXX ↘2022
Tannhäuser ↘2014
Travelogue I – Twenty to eight ↘1993
Travelogue II – Tears break fast ↘1994
Travelogue III – All ways six steps ↘1995
Women ↘2017
Zweiland ↘1997
Zuhören #1: Continu und Gespräche ↘2016
Zuhören #2: Improvisationen und Gespräche ↘2016
Zuhören #3: The Art of Resistance & Empowerment of Communities ↘2017
Zuhören #4: Climate change & democracy. From complexity to action ↘2019
Zuhören #5: In B ↘2021

Photographers
Fotograf:innen

Ackermann, Michael ↘ pp. 44 A, 121 E, 176 D, 190 A
Annigoni, Otello ↘ p. 120 B
Bak, Jeanette ↘ pp. 143 F, 320
Baltzer, David ↘ pp. 43 G, 52 D, 58 C, 82 D, 94 D, 109 F, 133 D, 166, 168 A, 177 E, 197 C, 215 F+G, 226 A, 241, 272, 284 A
Bleicker, Dirk ↘ pp. 56 C, 108 C, 182 A, 230 A, 233
Bolesch, Sebastian ↘ pp. 29 D, 30 A+B, 32 C, 33 F, 34 A, 40 A, 43 H, 44 B, 50 B, 53 J, 56 B, 57 E, 58 A, 62 A+D, 63 G, 76 A+C, 78 A, 80 C, 81 D, 83 G, 88 C, 90 B, 94 A, 102, 104 A, 105 E, 108 A, 109 G, 114 C, 120 C, 121 D, 122, 137 F, 140 A, 141 B+C+E, 142 B, 148 B, 150 C, 151 E–G, 152 A, 156 C, 160 A, 161 H, 165 E, 169 F, 171 C, 173 C, 175 D, 176 B, 178 C+D, 181 E, 182 B, 183 E+F, 187 F+G, 192 D, 200 D, 201 E, 205 B, 206 A+B, 210 A+B, 211 E+F, 262 A, 263, 266, 268 B, 269, 273, 277, 280 A–F, 281, 299, 305, 318 B, 323
Brandt, David ↘ pp. 53 I, 96 D, 198 D, 227
Bregeon, Cris ↘ p. 46 D
Cervantes, Julieta ↘ pp. 116 D, 125 G, 293
Dera, Phil ↘ pp. 98, 147 J, 194 B, 289
Döring, Steffen ↘ p. 128 A
Dümcke, Philipp ↘ pp. 193 G, 313
Escher, Rodolphe ↘ p. 156 D
Fatehpuria, Anubha ↘ p. 160 C
Giarbardo, Luca ↘ p. 274 A+B
Glinka, Jo ↘ pp. 22, 32 A
Gogatishvili, Gia ↘ p. 57 H
Grünschloss, Felix ↘ pp. 68, 112 A
Guérin, Emilie ↘ pp. 179 G, 298 C
Hartwig, Dieter ↘ p. 310 A
Hauk, Martin ↘ p. 308 A
Hentschel, Bernd ↘ pp. 67 C, 77 G
Isla, Yanina ↘ p. 315
Jansch, Jirka ↘ pp. 41 D, 205 F
Kaczmarz, Anna ↘ p. 92 C
Kaufmann, Ursula ↘ pp. 35 E, 80 B, 174 B
Kouskoutis, John ↘ p. 322 B+C
Kröll, Angela ↘ pp. 53 H, 197 F
Krüger, Jason ↘ p. 306 A
Le Pera, Achille ↘ pp. 53 G, 70 A, 92 A, 107 E, 175 C
Look, Oliver ↘ pp. 61 H, 84 A, 150 A, 220
Ludwig, Gerhard F. ↘ p. 240 A
Madvig, Bo ↘ p. 161 G
Martínez, Francisco ↘ p. 324 A
Martins, César ↘ pp. 8, 16
Mentzos, Dominik ↘ p. 275
Metzner, Jörg ↘ p. 43 F
Miklaszewskadz, Joanna ↘ pp. 101 C, 129 E, 146 F, 193 H
Pfisterer, Reiner ↘ pp. 1, 316
Pilick, Stephanie ↘ pp. 61 E, 82 B+C, 150 D, 188 B, 300 A+B, 301
Radünzel, Eva ↘ pp. 113 B, 124 B+C, 198 B, 199 H+I, 205 C, 215 C, 222
Real, Javier & Elena del ↘ p. 296
Rittershaus, Monika ↘ pp. 286 A+B, 287
Rival, André ↘ pp. 29 E, 56 D, 160 E, 218, 248 A, 252 A, 257, 344
Röder, Julian ↘ pp. 119 C, 133 E, 157 E, 158, 170 B, 172 A, 199 F, 309
Roy, Natascha ↘ p. 298 B
Saage, Carolin ↘ pp. 37 F, 44 C, 52 B, 53 E, 54, 59 D, 61 F, 62 B, 70 B+F, 115 F, 120 A, 127 E, 143 D, 184, 188 A, 197 B+E, 207 D, 307
Sandig, Jochen ↘ pp. 40 B, 57 F, 66 B, 129 D, 150 B, 179 H, 186 A, 198 C, 238 A+B, 252 B, 253, 256 A, 259, 270 C, 294 A, 339
Sandig, Sophia ↘ p. 146 C
Schenk, Thomas ↘ pp. 53 F, 256 B, 270 A+B
Schuppelius, Heike ↘ pp. 61 G, 88 D, 125 F
Talneau, Stephan ↘ pp. 73 D, 169 D, 314 A–C
Thorborg, Carl ↘ p. 139 H
Tsatsos, Stylianos ↘ pp. 45 D, 90 D, 104 C, 146 A, 178 B, 186 C, 194 D, 201 F, 210 C, 312
Uhlig, Bernd ↘ pp. 18, 20, 28 B, 33 E, 34 B, 35 C, 36 C, 40 C, 42 A+C, 48 A, 50 A, 51 D, 59 G, 60 B, 64, 71 J, 74, 77 E, 83 I, 89 E+F, 91 H, 93 D, 95 E, 96 C, 97 E, 101 B, 104 D, 106 A, 107 F, 109 E, 110, 114 A, 115 D, 117 E, 118 B, 124 A, 130, 132 B+C, 136 C+D, 139 E+F, 142 C, 146 D, 153 E, 154, 162 A, 163 C, 168 B, 169 C, 171 D, 177 F+G, 178 A, 179 E+F, 180 A+C, 181 D+F, 182 C, 186 D, 188 D, 189 E, 192 A, 193 F, 194 A, 195 E, 200 A+C, 201 G, 202, 204 A, 210 D, 212, 214 A, 217 B, 234, 242 A+B, 243, 244, 248 B, 249, 250, 254 A+B, 255, 258 A+B, 261, 271, 282, 284 B, 285, 288, 290 B, 291, 295, 302 A–D, 303, 319, 325, 326
Ulmann, Gerald ↘ p. 322 A
Voormann, Michael ↘ p. 76 B
Wagenhan, Martin ↘ pp. 48 B, 82 E, 290 A, 292
Wagner, Florian ↘ p. 321
Walde, Martin ↘ pp. 57 I, 63 E
Waltz, Sasha ↘ pp. 58 B, 71 H, 139 G, 238 C, 276 A, 306 B
Weigelt, Gert ↘ pp. 56 A, 72 C, 160 B, 189 G, 206 C, 214 B, 215 E, 264
Wizisla, Reinhard ↘ pp. 308 B+C, 318 A
Zölle, Matthias ↘ pp. 72 B, 83 F, 108 B, 228, 231, 232 A+B, 236 A+B, 237, 239
Zscharnt, Luna ↘ pp. 86, 94 B, 109 H, 116 A, 128 B, 129 C, 146 B, 147 G+H, 149 E, 161 F, 187 H
Zscharnt, Ute ↘ pp. 46 E, 47 J, 49 F, 52 C, 61 D, 66 A, 91 G, 100 A, 109 H, 136 A, 138 A, 144, 149 E, 173 B, 276 B, 278, 304

Authors
Autor:innen

Assmann, Aleida, Cultural Scientist / Kulturwissenschaftlerin ↘ p. 174
Assmann, Jan, Cultural Scientist / Kulturwissenschaftler ↘ p. 60
Borries, Friedrich von, Hochschullehrer, Architektur- und Designtheoretiker / Professor, Architecture and Design Theorist ↘ pp. 56, 170
Breitz, Candice, Artist / Künstlerin ↘ p. 58
Deluy, Clémentine, Dancer / Tänzerin ↘ pp. 30, 85, 157
Dübgen, Hannah, Writer and Librettist of the Opera »Matsukaze« / Schriftstellerin und Librettistin der Oper »Matsukaze« ↘ pp. 36, 124, 196
Eberlein, Undine, Philosopher / Philosophin ↘ pp. 35, 73, 101, 140
Eikmeyer, Robert, Art Historian and Cultural Scientist / Kunst- und Kulturwissenschaftler ↘ pp. 149, 150, 194
Franck, Julia, Novelist and Essayist / Schriftstellerin ↘ pp. 128, 162
Hapeyeva, Volha, Poet and Artist / Dichterin und Künstlerin ↘ p. 66
Jones, Hannah, Architect / Architektin ↘ pp. 40, 189
Karim Khani, Behzad, Writer / Schriftsteller ↘ p. 173
Kirschbaum, Heinrich, Philologe / Philologist ↘ p. 178
Lian, Yang, Poet / Dichter ↘ pp. 142, 187
Merei, Yasmine Nayef, Journalist / Journalistin ↘ pp. 80, 160
Müller, Katrin Bettina, Journalist for Arts / Journalistin für Kultur ↘ p. 247
Petrowskaja, Katja, Writer / Schriftstellerin ↘ p. 136
Rosa, Hartmut, Sociologist and Political Scientist / Soziologe und Politikwissenschaftler ↘ p. 201
Ruzicska, Christian, Publisher / Verleger ↘ pp. 78, 113, 152, 193
Sandig, Jochen, Director and Cultural Entrepreneur / Regisseur und Kulturunternehmer ↘ pp. 7, 227–44, 249–63, 267
Sandig, László, Dancer, Philosopher / Tänzer, Philosoph ↘ pp. 49, 116, 216, 227–33, 237–44, 249–64, 269–326
Scherer, Agnes, Artist and Researcher for Sasha Waltz & Guests 2018–21 / Künstlerin und Rechercheurin für Sasha Waltz & Guests 2018–21 ↘ p. 126
Serpa Soares, Claudia de, Dancer / Tänzerin ↘ p. 47
Varatharajah, Senthuran, Writer, Philosopher and Theologian / Schriftsteller, Philosoph und Theologe ↘ pp. 10–14, 104, 106
Waltz, Sasha, Choreographer, Director, Dancer / Choreographin, Regisseurin, Tänzerin ↘ pp. 7, 28, 120, 191, 227–33, 237–44, 249–64, 269–326
Zouk, Sigal, Dancer / Tänzerin ↘ p. 47

Colophon
Impressum

Editors / Herausgeber
Sasha Waltz, Jochen Sandig

Managing editors / Redaktion
Stephanie Bender, Sibah Pomplun, Sasha Waltz
with the collaboration of / unter Mitarbeit von
Christopher Drum, Kira Schmitz

Graphic design / Gestaltung
Daniel Wiesmann
with the collaboration of / unter Mitarbeit von
Tom Neubauer, Jule Erner, Robert Radziejewski

Copyediting / Lektorat
Sasha Waltz & Guests

Image rights / Bildrechte
Sibah Pomplun, Kira Schmitz, Tomoko Mamine

Translation / Übersetzung
Christina Oberstebrink, Nat Shockley, Imogen Taylor, Alexandra Titze-Grabec, unless otherwise noted / sofern nicht anders vermerkt ↘ p. 333

Lithography / Lithografie
DruckConcept, Berlin

Reproduction / Reproduktion
Daniel Wiesmann, unless otherwise noted / sofern nicht anders vermerkt ↘ pp. 328–33

Project management Hatje Cantz / Projektleitung Verlag
Anna Warnow, Sophie Pechhacker

Production / Herstellung
Thomas Lemaître

Printing and binding / Druck und Bindung
Livonia Print, Riga

Paper / Papier
Magno Volume, 115 g/m²
Munken Lynx Rough, 120 g/m²

Typeface / Schrift
Akzidenz-Grotesk Pro Light & Medium

Editorial deadline / Redaktionsschluss
January 2025

Cover design / Umschlaggestaltung
Daniel Wiesmann

Cover photo / Umschlagfoto
Sasha Waltz, »rauschen«, close-up, 2018/19
© César Martins

Sasha Waltz & Guests GmbH
Sophienstraße 3
10178 Berlin, Germany
www.sashawaltz.de

Published by
Hatje Cantz Verlag GmbH
Mommsenstraße 27
10629 Berlin, Germany
contact@hatjecantz.de
www.hatjecantz.com
A Ganske Publishing Group Company

ISBN 978-3-7757-5526-9

Printed in Europe

Sasha Waltz & Guests is supported by the Berlin Senate Department for Culture and Social Cohesion. / Sasha Waltz & Guests wird gefördert von der Berliner Senatsverwaltung für Kultur und Gesellschaftlichen Zusammenhalt.

Senatsverwaltung für Kultur und Gesellschaftlichen Zusammenhalt BERLIN

sashawaltz.de